D0217579

Shaping Abortion Discourse

Democracy and the Public Sphere in Germany and the United States

Using controversy over abortion as a lens through which to compare the political process and the role of the media in these two very different democracies, this book examines the contest over meaning that is being waged by social movements, political parties, churches, and other social actors. Abortion is a critical battleground for debates over social values in both countries, but the constitutional premises on which arguments rest differ, as do the strategies that movements and parties adopt and the opportunities for influence that are open to them. By examining how these debates are conducted, and by whom, in light of the normative claims made by democratic theorists, the book also offers a means of judging how well either country lives up to the ideals of democratic debate in practice.

Myra Marx Ferree is Professor of Sociology at the University of Wisconsin–Madison. She is the co-author of *Controversy and Coalition: The New Women's Movement Across Three Decades of Change* (2000) and co-editor of *Re-visioning Gender* (1998).

William Anthony Gamson is Professor of Sociology and co-directs the Media Research and Action Project (MRAP) at Boston College. He is the author of *Talking Politics* (1992) and *The Strategy of Social Protest* (2nd edition, 1990).

Jürgen Gerhards is Professor of Sociology at the University of Leipzig. His many publications include *Die Vermessung kultureller Unterschiede. Deutschland und USA im Vergleich* (*Measuring Cultural Differences: Germany and the U.S. in a Comparative Perspective*) (2000).

Dieter Rucht is Professor of Sociology at the Social Science Research Center, Berlin. His many publications include *Jugendkulturen, Politik und Protest* (*Youth Cultures, Politics, and Protest*) (2000).

Politics and relations among individuals in societies across the world are being transformed by new technologies for targeting individuals and sophisticated methods for shaping personalized messages. The new technologies challenge boundaries of many kinds – between news, information, entertainment, and advertising; between media, with the arrival of the World Wide Web; and even between nations. *Communication, Society and Politics* probes the political and social impacts of these new communication systems in national, comparative, and global perspective.

Shaping Abortion Discourse

DEMOCRACY AND THE PUBLIC SPHERE IN GERMANY AND THE UNITED STATES

Myra Marx Ferree
University of Wisconsin, Madison

William Anthony Gamson
Boston College

Jürgen Gerhards
Universität Leipzig

Dieter Rucht
Wissenschaftszentrum Berlin

CAMBRIDGE
UNIVERSITY PRESS

CAMBRIDGE UNIVERSITY PRESS
Cambridge, New York, Melbourne, Madrid, Cape Town, Singapore, São Paulo

Cambridge University Press
The Edinburgh Building, Cambridge CB2 8RU, UK

Published in the United States of America by Cambridge University Press, New York

www.cambridge.org
Information on this title: www.cambridge.org/9780521790451

First published 2002

A catalogue record for this publication is available from the British Library

Library of Congress Cataloguing in Publication data

Shaping abortion discourse: democracy and the public sphere in Germany and the United
States / Myra Marx Ferree . . . [et al.].
p.   cm. – (Communication, society, and politics)
Includes bibliographical references and index.
ISBN 0-521-79045-X – ISBN 0-521-79384-X (pb.)
1. Abortion – Political aspects – Germany.   2. Abortion – Political aspects – United States.
3. Abortion – Press coverage – Germany.   4. Abortion – Press coverage – United States.
5. Pro-choice movement – Germany.   6. Pro-choice movement – United States.
7. Pro-life movement – Germany.   8. Pro-life movement – United States.
9. Germany – Politics and government – 20th century.
10. United States – Politics and government – 20th century.
I. Ferree, Myra Marx.   II. Series.

HQ767.5.G3 S53 2002
363.46′0943–dc21   2001037366

ISBN 978-0-521-79045-1 hardback
ISBN 978-0-521-79384-1 paperback

Transferred to digital printing 2007

Contents

Tables and Figures

TABLES

FIGURES

Foreword

Friedhelm Neidhardt

Shaping Abortion Discourse supplies the reader with a highly condensed product of a long and complicated research process that generated a great mass of data. Literally thousands of newspaper articles and hundreds of documents about the abortion conflict in Germany and the United States were systematically analyzed, and thousands of speakers, utterances, and ideas were identified and interpreted. In addition, many interviews with actors and observers of the abortion issue were carried out. All of this covered an almost three-decade period of public abortion discourse in two countries, carried out by a U.S./German research team with the idea that in the end a monograph should be jointly written to present the core results of the comparative research.

The demand for consensus set by this ambitious goal required an unusual level of transatlantic cooperation. The "same codebook for content analysis, the same survey questionnaire, and to some extent the same interview schedule" had to be designed and agreed upon. Working with these instruments brought up many practical questions that had to be solved with balanced procedures on both sides. And because data produced by these procedures do not speak for themselves, a difficult and sometimes controversial discussion among the authors about the cross-cultural meaning of these data had to be carried out in order to develop a single line of describing and interpreting the research findings.

At the beginning, I myself was heavily involved in the research project. Then I was elected to an office that so much absorbed my capacity that I was not able to stay on as a member of the research team. But I remained in contact with my colleagues, heard this and that, and became more and more curious about the comparative outcome of the project. Would they be able to do it at all? And what could be learned from the final product? Was it worthwhile investing so much man- and womanpower into the joint effort?

This first answer is clear: They did it; the book is finished. The second answer is clear for me: It is a good book with exceptional data quality and many interesting findings and ideas. I am surprised by how much we can learn about two countries when a single issue is analyzed. Of course, one must be careful not to overgeneralize the findings about the abortion conflict in Germany and the United States. The abortion case is an extraordinarily moralized issue in both countries, mobilizing questions, actors, and constellations not typical for social and political business as usual. But not being part of "business as usual" brings, in this case, the advantage of demonstrating underlying cultural dimensions of the social and political routines that are always relevant, even if they usually cannot be seen. One does not need to agree with all of the arguments and interpretations of the authors to find their book instructive far beyond the abortion issue.

The illuminating quality of the book is not only the effect of the issue and the empirical data gathered about it in Germany and the United States. The quality of the findings about this debate is also dependent on the quality of the questions asked and the analytical framework used by the researchers. Let me outline very selectively what seems to me theoretically remarkable and convincingly demonstrated by the analysis described in this book.

I was skeptical when Bill Gamson, at the beginning of the project, came up with the proposal to use the concept of *frames* in order to analyze the thematic content of the abortion discourse expressed in American and German newspapers. This concept seemed to me to be too loose and scarcely usable in a mass-data enterprise. In the meantime, I learned that it is possible to work practically with the concept. Furthermore, the book demonstrates that it makes sense to use it for description and explanation. Understood as a "thought organizer," framing "deals with the *gestalt* or pattern-organizing aspect of meaning." For understanding meaning processes the concept of frame has similar functions to the concept of social structure for understanding interaction processes. Although they do not logically fix concrete norms and positions, frames privilege certain meaning elements at the cost of others. If speakers in the abortion dispute, for example, choose the Fetal Life frame to argue their case, this does not force them to vote in favor of restrictive abortion regulations, but there is a rather strong tendency for them to do so. It is easier for an actor to be in line with the built-in preference structure of the frame chosen.

Because of the more or less strongly articulated "loading" of a frame, disputes about certain decisions that have to be made can be understood as a competition between frames. Of course, frames do not compete by themselves. They have to be constructed and communicated by certain speakers. To understand the dynamics of a discourse, it is therefore necessary to ask about the actors who are meeting within the arena of public discourse, an arena that is most effectively organized and structured by mass media in modern societies. It is a highlight of *Shaping Abortion Discourse* that this book systematically deals with the ensemble of the speakers that shaped public controversy in both countries during the last decades, investigating the relative *standing* of different categories of speakers, finding very strong differences in this respect between the composition of the American and German public arenas, and asking for explanations for these differences.

In Germany, state actors and the political parties are by far the most influential actors within the abortion debate, while in the United States actors of the political periphery, above all movement organizations, have a very strong voice in "the master forum" of the mass media, much more so than in Germany. It is right to conclude, as the authors do, that the participatory elements of public life that provide for some sorts of "popular inclusion" are significantly more developed in the United States. And this circumstance influences the status of the mass media as well as the quality of the discourse and its outcome. The authors discuss this in the context of different *democratic theories of the public sphere*, focusing on divergent criteria for normative evaluation. Concerning the quality of the discourse and its outcomes, they operationalize and use criteria dealing with the dialogical structure of the ongoing communications of speakers, with the degree of civility with which they treat each other, with the range of communicative styles that they use, and with the conditions that lead to "closure" in the discourse and the degree of consensus finally reached by the actors involved. Once again, one need not completely agree with all of the methodological procedures and analytical judgments of the authors to find this analysis, too, fruitful and instructive.

I find very convincing the authors' explanation of the, in part, considerable differences between American and German characteristics of their public sectors. In this respect, the heuristic function of the concept of *discursive opportunity structure* proves extremely valuable. In *Shaping Abortion Discourse*, the socio-cultural, political, and mass media components of "discursive opportunity structure" seem to me intelligently developed in order to identify certain background factors for framing and standing characteristics. The career of these frames as well as the standing of the speakers competing for voice in the public sphere are, of course, dependent on the strategies and the talent of the speakers themselves.

But they operate under circumstances that selectively privilege or restrict certain classes of actors as well as certain frames. It becomes obvious that those circumstances are deeply rooted in long-standing cultural traditions and institutionalized patterns. With the authors, I am struck by the power of history that can be found in a wide range of national peculiarities. Asking what the background factors are that help to explain the dominant status of political and legal state actors among the speakers and the dominant status of the Fetal Life frame within the public debates in Germany brings up impressive examples for the concept of "path-dependency." It is necessary to understand this country's *Rechtsstaat* and welfare state tradition and to take into account the German traumata caused by the Nazi period to understand certain features of standing and framing relationships that differ from American ones, for better or worse. It is a sign of the quality of *Shaping Abortion Discourse* that those dimensions are addressed systematically.

Having read the manuscript of *Shaping Abortion Discourse*, I regret not having been with Myra Marx Ferree, William A. Gamson, Jürgen Gerhards, and Dieter Rucht when they wrote the book, although I know that it was not easy for them to bring this ambitious project to its end. I would have been proud to be a co-author with them.

Preface

This book represents a collaboration in the fullest sense of that word. All four of us were heavily involved in every stage of the work – in the theoretical development and research design, in the development of research instruments, in the lengthy data collection process, and in the analysis and interpretation of results.

Close collaborations among any set of four people are complicated and difficult, but this one was especially challenging. We had to face complicated and subtle differences across lines of national cultures, gender, and epistemological approach. At numerous times, we all harbored doubts about our ability to produce a collective product. But we persevered and, in the end, we believe that we have produced a book that reflects us all and is richer than anything we could have produced individually.[1]

In a book that focuses on the shaping of discourse, we have had to be especially self-conscious about our choice of language. What does one call the antagonists on the issue of abortion? How does one refer to the organism growing in the womb of a pregnant woman? There are no frame-free answers to these questions. Our solution has been to use the language of the two U.S. newspapers that we analyzed, *The New York Times* and *The Los Angeles Times*.

This means that we use "pro-abortion–rights" to refer to those who would lessen or remove legal or practical restrictions on abortion. We use "anti-abortion" to refer to those who would increase legal or practical restrictions (or defend those that exist from liberalization).

---

[1] For earlier publications stemming from this project, see Ferree and Gamson (1999, 2002); Franz (1999); Gamson (1999, 2001); Gerhards (1996, 1997, 1999); Gerhards, Neidhardt, and Rucht (1998); Gerhards and Rucht (2000); and Neidhardt (1996).

Often we will use the shorthand terms of "Pros" and "Antis" for the two sides.

Following journalistic practice, we call the organism in the womb of a pregnant woman a "fetus." We recognize that these labels, and others such as "partial birth abortion," are not neutral and frame-free, but (unlike labels such as "pro-choice" or "anti §218") they are comprehensible in both countries and reflect our own efforts (like those of U.S. journalists) to seek neutral language in a discourse where it typically does not exist.

We have tried to make what we have to say as accessible as possible, and this means, among other things, avoiding the use of unfamiliar acronyms. However, political parties in Germany and various organizations in the United States are often better known by their acronyms than their full names, and the reader will still encounter a fair number. To make things easier, we have included a glossary of frequently used acronyms for easy reference.

In a project that has taken us most of the past decade to complete, we have accumulated a long list of institutions and people to whom we are indebted. On the German side, we wish to thank the Fritz Thyssen Stiftung, which has generously financed a great deal of data collection. We are also grateful to our former colleague, Monika Lindgens, who collaborated with us in an early period of the research; Barbara S. Franz, who supervised the coders; Bettina Becker, Uwe Breitenborn, Sabine Hödt, and Inken Schröder, who did the hard work of coding more than 1400 articles; Verena Rösner, who organized the standardized survey of the collective actors in Germany; Anne Hampele, who conducted interviews with a subsample of these actors; and Andreas Dams, who was responsible for large parts of the data management.

On the U.S. side, we thank the National Science Foundation (grant SBR-9301617) for its financial support for three years of data collection. We particularly want to extend our thanks to Lynn Resnick DuFour, Julia McQuillan, Silke Roth, and Joan Twiggs, who at various times handled overall project scheduling and management; codebook development; coder training and supervision; reliability testing; in-person interviewing; survey formatting and mailing; and data cleaning, entry, and management – a wide variety of complex and challenging work. At Boston College, Michelle Carpentieri, Karen Ferroggiarro, Janine Berkowitz Minkler, and Christine Schneider contributed in numerous ways in the data collection process. Other graduate students have also contributed significantly to particular parts of the project at different times: Mark Swiencicki as a coder, Danielle Currier and Mary Murphy as interviewers, and Cory Lebson as a data manager. David Merrill has been invaluable in the final stages of this project, cleaning up past errors, preparing tables and charts for publication, documenting the various decisions and stages of work, and creating the Web site for future references.

As graduate students, they took on the demanding day-to-day responsibility for organizing reams of data and supervising dozens of undergraduate coders, as well as pitching in to code, clean, check, and enter data when needed. Without their skills and efforts, we might well have been swept away by the tide of data that we were generating. We reached many practical decisions collaboratively in team meetings, and their insights as well as hard work contributed much to bringing this massive endeavor to a successful conclusion.

Moreover, we are indebted to the German American Academic Council, which has supported our collaborative effort by financing, among other things, travel expenses for joint meetings in both the United States and Germany and technical assistance to put this book together.

Finally, we are grateful to a number of readers who have commented on the manuscript in various stages: Lee Ann Banaszak, Sabine Berghahn, Christine Bose, Lisa D. Brush, Gene Burns, Carol Hagemann-White, Paul Lichterman, Jenny Mansbridge, Patricia Yancey Martin, David Meyer, Sandra R. Levitsky, Friedhelm Neidhardt, Silke Roth, Frances Rothstein, and Carol Turbin.

Glossary

We have tried to minimize our use of acronyms, but many political parties and organizations are better known by their acronyms than by their full names. For reference, we provide this glossary of frequently used acronyms.

§218 = The section or paragraph of the German criminal code, going back to the formation of the German state in 1871, that makes abortion illegal

ACLU = American Civil Liberties Union

ALI = The American Law Institute, an organization that developed and disseminated a model abortion law as part of the abortion reform movement of the 1960s

AWO = *Arbeiterwohlfahrt*, a welfare organization associated with the German Social Democratic Party

CDU = The Christian Democratic Union, a political party that, in alliance with the independent CSU in Bavaria, forms the Christian Union in Germany

CFFC = Catholics for a Free Choice, a U.S. organization

CSU = Christian Social Union, the Bavarian Christian Democratic Party, which with the CDU forms the Christian Union in Germany

FAZ = The *Frankfurter Allgemeine Zeitung*, one of the two German newspapers analyzed

FDP = The Free Democratic Party, a German classical liberal party

FRG = Federal Republic of Germany, "West Germany" before unification

GDR = German Democratic Republic, the former "East Germany"

KPD = The Communist Party of Germany that was declared to be "unconstitutional" in 1956 (we only refer to it in the Weimar period)

LAT = *The Los Angeles Times*, one of the two U.S. newspapers analyzed

NARAL = The National Abortion Rights Action League, later the National Abortion and Reproductive Rights Action League

NCCB = National Conference of Catholic Bishops (U.S.)

NOW = National Organization for Women (U.S.)

NRLC = The National Right to Life Committee (U.S.)

NYT = *The New York Times*, one of the two U.S. newspapers analyzed

PDS = Party of Democratic Socialism, the successor to the Socialist Unity (Communist) Party in Germany following unification

RCAR = Religious Coalition for Abortion Rights; later RCRC for the Religious Coalition for Reproductive Choice (U.S.)

R2N2 = Reproductive Rights National Network (U.S.)

SZ = The *Süddeutsche Zeitung*, one of the two German newspapers analyzed

SPD = The Social Democratic Party in Germany

taz = *die tageszeitung, The Daily Newspaper*, a left-alternative newspaper based in Berlin, created in 1978

Part I

Introduction

The three chapters in Part I set the stage. Chapter One previews the two interwoven stories of the book. The first story is about the cultural contest in which abortion talk is shaped; the second is about whether the quality of abortion talk serves the needs of a democracy. This chapter also presents a way of thinking and a set of concepts for an analysis of discourse that can be applied to many other issues. In particular, we emphasize the way that groups work to frame issues to their advantage, attempting to mesh strategy with opportunity.

Chapter Two presents the historical context for understanding the contemporary debate on abortion in Germany and the United States. In Germany, unlike the United States, abortion has been a political issue since early in the twentieth century. Also, the highest constitutional courts in each country took different courses in their key abortion decisions in the early 1970s. The U.S. Court emphasized privacy as the central issue while the German Court emphasized the state's responsibility to protect life. These contrasts make the countries exceptionally well suited for our comparative study.

Chapter Three presents the nature of the data that we gathered in carrying out this research. General readers interested in the content of our argument may wish to skim or skip some of the discussion of the methodological issues that we confronted and how we resolved them.

CHAPTER ONE

Two Related Stories

*Es [das sich im Mutterleib entwickelnde Leben] genießt
grundsätzlich für die gesamte Dauer der Schwangerschaft
Vorrang vor dem Selbstbestimmungsrecht der Schwan-
geren.* It [the life developing in the mother's body] fundamentally takes priority over the pregnant woman's
right to self-determination throughout the entire period of pregnancy.

(German Constitutional Court 1975, BVerG 1, 44)

The right to privacy, whether it be founded in the Four-
teenth Amendment's concept of personal liberty and
restrictions upon state action or in the Ninth Amendment's reservation of the rights to the people, is broad
enough to encompass a woman's decision whether or
not to terminate her pregnancy.

(*Roe v. Wade* 1973, 410 U.S. 177)

At the beginning of a new century, Germany and the United States have
arrived at uneasy policy compromises on the vexed issue of abortion. The
compromises are in some regards surprisingly similar: In Germany, a
woman with an unwanted pregnancy can decide to have an abortion in
the first trimester, although she is required to have counseling designed
to encourage her to have the child. Access to abortion is relatively simple
after a short waiting period. In the United States, the choice of abortion
also rests with the woman in the first trimester. The 50 individual states
may impose various restrictions as long as these do not place an undue
burden on the woman's decision to end an unwanted pregnancy.

In other respects, the situations are sharply different. The similarity of practical outcomes is surprising because the public discussion of abortion and the constellation of actors attempting to shape it provide dramatic contrasts. The intensity of the debate and its ability to mobilize political passions in the United States are not matched in Germany; only the United States has experienced relatively widespread political violence over the abortion issue. As our opening citations suggest, the courts in each country chose a different route in laying out the constitutional framework for the acceptability of moral claims. Public speakers in each country have different historical and cultural traditions on which to draw as well. Some claims made in one country find no counterpart in the other and defy translation into such a different context. The comparison of public discourse on abortion is especially compelling in providing a lens in which the taken-for-granted in each country is rendered visible.

Our story is about the evolution and content of abortion *talk* rather than abortion *policy*. We interweave two closely related stories. The first is about the cultural contest in which abortion discourse is shaped. Here we ask who the major players are; what voice they have in the media; and how their framing strategies, interacting with a nationally specific constellation of opportunities and constraints, account for the differences that we observe in mass media discussions of the issue. It is a story about who says what to produce the outcomes that we observe and why some actors are more successful in promoting their preferred frames.

The second story is about the *quality* of abortion talk. Here we draw on democratic theory about the nature of the public sphere and what various theorists suggest that it should be to serve the needs of democracy. We look at how well the normative criteria suggested by different theoretical traditions – for example, *inclusiveness* or *civility* – are reflected in media discourse on abortion in Germany and the United States. In this we follow Susan Gal's (1994) suggestion that the nature of abortion talk tells a great deal, not only about reproductive rights and women, but also about the nature and concerns of democracy as a whole.

Both stories rely on the same data: a content analysis of a random sample of articles drawn from four elite newspapers, a survey of organizations attempting to influence the discourse, interviews with spokespersons for some of these organizations describing their efforts and their perceptions of successs, and, finally, interviews with journalists who most often wrote on abortion in the newspapers sampled. In the first story we describe and explain media discourse as the outcome of a contest over meaning; in the second story we use this outcome as a way of evaluating the quality of debate in the public sphere as it is reflected on this issue.

Both of these stories are built on a comparative framework. We are comparing two countries that are very similar in some important respects. They are both highly industrialized, democratic states with cultural roots in the enlightenment. They are members of the same family of what Max Weber called "occidental societies."

On the other hand, they are so different. The United States is a decentralized, presidential democracy with a weak welfare state and a strong civil society. Germany is a modestly centralized parliamentary democracy with a strong welfare state and a weak civil society. Church and state are institutionally and normatively separated in the United States and somewhat intertwined in Germany. But culturally, religion and politics are more intertwined in the United States compared to a more secular Germany. German journalists provide access primarily to state and party actors and their institutional allies, while U.S. journalists are much more open to grassroots actors and ordinary individuals and place a higher value on personalization and narrative in constructing the news.

Feminism is more differentiated from the broader women's movement in Germany, and feminist groups are much more decentralized. The German women's movement is reflected in a variety of party-based organizations as well as by women's civic organizations. In the United States, national feminist groups take up a wide range of issues and have the potential for both cooperation and competition with other national interest groups, but they have no strong organizational base in the political parties as such.

This combination – Germany and the United States are so alike and yet so different – is particularly useful for teasing out the invisible assumptions that participants inside each single system take for granted. By adopting a comparative perspective, we use each country as a lens through which we can make visible the assumptions of the other. The comparative perspective also provides a valuable standard against which we can measure the discourse in each country – not, for example, as "inclusive" or "civil" in absolute terms, but as relatively inclusive or civil compared to the other country.

In addition to these generic advantages of comparative analysis, the abortion issue has several specific virtues. First, it has been a topic of public controversy in both countries for approximately the same time period, with major events that are roughly parallel in their timing. In both countries, the abortion issue rose in salience and significance in the early 1970s, elicited an important decision from the highest court of the land, and then was re-visited by the court about 16 years later. In both countries, the courts reaffirmed their original principles but modified their practical application when they took it up again. Many other issues are on the public agenda of one country and not the other, but abortion has been a matter of controversy in both countries over approximately the same time period.

Second, abortion is an issue that engages women deeply in both countries and thus potentially offers a window into women's role in the political process that few other issues would so clearly reveal. The historical development of democracies left women on the sidelines for generations, and the extent and nature of women's citizenship in modern democratic states remains an important question. How women are spoken about, as well as how women as actors speak on this issue, provide clues to women's position in the public sphere more generally.

Third, the abortion issue, having been hotly contested in both countries over a 25-year time period, has given many different political actors the opportunity to settle – and sometimes change – their positions. As a contemporary issue, abortion reform emerged in the United States during the 1960s, while public discussion of abortion reform re-entered the public agenda in Germany during the early 1970s, after a relative period of quiet since the early 1930s. In the United States the visibility of the abortion issue in politics has risen fairly steadily since the mid-1960s, while in Germany intense discussion has come in two waves, in the first half of the 1970s and again in the early 1990s. Hence, the specific content and the overall quality of the discourse are observable over a period long enough to see what change, if any, has occurred.

Fourth, abortion invokes existential issues of life and death and taps into the deepest level of cultural beliefs: about the role of women, the role of the state as a moral agent, the sanctity of human life, the right to privacy, the nature of democracy, and society's obligations to those in need. Many have suggested that value conflicts pose special challenges to democratic processes of conflict resolution (Aubert 1972). Just which values are in conflict and whether and how they are reconciled becomes an empirical question when we take a comparative perspective on the issue. We can look at what values are most central in the discourse in each country and at how this changes over time. One need only look back at the opening quotations to see how differently the highest court in each country framed the question of what values are at stake. Comparing media discourse on abortion is an opportunity to see how fundamental values can be handled in different ways in the public talk of different democracies.

Fifth, abortion also offers an opportunity to compare the role of social movements, political parties, and other actors in relation to each other. Many studies of political issues focus exclusively on the policy-making process or on the mobilization of protest outside of conventional institutions. The long time span of our data and comparative nature of our approach allow us to see how various social actors – government agencies, political parties, and advocacy organizations – enter and influence the public sphere in competition with each other. This interactive process between institutional politics and protestors is often viewed from only one side or the other in separated fields of study, whether conventional political science or social movements research. Looking at the public arena in which parties and movements contend allows us to see the common factors that impact both, as well as the ongoing process by which their influence relative to each other is achieved.

Finally, studying the shaping of media content is a way of assessing cultural impact: how the constellation of opportunities and constraints shape the strategies and use of symbols by those who seek to influence public discourse and how successful they are. Cultural change in civil society is often separated from institutional political change as if only one of these at a time could be the target of actors' deliberate strategy or social concern. Looking at culture as political and contested, as it so obviously is in regard to abortion, reconnects these dimensions. Similarly, it enables us to evaluate the content of public discourse where the challenge is greatest – on an issue fraught with moral dilemmas and conflicts.

In the following section we provide a framework that helps us to analyze the cultural contest in which abortion discourse is shaped, our first story; we then offer a framework for the analysis of the quality of abortion talk and the nature of democracy, our second story.

SHAPING PUBLIC DISCOURSE

We need to set the stage for our two stories, but a preview of the content is in order. Our first story will show how different types of actors play leading roles. In Germany, political parties and state actors dominate the stage; in the United States, the political parties are mostly backstage, and advocacy organizations are major players.

Groups with the same policy position often talk and think about the issue in quite different ways. To convey the flavor of the differences that we will be discussing in detail in the followings pages, consider the contrasts in these quotations, all drawn from advocates of a woman's right to choose:

> All efforts to protect unborn life in the body of the mother must be directed to doing so with the cooperation of the woman and not in opposition to her. In no way, including through the law, can the protection of unborn life be coerced. (German Lutheran Bishop Martin Kruse, 1990)

> Mein Bauch gehört mir! (My belly belongs to me!) (Slogan used by German feminist groups in the 1970s)

> No one can remove the decision about the continuation or termination of a pregnancy from the unwillingly pregnant woman. The church distances itself from its murderous and inhumane history and forgets the persecutions of the witches, the deaths of women from illegal abortions and the countless unwanted pregnancies that resulted from the church's prohibition of contraception. (Verena Krieger, the Green Party, quoted in FAZ, 12/29/89)

> The final decison about the termination of pregnancy should remain with the woman, but . . . the constitution [should] be expanded with a clause that expressly encompasses the protection of unborn life . . . this [law protecting life] would secure the claim that women would have on counselling and financial assistance (Rita Süssmuth, leading feminist member of the CDU, quoted in FAZ, 7/24/90).

> Jesus himself was feminist and believed that women were moral decision-makers . . . The Church itself, in becoming a patriarchal model, got away from that. We as women are calling the Church back to a belief that women are, in fact, moral decision-makers about our own lives and the lives of our families. (Jane Hull Harvey, *Methodist Church, General Board of Church and Society*, interview, Sept., 1997)

Instead of debating whether or not abortion is legal, we should be discussing what the concrete reality is if abortion is illegal. *Who* is it who suffers? . . . There are race and class issues related to that, as opposed to moral issues which don't have any bearing on what's concretely going to happen – if abortion is [not] safe, legal, and accessible. Because rich women will always have the right to go somewhere and find some means. . . . That should be where the debate should be, not on the morality. (Jana, *Refuse and Resist,* quoted from interview.)

Roe v. Wade found that abortion is so personal, so consequential that the public has no right to decide for the burdened woman. That principle deserves to rest undisturbed. (*New York Times* editorial, 1/21/89)

Take your rosaries off our ovaries! (Slogan used by American feminist protestors quoted in *The New York Times* 6/14/92)

In these quotes, speakers in each country frame the roles of women, church, and state in terms that are in part familiar and in part scarcely understandable to listeners in the other. But even within a single country the speakers differ significantly in the meaning they give to abortion regulations in spite of their common support for less restrictive abortion policies. Anti-abortion speakers are no less various in their repertoires of talk. Public discourse thus provides a window in the way that issue meanings are both shared and disputed within a political culture.

THEORETICAL FRAMEWORK

We believe that the general framework and set of tools for analysis that we offer here can be applied to other politically contentious issues, such as welfare reform or worker rights. *Public discourse* is public communication about topics and actors related to either some particular policy domain or to the broader interests and values that are engaged. It includes not only information and argumentation but images, metaphors, and other condensing symbols.

Public discourse is carried out in various *forums.* A forum includes an *arena* in which individual or collective actors engage in public speech acts; an active audience or *gallery* observing what is going on in the arena; and a *backstage,* where the would-be players in the arena work out their ideas and strategize over how they are to be presented, make alliances, and do the everyday work of cultural production. Figure 1.1 presents this visually, using a stadium metaphor.

There are different forums in which public discourse takes place: mass media, parliaments, courts, party conventions, town hall assemblies, scientific congresses, streets, and the like. We define the *public sphere* as the set of all forums. In the current era, there is one forum that overshadows all others, making them sideshows. For various reasons, general-audience *mass media* provide a master forum. The players in every other forum also use the mass media, either as players or as part of the gallery. The mass media gallery includes virtually everyone. All collective actors must assume that their own constituents are part of the mass media gallery and the messages that their supporters hear cannot be ignored, no matter how extensive the actors' own alternative media may be.

Second, the mass media forum is *the* major site of political contest because all of the players in the policy process *assume* its pervasive influence (whether justified or not). The mass media present – often in a highly selective and simplified way – discourse from other forums. The participants in these other forums look to the mass media forum to assess their effectiveness, measuring success by whether a speech in the legislative forum, for example, is featured prominently in *The New York Times* or the *FAZ* and whether it is commented on in a positive or negative way.

Finally, the mass media forum is not simply a site where one can read relative success in cultural contests. It is not merely an indicator of broader cultural changes in the civil society but also influences them, spreading changes in language use and political consciousness to the workplace and other settings in which people go about the public part of their daily lives. When a cultural code is being challenged, a change in the media forum both signals and spreads the change. To have one's preferred framing of an issue increase significantly in the mass media forum is both an important outcome in itself and carries a strong promise of a ripple effect.

The three parts of the mass media forum – arena, gallery, and backstage – require some elaboration.

THE ARENA The arena is a place where participants engage in speech acts of various sorts. The speech acts are intended to convey a message about either the policy issue under discussion or the organization that they are speaking for. Commentary on the issue is an attempt to convey a preferred way of framing it and to increase the relative prominence of the preferred frames in the mass media arena.

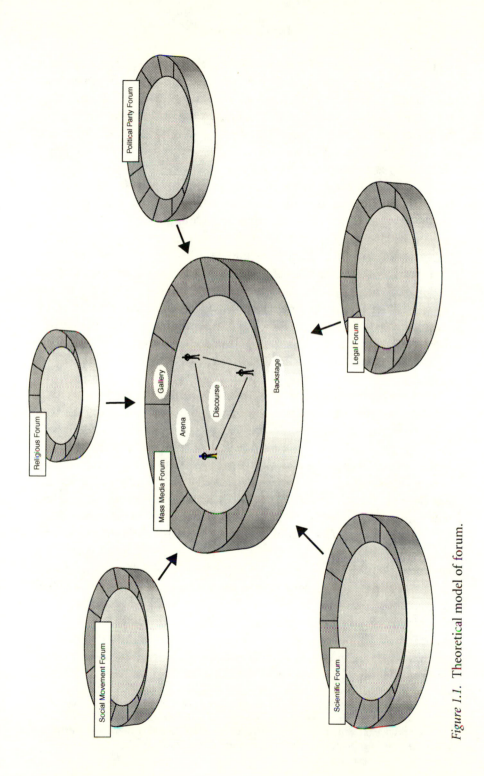

Figure 1.1. Theoretical model of forum.

Those who are quoted are overwhelmingly spokespersons for collective actors – government ministries, political parties, or organizations that claim to represent the interests or values of some constituency, speaking for or on behalf of them. These players speak for an organization or advocacy network that in turn claims to speak for some section of the gallery. Whether gallery members in fact accept such representation is an empirical matter.

Journalists play a dual role in this arena. First, they are gatekeepers. By including quotations and paraphrases from various spokespersons, journalists decide which collective actors should be taken seriously as important players. However, journalists are not *merely* gatekeepers in this process. They are themselves players who comment on the positions that other actors take, and they participate in framing the issue under discussion. They can interpret and provide their own meaning when they choose to, operating within the constraints provided by accepted journalistic practice in their respective countries. Journalists, then, play a double role both as purveyors of meaning in their own right and as gatekeepers who grant access or withhold it from other speakers.[2]

Our stadium metaphor is misleading if it suggests that the playing field in this arena is like the flat, orderly, and well-marked field in a soccer stadium. The field in which framing contests occur is full of hills and valleys, sinkholes, promontories, and impenetrable jungles. To make matters even more complicated, the contours of the playing field can change suddenly in the middle of the contest because of events that lay beyond the control of the players; and players can themselves sometimes change the contours through actions that create new discursive opportunities. This complex playing field provides advantages and disadvantages in an uneven way to the various contestants in framing contests.

THE GALLERY The gallery is not just a bunch of individuals. Most of those watching the media carry around with them various collective identities – solidarity groups with whom they personally identify. Anderson (1991) captures the idea best with his concept of *imagined communities*. Examples would include women, workers, Christians, environmentalists, conservatives, Latinos, the "left," and many others.

---

[2] The complex interaction between institutionalized political actors, social movements, and media has only begun to be studied as a triad of influence in which all three types of actors have interests and routine practices that affect the work of each of the others. See for example the discussion in Oliver and Maney (2000).

Since people have multiple identities, they are potentially part of many imagined communities.

Imagined communities are not collective actors. They can only speak through some form of organization or advocacy network that attempts to generate, aggregate, transform, and articulate their concerns.[3] These carriers attempt to represent and make claims on behalf of the interests and values of particular communities that become their constituencies. Often rival carriers compete for the same constituency offering different and even contradictory claims about the "real" interests of the general public or some more specific constituency such as women or Christians.

BACKSTAGE Although a small minority of the speakers in the arena are individuals speaking only for themselves, generally those with standing are spokespersons for collective actors. These speakers have the advantage of being able to prepare backstage with the help of an organized production center. Their organization may provide material resources, strategic analyses of the playing field and the opportunities and constraints that it provides, professional know-how in the ways of the media, and useful alliances in the presentation of preferred frames in the arena. Speakers without such an organized production process behind them are severely handicapped against such competition.

Standing and Framing as Measures of Success

We measure success in the mass media forum by two criteria: standing and framing. By *standing*, we mean having a voice in the media. In news accounts, it refers to gaining the status of a regular media source whose interpretations are directly quoted. Standing is not identical to receiving any sort of coverage or mention in the news; a group may appear when it is described or criticized but still have no opportunity to provide its own interpretation and meaning to the events in which it is involved. Standing refers to a group being treated as an actor with voice, not merely as an object being discussed by others.

Even if a player gains standing, there is no guarantee that the media will report what the organization would like. Success is also measured by the degree to which its preferred frames are prominently displayed relative to rival frames and how this relative prominence increases over time. A *frame* is a thought organizer.

---

[3] This discussion draws heavily on Rucht (1995).

There are three principal meanings of frame in the English language, the first two of which apply to our use here. The first, as in a picture frame, is a rim for encasing, holding, or bordering something, distinguishing it from what is around it. A frame in this sense specifies what is relevant and what should be ignored. A second meaning, as in a building frame, is a basic or skeletal structure, designed to give shape or support. The frame of a building, covered by walls and insulation, is invisible once construction is completed. Although we do not actually see it, we can infer its presence in the finished product from its visible manifestations.[4]

As a social science concept, both of these meanings apply. Issue frames call our attention to certain events and their underlying causes and consequences and direct our attention away from others. At the same time, they organize and make coherent an apparently diverse array of symbols, images, and arguments, linking them through an underlying organizing idea that suggests what is at stake on the issue. Framing deals with the *gestalt* or pattern-organizing aspect of meaning.

There is a large and growing social science literature using the concept that we will review here quite selectively.[5] "Media frames," Gitlin (1980, p. 7) writes, "largely unspoken and unacknowledged, organize the world both for journalists who report it and, in some important degree, for us who rely on their reports." This usage of the term "frame" implies a range of positions rather than any single one, allowing for a degree of controversy among those who share a common frame. One can see in these quotations how differently supporters of less restrictive abortion policies can frame what is at stake on the abortion issue.

Media Discourse, Public Policy, and Everyday Life

Although success in having an impact on media discourse is important, it does not necessarily translate into impact on either public policy or on the everyday lives and practices of people in the gallery. With respect to public policy, decision-makers in the political system are

---

[4] The third meaning, largely irrelevant for our usage, is to rig evidence or events to incriminate someone falsely. It has some echoes in the strategic use of frames to make one's opponent's ideas "unspeakable" (Zirakzadeh 2000).

[5] For more extensive discussions see especially Goffman (1975), Bennett (1975), Tuchman (1978), Gitlin (1980), Gamson and Modigliani (1989), Ryan (1991), Gamson (1992), Snow and Benford (1988, 1992), Gerhards and Rucht (1992), Gerhards (1995), and Oliver and Johnston (1999).

clearly an attentive part of the gallery and may be influenced directly by the metaphors, images, and arguments that they see in the media. But other forums may be more important in influencing their thinking – including policy forums where the gallery is less the general public and more those with professional work interests and responsibilities in the policy domain.

Most of the impact of the media forum on decision makers is indirect, mediated by the perceived or actual impact of media discourse on the distribution of individual opinions among voters. To the extent that media discourse shapes opinions on issues that are electorally relevant, it will constrain political decision-makers or induce them to follow dominant tendencies to avoid defeat at the next election. This argument can be seen as a version of the two-step flow of influence – in this case, from the media to voters to policy-makers.

But the opinions of voters – whether in the form of sample surveys or the words of one's taxi driver – are open to interpretation. Various speakers compete to give their spin on what the "public" really thinks. For issue advocates in the policy arena, media discourse may be primarily a cultural tool whose content they can use in their own efforts to garner support rather than something by which they are influenced directly.[6]

Policy processes, however, are not driven only or even primarily by ideas. Decision-makers may be influenced by many other factors that operate with substantial insulation from public discourse – for example, the exchange relationships and deal-making of political insiders, support from influential political actors who may have substantial material interests engaged, and the demands of party discipline. It is quite possible to win the battle of public discourse without being able to convert this into the new advantages that flow from actually changing public policy. It is also possible to lose the battle of public discourse but successfully defend one's own cause by other means, for example, by lobbying legislators or winning in court.

As a rule, however, doing badly in mass media discourse creates vulnerability in pursuing policy interests. Political parties and individual politicians looking for issues that will attract voters and embarrass or divide their opponents may make the issue electorally relevant. For supporters of existing policies, the success of challengers in the mass media

---

[6] This is the sense in which framing evokes its linguistic rig-the-evidence roots as well.

forum puts them on the defensive and complicates their work. They are left vulnerable when their would-be allies are worried that their policy choices will become an issue that opponents are likely to use against them in the next election. If challengers are sufficiently successful in defining the terms of debate in media discourse, the support of a powerful but discredited interest group may stigmatize those who help them in policy disputes. The weakened position of tobacco companies in American politics provides a current example of how adverse framing in the media can make other resources less usable.

The link between mass media success and policy outcomes is further mediated by the complicated relationship of media discourse to the attitudes and understanding of people in the gallery. Gamson (1992, p. 179) likens people's efforts to make sense of issues to finding their way through a forest:"The various frames offered in media discourse provide maps indicating useful points of entry, and signposts at various crossroads highlight the significant landmarks and warn of the perils of other paths." In their attempts to make sense of the world of public affairs, ordinary people are only partially dependent on media discourse. Their dependency varies widely among different issue domains.

On certain issues, media discourse may be a first resort and the primary resource for making meaning, but even then people typically will find multiple frames available. The openness of the media text requires that they use other resources as well to complete the task. People control their media dependence in part through their willingness and ability to draw on popular wisdom and experiential knowledge to supplement what they are offered. In most cases, this is not only a reflection of an isolated individual but a social process by which people discuss and weigh their perceptions and experiences in light of those of their peers, friends, or family members, and in view of their other political, social, and religious commitments. If media dependence is only partial when media discourse serves as the starting point, it is even less so on an issue such as abortion, where experiential knowledge is likely to be a primary resource for finding a path through the forest.

Finally, success in media discourse also fails to guarantee that broader cultural and institutional practices will change. One may win the battle of words while practices remain unchanged or even change for the worse. Here, the abortion issue will serve well as an illustration. Most studies of media discourse on abortion, including this one, suggest that in the United States the proponents of frames emphasizing rights of individual privacy and women's self-determination do very well. At the same time, access to abortion is not increasing anywhere and has already declined in some areas. As of 1992, 84% of all counties in the United States had no known abortion provider and only 12% of residency programs required doctors-in-training to learn how to perform first-trimester abortions (Monangle 1995). Some states have only a single abortion provider, requiring women to travel great distances. The symbolic contest over the framing of abortion may be very far from the minds of potential abortion providers who are deterred by the fear that they may become the target of anti-abortion violence – regardless of whether such violence is roundly condemned in media discourse and public opinion.

EVALUATING PUBLIC DISCOURSE

[The discussion of abortion] has become stuck in the jungle of principles and emotions. . . . It is time to pull the debate back out into coolness, into pragmatism. (*Frankfurter Allgemeine Zeitung* (*FAZ*), July 30, 1971)

Civil discourse on this issue is really important and is sorely lacking. (pause) Sorely lacking. (Frances Kissling, Catholics for a Free Choice, Interview, May 1997)

It seems to be basic journalism that you really try to paint black and white because grey is not really that interesting. The business of the media is to paint polar opposites, [not] to create solutions. (Serrin Foster, Feminists for Life, Interview, July 1997)

Every effort to present a political opponent as a criminal is wicked. But, on the other side, tough arguments are quite appropriate. Politics is not a choral society full of harmony. If I want to change something in society, then I have to be able to stand the battle. (Stephan-Andreas Casdorff, *Die Süddeutsche Zeitung* (*SZ*), Interview, March 2000)

You are always more likely to get people to read your story if you can humanize it and personalize it. But you have to be careful in the process not to trivialize and sensationalize it. . . . I think you run the risk of sensationalizing it if you lose sight of the fact that we are talking about a serious public policy issue. You just have to strike a balance. (David Shaw, *The Los Angeles Times*, Interview, May 1998)

On the abortion issue, it is always important to keep the focus on what the issue is about, which is the lives of women and the quality of lives of women, in my opinion. I think this sometimes gets lost in the day to day reporting or the political rhetoric, or the latest wrinkle on the story. (Linda Greenhouse, *The New York Times*, Interview, June 1998)

Do the mass media provide the tools we need for democratic public life? The answer to this big question clearly depends on the theory of democratic politics with which one begins. More specifically, it depends on what role the model envisions for citizens, and, on this question, there is a long history of controversy with little normative consensus.

In spite of this lack of consensus on what the normative criteria should be, there seems to be a surprising amount of agreement that the mass media as they currently operate are seriously inadequate. The complaints are diverse and sometimes contradictory, especially if the target includes not only elite news media but also a broader spectrum of the popular press and television. No one seems to think that the media provides what citizens need to sustain a vital democracy.

With differing emphases in each country, political commentators suggest that most media discourse:

- is irrational and lacks reasoned argumentation;
- contains lies, distortions, and deliberate misinformation;
- shows a lack of civility and mutual respect;
- polarizes issues and discourages dialogue among those with differing opinions;
- appeals to the emotions rather than to the brain;
- is superficial, contains gross oversimplifications, and lacks subtlety and nuance;
- excludes many voices and lacks openness to many perspectives, especially those held by groups with fewer resources and less cultural power;
- encourages passivity, quiescence, and nonparticipation on the part of the citizenry.

How does one assess such claims? We use theories of democracy and the public sphere to suggest the relevant criteria. All theories of democracy start from the assumption that subjecting political decisions to public debate is a key element of the democratic processes. It is codified in existing democracies by rules about freedom of opinion, assembly, speech, and media intended to secure the public sphere. However, the questions of *who* should participate in public discourse, *when, how,* and *what* constitutes the most desirable *process* and *outcome* are all contested issues.

For convenience, we have divided democratic theory into four traditions: *Representative Liberal* (with its roots in Burke [1790], Mill [1861], and Schumpeter [1942]); *Participatory Liberal* (for example, Barber [1984]); *Discursive* (especially Habermas [1962, 1984, 1992, 1996]); and *Constructionist/Feminist* (for example, Benhabib [1996], Fraser [1997a], and Young [1996]). We often find different traditions calling attention to similar criteria, and sometimes there are different emphases among theorists we are grouping together and calling a tradition. Our purpose here is not to draw boundaries but to highlight normative criteria that are either matters of debate or consensus, looking at what democratic theories collectively imply.

We organize the criteria around the norms for participation (who should speak and when), content and style (what and how), process, and outcomes. The criteria that emerge from this analysis are *inclusiveness, civility, dialogue, argumentation, narrative, empowerment, closure,* and *consensus.* Our second story is about operationalizing these criteria using abortion discourse, comparing how well each of them is met in Germany and the United States. As we will see as the analysis unfolds, Germany does relatively better on those emphasized by the representative liberal tradition, while the United States does better on those emphasized by the participatory liberal and constructionist/feminist traditions. But there is much more to be told in later chapters.

PLAN OF THE BOOK

In the first section of the book, Chapter Two opens the way by providing some historical context for understanding the contemporary debate on abortion in each country. It is necessarily an abbreviated history, highlighting the major events that led to a wave of reform in the late 1960s and early to mid-1970s and what has happened in each country since then. The major court and legislative decisions of the 1970s were both a response to the reform wave and shaped the context for later discourse. We identify three main stages of debate in both countries and draw out both parallels and differences between the two countries that make them especially well suited for this comparative analysis.

In Chapter Three we describe the nature of our data for the general reader, with additional detail for methodological specialists included in an appendix as well as on the Web ⟨www.ssc.wisc.edu/abortionstudy⟩. We explain our focus on newspapers and the choice of the four newspapers in our sample: *The New York Times*, *The Los Angeles Times*, *Die Süddeutsche Zeitung*, and the *Frankfurter Allgemeine Zeitung*. We describe our complicated procedures for coding a sample of about 2500 articles, about one-half from each country. We carefully recorded who was given voice in these articles to articulate their own views. We also coded the frames displayed by both those who were quoted and by the authors of the articles.

In addition, we surveyed organizations involved in producing this media content, 94 in Germany and 55 in the United States. The survey tells us about the resources available to these organizations, their sophistication and professionalism in dealing with the mass media, their own perspective on the abortion discourse, and their sense of success or failure in shaping it. In selecting organizations to survey we made an effort to include "backstage" actors who chose less visibility and those whose voice was largely excluded from mainstream media. We also interviewed a selective sample of spokespersons for some of these organizations, either because they were central players or because of other characteristics that make them theoretically interesting. Finally, we interviewed a small number of journalists who wrote extensively about the abortion issue in the newspapers that we sampled.

The second part of the book provides a comparative overview of the framing contest as a whole – the framework of opportunities in which it is waged, the main players involved, and the leading frames used in both countries – highlighting the similarities and differences that we found. Chapter Four looks at some of the differences in the politics and culture of Germany and the United States that shape and constrain different types of actors, inevitably influencing who receives voice and what frames are easy or difficult to express. Here we describe the discursive opportunity structure in the two countries as it applies to collective actors in general, not only on the abortion issue. This includes especially the differences in the role of political parties in the two countries, in the diffusion and decentralization of government authority, in the cultural acceptance of the welfare state, in the politics of gender in and outside of government, in the relations of church and state, in the handling of social justice claims, and in mass media norms and practices.

In Chapter Five we examine which actors receive standing in the mass media in the two countries – that is, which actors are used as quoted or paraphrased sources in news reports and commentary on abortion – and how this has changed over time. We show how quite different types of actors are given significant voice in the two countries on this issue – emphasizing the different roles of political parties and social movement organizations in particular. We compare the organization, resources, and media relations skills of similar types of actors in each country as a way of understanding why some are more successful, even when recognizing that the playing field is more advantageous for some than for others.

Chapter Six provides an overview of the framing contest on abortion in the two countries and how the careers of different frames have changed over time. We find that different frames are dominant in the discourse of the two countries and that, somewhat to our surprise, the "clash of absolutes" (Tribe 1990) is more evident in Germany, even though the German debate has been more tempered in many ways and unmarred by the wave of anti-abortion violence found in the United States. At the same time, there are certain elements of consensus in German discourse that are not present in the United States. The United States discourse includes many more claims about the role of the individual and the state and more strongly polarized claims about the morality involved in abortion. We also find that the German discourse has generally moved toward a more anti-abortion framing of what the issues are and the American debate has moved in a more pro-abortion-rights direction from the beginning of the period.

The third part of the book explores the representation of the discursive interests of three major constituencies on the abortion issue. We examine who makes claims on behalf of each constituency – and their relative success in shaping abortion discourse. In Chapter Seven, we look at who attempts to represent women's claims. In both countries, there is an active women's movement that seeks to connect abortion rights to women's rights, but the movements differ in significant ways and have differential success. We examine both the voice that women have as speakers in the media discourse and the career of gendered frames sponsored by different mediators. We find that abortion is a more gender-polarized and gender-identified issue in Germany than in the United States, and has been from the very beginning of the period we study.

In Chapter Eight we examine the nature of the religious constituency and the relative success of those promoting religious frames in shaping the abortion discourse. We particularly focus on the churches, active in both countries, and on the successful mobilization of the Christian Right constituency in the United States. There is much less of a social movement component in the field of actors speaking against abortion on religious grounds in Germany, leaving the institutional churches, particularly the Catholic Church, as the major spokespersons for a religious constituency. The United States not only has a variety of anti-abortion actors for a religious constituency but also has pro-abortion-rights speakers who are invoking a sacred canopy, arguing that abortion can be a moral choice for a religious person under some circumstances. United States speakers invoke religious pluralism and the diversity of moral values to legitimate choice, while German speakers assume a moral consensus from which they are more or less willing to countenance exceptions. There is also less ambivalence in Germany about the state as the guardian of morality and as a moral actor.

Chapter Nine considers what we have labeled the tradition of the left, a constituency that emphasizes inequality based on class, race, or ethnicity as well as gender, and responds in terms of meeting needs and supporting autonomy for disadvantaged groups as well as making claims for social justice. We examine the impact of the would-be mediators of the tradition of the left in shaping abortion discourse, focusing on the left–right continuum in politics and the alignment of political parties as representatives of "the disadvantaged." The abortion issue in Germany was historically part of class politics, and from the beginning of the period that we study the German parties had clearly divergent positions. In the United States, abortion has also been a partisan issue, and in both major parties' efforts to preempt the middle, advocacy for the poor or for racial and ethnic minorities often must come from social movement organizations. We look at the discursive obstacles that lead American groups to back away from such advocacy. In Germany, the framing of abortion as help for the needy, in this case pregnant women, also raises issues of state paternalism and women's autonomous decision making that are sources of controversy in and for the imagined community of the left.

In the fourth part of the book we turn from the task of explaining how abortion discourse has been shaped to an evaluation of what these outcomes mean for the functioning of democracy in the two countries. In Chapter Ten we mine different theoretical traditions for their normative criteria about what are desirable qualities in a democratic public sphere and in the particular forum that concerns us here: the mass media. In some cases, different traditions point to similar or overlapping criteria; in other cases, there are theoretical controversies and a lack of normative consensus. We use this chapter to delineate four basic traditions – *Representative Liberal, Participatory Liberal, Discursive,* and *Constructionist/Feminist* – and to outline what each tradition would highlight as the most desirable criteria for a well-functioning public sphere.

In Chapter Eleven we operationalize these criteria for good public discourse, measuring them in the ways that our data allow. We then compare German and United States discourse on how closely the different criteria are met and whether there are any visible trends over time in how well they are met. Where there is a lack of normative consensus on the desirability of a criterion, we leave the reader to judge whether meeting this standard reflects positively or negatively on the society that does.

In Chapter Twelve we look at what the participants and journalists involved in the abortion issue have to say about the quality of discourse. Here, our data on actor observations come from a survey of organizations and interviews with organizational spokespersons. Our data on journalist observations come from our interviews with journalists who covered the abortion issue and other journalists' comments on the quality of the discourse that appeared in our newspaper sample. In general, the actors and journalists involved tend to see the discourse accurately as it is reflected in our analysis, but they see it selectively, missing much of what is there.

In a final concluding chapter we review the various findings in the two main sections of the book and examine their implications for understanding cultural change and democratic theories of the public sphere.

CHAPTER TWO

Historical Context

If Germany and the United States have reached somewhat similar compromises on abortion policy, they have arrived there by quite different historical paths.[7] In this chapter we trace the paths by which law and policy were shaped in each country over the past century. Perhaps the most fundamental difference is that Germany went through intense debates on abortion in the first third of the twentieth century while the United States witnessed what Luker (1984) aptly labeled a "century of silence."

Abortion emerged (or, in the case of Germany, reemerged) as a controversial public issue in the last third of the twentieth century. We will review the "critical discourse moments" that have occurred in both countries during the contemporary period. *Critical discourse moments* are events that stimulate news articles and commentary in various public forums – in this case, especially legislative actions and court decisions.[8] These events sometimes change the discursive opportunity structure and, therefore, necessarily require the would-be players to interpret the event in terms of their preferred frame and, in some cases, to reevaluate their discursive strategy.

PROLOGUE

UNITED STATES

In the first two-thirds of the nineteenth century, abortion was largely unregulated in the United States, especially before "quick-

---

[7] Rucht (1994, Chapter Eight) provides a fuller comparative history. Other good historical accounts for the United States are available in Burns (2002), Luker (1984), and Solinger (1998) and for Germany in Jochimsen (1971) and Grossman (1995).

[8] For a discussion of the concept of critical discourse moments, see Chilton (1987).

ening."[9] It was not a matter to be discussed openly in public although abortion providers advertised their services in coded form (see Olasky 1988). A movement in the last third of the century changed this situation, making abortion illegal except under special circumstances.

This movement was part of a broader effort by physicians to secure their medical authority against the competition of other healers by delegitimizing them as "quacks" and "charlatans." Their successful campaign on abortion took a practice that had been tacitly allowed and made it illegal except when physicians, and only physicians, decided that it was medically necessary. Churches, including the Catholic Church, were not involved in the nineteenth-century "physicians' crusade" (Mohr 1978, p. 147) to make abortion illegal.

Each of the states made its own regulations, and they varied widely. In some states no exceptions were permitted, but in most cases the only legal exceptions (for "therapeutic" abortions) were to be made by hospital committees on grounds that a continuation of the pregnancy endangered the life of the woman. Illegal abortions flourished, sometimes with tragic results, despite occasional prosecutions of unauthorized abortion providers.

There was virtually no public discussion of abortion from 1890, at which point nearly every state had passed some form of restrictive legislation, until the late 1950s. Planned Parenthood was one of the few organizations that did not accept the status quo.[10] The organization initially took a position that emphasized women's own decision making about childbearing, but it soon found itself drawn into alliances with doctors who stressed eugenic themes. In Gordon's (1977, 1982) analyses, their understanding of issues of reproduction gradually shifted from affirming birth control (by women) to supporting population control (by doctors and public officials). During this period, Planned Parenthood never affirmed abortion as a woman's right or defended the illegal abortion providers who were sporadically prosecuted.[11]

In 1957, Planned Parenthood held a conference on the medical practice of abortion as it currently existed. This conference made public a

[9] *Quickening* is the moment when the pregnant woman first experiences movement by the fetus.
[10] Planned Parenthood emerged out of the complicated birth control movement of the 1920s and 1930s (see Burns 2002).
[11] Despite the popular perception of illegal abortion providers as unqualified and dangerous practitioners who were exploiting women's distress for their profit, some unknown proportion of them were both competent and principled (Joffe 1995; Solinger 1998).

"secret" that was previously known only to doctors and countless women who did not talk about it. The secret was the fact that medically approved abortions were frequently occurring in cases of rape and incest, mental illnesses such as depression, medical complications that were not life-threatening for the mother, and at times for fetal deformity as well.

This widespread practice was clearly going beyond what the laws in various states allowed. A major outgrowth of the conference was an effort carried out by the American Law Institute (ALI) to create a model abortion law. This proposed legislation would, if adopted, bring the law more into accord with actual practice by creating legal exceptions for these grave circumstances. The century of silence was ending but the abortion issue had not quite become visible.

GERMANY

There was no century of silence in Germany. The legal starting point began with the formation of Germany as a state in 1871. In its criminal code, §218 defined abortion as a felony punishable with five years imprisonment. Abortion became a public issue by the late nineteenth century with the efforts of social reformers – socialists, feminists, and liberals – to put birth control and population control issues on the political agenda.

By the turn of the century, this had blossomed into a broad challenge that included lessening or removing restrictions on abortion, offering support for unwed mothers, and supporting women's right to choose whether or not to bear children (Wobbe 1989). The *Bund für Mütterschutz und Sexualreform* (League for the Protection of Mothers and for Sexual Reform) was founded in 1904. Evans (1976, p. 134) describes the group as notable for "drawing the consequences of their liberal individualism and applying them to personal life." They sought legal equality in marriage, easier divorce, an end to police interference in breaking up "free unions," and equal rights for children born out of wedlock.

The *Bund* was the first group to call for the elimination of §218. They struggled for the legalization of abortion "in the name of the right to self-determination, in the name of the free personality of women" (Evans 1976, p. 134) and offered an unusually extensive analysis of gender politics. They connected abortion rights to financial and moral support for unwed mothers and framed such rights as essential to women's control over the conditions of their existence (Allen 1985). While many separate women's groups supported their cause, in 1908 the broad umbrella organization of the liberal women's movement narrowly rejected taking up the campaign for elimination of §218, even though more radical feminists continued to agitate for change (Grossman 1995).

It fell to communist and socialist parties to take up this issue politically in the Weimar Republic (Wobbe 1989). In 1920, the left socialists (USPD) introduced a bill for the complete elimination of §218, but it failed to pass, as did a similar bill introduced by the Communist Party (KPD) in 1922. Throughout the 1920s, abortion remained an important political issue, particularly presented in terms of class conflict and the unjust prosecution of poor women with no practical alternatives to abortion.

Prosecutions of women rose from 411 in 1902 to 1884 in 1916 to 7193 in 1924. Reformers argued that no rich women were among the many thousands being sent to prison under the law (Jochimsen 1971). Between 1919 and 1932 there were 60,000 cases in which women were prosecuted for illegal abortions. Yet the reformers were only able to widen slightly the exceptions under which abortion might be legal – to include, in 1926, serious threats to maternal health, with the concurrence of a medical commission.

The conflict escalated in the late 1920s, as protest groups formed to defend two doctors charged with performing illegal abortions, Else Kienle and Friedrich Wolf, who were noted for their work among the poor. In 1929–1930 there were over 800 local protest groups and 1500 mass demonstrations against §218 recorded (Augstein 1983). The left socialists (USPD) and communists (KPD) led the battle, and the main body of the Social Democrats (SPD) came along only "lamely, with hesitation and resistance," one participant complained (Arendt 1970, p. 96). The debate was smothered by the Nazi acquisition of power in 1933.

Nazi abortion law sharply distinguished between life that was worthy of life and "unworthy lives" (*lebensunwertes Leben*), forbidding abortion in the former but demanding it in the latter case. In 1935, the Nazis introduced a "eugenic justification" for abortion into the criminal code, and in 1943 they supplemented §218 with a clause demanding the death penalty for abortion "in cases where the vitality (*Lebenskraft*) of the German people is threatened" (Koonz 1986). During the occupation after the war, the three Western powers reactivated the 1926 version of §218 in the sections of Germany that they controlled. However, little was done to enforce it.

The Federal Republic of Germany (FRG) was founded in the zones occupied by the three Western powers in 1949; the German Democratic Republic (GDR) was founded in the Soviet-occupied zone in the same year. The FRG's constitution, the Basic Law, was written in the context of the omnipresent memory of the Nazi regime and the emergent Cold War. Its second provision proclaimed the fundamental obligation of the state to protect life. This provision was not explicitly connected to any position on abortion, although abortion was certainly not an unfamiliar issue to the constitutional committee.

The FRG returned to the pre-war criminal code, including §218, rejecting proposals that would have permitted abortion in cases of rape, although the continued presence of occupying armies made this a visible political issue. The number of successful prosecutions for abortion, however, steadily declined – from 1033 in 1955 to 276 in 1969. Most women received light sentences.

ACT ONE: THE (RE)EMERGENCE

UNITED STATES

Two events in 1962 marked the end of the public silence in the United States. One was a fictional dramatization, "The Benefactor," shown on a popular prime-time television show, "The Defenders." The protagonist was on trial for having performed an illegal abortion and was presented as a highly attractive and principled man. The second was a human interest story about the dilemmas of a woman, Sherri Finkbine, a married, white, middle-class mother of four who had taken Thalidomide, a drug discovered to cause major birth defects, and faced the likely prospect of bearing a severely deformed child. These complex narratives have been described in detail by Condit (1990) and others (Gamson 1999), and we will not repeat them here. The two media stories, both of them lasting over several weeks, clearly established abortion reform as a publicly discussible topic and gave a boost to the reform effort.

By 1967, the ALI model abortion law was on the agenda of half the state legislatures and had already been passed in California, North Carolina, and Colorado. Between 1967 and 1970, a number of other states, especially in the South, where the Catholic Church had little political presence, adopted the ALI law with little controversy (Burns 2002).

However, this was not the case in New York, where a heated controversy between 1967 and 1970 resulted – partly through missteps on the part of opponents of reform – in a sweeping law far beyond what the ALI had proposed. The New York law essentially legalized abortion in the first trimester, creating an entirely different legal climate for abortion providers as well as providing access to legal, medically safe abortions for pregnant women from other states – if they had the means to travel. The controversy over the New York law also led to the mobilization of the anti-abortion movement, which will be described in more detail later.

Meanwhile, the abortion reform movement was rapidly broadening as a new wave of the women's movement began to emerge. While the ALI law reinforced medical authority over abortions, the new players challenged it. Repeal rather than reform became their goal, and they framed the issue in a new way. The formation of NARAL in 1969 is a good marker. In those days, the acronym stood for the National Association for the Repeal of Abortion Laws. NARAL demanded women's right to make the decision rather than merely extending the discretion of doctors and hospital committees over a wider set of circumstances that could justify legal abortions. The women's movement during this period also included groups less interested in changing laws and more interested in making medically safe abortions available to women who sought them at a reasonable cost.

The clandestine abortion service called Jane provided one such form of resistance (Kaplan 1995). Newly emerging feminist grassroots groups also brought protest into elite forums, demanding a voice in panels and expert commissions where no women sat (Cisler 1970, p. 278). Some began to take their protest to the streets as well. The *NYT* reported: "More than 15,000 demonstrators, most of them young, white and female and wearing bell-bottom pants, startled Easter shoppers yesterday afternoon by marching across 34th Street to protest abortion laws. The march, from First Avenue to Broadway, was part of a day-long series of demonstrations organized by People to Abolish Abortion Laws, a coalition of groups including many militant feminist organizations and several Manhattan Democratic clubs." (*NYT*, 3/29/70).

Despite this and other instances of early Democratic involvement in the abortion rights movement, the alignment of the abortion issue with the political party position was not entirely clear during this phase of the discourse. Catholics were largely a Democratic party constituency, and the Catholic Church was the leading voice of opposition to abortion reform. A majority of the early right-to-life activists were Democrats, and Ellen McCormick founded the New York Right-to-Life party only when she failed to convince the Democratic Party to take up the cause (Kelly 1992). Only the veto of a Republican governor, Nelson Rockefeller, saved the New York abortion law from repeal in 1972. Feminist groups were divided in their party allegiances, if they had any at all. Abortion was not a defining issue for either party.

This was the context in which the Supreme Court agreed to hear challenges to abortion laws in Texas (*Roe v. Wade*) and Georgia (*Doe v. Bolton*) in 1972. By its decisions in these cases, the Supreme Court essentially moved the arena from the state to the national level, thus beginning a new phase of conflict, transforming the character of the debate, and involving new protagonists.

On January 22, 1973, the Supreme Court presented a 7–2 decision in the case of *Roe v. Wade* in which a pseudonymous plaintiff, Jane Roe, sued the state of Texas for the right to have a legal abortion. The court found for the plaintiff, and Justice Blackmun, writing for the majority, accepted her attorney's argument that the 1963 Court decision, *Griswold v. Connecticut*, was the appropriate precedent.[12]

Blackmun and the majority found that the right to privacy of a married couple that had been affirmed in *Griswold* also extended to cover the decision of an individual woman to terminate a pregnancy. The court further defined the limits to this right to privacy by dividing a pregnancy into three equal stages or trimesters. It balanced the right to self-determination against the state's legitimate interest in the health and safety of the mother in the second trimester and affirmed the state's legitimate interest in the life of the fetus as well in the third trimester. The court defined "the woman and her doctor" as a unit with an absolute right to decide on the appropriateness of abortion in the first trimester. In doing so, it invalidated state laws in 46 of the 50 states,[13] including those that had adopted the ALI reform law. It took the regulation of abortion in the first two trimesters largely out of the hands of individual state legislatures.

This did not stop state legislatures from attempting to write restrictive regulations, and there was an immediate legislative mobilization after *Roe* at the state level. Indeed, according to Halva-Neubauer (1993),

---

[12] In that case, the court had invalidated a Connecticut law prohibiting the sale of contraceptives to married women on the grounds that this was state interference in what ought properly to be the private decision of a family and was constitutionally prohibited. The right to be secure in one's person or in one's household from state intrusions constituted a general right to privacy, the court argued.

[13] The exceptions were Alaska, Hawaii, New York, and Washington.

more state legislatures debated abortion bills in the three years follow-ing *Roe* than in any other period. Among the most popular bills were the so-called "conscience clauses" that allowed individual hospitals, doctors, nurses, or other medical personnel to refuse to participate in abortions without penalty. These bills also included consent require-ments that the pregnant woman be given specific information about the procedure and the fetus and/or that she secure the consent of her parents or husband.

In addition, states passed laws requiring physicians to save fetuses born alive, prohibiting certain procedures, and defining who could perform abortions and in what settings. Some state bills called on the U.S. Congress to pass a Human Life Amendment that would nullify the *Roe* decision by amending the constitution. State and federal courts were asked repeatedly to rule on the constitutionality of these specific laws. The decision in *Roe* thus stimulated rather than ended legislative debates on the rights that women had over the decision to terminate a pregnancy.

Roe v. Wade also initiated a wider public mobilization than the United States had ever experienced with regard to abortion. Imme-diately following the decision, the informal National Right to Life Committee incorporated as an independent nondenominational organization. The Catholic bishops sought a concerted national strategy and shifted their attention from merely supporting or resist-ing state-level initiatives to advocating a constitutional amendment and flooding Congress and the Supreme Court with letters of protest. The first conservative Protestant right-to-life organization, the Christian Action Council, was founded by a group that included the prominent television evangelist, the Rev. Billy Graham (Kelly 1992, p. 158).

On the other side, NARAL renamed itself the National Abortion Rights Action League in 1973 and, together with allies such as Planned Parenthood and the American Civil Liberties Union, "regrouped for the next round in the conflict" (Staggenborg 1991, p. 58). Women's health centers began to offer legal abortion as one of a number of health ser-vices provided in a feminist context of woman-centered care (Ruzek 1978; Simonds 1996). Catholic feminists founded Catholics for a Free Choice in 1973 and the Religious Coalition for Abortion Rights, repre-senting national religious organizations drawn from various Protestant denominations and Reform Judaism, was founded in 1974 "to protect the option of legal abortion" (Segers 1992, p. 171).

The Supreme Court's *Roe* decision, then, was not the beginning but the end of Act One. It changed the playing field for a new political struggle between those who would impose new restrictions on abortion and those who sought to defend the new status quo (McCarthy 1987).

GERMANY

Abortion never fully disappeared as a political issue in Germany, but it began to reemerge in the 1960s (Gante 1991). Liberal lawyers, notably the *Humanistische Union* (HU), began to call for reform of §218 that would recognize advances in prenatal testing and counseling by providing eugenic exceptions as well as an exception for rape. The Social Democratic Party (SPD), after its electoral victory in 1969 and newly formed governing coalition with the liberal FDP, announced that it would take up the problem of reform of §218. The government appointed a commission of law professors to provide a suitable reform, but the group returned with a divided recommendation.

A majority proposed legalizing abortion in the first trimester, with counseling required beforehand (the *Fristenlösung*). A minority proposed a wider set of permissible justifications (or "indications") for abortion but would leave the decision in the hands of medical authorities (the *Indikationslösung*). Women's groups such as the Women's Law Association and the Women's Caucus of the SPD pressed for legalization in the first trimester, and emerging autonomous feminist women's groups at the local level, such as the *Frauenaktion '70* in Frankfurt, pushed further by calling for the complete elimination of §218, reviving the demand that had energized the movement in the 1920s. The political parties all took formal positions on the reform, as did the churches, but it was at first essentially an elite debate.

Public interest in the issue was especially stimulated by a creative protest action. Drawing on the example of a similar protest in Paris the previous month, Alice Schwarzer, a feminist and journalist, orchestrated a public declaration by women celebrities that they had had abortions. In June 1971, in the widely read weekly magazine *Stern*, 374 women publicly claimed to have had an abortion and dared the government to prosecute.[14] Although investigations of some of the women followed, no actual prosecutions resulted, and six weeks later there were over 86,000 similar written claims from less well-known women.

---

[14] The participants believed that it was irrelevant for this collective action whether they actually did or did not have an abortion.

This action, and the public campaign for eliminating §218 that followed, was clearly associated with feminist groups and action committees on the local level. Protesters often raised the issue of the exclusion of women from the hearing rooms and parliamentary committees where reforms were being debated (for example, in May 1972 in Cologne). Doctors followed the feminists' lead with their own public declarations of having broken the abortion law (329 made such declarations in an article in the newsmagazine, *Der Spiegel*, in 1974) and a few faced disciplinary proceedings and lost their jobs as a result.

Opponents of liberalization also mobilized during this period. As in the United States, the Catholic Church was in the forefront. In 1973, *Aktion für das Leben* (Pro Life Action) was founded, and the church itself mustered substantial demonstrations in several cities in the same year. In Germany, unlike in the United States, however, the closest political allies of the Catholic Church were the Christian Democratic Party (CDU)[15] and the Christian Social Party (CSU). The latter, restricted exclusively to Bavaria, is a more thoroughly Catholic and deeply conservative party than the CDU, with whom it enters into coalition at the national level.

Because most of the more Protestant parts of Germany fell into the Soviet occupation zone and became the GDR, Catholics were a majority in the CDU. The minority of Protestant (Lutheran) members had their own working group. In the color symbolism that is widely used and understood in Germany, the CDU is "black" or clerical, in opposition to the "red" Social Democrats. Thus in Germany, unlike in the United States, abortion could be clearly mapped onto the prevailing division of party interests – based on both the extensive history of engagement of "the left" with this issue and the unquestioned affinity of the Catholic Church for the party of "the right."

Meanwhile, in East Germany, reform came quietly in 1972. With state- and party-controlled media providing little or no public discussion of the issue, abortion was legalized in the first trimester[16] by the national legislature. The Catholic Church raised objections, but only privately. There was a minority vote against the law by Christian Democrats (14 against and 8 abstentions), the first minority vote in the

---

[15] The CDU was formed in the postwar period as the nondenominational successor to the Catholic party of the Weimar period, the *Zentrum*, and is the dominant conservative force.

[16] Second-trimester abortions were permitted with the consent of a hospital committee when warranted by the medical condition of either the mother or the fetus.

GDR parliament, but no public debate or media coverage. At the same time, contraception in the form of the birth control pill was made available at no cost. Abortion was, like all medical care, available at no cost, but it was allowed only on an in-patient basis. A variety of social support measures for mothers were also passed around this time, including extensive public childcare and paid leave for mothers in the first year after birth.[17]

In West Germany, the public mobilization around abortion pushed the government toward reform. But with no consensus within the SPD, the government was having difficulty coming up with a specific proposal; by the spring of 1973, four different bills lay before the *Bundestag*. For the first time in the history of the *Bundestag*, individual votes had to be tallied, and decriminalization in the first trimester passed with a very narrow majority (247 to 233) in 1974. The only limits were that abortions needed to be performed by a doctor after counseling. Medical grounds were acceptable at any point and eugenic grounds were sufficient up to 22 weeks. This was essentially the *Fristenlösung* option.

After further legislative battles left the new law standing, five CDU/CSU state governments and 193 conservative members of the *Bundestag* appealed to the Constitutional Court to overturn the decision. In February 1975, by a vote of 5 to 3, the Court held that "the right of developing life must take priority" over the woman's right of self-determination[18] and directed the *Bundestag* to rewrite the law accordingly (Döbert 1996).

The Court decision was not accepted passively. Demonstrations against it included burning judges in effigy and stone-throwing by demonstrators; the police responded with tear gas and clubs. In July 1975, a police search of the Women's Center in Frankfurt, and confiscation of their list of doctors, evoked a wave of protest, including well-publicized, feminist-organized bus trips to abortion clinics in the Netherlands.

But the federal legislature, seeing itself as constrained by the Constitutional Court decision, worked to produce an acceptable alternative. In February 1976, the *Bundestag* passed an *Indikationslösung* law, accepting four grounds for legal abortions – criminal, medical, eugenic,

---

[17] See Ferree (1993) and Penrose (1990) for more details on the policy of supporting rather than coercing motherhood as central to this wave of legislation.

[18] This latter right derives from the constitutional provision for "the free development of the personality of each individual."

and "social."[19] This law so contentiously arrived at finally went into effect at the end of June, 1976.

In addition to specifying acceptable reasons, the new law also required a counseling session with a doctor other than the one who would perform the abortion, at least a three-day waiting period between the counseling and the abortion, and only allowed abortions in "a hospital or licensed institution." Abortions that failed to meet any of these conditions were punishable with up to a year in prison for the pregnant woman and up to three years for any other participating party.

Publicized, deliberately provocative trips to the Netherlands to circumvent the law by obtaining abortions there continued until the end of 1977, and critics on both sides found the reform unsatisfying. But the court's decision placed the long-sought goal of the repeal of §218 apparently out of reach and changed the discursive opportunity structure for the next phase. At the end of Act One, public controversy about abortion dropped dramatically in West Germany, even as the debate in the United States began to heat up.

ACT TWO: THE CONTINUING STRUGGLE

UNITED STATES

In addition to the attempts in various state legislatures to introduce new restrictions on abortion following *Roe*, anti-abortion groups launched a national campaign for a "Right-to-Life" amendment to the constitution. By 1976, such efforts had largely stalled. However, in one of its many decisions upholding the legality of abortion and throwing out various restrictive state laws, the Court left open a new opportunity for opponents of abortion. State governments, the Court ruled, were not obliged to pay for abortions for poor women.

This decision opened a new avenue for federal action. In 1976, Henry Hyde, a Republican from Illinois, introduced an amendment to the appropriations bill for Health and Human Services for the following year. The Hyde Amendment prohibited all federal funding for abortions through federal programs such as Medicaid[20] except when the life of the

---

[19] "Soziale" Indikation was a convenient label for what officially was termed "allgemeine Notlagenindikation" (a general state of need).

[20] The Hyde Amendment was first passed in 1976 but initially blocked by court injunction from being implemented. Medicaid is a means-based program for people below the poverty line and covers many women in their childbearing years. Some versions

mother was endangered or, in later years, for rape and incest. In two cases in 1977 (*Beal v. Doe, 432 US 438* and *Maher v. Roe, 432 US 464*), the Supreme Court affirmed the constitutionality of individual states limiting use of Medicaid for only "medically necessary" abortions. In a 5–4 opinion in 1980, the Court then accepted the Hyde Amendment in *Harris v. McRae (448 US 297)*. Funding restrictions at both the state and federal levels became ubiquitous. Congress added a version of the Hyde Amendment to each year's appropriations bills through 1989 (Mezey 1992).

The late 1970s also saw the rise of the Christian Right, which we discuss in detail in Chapter Eight. When Ronald Reagan won the Republican Party nomination in 1980 with strong Christian Right support, the party platform adopted, for the first time, a plank calling for a constitutional amendment to prohibit abortion. The combination of the party's formal position, the public endorsement by Reagan of a Human Life Amendment to the constitution, and the recurrent drama of Supreme Court confirmation hearings focused on the nominee's position on *Roe* produced a clearer partisan alignment on the abortion issue than had been present during the first phase of the discourse.

The late 1970s also saw the rise of the first anti-abortion violence, beginning with bombing and setting fire to clinics, kidnappings of personnel, and death threats. The National Abortion Federation (NAF), a coalition of abortion provider organizations, began keeping statistics at this point. It later reported more than 1100 acts of violence in the period of 1977 to 1992 (National Abortion Federation 1993).

By the end of 1988, most of the mobilization against abortion had moved in two distinct directions. Part of the movement had taken up nonviolent, direct action by attempting to physically block access to clinics where abortions were performed. Other parts of the movement played an insider game, focusing especially on the Republican Party, as described in Chapter Eight. The movement had achieved some favorable Supreme Court appointments and decisions, but *Roe v. Wade* still stood, although it appeared to "hang by a thread" in the lingo of the day. Abortion rights supporters responded defensively, attempting to

---

of the Hyde Amendment also blocked women in military service from receiving abortions in military hospitals (where their medical care is generally provided at no cost to them).

block anti-abortion Court nominees, providing escorts for women entering blockaded clinics, and lobbying state legislatures to prevent additional restrictions from being adopted.

The Supreme Court, at this point, elected to hear the case of *Webster v. Reproductive Health Services*. The plaintiffs were challenging a restrictive Missouri law that they claimed violated the Court's *Roe* decision. The outcome was in doubt since, for the first time, the combination of justices who had originally voted against *Roe* with those appointed by Reagan now constituted a narrow majority of the Court. The stage was set for Act Three.

GERMANY

The abortion struggle in Germany during this phase was much less intense but continued in arenas outside of the legislature and judiciary. Under the 1976 law, more than 80% of legal abortions were carried out under the social need exception to the prohibition. Nevertheless, the restrictions were often burdensome, requiring the permission of two doctors, a waiting period, and counseling. Approval was uncertain, especially in Catholic areas, and the threat of prosecution was never completely absent. Charges were brought against an increasing number of women for illegal abortions, and doctors were sometimes prosecuted for certifying abortions too easily to suit a particular legislator, prosecutor, or police department.

"Abortion tourism" to the Netherlands remained quite common, especially for women from states with a more restrictive position on interpreting the social justification. The degree of enforcement affected the actual availability of legal abortions from place to place and over time. In two cities of comparable size – Stuttgart and Dortmund – the number of legally registered abortions were, respectively, 18 and 4124 in 1989.

In predominantly Catholic parts of Germany, abortion was not merely difficult to obtain but potentially risky. Between 1983 and 1988, there were an average of 170 prosecutions a year against women who obtained illegal abortions, although in most years 10 or fewer convictions resulted (Vultejus 1990). In 1988, Horst Theissen, a doctor in the small Bavarian town of Memmingen, was prosecuted for unwarranted use of the social need justification in 156 cases. His confidential records were opened and the individual women and their abortions were publicized (Friedrichsen 1991). This Memmingen trial was portrayed in the national newsmagazine *Der Spiegel* as a "witchhunt" in a cover that

screamed its concern in red and black. The case, unlike the earlier prosecutions in the 1980s, became a *cause celebre*.

Some estimates for the period suggest that two-thirds of all abortions
on West German women were performed illegally. Even the number of
claims for payment submitted by doctors to the patients' insurance
companies regularly exceeded the number of legally registered abortions. Women who went to the Netherlands for abortions were occasionally subjected to forced gynecological examinations at the
German–Dutch border on their return to determine if an illegal abortion[21] had taken place (Maleck-Lewy 1994).

Neither side was happy with the situation. Feminists continued to
argue for the repeal of §218, but their proclamations and moderate-size
demonstrations were routinely ignored. At the same time, a broader
women's movement working through the political parties was gaining
strength. A striking indicator of this rising influence was the appointment by the CDU in 1986 of Rita Süßmuth, a self-identified feminist,
to head the newly re-named and re-organized ministry for Women,
Health, and Family.

By 1989, the abortion law in West Germany was depicted by all
sides as a force for political hypocrisy. The law itself was seen as unsat-
isfactory by liberals, who thought it ineffective in encouraging childbirth and demeaning to women; by conservatives, who thought it
inadequately enforced; and by feminists, who thought it wrong in
principle.

In East Germany, the "silent liberalization" of 1972 was followed
largely by more silence on the topic of abortion (Harsch 1997). In the
1980s, publication of Charlotte Worgitsky's novel, *Meine ungeborenen
Kinder* (*My Unborn Children*), provided the first opportunity for some
limited discussion of the meaning of women's choice of abortion in the
GDR. The circumstances and needs that led her protagonist to multiple abortions were used as a vehicle for raising such questions as: What
is a responsible decision for abortion? How is sexual repression associated with undesired pregnancy? When and how do women actually
decide on abortion? (Worgitsky 1992). By 1989, GDR women had a generation of experience with legal abortion in the first trimester but only
a modest start on forming a social evaluation of the meaning of that
experience (Maleck-Lewy 1994).

---

[21] Even going abroad for an abortion was illegal under German law, though it never
was under U.S. law.

ACT THREE: AN UNEASY COMPROMISE

United States

In June 1989, the Supreme Court reorganized the playing field again. In its *Webster* decision it held that some restrictions were allowable, but they had to meet an ambiguous standard of not creating "an undue burden" on the pregnant woman. The Court decision did not give a definitive answer to what restrictions would constitute such a burden, but they gave some direction by approving some of the restrictions in the Missouri law while throwing out others. Tribe (1990) called the decision "not a model of clarity," but it made certain things very clear: Henceforth, state legislatures would become a more significant arena for efforts to adopt new abortion restrictions and there would undoubtedly be future federal cases testing the boundaries of an "undue burden." The decision also made clear that this particular constellation of justices was not going to overturn *Roe v. Wade*.

Neither side was happy with the result. Anti-abortion forces were disappointed that the Reagan appointees did not all join with the earlier *Roe* dissenters to overturn the earlier decision. Abortion-rights supporters were dismayed at what appeared to be an invitation to state legislatures to pass restrictive legislation that might pass muster as not being an undue burden. The response was a sharply renewed mobilization by the Pro side and a period of re-examination of strategy by the Anti side, processes that we describe in detail in later chapters.

State legislatures responded to the new opportunity in a variety of ways. Some states – such as Pennsylvania and Louisiana – that had previously challenged *Roe* continued to do so; others had strong majorities in favor of abortion rights and did nothing or, in some cases, reaffirmed the right of a pregnant woman to choose to have an abortion in the first trimester. In 1992, the Supreme Court agreed to review the constitutionality of a new Pennsylvania law. In its *Casey v. Planned Parenthood of Pennsylvania* decision, it again accepted some restrictions and threw out others, providing some additional clues on where this particular court drew the undue burden line.

The first Bush administration provided additional opportunities to debate abortion by issuing an executive order forbidding health care providers paid by federal funds from mentioning the abortion option to their patients. Abortion rights advocates labeled it a "gag rule" and doctors were angered by its intrusion on medical autonomy. By the time of the 1992 presidential election, the abortion issue had become highly salient with clear lines differentiating parties and candidates. Abortion rights groups mobilized strongly in support of the Democratic candidate, Bill Clinton, not only marching in great numbers on the Washington mall, but also working to turn out the vote.

With Clinton's election, the playing field changed yet again. His appointment of two new Supreme Court justices, Stephen Breyer and Ruth Bader Ginsburg, solidified the *Roe* majority. The anti-abortion movement goals of having the Court overturn *Roe* or pass a right-to-life constitutional amendment seemed more remote and unachievable.

Opposition to abortion through violent and nonviolent actions grew steadily following the *Webster* decision. Anti-abortion protesters invaded clinics and blockaded entrances, sometimes chaining themselves to doors. The National Abortion Federation reported 541 such incidents between 1987 to 1992 and another 264 in 1993 alone. The first murder of a physician who performed abortions, David Gunn, occurred in Pensacola, Florida, in March 1993. Death threats were common and further shootings and several murders of physicians and of staff at clinics providing abortions followed.

The *Webster* decision opened the door for new legal limitations on abortion rights, but the practical effect in state laws was less than many had anticipated. By contrast, the effects of anti-abortion protest, both peaceful and violent, were effectively deterring abortion providers. For women seeking legal abortions, access became more focused on fewer providers, and the usual costs of an abortion rose to reflect the insurance and security burdens that clinics faced. Variation in access to abortion between states was increasing, (but unlike Germany) not only because of state action.[22]

GERMANY

In Germany, Act Three begins with *die Wende* (the "turning point"), the collapse of the GDR and the ensuing unification process. With two different abortion laws and practices to reconcile in a single state, the issue was inescapably on the state agenda. Between the aftermath of the Memmingen trial and the effort of the Bavarian state government to stop paying for legal abortions, the issue had already heated up; now it reached a flash point.

[22] As of 1999, 29 states have passed legislation requiring parental consent for minor's abortions, 14 require a waiting period after some type of state-directed counseling, 13 restrict private and/or public insurance coverage, and 26 restrict or prohibit postviability abortion (Alan Guttmacher Institute 1999).

In the former GDR, the Independent Women's Association (UFV) emerged as an active feminist participant on the issue. The group opposed simply imposing West German law on East Germany and gathered about 100,000 signatures calling for a new law on abortion rather than the adoption of the existing FRG law, as was happening with other sections of the criminal code (Hampele-Ulrich 2000, p. 203). Controversy over what abortion law would become was sufficiently widespread that it threatened to derail the entire unification process. To prevent this from happening, the unification treaty, signed in October 1990, deferred the resolution of the controversy, obliging the new *Bundestag* to find a regulation "that, by means of legally securing the claims of women, particularly for counseling and social support, better guarantees the protection of unborn life and the constitutionally acceptable management of a conflict situation for women than is now the case in either part of Germany."

This language was more constraining than was generally recognized at the time: It did not mention any self-determination rights of women, it gave primacy to the protection of unborn life, defined unwanted pregnancies as "conflicts" for women, and left the specification of who would manage the conflict undefined. It also demanded that resolutions be "constitutionally correct," thereby accepting the guidelines set earlier by the West German constitutional court (Maleck-Lewy and Ferree 2000; Mushaben, Lennox, and Giles 1997). While the operative phrase in the unification treaty appeared to respect both the "protection of unborn life" and "the claims of women" and so to criticize both German states equally, it set the terms of debate for the new law in a West German constitutional framework. By deferring the final decision, the treaty provided an opportunity for both sides of the debate to mobilize their forces.

The Pro side was somewhat divided on strategy. Some feminists focused on the adoption of the former GDR's trimester rule (the *Fristenlösung* approach discussed earlier). Other West German feminists active in local autonomous projects and in the Green Party were committed to the now-traditional demand for the repeal of §218. There were tensions within the women's movement between East and West, older and younger women, and those opposed to and those supportive of new reproductive technologies (Maleck-Lewy and Ferree 2000; Ulrich 1998; Wuerth 1996).

Each party in the new *Bundestag* submitted its own proposal for a new law. The parties of the left called for unqualified legal abortion in the first trimester along with social measures to support mothers and children. The liberal party (FDP), a pivotal party that sometimes joined in governments with the SPD and other times with the CDU, insisted on some form of counseling. The Christian Democrats were split – some wanted to maintain the existing West German law and others pushed for eliminating the social necessity "loophole."

Women members of parliament from the more moderate part of the CDU joined women from the FDP and SPD in crafting a parliamentary compromise, called the "group bill." It included mandatory counseling and a waiting period but left the ultimate decision with the pregnant woman in the first trimester. The bill also offered additional social support measures, such as increased funding for kindergartens, that were intended to encourage childbearing as an option. As Mushaben (1993) points out, both the existence of a cross-party coalition and the prominence of women legislators were highly unusual in German politics.

The group bill was passed on June 26, 1992, after a 14- hour debate by a vote of 355 to 283 with 16 abstentions. The parties technically released their representatives from party discipline, but there was considerable informal pressure; nevertheless, 32 members of the CDU (20 of them from the former GDR) voted for the bill in defiance of the party leadership. Almost immediately, 249 Christian Democrats appealed to the Constitutional Court to prevent the law from going into effect.

In a 5–3 decision in May 1993, the Court overturned the new law on grounds that it offered insufficient protection to human life. The court insisted that abortion remain a felony (with a penalty of 1–3 years in prison) unless justified by rape, incest, or a threat to the life of the mother. The Court ruled that the mandatory state-licensed counseling be directed toward preserving the life of the unborn child and not be carried out by any person or organization that provided abortions. Women who underwent such counseling and subsequently chose to have an abortion were then to be exempted from legal prosecution, although their action was still defined as criminal. The most ambiguous part of the Court's decision concerned the nature of the counseling, which the justices argued needed to be "goal-oriented" in protecting the life of the fetus, but "outcome-open" in style, encouraging but not forcing women to continue their pregnancies.

In June 1995, the *Bundestag* turned the Court decision into law with minor modifications. State health insurance would pay for abortions that were "legal" in the sense that they were carried out for reasons of rape, incest, or serious threat to the woman's life or health – and not merely nonprosecutable because of the women having undergone mandatory counseling. The new law intensified both state control and moral pressure on abortion providers as well as on women seeking abortions.

Counselors were tested and certified every two years and had to write up an account of each counseling session, but without identifying the woman being counseled. In 1996, the Bavarian state legislature passed a more restrictive state law forbidding outpatient abortions and allowing physician's homes and offices to be searched for evidence of illegal abortions – a law that was subsequently overruled by the Constitutional Court.

In 1999, the Vatican demanded that the Catholic Church officially withdraw from offering counseling that could result in a certificate entitling women to a nonprosecuted abortion, and Catholic lay groups took over instead.[23] The availability of abortion in practice still varied considerably by state, but the federal requirement that all states provide the necessary formal counseling reduced these disparities somewhat.

This uneasy compromise appears to have, at least temporarily, settled the issue without satisfying either side. In contrast to the United States, mobilization around the abortion issue has faded.

CONCLUSION

While U.S. abortion politics moved from silence to screaming, the course of the conflict in the past century in Germany has been toward less confrontation. Contrary to the stereotypes of uncompromising forces facing off across an unbridgeable divide, in both Germany and the United States much of the legislative activity around abortion has been a politics of incremental change. The application of the undue burden criterion or of counseling that is directed toward preserving the life of the fetus but is outcome-open is not a clash of absolutes but a search for an elusive, delicate balance.

The Epilogue is still to be written. The abortion issue remains very much politically relevant in the United States. As of the fall of 2000, the U.S. Federal Drug Administration has approved RU-486, a pill that induces abortions in the early stages of pregnancy, for distribution by

---

[23] With the exception of the diocese of Limburg, where the bishop decided not to follow the Vatican's orders.

the nonprofit Population Council. This decision, along with the question of appointments to the Supreme Court that might shift its narrow majority, immediately became an important campaign issue. The disputed election of George W. Bush further promises to focus the attention of both sides on court nominees who might still overturn *Roe v. Wade*.

In Germany, RU-486 was legalized in the late 1990s by the SPD-led coalition government without much controversy. Health insurers, however, treated it as a prescription drug and refused to pay for the medical supervision necessary for this less than risk-free drug. At the time of this writing, the only company that had been producing and distributing the drug announced that they would cease to do so in the future. The issue is quiet for the moment, but the status quo is only grudgingly accepted by German feminists and the broader German women's movement or by the Catholic Church.

There may yet be more to come in the absence of a genuine consensus in either country. Understanding the possible range of change, and the likely responses from those affected, requires an understanding of the meanings given to what has gone before. Analyzing the shifting discourses of interpretation in the three acts of the drama described is the goal of the rest of the book.

CHAPTER THREE

Methods

O ur research findings are based on an unusually complicated data set, using multiple methods, including content analysis of newspapers and organizational documents, a survey of organizations, and intensive interviews. In this chapter we attempt to provide the general reader with enough information to assess its strengths and limitations. Important details for those with methodological interests are relegated to an appendix and to the Web (www.ssc.wisc.edu/abortionstudy).

THE CONTENT ANALYSIS

Our two major outcome variables – standing and framing – are both based on a content analysis of two major newspapers in each country. In the United States, we sampled *The New York Times* (*NYT*) and *The Los Angeles Times* (*LAT*); for Germany, we sampled the *Frankfurter Allgemeine Zeitung* (*FAZ*) and the *Süddeutsche Zeitung* (*SZ*). These newspapers are similar in targeting a national rather than a more regional audience and in being oriented toward policy-making elites. While they all cover national news, the papers we chose in each country also cover different geographical regions, giving us a way to pick up different local events, actors, and frames. We were not interested in differences between newspapers but in producing a data set that was independent of the possible idiosyncrasies of any single source. While we would have liked to include tabloids, TV, and magazine coverage, we discovered that many sources, particularly in Germany, were not archived as far back as we wished to go. We decided to focus on a narrower range of media for a longer period to focus on the comparative analysis of changes over time.

There are some small ideological differences, particularly between the German papers. The *SZ*, although it is published in a more conservative region, is more oriented to center-left readers; the *FAZ*, though in a more liberal region, is oriented to center-right readers. However, when we checked our results on standing and framing in their news articles, we found no generally important differences.[24] Comparing the *NYT* and the *LAT*, one would be hard put to find any editorial differences on abortion policy, and we found no significant differences here on measures of standing or framing.

These newspapers are a small and specialized sample of the mass media in each country, and the reader should keep this limitation in mind, even when we use shorthand to talk about "media" standing or framing. The *FAZ* and the *SZ* have daily circulations of around 400,000 copies each, but Germany had about 400 daily newspapers with a combined circulation of 25 million in the 1990s. (Most German newspapers do not have Sunday editions.) The *Bild*, a Hamburg-based tabloid, has a circulation of more than 4 million. A weekly newsmagazine, *Der Spiegel*, has a circulation over a million and a more business-oriented competitor, *Focus*, has a circulation of about 800,000. There are also television and other mass media as well.

The New York Times and *The Los Angeles Times* each have relatively comparable circulation figures (about a million daily and 1.4 to 1.6 million on Sundays). While these two are important and well-regarded papers in their own right, they are also the source for many syndicated news articles and commentaries that appear widely in other newspapers – a practice that does not exist in Germany. In fact, when we attempted a small test study of how newspapers in the U.S. South might differ from these giant papers, we quickly found that a great deal of the news reporting and even commentary on national issues came from these sources, although sometimes with a day or two delay.

While there are almost 1500 U.S. daily newspapers with a combined circulation of approximately 56 million, there are not nearly as many unique stories or points of view as these figures would suggest. Nonetheless, the *NYT* and *LAT* are far from representing *the* mass media in the United States. There are many other broadsheets and tabloids, weekly newspapers, radio and television news and talk shows, and it is important to bear this in mind when we speak of "the media" or "the discourse."

---

[24] The book dealing only with the German data pays more attention to the small differences between the newspapers that can be identified; see Gerhards, Neidhardt, and Rucht (1998).

Table 3.1. *Total Number of Articles Published and Sampled by Years by Newspaper*

Newspaper	All articles	Articles in sample	Years
LAT	1884	554	1972–94[a]
NYT	3886	689	1962, 1967, 1970–94
FAZ	867	678	1970–94
SZ	959	747	1970–94

[a] The *LAT* is not indexed before 1972.

With this caveat in mind, these newspapers remain important *validators* for other media. They signal who is to be taken seriously as a player and what ideas are important enough to be considered seriously. Even when their stories are not directly reprinted in other newspapers, editors and publishers look to their coverage as an indicator of what is "newsworthy." Achieving standing and having one's frame featured prominently in these particular papers is an important achievement, with broad repercussions that reach beyond their particular readers.

THE SAMPLE OF ARTICLES

Table 3.1 shows the total number of articles we found that qualified as being "about abortion" (half or more of the content focused on abortion-related issues). In the United States, we could use the newspaper's own index to lead us to appropriate articles, although we also rejected some articles that were indexed under "abortion" as having too little relevant content to qualify. Especially in the early years of our sample, we checked other related topics (thalidomide, birth defects, contraception) in the index to find articles that met our criteria. Since the *NYT* index went back into the 1960s and the *LAT* index only began in 1972, we selected two earlier years (1962 and 1967) from the *NYT* and began our continuous series from 1970 in the *NYT* and 1972 in the *LAT*.

Sampled articles had to meet a number of other screening criteria to be in our sample. In the United States, we excluded articles of less than three paragraphs, preferring to code the content-richer, longer articles. This means that in some comparisons of discourse style we also excluded the short news reports in the German sample in order to be comparing only similar types of articles. In both countries, editorials, op-ed columns, news analyses, and news accounts were included, but book reviews and letters to the editor were not.

As Table 3.1 shows, there were many more articles available about abortion in the United States than in Germany. Since we wanted actual sample sizes that were approximately equal in each country (we were aiming for about 1200 articles in each), we adopted different sampling strategies in each country. In the United States, we used a sampling strategy that aimed to produce a minimum of 20 articles per year, with roughly equal numbers of articles from each newspaper, and would not overly concentrate our sample on the explosion of abortion-related articles that appeared around the 1989 *Webster* decision. This meant taking a higher proportion of articles in slow years and a lower proportion in others. It also meant that we took a somewhat larger fraction of *LAT* articles than those from the *NYT*. *The New York Times* index, for example, showed 85 articles on abortion in 1987 and 377 articles in 1989. We thus set a variable sampling fraction for each year and newspaper and drew our articles randomly within each subset to achieve that number. Thus, while we chose a random sample of one in four 1987 articles, we sampled only one in eight of the 1989 set.

To select the articles dealing with the abortion issue in the *FAZ* and *SZ* we made use of the index of the archive of the German *Bundestag*. To be sure that the selection criteria of this archive were not biased, for example, in favor of parties that are members of the *Bundestag*, we checked six different weeks to see whether the articles that we found in the archive were identical with the articles on abortion in the two newspapers. We did not find any bias. There were fewer articles in Germany than in the United States overall, even in years such as 1990–1992, when there was intense coverage. As a result, the German sample was created by taking every other article in the period 1970–1979 and every article in the 1980–1994 period.

This oversampling of articles in slow years in the United States and in recent years in Germany does not affect our comparisons of changes over time because we then weighted the data to reflect the true proportions of articles in the population. For example, the sampled articles in the first period in Germany were weighted by a factor of two. If we were to use unweighted numbers, this would impart a bias to our estimates of overall standing or frame prominence in a country by over-counting certain years or certain newspapers. But by weighting data based on the sampling fraction and then "deflating" the numbers back

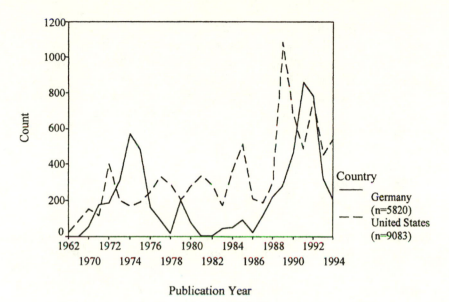

Figure 3.1. Number of articles in sampling frame by year by country. (Note: The *n* for each country are the number of articles in the sampling frame.)

to the actual sample size, we both captured the actual distribution over time and preserved a fair estimate of statistical significance.[25]

Because the numbers of articles are so small in some years, our analysis typically groups the data into six larger and unequal periods that reflect these distributions and important turning points. This allows us enough cases for analysis in even slower news periods and also makes the time periods align comparably in the two countries, even though there are small differences within each period with regard to when each country acted.[26]

As Figure 3.1 shows, the actual distribution of articles over time is quite different in the United States and in Germany. The German coverage of the abortion issue is largely concentrated in the two primary periods when reform debates were occurring in the national legislature, and coverage is very light in the intervening period. Thus, the German

[25] The details on sampling procedures and sample sizes and weights for each of the four newspapers by year are available on the Web at www.ssc.wisc.edu/abortionstudy.

[26] Thus the period 1973–1976 encompasses both the 1973 *Roe* decision in the United States and the 1974 *Bundestag* decision, the 1975 court reversal and the 1976 revised law in Germany that set the parameters of reform for future years (see Chapter Two).

distribution of articles has two widely separated but roughly equal peaks. In the United States, coverage increases over time, rising to a single, very pronounced peak in the period when the Supreme Court was considering the *Webster* and *Casey* cases. The two different distributions of the extent of news coverage over time is itself an interesting fact about the discourses of the two countries that we will discuss mainly in Chapter Eleven.

UNIT OF ANALYSIS

THE ARTICLE. For some purposes, the article makes sense as the unit of analysis. Looking at an article as a whole allows us to ask what percentage of articles quote a particular organization or type of organization or include certain mixes of speakers. But we analyze the data primarily by looking at units smaller than the article as a whole.

THE UTTERANCE. An utterance is a speech act or statement by a single speaker. A single article can contain multiple utterances by the same person or organization, separated in different paragraphs, each of which is coded separately. Sometimes we measured the prominence of a particular idea or frame by its rate per utterance – that is, by how often it appeared on average across all utterances by speakers of a certain sort. For example, a rate per utterance of .18 means that this idea would appear 18 times in 100 utterances of this type on the average. The rate at which an idea is expressed reflects the value of that idea to a speaker, not its relative share of attention compared to other ideas being expressed. Thus, just because an actor uses more different ideas in an utterance, or a type of actor using a certain idea has longer, more complex utterances, the rate of appearance of that idea does not go down – although its share relative to other ideas would. Since the utterance is our fundamental coding unit, in Figure 3.2 we present the overall distribution (weighted as described above) of utterances by country and year.

THE SPEAKER. Speakers are units constructed from all utterances in a single article that can be attributed to a single source. Since journalists are the ones constructing articles, they may be separating utterances into different short paragraphs rather arbitrarily. Many ideas that a speaker wishes to express may be part of a longer, more complex argument that runs across several paragraphs. Thus for many purposes it made sense to consider the speaker as a whole as he or she was presented in the entire article.

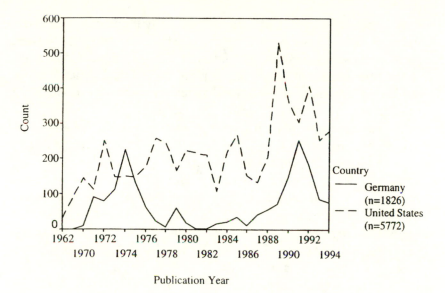

Figure 3.2. Number of utterances by year by country. (Note: The number of utterances was weighted by the sampling fraction and sample size.)

In some cases, the same source may have actually been represented in utterances by two different individuals (e.g., the president and his press secretary). However, the same individual (for example, Kate Michelman) was counted as a different speaker each time she was quoted in each different article. To be counted as the same speaker, different individuals had to represent the same organization, political party (if relevant), and gender (if given), but speakers were never combined across articles.

In some analyses, the relevant comparison was the percentage of speakers of a certain type who included a particular framing idea at all. Unlike a percentage of ideas in individual utterances, this measure is not sensitive to how many other ideas do or do not occur in the utterances. It is a measure of absolute rather than relative prominence. Unlike rate, which has the advantage of counting repeated uses of arguments in the same frame by a single speaker, this measure allows us to construct indicators of complex argumentation – for example, whether a speaker includes opposing arguments.

Not all utterances and not all speakers included substantive statements that frame what abortion is about. While we counted all utterances and speakers, regardless of the specific content of what they had to say, in our measures of standing we generally focused on just those utterances and speakers who were saying what they thought abortion means when we do an analysis of framing. This means that the speakers and utterances that comment only on the political situation ("we are winning this battle" or "they need a great many more votes to win") or the morale of the actors ("we are prepared for the long haul") or say nothing substantive at all ("no comment") were used to calculate standing but were dropped from the analysis when we calculated the rate of use of an idea or the proportions of speakers who included it.

THE IDEA ELEMENT. Each particular idea element – for example, "Women need protection from coercion to have an abortion" – was given a unique three-digit code. These codes were constructed so that the first digit represented a broad idea about abortion (such as framing it as being about the life of the fetus), the second digit represented a particular subtype of argument within this frame (such as the claim that the fetus has a right to life), and the third digit was an even more specific idea within that (such as the argument that science proves that the fetus is a human being and therefore has a right to life).

A given utterance may contain multiple ideas, each of which was coded separately. The idea element is really a property of the utterance (something it does or does not contain) rather than a real unit, since we did not keep coding the same idea over and over if it appeared multiple times in the same utterance. Therefore, when we look at the relative share of the total ideas that reflect a particular frame, comparing it to some other frame, treating idea elements as if they were units, this is the same thing as counting the percentage of utterances that contain *any* ideas of this type compared to those containing other ideas. But we express this as the proportion of idea elements because this is an easy way to see what is going on.

Different units of analysis are appropriate for different questions, and we will make clear whether it is the article, the speaker, the utterance, or the idea level that is relevant for any particular analysis. Table 3.2 summarizes the number of articles and the weighted number of speakers, utterances, and ideas by newspaper for each country.

CODING PROCEDURES

We used the same codebook and data entry program in both countries, translated into the appropriate language. In the initial preparation of the codebook, we drew ideas from articles in both countries and looked for comparable meanings in different phrases and differences

Table 3.2. *Weighted Number of Articles, Speakers, Utterances, and Ideas by Newspaper*

Newspapers	Articles	Speakers	Utterances	Ideas
LAT	406	1,652	3,344	5,418
NYT	837	3,111	5,738	9,051
FAZ	677	1,813	3,069	3,792
SZ	748	1,924	2,750	3,140
Totals	2,668	8,500	14,901	21,401

in meaning of similar words by translating our translations back to the original. In early stages of constructing the codebook we used bilingual coders to code both the German and U.S. articles. Some particular ideas were relevant for only one country – for example, "the proposal is unfair to East German women." Nevertheless, they appear in the all-inclusive common codebook.

Coders in both countries used a customized database program for data entry, following prompts to enter codes on-screen with pull-down menus of choices. The same rules were applied, with minor modifications, for some differences in contexts. The program was set up so that the coding was done hierarchically: First, data for the article as a whole were entered, such as its date and type (news, editorial, feature, etc.), and the author and focus of the story. Then each utterance was coded with regard to the speaker who made it (in terms of the organization being represented, if any, or political party and gender, if identifiable) and the ideas that it contained.

In coding the ideas contained in any given utterance, the coders selected a three-digit number. The first digit reflected the frame, the second digit a subframe and/or position, and the third digit a more specific idea within that subframe. Speakers were coded as using an idea even if they were not endorsing that idea or the policy it tended to favor because they were nonetheless giving that particular way of thinking about the issue more prominence in the discourse.

Coders received extensive supervised training, and we were able to achieve reliabilities of better than 80% by independent coders up to the second-digit level. We checked the comparability of coding between the two countries by using English-speaking coders to code some German articles in translation, and we also revised the common codebook when coders in either country identified missing or ambiguous codes in the first phases of coding. We also went through a phase of data-cleaning and consistency-checking at the end, correcting some coding that had become inconsistent over time.

In the data analysis, we typically combined the specific three-digit idea codes into broader, even more reliable groups. We treated ideas most often as expressing a specific frame plus the direction of the idea. The first digit indicates the frame and the second and third digits are combined into just three groups: Pro, Anti, and Neutral. We use the designation Pro for ideas that are what Americans would call "pro-choice" or "pro-abortion-rights" and Germans would call "pro-liberalization." Anti is the designation we give to ideas that are anti-abortion; they are frames that suggest opposition to relaxing the state's regulation of abortion by criminal law or give a favorable cast to imposing more stringent and restrictive laws. Neutral ideas are those that are either ambiguous (such as saying that abortion is about the relation between the individual and the state without indicating what that relation should be) or that imply different things in different contexts (such as the idea that adult women do not need counseling but teenagers always do, which is an idea supporting more restriction in the United States and less restriction in Germany). In addition, we sometimes grouped ideas into clusters that were similar even across different frames and directions (for example, all ideas about women needing help and support).

Organizational Documents

In the survey of organizations described, we also asked for documents in which the organization set forth its views on the abortion issue. Using the same three-digit idea codes, we coded up to a two-page sample from these organizational documents.[27] This enabled us to operationalize the organization's preferred frame on the abortion issue based on its own public presentation, independently of how it was quoted (or not quoted) in the media sample.

THE ORGANIZATIONAL SURVEY

In our model of framing contests, the agents who were trying to shape the discourse were overwhelmingly collective actors – state and party actors, churches, grassroots advocacy organizations and networks, and

---

[27] We coded 100 actor documents in Germany and 90 in the United States.

other civil society actors. In order to reconstruct the backstage of the media forum, we thought it wise to solicit their own understanding of the process and their view of mass media discourse, asking about their strategies for influencing the media, their activities and resources. We focused our attention on groups that were significant in Act Three – that is, from 1989 to 1994 – and we excluded actors who were speaking for the government in any official capacity. Even though government officials are often important players, we judged it unlikely that a survey of such formal power-holders would be answered at all, let alone with the level of frankness that would be needed to gain any insight into their role. We included not only national-level actors but also state-level and local-level groups from the states where our newspapers were located (in Germany this meant the states of Hessen and Bavaria and the cities of Frankfurt and Munich); in the United States we focused on the tri-state region (New York, New Jersey, and Connecticut), California, New York City, and Los Angeles.

We sought the views not only of those who had achieved significant media standing but also of more marginalized and behind the scene groups as well. Our standing data for the period 1989–1992 provided us with the major and more occasional players, but we turned to other sources as well in making our selection. There are excellent histories of the Anti and Pro movements on the abortion issue discussing the role of various organizations, and, from these sources, we added to our list several groups that were rarely or never quoted in the newspapers that we sampled. Finally, we circulated our list to scholars familiar with the framing contest, asking them to suggest any significant groups that were omitted.

Our final list in Germany had 150 organizations, and we were able to obtain completed questionnaires from 94 of them (63%); in the United States, we identified 70 groups and ended up with 55 completed questionnaires (79%). On the nonresponses, some of the organizations that we identified were no longer in existence, a few we were unable to locate, and others promised to respond but never got around to it in spite of nagging phone calls. A complete list of the organizations that completed the survey can be found at www.ssc.wisc.edu/abortionstudy.

With minor modifications for context, we used the same detailed questionnaire in both countries (it is also available at www.ssc.wisc.edu/abortionstudy). Groups were asked about their goals on the abortion issue, changes in these goals, and the specific activities that they had engaged in to achieve them. They were asked about the centrality of the mass media in their efforts and about their interaction with journalists. They were asked for their own assessment of the most important players in shaping media discourse. They were asked about their alliances and how they understood their role in a broader organizational field. Finally, they were asked about their own internal organization and allocation of staff time and resources to media relations.

INTENSIVE INTERVIEWS

PARTICIPANTS

For a number of groups, we felt that we needed a more nuanced understanding of the collective actors' thinking, and this required a more intensive follow-up interview. We particularly targeted groups that were unusual in some ways, by being especially prominent, or by having changed over time in their approach, or by representing a point of view that the media seemed to neglect. We were interested in seeing whether less coverage reflected their own choices to focus their efforts elsewhere or whether they attempted to get into the media but did not succeed. Thus our selection of groups in the two countries was less completely parallel than our selection of newspaper articles because it was targeted to explaining the gaps and differences in coverage that we found.

We conducted such interviews with leaders and/or media directors of 20 U.S. and 23 German organizations. Nearly all of the major players were included, plus a number of organizations with more specialized, less public roles. These interviews were more conversational in style and less standardized than the survey. The interviewers – including the authors – had a schedule of topics, some of which were special to the organization in question. They were invited to probe answers that were vague or unclear. The Methodological Appendix lists those who were kind enough to give us their time and thoughtful answers to interviews that often ran more than an hour.

JOURNALISTS

The authors also conducted intensive interviews with a small group of journalists who had written extensively on the abortion issue for the four newspapers in our sample. In Germany, we interviewed Heidrun Graupner from the *Süddeutsche Zeitung* and Stephan-Andreas Casdorff (formerly from the *SZ*), and Friedrich Karl Fromme and Günther Bannas from the *Frankfurter Allgemeine Zeitung*. These four journalists were among the most frequently by-lined authors of articles and commentary about abortion in the late 1980s in our dataset.

In the United States, we interviewed Karen Tumulty, the congressional correspondent for *Time Magazine* who had formerly been on the staff of *The Los Angeles Times* and had written extensively on abortion during the years of our content analysis. We also interviewed David Shaw of *The Los Angeles Times*, who had earlier published a major four-part series on abortion and the media. Finally, we interviewed Linda Greenhouse, who covers the Supreme Court for *The New York Times* and had written extensively on the Court's complicated abortion decisions.

The interview explored their views on the overall quality of media coverage of the abortion issue, who they saw as the major players, who they turned to as sources to interview on the issue and why they chose them. We asked them about whether they believed that the significant players and prominent ideas had changed over time. We asked about their choice of language in labeling the sides and in talking about various aspects of the issue. We draw on these interviews especially in Chapter Twelve, where we examine *metatalk* – commentary on abortion discourse rather than on abortion itself.

CONCLUSION

Many comparative studies involve researchers in different countries exploring the same general issues, with each team designing its own data-gathering methods. This study is unusual in its use of common instruments – the same codebook for content analysis, the same survey questionnaire, and to some extent the same interview schedule. We not only designed the instruments together, we checked on the applicability and reliability of the coding between the two countries as it was going on. These procedures allow us to feel unusually confident that any differences that we find between countries are really there and are not an artifact of different methods.

Part II

Major Outcomes

This part analyzes the different playing fields in Germany and the United States on which various collective actors attempt to shape the meaning of abortion and presents the results on our two major outcome variables: standing and framing. Chapter Four focuses on the playing fields themselves and looks at how the politics and culture of the two countries vary in ways that inevitably influence who receives standing and which frames are easy or difficult to express. We emphasize not only the formal institutional roles of churches and parties but also media expectations. Also, German political culture gives the state more generally accepted responsibility for the welfare and support for families.

Chapter Five looks at which actors receive standing in the mass media and how this has changed over time. Standing, or the ability to have one's views transmitted through the media, is a resource that is conferred more on political parties in Germany and shared more equally with social movements in the United States. This chapter compares the organization, resources, and media relations skills of similar groups of actors in each country as a way of understanding why some are more successful, even when recognizing that the playing field is more advantageous for some than for others.

Chapter Six provides an overview of the framing contest on abortion in the two countries and how the careers of different frames have changed over time. We see some differences that we would expect. The different framing by the courts is reflected in a more Fetal Life framing in the mass media discourse in Germany and a more Individual and State framing in U.S. media discourse. We also find some surprises – in particular, that the "clash of absolutes" is more evident in Germany, even though the politics of abortion is more tempered in many ways and unmarred by the wave of anti-abortion violence found in the United States.

CHAPTER FOUR

The Discursive Opportunity Structure

In 1931, a lively framing contest over abortion policy in Germany reached a peak. Hundreds of new groups were created, and there were more than 1000 local demonstrations in support of lessening or removing legal restrictions on abortion, with appropriate coverage in the mass media of the day. Move the clock forward two years, after the Nazis seized power, and the whole scene seems unimaginable. The playing field in which any framing contest about abortion that was being waged was so radically different that the once taken-for-granted became unthinkable. The idea that one could further abortion reform through mass demonstrations and public discourse might as well have come from the moon.

Under the new regime, abortion was framed as a tool for "race hygiene" (Czarnowski 1997; Koonz 1986). Coercive sterilization and abortion were means for preventing inferior races from reproducing. Aryan women, in contrast, had a responsibility to the state to reproduce, and abortion was a criminal act. In 1943, a woman who had more than one abortion was threatened with capital punishment for "repeatedly undermining the vitality (*Lebenskraft*) of the German people." No alternative frames were permitted in this arena (Koonz 1986).

The shift from the Weimar Republic to the Nazi regime is an extreme case of a changing context for abortion discourse. The differences between the United States and Germany and the changes over the past 30 years are certainly less dramatic. After all, we have two modern industrial democracies with a federal structure; similar economic systems; independent judiciaries with powers of reviewing laws passed by legislatures; and privately owned, politically independent newspapers. Nor have they changed very much on these dimensions in the time period that we are examining. But as one zooms in on their respective playing fields and analyzes the components, the differences and changes become striking. Many of the findings that we will report cannot be understood without a clear sense of the special features of the context in which the framing contest in each country was occurring.

We use the term *discursive opportunity structure* as an umbrella term for this context.[28] Using our stadium model from Chapter One, it refers to the character of the arena. Unlike the flat, orderly, and well-marked field in a soccer stadium, the field in which framing contests occur is full of hills and valleys, barriers, traps, and impenetrable jungles. To make matters even more complicated, the contours of the playing field can change suddenly in the middle of the contest because of events that lay beyond the control of the players; and players can themselves sometimes change the contours through actions that create new discursive opportunities. This complex playing field provides advantages and disadvantages in an uneven way to the various contestants in framing contests.

The discursive opportunity structure is part of the broader political opportunity structure. The latter concept refers to all of the institutional and cultural access points that actors can seize upon to attempt to bring their claims into the political forum, and it has been used to explain the frequency and timing of protest events such as demonstrations and rallies. The discursive opportunity structure is limited to the framework of ideas and meaning-making institutions in a particular society. It provides a similar tool for understanding why certain actors and frames are more prominent in public discourse than others. The mass media are clearly central to this meaning-making process, but they are only a part of the institutional and cultural structures that channel and organize discourse.

Distinctions applied to the political opportunity structure more generally also apply to the discursive opportunity structure. Structure implies stability, but it is useful to treat stability as a variable element, running from highly inert components that are more or less permanent features of the terrain to windows of opportunity that may be open only briefly (see Gamson and Meyer 1996). The more volatile components of opportunity can be influenced by the agents who are attempting to shape the discourse. Some aspects of opportunity apply across many

---

[28] We developed the concept of a discursive opportunity structure in our collaborative discussions, and it has already been taken up and developed in Koopmans and Kriesi (1997) and Koopmans and Statham (2000).

issues and are general features of the playing field, while others are issue-specific or are relevant for only a limited range of framing contests. Finally, we use structure here to include both cultural (e.g., values, belief systems, images, etc.) and institutional (e.g., electoral and party systems) elements. We will pay attention to both aspects of opportunity as we examine various more specific components in the two countries.

THE PUBLIC SPHERE IN GERMANY AND THE UNITED STATES

Hallin and Mancini (1984, p. 841), building on Habermas' arguments about the structural transformation of the public sphere, compare the nature of the public sphere in Italy and the United States. We can apply their argument to German–U.S. differences as well. They note the replacement of a participatory, decentralized bourgeois public sphere "by a process of political communication dominated by large scale institutions." Political interpretation in Germany is provided by the institutionalized actors who have traditionally dominated the modern public sphere: political parties, unions, industrial associations, and organized religion. In such a situation, the journalist does not need to play a very active role as an interpreter of meaning.

In the United States, in contrast, these institutionalized actors are weaker. Political parties are loose coalitions organized to compete for public office, not for expressing unified frames. As a result of this relative vacuum, they argue, the mass media become *the* primary actor of the U.S. public sphere in performing the function of providing political interpretation. This broad difference in the nature of the public sphere is expressed through several of the specific components analyzed in the following paragraphs. The many important differences in historical context are also embedded in these specific components and are central to understanding some of the differences between the countries as well as changes over time.

For convenience, we organized these components under three rubrics: political, socio-cultural, and mass media. Here, we will postpone the discussion of how they apply to abortion, focusing instead on aspects that apply across a range of issues and are relatively stable over time in the two countries. The specific uses made of these opportunities with regard to the abortion issue, then, form the core of the analysis of the rest of the book. The two political components – *legal/judicial* and *party/state* – are examined more closely in the two chapters that follow on standing (Chapter Five) and framing (Chapter Six). The three socio-cultural components – *gender, moral/religious*, and *justice* – are each examined closely on how they apply to the abortion issue in three separate chapters in Part III. The mass media component, looking at how the structures, norms, and practices differ in the two countries, thereby advantaging some actors and their preferred frames over others, forms part of our consideration of the quality of discourse and how it is evaluated by those who are part of it. This is the last section of the book.

POLITICAL COMPONENTS

All of the components are about politics in the broader sense of who gets what, when, and how. In this section we use "political" in the narrower sense of government and the role of the state and political parties in society. We focus on two components – one involving the legal and judicial context in which an issue discourse occurs and one involving the role of the state in society and its relation to political parties. Important differences between Germany and the United States exist in both components.

LEGAL/JUDICIAL

There are two major differences between the two countries in the operation of their judicial systems: (a) The German Federal Court has a broader and less restricted role in setting the rules than does the U.S. Supreme Court, and (b) lower courts play a much more significant role as sites of contention in the United States than in Germany. Hence, the U.S. judicial system as a whole has what Hilgartner and Bosk (1988) call a greater "carrying capacity."

U.S. courts are case-oriented. Their decisions focus on issues presented in a particular case, and higher courts must wait until a suitable case reaches them on appeal from lower courts before they can make a decision. The Supreme Court has wide discretion over what cases it hears and typically seeks cases that present issues in as pure a form as possible, avoiding those that present a tangle of complex issues. "Hard cases make bad law," is the prevalent judicial philosophy. Compared to Germany, U.S. courts are normally more proscriptive – saying what is not allowed – and less prescriptive – saying what a proper law should look like. On some issues, this requires a trial-and-error process to determine, for example, what kind of abortion restrictions might place "an undue burden" on the pregnant woman and are, thereby, unconstitutional.

The jurisdiction of the German Federal Court, although in practice often triggered by particular cases, is not case-bound and is free to address the full range of issues that it deems appropriate. Its rulings are not merely proscriptive but often prescriptive as well, outlining the provisions that a constitutional law should include or address. In effect, it provides legislative guidelines that must be followed.

In addition, the selection process for judges creates a different aura around the Court in the two countries. German judges are selected by a parliamentary committee meeting in closed session rather than in public hearings. Most Germans have little inkling of the selection process. In fact, the parties operate with a tacit agreement of taking turns between the major parties, but the nominees must be acceptable to both.[29] The less visible nature of the process makes the German Court decisions appear more as *ex cathedra*, the ultimate judgments of an abstract institution rather than the particular opinions of a specific group of men and women. The impersonality of the court is underlined by the fact that it actually consists of two separate, interchangable, and equally empowered panels, each of which is considered "the Court" as a whole when it hears a case. Landfried (1988, p. 12), comparing judicial systems in different countries, calls attention to the "high confidence of Germans – compared with citizens of other nations – in their legal system and in the Constitutional Court." This leads, in her view, to "the danger of juridification of politics by judicial review."

Supreme Court justices in the United States are chosen by the president with the advice and consent of the U.S. Senate. Confirmation hearings are open and on controversial nominees often draw extensive media coverage. Court decisions often feature minority opinions, and the votes of the nine justices are public information. The individuals who make up the Court are well-known. Their personal backgrounds as well as their records of public statements and past decisions are subjected to close scrutiny, not only during the confirmation process but

---

[29] An interparty agreement in 1975 specified that one-fourth of the judges should not be affiliated with any party.

also whenever the media attempts to predict their votes in a pending case. U.S. Court decisions, then, are more likely to appear as the contingent outcome of the group process of nine individuals rather than any kind of ultimate judgment.

In addition to these differences at the federal level, lower courts play a much stronger role in the process in the United States. On an issue such as abortion, the federal court has sole jurisdiction in Germany. It also has considerable discretion in choosing which cases to hear and often acts at the request of state governments and legislatures. Statistics kept until 1990 show that one out of eight federal laws were brought to the Court for review (Billig 2000).

In the United States, 50 State Supreme Courts may be called on to rule on laws passed by their respective legislatures. These multiple potential battlegrounds provide a discursive opportunity for a wide variety of grassroots groups to contest issues, choosing cases and sites where they judge the legislative and judicial climate to be most favorable. Many social movements have used legal challenges, including class action suits, as a means for pursuing policy changes and challenging once dominant frames in public discourse. "Legal defense funds," with tax-exempt status, are a device used by a wide range of political organizations to support such efforts. Multiple venues mean multiple opportunities.

STATE/PARTY

A positive view of the state in Germany – that the state can and should be a force for good in social life – contrasts with a contested and distrustful discourse on the role of the state in the United States. In the Hegelian philosophy of law (*Staatsrechtslehre*) that dominated German thought in the nineteenth and first part of the twentieth centuries, the state should be an impartial institution "above" society. Its role is to enhance society by imposing certain moral standards, regulating civil life, mitigating social conflicts, and taking responsibility for the well-being of its citizens.

The underlying idea is expressed colloquially in the idea of a "father state" – that is, a caring and protecting state that one can trust and should obey. Fuchs (2000, p. 33) contrasts the "solidaristic statism" (*solidarischer Etatismus*) of Germany with the competitive individualism in the United States. This gendered concept, German feminists have argued, sees the solidarity of the German state as that of a "brotherhood" of sons who share the authority of the once dominant authoritarian monarchs without challenging the exclusion of women and ethnic minorities who are not part of the "family."[30]

The U.S. state was born in a revolution against a colonial state that, in the minds of the founders, had repeatedly abused its power. In this libertarian tradition, the state is perceived as a necessary evil whose role should be kept to a minimum. Its role is to foster individual freedom, limited only by making sure that people's choices do not interfere with the freedom of other people or the ability of the state to carry out basic functions of maintaining order.

The New Deal challenged this view of government. Most U.S. citizens welcomed the basic elements of the welfare state, and opposition to such programs as Social Security or Medicare has disappeared. Today, the parties compete on their ability to "save" these parts of the welfare state. But the historical legacy of distrust, which is often shared across the political spectrum, left the cultural support for a welfare state vulnerable and subject to a highly successful counterattack. Framing the government as "Big Brother," as part of the problem rather than part of the solution, as a thing to get off our backs – all have a resonance with the liberal tradition (Harrington 1999). The New Deal cultural legacy of a helpful state has been so thoroughly undermined by this attack that the "new" Democrats, symbolized by Clinton and Gore, have largely abandoned its defense. Opponents of the welfare state have succeeded in making the line, "I'm from the government and I'm here to help," seem an ironical joke.

In addition to this sharp cultural difference on the view of the state, there is an equally clear difference in the legitimacy and quasi-state role of political parties. German political parties have a constitutionally recognized role in the formation of a government, with defined rights and responsibilities. U.S. political parties were viewed with suspicion by the framers of the U.S. Constitution and are weakly institutionalized; party discipline is weak and the desire to maintain unity often leads to the avoidance of statements on issues that might provoke internal divisions.

In Germany, elected political representatives are heavily dependent on parties. Half of the members of the *Bundestag* are not elected by a local constituency but at large, based on their party's nationwide share of the vote. Where they appear on the party list determines their chances

---

[30] See Pateman (1988) for the general argument and Young (1999) for its special applicability to the "corporatist" German state.

of election. Those who fail to accept party discipline on major issues are not likely to end up on the list.

The German political parties are at the heart of the entire process of interest aggregation and political decision making. Their status is secured by constitutional rules – Clause 21 of the Constitution states that political parties contribute to the formation of the people's political will. Additional laws regulate the parties' rights and duties and prescribe such features as democratic procedures and financial accountability. Parties get large public subsidies, partly based on the number of votes that they attract in elections. Parties are officially represented in many quasi-state institutions such as committees that supervise public radio and television. Overall, parties play such a strong role in the political system as a whole that Leibholz's (1967) characterization of Germany as a "party state" is a common wisdom of contemporary political science (von Beyme 1991).

German parties are coherent and hierarchical organizations with sections on the local, district, state, and national levels. The two largest parties, the Social Democrats (SPD) and Christian Democrats (the CDU plus, in Bavaria, the organizationally separate CSU), each have about 800,000 enrolled fee-paying members. The smaller parties, including the Free Democrats (FDP), the Greens (founded in 1980), and the Party of Democratic Socialism (PDS, the successor of the former East German Communist Party), are also well organized with around 68,000, 48,000, and 90,000 members, respectively, in the late 1990s.

In spite of many internal disputes, the parties are relatively coherent ideologically and exert considerable control over their different units and branches. On parliamentary votes, unless there is an explicit understanding that members are free to vote their conscience, they vote as a unit according to the party line. Essential ideological and strategic differences on most political matters are between parties, not within them. Other organizations that are closely allied and identified with a political party have a great access advantage over those who lack such party ties. The Catholic Church has this kind of privileged access to the Christian Democrats while the trade unions and their affiliated social welfare organizations have this access to the Social Democrats.

U.S. political parties play a very different role. With only two parties, each becomes an arena of contest among different constituencies rather than an organizationally and ideologically coherent actor. Candidates for political office are not dependent on the party's endorsement and are chosen in primaries in which the party leadership's choice may lose to an outsider with a nominal affiliation. Individual candidates may get some financial help from the party's national committee in funding their campaign, but they create their own campaign committees to collect funds directly from contributors, as well as funding their campaigns from their personal wealth. Many candidate advertisements in statewide election campaigns don't even mention the candidate's political party. With so little control of the selection process, it is hard for parties to discipline mavericks, and they rarely even try. Organizationally, the national party has little control over the 50 different state parties who operate pretty much as independent organizations.

After the election, the party may control committee assignments and other perks that provide some basis for enforcing party discipline, but it is a very rare occurrence when parties vote as a block in the U.S. Congress. With each party trying to please multiple constituencies, other organizations are wary of being too heavily aligned with a particular party lest they be taken for granted. They may be discounted if they have no place to go when they do not get what they want. The most typical strategy is to keep one's lines of access open to both parties; or, if this is unrealistic, to threaten to support third-party candidacies or to simply stay home on election day. There is not a lot to gain by a sustained marriage to any one party in the United States.

Finally, there are the basic differences between a presidential democracy with an executive and legislature, which are each elected directly and have separate powers, and a parliamentary democracy in which the leader of the largest party in the legislature forms a government and can be unseated by parliamentary vote. The German version of parliamentary democracy is strongly centralized at the federal level, with state and local parties exercising little independent control. The U.S. presidential democracy is strongly decentralized with 50 governors and state legislatures that act independently of who is in control at the federal level.

The result of this much more bifurcated and decentralized U.S. political system is the creation of many more points of access for political contests in the United States. As with the court system, issues that are not on the federal agenda may be engaged in a more favorable state venue, either through pressing for legislation or through referenda. Battles over issues in particular states often stimulate national discourse as test cases that highlight the acceptability of given policies that might be extended to other places and eventually to the national level. The *Bundestag* is the central arena in Germany, but the U.S. Congress is only one of many discursive battlegrounds.

SOCIO-CULTURAL COMPONENTS

Worldviews and values, and the more specific norms, ways of thinking, practices, resources, and rules that support them, provide a pool of potential legitimating devices for particular ways of framing an issue and justifying one's position on it. They offer discursive opportunities as rivals compete in linking their framing of an issue with broader cultural symbols, themes, and narratives. "In all public arenas," Hilgartner and Bosk (1988, p. 71) argue, "social problems that can be related to deep mythic themes or broad cultural preoccupations have a higher probability of competing successfully."

Some frames have a natural advantage because their ideas and language resonate with the broader culture. Resonances increase the appeal of a frame by making it appear natural and familiar. "Those who respond to the larger cultural theme will find it easier to respond to a frame with the same sonorities," writes Gamson (1992, p. 135). Snow and Benford (1988, p. 210) make a similar point in discussing the concept of "narrative fidelity." Some frames, they write, "resonate with cultural narrations, that is, with stories, myths, and folk tales that are part and parcel of one's cultural heritage."

Gamson (1992, p. 135) argues for the dialectical character of these cultural themes:

> There is no theme without a countertheme. Themes are safe, conventional, and normative; one can invoke them as pieties on ceremonial occasions with the assumption of general social approval, albeit some private cynicism. Counterthemes typically share many of the same taken-for-granted assumptions but challenge some specific aspect of the mainstream culture; they are adversarial, contentious, oppositional. Themes and counterthemes are paired with each other so that whenever one is invoked, the other is always present in latent form, ready to be activated with the proper cue.

The socio-cultural aspect of discursive opportunity structure also has its institutional aspects. Each of the themes and counterthemes that make up the cultural chorus is carried by specific organizational representatives who may have more or less regularized access to the political-legal system. Each of the various components of the discursive opportunity structure provides its own realm of relative advantages and disadvantages for certain actors and their preferred frames. To be effective, their strategic choices in presenting their images and arguments must take into account and be shaped by the specific features of the complicated landscape on which they compete.

GENDER

The exclusion of women from citizenship until the early twentieth century in both countries, and even now from equivalent political representation, makes it necessary for women in both Germany and the United States to struggle to have a voice on any political issues. Attention to gender as a political category has grown internationally over the past three decades, and women have gained more voice over time in both countries. But increases in official political representation have been much more pronounced in Germany than in the United States. Between 1980 and 1994, for example, the proportion of the *Bundestag* members who are women rose from 8% to 26%, while in the United States the proportion of women legislators in the House of Representatives rose only from 7% to 12% (and is even less in the U.S. Senate).

U.S. feminists, unlike European feminists, cannot turn to a strong party system to gain legislative access and a voice in government. Party quotas have been successful in many European parliamentary systems, as in Germany's, in providing a structure for the representation of gender interests (Lovenduski and Norris 1993), but it would not work in candidate-based U.S. elections. Even though many U.S. feminists began to organize in small, grassroots, face-to-face groups, they soon, like most social movements in the United States, formed large voluntary associations that echoed the federal, state, and local organizations of political decision making (Skocpol 1997). As Clemens (1997) shows, the lobby structure taken by many social movements, including feminists, evolved historically to represent interests that parties did not.

U.S. feminists continue to run some nonhierarchical, local projects, but even radical feminists with roots in the civil rights movement and new left developed larger associations that focus on lobbying state and national governments and pressing for legal changes on issues such as sexual harassment, wage discrimination, and violence against women. The National Organization for Women (NOW) is one such group. They are represented in Washington, have well-staffed offices, and usually work as part of a coalition of interest groups. These feminist groups have always, as a matter of principle, included men as members – NOW makes a point of being an organization *for* women, not *of* women. Feminist organizations are interest groups in the specifically American sense (Clemens 1997).

Feminist organizations born in the 1960s and 1970s are thus not much different organizationally today from those that were already in place from the earlier waves of feminist mobilization in the 1920s (such as the League of Women Voters). The early distinction that could be made between "younger branch" anti-hierarchical activists and "older branch" feminists engaged in institutional politics was already obsolete in the early 1980s (Ferree and Hess 2000). U.S. feminist organizations are national "players" involved in coalitions and coordinating groups with other interest groups and their legislative supporters (Peattie and Rein 1983; Spalter-Roth and Schreiber 1995). They are allied on many issues with other women's organizations, such as the YWCA or the Girl Scouts, but also with many non-gender-specific associations, such as the ACLU or the unions, depending on their understanding of common interests on specific issues.

For many U.S. feminists, unlike German feminists, liberal ideas of individual rights and equal treatment are central values; even radical arguments for redefining issues such as sexual harassment are framed in these terms (Zippel 2000). The entire women's movement in Germany, not just its feminist wing, has a history of skepticism toward ideas of equal rights and equal treatment. As Moeller (1993) shows for the development of family policy in Germany in the 1950s, even SPD and FDP women used the idea of "treating women like men" as something wholly undesirable, and conservatives associated this with GDR policies to discredit the very notion of gender equality. Moeller concludes, "A rhetoric of individual rights had never been central to the politics of German liberalism or to the bourgeois feminist movement, and the fifties was no time for its efflorescence in Germany. The constant refrains of security and protection that ran through much of the political discussion of women's status [in the 50s] implied that in a new Germany there would be [male] protectors" (1993, pp. 221–222). Most German advocates for women in the postwar years were careful to maintain their distance from anything that would suggest a classical liberal view of equal rights.

The rejection of equal rights language as bourgeois and limiting was also a theme as German feminists mobilized in the late 1960s and early 1970s, with many of the activists coming from the student milieu of the New Left. These new, young German feminists, in contrast to their U.S.

counterparts, resisted forming any sort of enduring national organization (Ferree 1987; Kaplan 1992). Committed to the principle that nonhierarchical, grassroots organization is the only appropriate means to
challenge patriarchy, German feminists centered their organizational
efforts on small, local projects and temporary networks among such
local groups and projects. These groups also were designed to be exclusively of and for women, emphasizing the differences between women
and men in their social locations and perspectives on the issues (Ferree
1987). "Feminist" is a term that applies exclusively to women, and connections between feminists and mixed-sex organizations like unions are
weak (Ferree and Roth 1998).

Because such collectivist organizations remained resolutely local,
there are no national feminist groups outside of government dedicated
to representing a wide spectrum of women's concerns. There are some
women's organizations dedicated to challenging gender relations that
Americans would call "feminist" groups, but Germans would not
because they did not originate in the New Left and do not share the
style of organizing associated with it.[31]

Feminist organizations in Germany also differentiate themselves
from those women's rights groups that were originally founded before
the Nazi regime. Although only the new, local grassroots project groups
would be called "feminist" in Germany, we separate all autonomous
women's organizations centered on challenging gender relations
(including the UFV and Women's Law Association as well as local projects and networks) from the associations by and for women in parties,
churches, unions, and professions that we treat as part of a more diffuse
"women's movement."[32] This broader "women's movement" especially
includes associations of women in the parties. They are inspired by feminism but mobilized within rather than outside the institutions of

[31] These include the women's rights group, the German Women's Law Association
(*Deutscher Juristinnenbund*), and the UFV (Independent Women's Association), a
feminist umbrella organization that had been created in December 1989, shortly
before the collapse of that state. Although in the United States the terms "feminist"
and "women's movement" are typically used interchangably, in Germany (as in much
of the world) the word *feminist* implies a central focus on women's rights and changing gender relations while the *women's movement* is defined more broadly as including all organizations that organize women as women to make claims on any issue,
from environment to peace to workplace rights.

[32] These include such confessional organizations as the Catholic Lay Women's Association, professional women's groups such as the Association of Women Doctors,
and the umbrella organization of women's social and civic groups (the *Deutscher
Frauenring*).

politics. These organizations are especially significant in Germany compared to the United States.

The formation of new women's organizations within existing political parties, such as the Association of Social Democratic Women, the *AsF*, and the *Frauen-Union* for women in the conservative CDU-CSU, was an important shift in the opportunity structure for discussing gender issues. In the 1980s, some feminists became involved in forming and supporting the new Green political party and participating in campaigns for women's influence in German and European politics. The Greens introduced the "zipper list" (in which men's and women's names were alternated equally in the list of candidates to whom seats would be apportioned based on the proportional share of votes won by the party overall) into German politics, creating a competitive pressure on other parties to also recognize and include women.

When the Greens were in government, their appointments to ministries included non-party members who were active in social movements on the relevant issues. They thus became a vehicle for bringing feminists into state roles. Insofar as women seek a policy voice in Germany, the primary route that is open to them is the parties. However, not only party structures but all types of formal organizations remain highly controversial for feminists. As one put it:

> the women's movement . . . is not a group, not a formation, not
> an association, but rather an uprising, and that is something it
> acknowledges and desires: In Lower Saxony the periodic meeting
> of movement women is called the "Women's Uprising." The form
> in which feminist ideas and demands are presented matters. These
> issues resist the typical procedures of representation, they do not
> fit into the framework of political business, they are articulated by
> the mutterings of a female crowd that insists on being present and
> having the last word (Sichterman 1986, p. 134).

The label "feminist" is usually reserved in Germany for those groups who remain a "female crowd" without formal organization. However, throughout the 1980s there was a strong push by women inspired by the new feminism to enter into state and local politics. Both the Green party and the SPD established women's ministries in government, and all parties recruited women actively for local-level women's affairs offices. The CDU-CSU national government gave a formal mandate to cover women's affairs (along with families, youth, and senior citizens) to one cabinet minister, Rita Süßmuth, who was willing to be publicly identified as a feminist. This wider women's movement in the parties took up feminist issues but would not generally call itself feminist.

In sum, this overview of the gender component of the playing field indicates that across all issues U.S. feminists have more organization, resources, and potential allies outside of the formal political structures of parties and legislatures, and German women with feminist inclinations have relatively more organization, resources, and allies within the parties than outside them. Feminism is more differentiated from the women's movement in Germany, and feminist groups are much more decentralized. Equal rights language is probably more acceptable to U.S. feminists than to German feminists of all generations. Especially in the past decade, German feminist thinking has come to be reflected in a variety of party-based organizations and government positions as well as by grassroots groups.

In the United States, national feminist groups take up a wide range of issues and have the potential for both cooperation and competition with other national interest groups, within and across gender lines, but have no strong organizational base in the political parties and only a weak legislative presence.

MORAL/RELIGIOUS

German culture after 1945 defines itself in opposition to the Nazi period (Lepsius 1989). Since it was the Nazi state that so blatantly violated the principle of the protection of life (*Lebensschutz*), the anti-Nazi, democratic state should be in the forefront in upholding and enforcing it. Clause 2 of the (West) German Constitution states that "Everybody has the right to life and bodily integrity." The specter of the Holocaust hovers over the discussion of issues such as euthanasia and reproduction. The death penalty does not exist in Germany and is not an issue. One finds no German counterpart to U.S. conservatives who enthusiastically support capital punishment while vehemently opposing abortion. The Nazi experience to some degree haunts U.S. discourse as well, but the ghost is more distant and less threatening.

The different role of religion in the two countries is quite complicated and in some respects paradoxical. Institutionally, religion and politics are less separated in Germany than in the United States, but culturally they are more separated. This creates two quite complicated and contrasting playing fields for sponsors of religiously derived frames.

Many Germans are unconvinced that religion and government should be institutionally separate spheres. Churches provide religious instruction in the public schools and, unless they formally resign from church affiliation, people pay a church tax to the state that is then apportioned to the individual denominations on the basis of the proportion of taxpayers affiliated with them. Even most non-church-attending Germans who think of themselves as secular in orientation do not actively reject either the church tax or religious instruction in the schools.

Institutionally, the intertwined interests of religion and state are made explicit in the self-identification of some parties. The Christian Democratic Union and the Christian Social Union (CDU/CSU) see their own mandate in part as furthering the interests and values of the churches in politics. Nor does the Catholic Church hesitate to intervene directly in German politics when it can. Moeller (1993), for example, describes the successful political campaign led by the Catholic Church in the late 1940s and early 1950s to delegitimate women's paid employment and single motherhood, both of which had become widespread in the aftermath of the war. The campaign led to the addition of "protection of the family"[33] to the German Constitution as a responsibility of the state. Classifications of welfare states such as those of Esping-Anderson (1990) and Sainsbury (1994) place Germany in the "conservative Christian" category, reflecting the long-term success of the Christian Democrats in defining German social policy in the latter half of the twentieth century.

The rhetoric of the Cold War in Germany contrasted the Christian basis for the modern West German state with a "godless, atheistic" Eastern bloc (Moeller 1993). The opposition of the "red" (or socialist) parties with the "black" (clerical, Christian, conservative) parties was common throughout Europe, but because Germany sat directly on the geopolitical fault line that the Cold War produced, the Social Democratic Party was at a special disadvantage. The alignment of the churches, especially the Catholic Church, with the conservative parties that explicitly called themselves Christian was an important part of the self-image of those who defined themselves as "anti-communist."

In contrast, the United States has a competing normative principle with a constitutional sanction: Religion and politics ought to be inde-

---

[33] This provision was the basis on which the Constitutional Court decided in 1999 that tax laws needed to provide more support for parents of young children and directed the legislature to address this.

pendent spheres of activity with no official relationship between church and state. The principle is not uncontested, but those who do so are at a rhetorical disadvantage and face an uphill struggle. Even many deeply religious U.S. citizens would object to paying their church contributions in the form of taxes or having state schools provide classes in religion, as is the rule in Germany. Moreover, neither the Republican nor the Democratic Party has historically had a specific identification with Christianity as such, although the recent alliance of the Christian Right with the Republican Party threatens to change that. From these differences, it would appear that the carriers of explicitly religious frames should have greater discursive opportunity in Germany than in the United States.

The cultural separation of religion and politics is a different matter. By every measure, Germany is a more secular society than the United States. While the majority of Germans are nominally members of either the Catholic (35%) or Lutheran (36%) Church,[34] their affiliation plays only a moderate or even marginal role in orienting their personal lives. Attendance at weekly services had dropped by 1990 to 20% among Catholics and 5% among Protestants. The 1990 World Values Survey found more than two-fifths of U.S. respondents claiming to attend religious services once a week or more. The same survey shows more than one-third of Germans saying that they are atheists or not religious compared to about one-sixth of Americans who respond this way. A 1979 Gallup Poll asked Germans and Americans "How important are religious beliefs in your life?" Almost 60% of the Americans answered "Very Important" compared to only one-sixth of the Germans.

In addition, the United States is characterized by a broad and diverse religious pluralism instead of two dominant, established churches. The various religious congregations include many who are reacting against what they see as the increasing secularization of modern life. In this worldview, their adversaries' views on the role of women, homosexuality, prayer in schools, premarital sex, and abortion are viewed as symptoms of secular humanism, a more fundamental problem of moral decay. Not everyone who considers religion very important embraces a religious master frame to understand political issues, but there can be

---

[34] Most of the remainder have no religious affiliation. They are disproportionately concentrated in the former GDR. Most Muslims resident in Germany are not citizens, even if born in Germany, and do not appear in these statistics.

little doubt that the religious constituency is substantially larger and should therefore provide greater discursive opportunities for religious frames in the United States than in Germany.

However, in Germany the religious constituency has two, large well-institutionalized political representatives in the form of the Catholic and Lutheran Churches, while in the United States the issue of who can speak with the most legitimacy to represent a religious point of view is less structurally obvious and more open to competing claims.

JUSTICE

Every issue has a distributional dimension. There are always relative winners and losers, especially in the short run, even when framing strategies emphasize the collective benefits of particular policies. Justifications for policies in terms of their impact on economic growth, for example, often make use of the metaphor, "A rising tide lifts all boats." A rising tide, however, lifts all boats equally. Few would make such claims for economic growth; there are inevitable short-term winners and losers even if everybody gains some advantage in the long run.

The issue of social justice arises when the winners and losers from any specific policies follow more general lines of economic and social cleavage between the "haves" and "have-nots" in a society. The beginning of any analysis must be the centrality of class in German thinking about injustice compared to its secondary status in the United States. "Left" and "right" are defined in Germany by one's stance on class inequality, and political parties have historically been easy to locate on this continuum, for commentators and voters alike (Fuchs and Klingemann 1990). More than a century of battles in Germany between a left that speaks in the name of workers and the poor and a right that speaks for employers and the bourgeoisie have left a readily recognizable terrain of class conflict in which much, but not all, politics can be fitted.

In the United States, the language of "class warfare" is a countertheme rather than a dominant political cleavage. Issues of gender, race, religion, and sexuality provide alternative alignments of interests. American "exceptionalism" in regard to the absence of a socialist or social democratic party has long been noted as a distinctive aspect of U.S. political culture. This makes it more difficult to define precisely what the left is or stands for, and it also makes it easier for diverse groups to make appeals about social fairness in terms of their rights, without necessarily connecting their claims to any one broader alignment of political forces.

Because class is central to defining a single left–right continuum in Germany, the history of class struggles still significantly shapes its discursive opportunity structure today. The German state of the late nineteenth century pioneered social welfare provisions such as unemployment insurance and state-supported health care. Germany had the largest Social Democratic Party in the world in the 1890s and 1900s, and international social democratic theory and practice often emerged in Germany. Such thinking tended to define the true proletariat as the male working class employed in industrial jobs and to advocate policies that excluded women from employment but improved male workers' wages and ability to support and care for dependents.

Thus the definition of women as mothers and wives, dependent on male protection, is deeply anchored in the German welfare state. Even today German law not only permits but encourages employers to pay people in the same job differently based on how many dependents they have by making "dependent benefits" a norm in wage agreements. Industrial workers in general are seen as the disadvantaged group, and group benefits and protections are seen as the legitimate way of balancing the scale for them. For example, German social policy has long offered financial support for students of working class backgrounds (*Arbeiterkinder*) but is deeply suspicious of affirmative action for women or others.[35] In fact, legislation that sharply limits night hours or types of occupations for women in the name of protecting them from exploitation – but in fact also restricts women from competing with men and has kept their wages lower – is only now losing some of its legitimacy in Germany. U.S. courts in the early 1970s were already dismantling protective legislation for women as a discriminatory violation of equal treatment.

Compared to other industrial democracies, the United States has lagged in providing any sort of "social safety net" for the poor and continues to resist a self-definition of a "welfare state," culturally being more committed to individuals taking care of themselves through the market. U.S. social policy is also far more suspicious of any differences in treatment of "individuals." Together, these factors provide a partial

---

[35] For example, debates over giving equally qualified women preference in hiring decisions frequently suggested that the deplorable result would be advantaging unmarried women over men who were supporting families.

explanation of why the United States remains the only industrial country without government-supported paid maternity leave.

Treating people differently depending on whether they are married or single, have children or don't, is not usually seen as fair in the United States. Injustice claims based on group differences are culturally suspect in the United States while they seem natural and legitimate in Germany. Different treatment based on assessments of what social groups "need" is an accepted part of being a "social market economy" (Germany's preferred term for itself), and women are especially seen as wives and mothers and as needing state help and protection in these roles. In the United States, women fall more readily into the basic category of "individual," and individuals are usually discussed in terms of their rights, rather than their needs.

Political progressives in the United States who try to raise class issues often find themselves marginalized, attacked for speaking an "outmoded" language of "class warfare." Far from being resonant, framing an issue as being about class inequality is a challenge to the dominant political culture. This is even true when the group being identified is a conflated race-class category such as "the poor" and "the disadvantaged" or a racialized gender-class category like "welfare mothers." What everybody is seen to need, in American parlance, is the "opportunity" as an "individual" to make his or her own "choices" and then to live with the result. It is consequently hard to talk in the United States about groups having distinctive needs that the state ought to meet or about individuals who are not freely able to make choices.

Talking American is the apt title for Carbaugh's (1988) study of a popular television talkshow, "Donahue." His analysis focuses on what he calls the "equivocal enactment of individuality and community." It is seen most clearly in the symbol of the person as an "individual." This symbol, Carbaugh argues, allows speakers to transcend the differences that are implied when people are discussed as members of social groups – as men and women, blacks and whites, working people and middle-class professionals, or other collective categories. "By defining persons as individuals," he writes, "one asserts simultaneously that we are both all alike and each unique" (1988, p. 23).

In this discourse, persons as individuals may claim rights; social groups and institutions are moved to the rear. The assertion of injustices based on social inequalities must contend with a culturally normative response that asserts that we are all individuals, and it implicitly denies the relevance of social location and group differences. Such claims do not face a similar obstacle in German discourse, especially when the social location in question is class.

MASS MEDIA

German journalists accept and take for granted a public sphere dominated by political parties and the organizations closely associated with them. The choice of sources, for example, is obvious and established by long-standing political convention. "In Germany," Pfetsch observes, "it is not so much the daily response to public opinion data or the creation of highly visible pseudoevents that govern news management. Instead, the political response to the statements of coalition partners or political opponents through the media is the crucial characteristic of strategic communication. In this constellation, the media are used as vehicles to influence the discourse within the governmental system" (1998, p. 81; see also Pfetsch 2000).

In the United States, as Hallin and Mancini (1984) argue, the vacuum left by the absence of political parties as interpreters of meaning enhances the role of journalists in the process. The choice of sources is not simply the *pro forma* application of established conventions; there are guidelines, of course, but some journalistic judgment is required to apply them to particular cases. It also allows for a more active role for journalists themselves as players who help to shape meaning.

The four elite, broadsheet newspapers that we compare in this book are a small sample of the media discourse available and they are very similar on many dimensions. Economically, they are independently owned, commercial enterprises. In the case of *The New York Times* (*NYT*) and *The Los Angeles Times* (*LAT*), they are part of larger companies that own several other companies as well, mostly media related. They are heavily advertiser-dependent for income, and, on some issues, the economic interests and ideology of the owners might affect the discursive opportunity structure.

Ideologically, there are some small differences among them. The *Frankfurter Allgemeine Zeitung* (*FAZ*) has a center-right readership that is more likely to support the Christian Democrats. The *Süddeutsche Zeitung* (*SZ*) has a center-left audience that is more likely to support the Social Democrats. But they operate by very similar professional conventions that make their news reporting very similar. Greater differences, of course, are reflected in their editorial and opinion pieces, but news coverage is not ideologically driven (Gerhards, Neidhardt, and Rucht 1998, p. 97). For the U.S. newspapers, one would be hard put to characterize general ideological differences between the *LAT* and the *NYT*. Again, journalists who assemble the news operate as professionals following virtually identical norms and practices and both papers seek, more or less consciously, what they see as the ideological center.

The most important difference between the countries is in the greater openness of U.S. journalists to sources other than state and party actors, and particularly to grassroots actors. Gans (1980, p. 44), in discussing the dominant values in U.S. journalistic culture, writes that "Citizens should participate; and 'grassroots activity' is one of the most complimentary terms in the vocabulary of the news, particularly when it takes place to foil politicians or bureaucrats, or to eliminate the need for government action."

Perhaps related to this openness is a much higher value on the personalization of the news, human interest stories, and the voices of selected "ordinary" people whose claim to expertise is only their experiential knowledge. German commentary and opinion is intended to reflect the collective views of the newspaper staff while U.S. media commentary, aside from editorials, expresses the opinion of the individual writer, who may be a syndicated columnist or an invited op-ed writer rather than a member of the staff. Papers such as the *NYT* and *LAT* pride themselves on presenting a range of opinions on controversial issues, but they also define limits on what counts as legitimate discourse.

The net result of these differences is that the United States offers a more favorable media opportunity structure, even in elite newspapers, for the voices of movement groups and unaffiliated individuals than does the German media system and culture.

CONCLUSION

We have described the general contours of the playing fields in Germany and the United States on which their respective framing contests over abortion take place. The playing field, as we will emphasize throughout this book, does not determine the outcome of the contest, but it heavily influences it. The activities and choices of the players, if they are to be successful, require that they be able to read this playing field and make their choices with an awareness of the opportunities and constraints that it provides. If they make misjudgments, they will suffer the consequences. There is typically a lot of trial and error in prolonged symbolic contests.

This chapter provides our reading of the important differences in the discursive opportunities in the two countries. We have emphasized differences that are particularly important for the abortion issues, but they exist for every issue, even though the particular component may be much more relevant for one particular subset than another. To summarize:

As part of the broader set of political components, there exist more political and judicial access points in the United States compared to Germany, thus providing many more discursive opportunities for civil society actors, including social movement organizations. In addition, a German view of the state as a force for good in social life contrasts with a distrustful view of the state in the United States. The anti-statist, libertarian tradition in the United States provides a discursive advantage to frames that emphasize state intrusion into areas of private life and a disadvantage to frames that emphasize a supportive government role.

Political parties in Germany are relatively tight and centralized organizations that play a well-institutionalized role as interpreters of meaning. They take clear positions on policy issues and maintain party discipline. By contrast, political parties in the United States have no constitutional legitimacy and are decentralized umbrella organizations, more like a loose coalition than a single actor. They have multiple spokespersons, often with conflicting messages, and generally fudge their position on issues where there is internal party disagreement.

Regarding socio-cultural components, there are also some striking differences as well as similarities in the two countries in regard to the institutional and cultural opportunities that are available for raising issues in terms of gender, morality, or justice. The specter of the Holocaust hovers over all issues in Germany, but it can be especially salient for issues that have a central moral dimension. The Nazi experience often haunts U.S. moral discourse as well, but in Germany the ghost is much nearer and more threatening. In Germany, one major implication of defining itself in opposition to the Nazi period is to elevate the principle of *Lebensschutz* (the protection of life) to the top of a hierarchy of values. This provides a special discursive opportunity to frames that can tap such a theme.

Focusing attention on gender is not necessarily equivalent to acknowledging women as actors, but the former is unlikely without the latter. Because of institutional opportunities, women's efforts to represent gender politically have taken different forms in each country. In

Germany, some women inspired by feminism have entered the political parties while others have insisted on the necessity of remaining a grass-roots "female crowd." In the United States, feminist mobilization has been channeled largely into the federal–state–local structure that is typical of U.S. interest groups and work with allies both in the wider women's movement and in non-gender-specific organizations in civil society. Institutionally, women concerned about women's status are stronger within the German parties than outside of them, while the reverse is true for the United States. Culturally, only those groups that have remained outsiders are considered to be "feminists" in Germany, while the line between feminism and the broader women's movement is indistinct in the United States. Demands for equal rights and equal treatment are highly legitimate claims in U.S. gender politics, but they have long been viewed with suspicion in Germany by feminists and nonfeminists alike.

Religious frames are institutionally advantaged in Germany more than in the United States, but they are culturally disadvantaged. The institutional linking of the two major religious denominations in Germany with the Christian Democratic party means that actors with religious frames have greater access to the arena than those in the United States with its institutional separation of church and state. But the lesser importance of formal religious participation for Germans and the lesser importance of religion in their lives means that religious frames will have fewer cultural resonances. Here, it is the United States that provides a much better discursive opportunity for religious frames.

Frames that claim injustice along some major line of societal cleavage will have greater or lesser advantage depending on what dimension of social cleavage is advanced. In Germany, the natural fault line for injustice claims is social class; the right–left dimension is a major defining category for understanding German politics and has historically been understood primarily as a social class dimension. Injustice claims based on a social class cleavage are advantaged in German discourse. In the United States, injustice claims most commonly rest on a conflated ethnic/class category, and pure class claims are disadvantaged. But at a more fundamental level, all claims based on group injustice are disadvantaged in the United States against a cultural norm that social location is irrelevant and everyone should be judged as an individual. Individualism is generally suspect in German discourse, but particularly so when applied to women.

Finally, considering the mass media in both countries, we conclude that German journalists provide access primarily to state and party actors and their institutional allies. U.S. journalists are freer to choose who represents an issue and value the inclusion of grassroots actors and ordinary individuals more highly. U.S. newspaper writing styles place a higher value on personalization and narrative. As a result, there is greater discursive opportunity in the United States for nonstate and party actors and a greater receptivity to "human interest" as a reason to focus on the experiences of ordinary people. Newsworthiness in the United States generally is less constrained to follow institutional priorities.

The implications of this discursive opportunity structure for the framing contest over abortion are developed in the next five chapters in the form of specific propositions. In Chapters Five and Six, we present the major findings on our two major outcome measures: standing and framing. The interaction of the playing field on this issue with the characteristics and strategic choices of the players explain these results. In Chapters Seven through Nine we examine more closely how the gender, moral/religious, and justice components of discursive opportunity play out on the abortion issue.

CHAPTER FIVE

Standing

Not every actor has an equal chance to have a voice in public discourse. Not only are some actors better prepared and motivated to speak out on a particular topic, but the customary practices of news gathering make some speakers highly salient to the media while others are less so. By *standing*, we mean having a voice in the media.

The concept comes from legal discourse, where it refers to the right of a person or group to challenge in a judicial forum the conduct of another. Rather than a matter of clear definition, legal standing is a battleground. By analogy, media standing is also contested terrain. In news accounts, it refers to gaining the status of a media source whose interpretations are directly or indirectly quoted.

Standing is not the same as being covered or mentioned in the news; a group may be in the news in the sense that it is described or criticized but has no opportunity to provide interpretation and meaning to the events in which it is involved. Standing refers to a group being treated as an agent, not merely as an object being discussed by others.

From the standpoint of most journalists who are attempting to be "objective," the granting of standing is anything but arbitrary. Sources are selected, in this view, because they speak as or for serious players in any given policy domain: individuals or groups who have enough political power to make a potential difference in what happens. Most journalists would insist that their choice of sources to quote has nothing at all to do with their personal attitudes toward those sources. If they choose to call up Operation Rescue and quote its erstwhile spokesman, Randall Terry, on his reactions to a Supreme Court decision on abortion, this has nothing to do with whether they like or dislike Operation Rescue or Terry, or how they would depict this group. They would say that they are simply reflecting a reality that is out there – for better or worse, the group has enough power that it needs to be taken into account and Terry is able and willing to speak for them.

Linda Greenhouse, who covers the Supreme Court for *The New York Times*, speaks of "the imperative to quote somebody who is a spokesperson for a group with public name recognition because you have to discharge your duty." She distinguishes such sources from those whom she turns to "as a substantive resource to get some understanding" (Interview, June 1998). As one TV news producer put it, "Our job is to bring on guests who make the news – the players, in other words."[36] News, in this world view, is about those powerful enough to make a difference – "objective" reality is the basis of standing.

Having standing in certain media, however, also creates power. Being visible and quoted defines for other journalists and a broader public who really matters. Most journalists recognize that their choices also enhance or diminish the power of those to whom they offer or deny standing. Standing both reflects and enhances acceptance as a player on a given policy issue and thus is a measure of achieved cultural power.

THE SOURCES OF STANDING

We assume, then, that journalists operating in a media forum try to give standing based on their perceptions of who the key players are, but that their judgment reflects three broad sets of factors: (1) broader institutional and cultural assumptions that differ between Germany and the United States; (2) journalistic norms and practices; and (3) characteristics of the actors who compete for standing including their goals, resources, and professionalism.

Features of both government and civil society privilege certain actors on certain issues and de-privilege others. For example, political parties or religious groups may have certain institutional and cultural opportunities to speak on certain issues. Journalists tend to take these rules of the game for granted, without much consciousness or critical analysis. In granting standing to certain actors, they reflect broader societal expectations rather than those specific to the mass media. Advocacy organizations that lobby legislators are an institutionalized feature of U.S. politics, but they do not feature so prominently in German politics. Thus, the differences in stable aspects of the opportunity structure

---

[36] *Nightline* producer Richard Kaplan, quoted in Croteau and Hoynes (1994).

discussed in Chapter Four will help to account for some of the differences in who has standing on abortion in the two countries.

Beyond this, differences in journalistic news routines and cultural norms also play a role. What journalists believe about who makes a difference in general will lead to particular news routines and norms about source selection that will then be applied to specific issues such as abortion. These practices interact with those of potential sources, leading to the establishment of ongoing relationships with some sources and not others. U.S. journalists, more than their German counterparts, are driven by the need to supply spectacle and drama, and this gives a relative advantage to sources who provide good sound bites and colorful quotes.

In contests over meaning, sources are often chosen because they are seen as representing a particular perspective. Rather than being seen as representative in the sense of typical, they are chosen as prototypes who represent a particular cultural tendency in a compelling way. In this sense, standing still reflects a journalistic judgment about which movements make a difference, but such judgments vary over time as movements succeed or fail in establishing their political significance. In both the United States and Germany, the Catholic Church and the women's movement make claims on the abortion issue, but the legitimacy accorded these actors by journalists may vary both between countries and over time within them.

Finally, the different standing of organizational actors will be influenced by their own internal characteristics and concrete activities, in particular the resources that they make available for media relations, their choice of media strategies, and the professionalism and skill with which they implement them. This in turn is a reflection of organizational goals and priorities. The same type of group – for example, a social movement organization – may be more centrally organized in one country or at different points in time, may make more use of sophisticated media relations professionals who understand the news needs of the media, or in other ways influence its media standing.

Some media-savvy organizations combine both resources and experience to promote their standing in the media, but not all organizations either can or wish to develop a media strategy. Some resist the level of bureaucratization and specialization that are required to do so or have no organizational presence in the major media centers: New York, Los Angeles, and Washington, DC in the United States and Bonn, Berlin, Frankfurt, Hamburg, and Munich in Germany. U.S. social movements generally pursue media standing in a more active way than their German counterparts.

The issue of abortion has been, as we have seen, the basis of a continuing debate in both countries. The differences in who actually gets to speak on this issue and how standing changes over time are doubly revealing. These differences promise to tell us about how the process of acquiring standing works more generally, and to reveal who has standing on the issue of abortion, thereby allowing us to examine the relative importance of the different determinants.

At an operational level, standing is simply the appearance of a speaker who is being quoted or paraphrased in the media. A speaker may be either a collective actor (a government agency, political party, association, or social movement organization) or an individual (either an expert or some other person not acting as a spokesperson for any organization).[37] For a speaker to be coded as having standing, there must be an article about abortion in which he or she has something to say, even if what is said is not substantively meaningful (for example, "No comment"). Standing measures the *opportunity* to make a substantive comment about what abortion means, even if the occasion is not utilized to participate in framing. It indicates who is speaking in the article and how much they are quoted – that is, their number of utterances.

We present our results in three sections. First, we will focus on the relative importance of state and party actors in the discourse in the two countries and how this has changed over time. Second, we will compare the role of different civil society actors – particularly the Catholic Church and social movement organizations. Finally, we will look at the specific civil society actors who have achieved the most standing in the two countries.

STATE AND PARTY ACTORS

Proposition 5.1. *The standing of state actors is much higher in Germany than in the United States.*

By state actors, we include quotes from spokespersons for legislators, the courts, and for government agencies and ministries – that is,

---

[37] About 25% of the "speakers" whose words are being coded in the two countries are the authors of articles rather than an external source. Although we code these comments when we explore how the abortion issue is being framed, the utterances of these "speakers" are excluded from the analysis of standing.

Table 5.1. *Overall Standing by Country[a]*

Type of Speaker	Germany	United States
State	**58%**	**38%**
Executive	17%	18%
Legislative	33%	12%
Judicial	8%	8%
Political Party	**15%**	**2%**
Associations and Movements	**19%**	**43%**
Churches	12%	9%
Pro and Anti movement organizations	2%	23%
All other organizations	5%	10%
Individuals	**8%**	**18%**
Experts	7%	9%
Others	1%	9%
Total number of utterances	4479	6228

[a] Journalists were excluded.

government officials at any level or branch of government. In Table 5.1, well more than half (58%) of all utterances in abortion articles in Germany come from state actors, compared to slightly more than a third (38%) in the United States. While the percentages for the executive branch are about the same in both countries overall, the most striking difference is in utterances by legislative speakers (33% in Germany versus 12% in the United States).

We wondered whether this dramatic difference might reflect the wavelike nature of German abortion discourse noted earlier, compared to the more or less continuous coverage in the United States. German abortion discourse is heavily concentrated in the period when abortion law is being considered in the legislature; we might expect legislative speakers to have particularly high standing during the periods in which the legislature is the main site of political contest.

This explanation, however, is not sufficient to account for the U.S.–German differences. The greater prominence of state speakers in Germany holds even across periods when abortion is less actively on the state agenda. While the U.S. percentage of utterances from state actors is amazingly steady over time at around 40%, it ranges from 45% to 57% in Germany even in the less active periods and soars to 60% during the more intense waves of discourse. The share of utterances from state speakers in Germany is always higher than it is in the United States, even when no new proposal to regulate abortion is under consideration.

We also coded articles based on the arena in which the action for the story originated. Government action is a frequent arena in both countries but more so in Germany, where over two-thirds (68%) of all articles are stimulated by government action compared to half in the United States. This difference can account for at least part of the greater prominence of state actors in Germany, but again it is insufficient. Looking *only* at those articles stimulated by government action, we find that nearly three-quarters (73%) of the German utterances are from state actors, compared to just over half (57%) in the United States. Hence, whether government action is the springboard for coverage or not, the relative standing of state actors remains considerably higher in Germany.

Finally, state actors are much more likely to be the *exclusive* speakers in German articles, compared to having to share standing in the United States. About one-quarter (28%) of U.S. articles contain only state speakers, while a majority of German articles (51%) give standing only to state actors. Limiting the analysis to news articles (by excluding editorial and opinion pieces), nearly one-third (31%) of U.S. articles give standing to both state and nonstate actors, compared to only about one-eighth (12%) of German articles with this mix.

Proposition 5.2. *The standing of political parties is much higher in Germany than in the United States.*

As we noted in Chapter Four, political parties in Germany have a constitutionally recognized role in the German political system that they lack in the United States. They are formally defined as playing a role in the formation of government, and their rights and responsibilities are defined as well. German political parties are quasi-state actors. In contrast, political parties were viewed with suspicion by the framers of the U.S. Constitution and are weakly institutionalized compared to other democracies. Although political action is often driven by partisan concerns, U.S. political parties sometimes function mainly as vehicles for funding campaigns for individual candidates. Party discipline is weak and the desire to maintain unity often leads to the fudging of a clear position on potentially divisive issues such as abortion.

Given these differences, it is not surprising that German political parties have much higher media standing than their U.S. counterparts.

In Germany, parties as organizations offer 15% of all utterances compared to only 2% in the United States. German party speakers alone provide 40% of all nonstate utterances, while in the United States they are only a trivial 3% of those with standing aside from state actors.

In these figures, we are using those who speak for the party itself as an organization. If we take a wider group of speakers, those for whom the journalist provides a party affiliation,[38] we find a higher level of party-identified speakers in the United States but still a much smaller proportion of party-affiliated speakers than in Germany. In the United States only 12% of all utterances come from speakers who are identified with a party, but in Germany 47% do. In the legislative arena, speakers with any party identification at all (whether speaking as a person in state office or on behalf of a political party) provide two-thirds (67%) of all utterances in Germany but just one-quarter (25%) in the United States. All party-affiliated speakers in Germany play a considerably more prominent role in shaping the discourse than they do in the United States, not just those speaking for party organizations.

While the quasi-state nature of German political parties helps to account for the substantial difference in their overall standing, it cannot explain the substantial increase in the standing of German parties as organizations over time. Especially if one compares the two waves in which legislative action on abortion was on the agenda (1973–1979 and 1989–1992), party speakers are much more prominent in the second round of reform.

Figure 5.1 looks at standing only among nonstate speakers. German political parties jump to 50% in the latter period, compared to only 20% in the earlier reform wave. Furthermore, the standing of parties increases well before unification when the issue of abortion returns to the legislative agenda. The increases in numbers of utterances from German speakers with any party identification, whether in or out of state office, also rises from 36% to 72% over the period of our study, with the biggest jump coming between 1977–1982 and 1983–1988.

It is somewhat surprising that U.S. political parties do not show any similar large increase in standing. In 1980, the Republican Party added

---

[38] This includes cases where the party affiliation is not explicitly given but can be assumed (e.g., Jimmy Carter was coded as a Democrat, Ronald Reagan as a Republican, etc.).

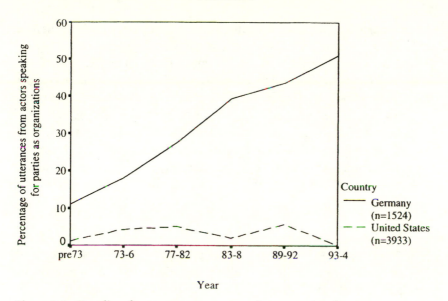

Figure 5.1. Standing for nonstate, party speakers over time by country. (Note: Journalists were excluded.)

an explicit anti-abortion plank to its party platform for the first time, and the Democratic Party began to position itself more clearly in favor of abortion rights. Nevertheless, the share of utterances from U.S. speakers with any party identification rises from only 13% before *Roe* to a high of 22% in the 1977–1982 period and to 21% in 1989–1992, in both cases times when presidential election campaigns (Reagan's and Clinton's) highlighted the abortion issue. The party organizations themselves remained nearly invisible as speakers throughout the whole period of the study.

These German and U.S. differences may also reflect differences in media practices, especially the way in which the balance norm is implemented. In Germany, balance can be provided by interviewing spokespersons for the spectrum of political parties; in the United States, where the parties are often reluctant to speak on abortion, journalists tend to look to advocacy organizations representing different positions.

In sum, both institutional position and journalistic norms combine to give state actors and political parties much greater standing in Germany than in the United States. This higher standing cannot be explained merely by the greater prominence of the legislative arena as a stimulus to discourse, nor does it occur only in the years in which the *Bundestag* was debating abortion reform. Even within this arena,

German articles give more standing to state and party speakers than do U.S. articles focusing on the legislative arena.

Furthermore, German articles are more likely to rely *exclusively* on state and party speakers. U.S. journalists typically put state, party, and nonstate speakers together in the same article; German journalists rarely do. However, the dominance of parties in Germany is not just a natural outgrowth of their constitutional position, either. Unlike the United States, where party-identified speakers have remained relatively stable in significance, German parties became the chief voices dominating the debate in the second round of reform as they had not been in the first.

CIVIL SOCIETY ACTORS

Standing is scarce. The success of one kind of actor is not simply a matter of its own strengths but also a question of the competition. In this section we look closely at the competition to state and party actors in the two countries – churches, social movement organizations and related advocacy groups, human service organizations, and experts and other individuals speaking only for themselves.

Proposition 5.3. *Social movement organizations have much higher standing in the United States than in Germany.*

Overall, advocates for anti-abortion- or pro-abortion-rights movement organizations account for almost one-quarter (23%) of the United States utterances compared to 2% in Germany. When we remove all state and party speakers from the total, controlling for their greater standing in German discourse, the figure for the United States rises to 38% and for Germany to 7%. Even within this narrower field, movement actors receive much higher standing in the United States. Furthermore, the high standing of movement actors has increased substantially in the United States, especially since 1983, reaching half of all civil society speakers in the most recent period, while it still remains at 10% in Germany.

One small part of this difference may be due to the arena that stimulates the particular article. About one-seventh (14%) of U.S. articles have some social movement action as their basis, compared to only 3% of German articles. But even when one looks only at the legislative arena, movement organizations have 20% of the utterances in the United States while comprising less than 1% in Germany.

Table 5.2. *Social Movement Organizations in Germany and the United States:*
Comparing Resources and Media Sophistication

	Germany	United States
Median budget in $1000's[a]	15.6	600
Median paid staff	0	3
Staff has media experience[b]	24%	64%
We contact journalists[b]	24%	64%
Journalists call us[b]	6%	77%
Mean press releases	3.6	8.7
Mean press conferences	.9	6.7
Mean journalist contacts	3.9	8.5
Media not interested in us[b]	65%	18%
Actively work to influence national media[b,c]	29%	86%
National media are central target[b]	35%	68%
Number of organizations surveyed	17	22

[a] $N = 10$ for Germany and 17 for the United States.
[b] Percentage saying "completely true" or "somewhat true."
[c] N for the United States is 21.

Most of the difference, we argue, can be accounted for by the greater resources and professionalism of the social movement sector in the United States compared to Germany. U.S. movement organizations are much larger, more bureaucratic, and more centralized than their German counterparts. As described in Chapter Three, we surveyed the nonstate actors who were active in the 1989–1992 period in both countries. If we look at just the social movement organizations, we find that the U.S. groups had a median budget of $600,000 per year and a median full-time staff of three compared to $15,600 and zero full-time staff in Germany. On virtually every measure of media sophistication and interest, the U.S. groups dwarf their German counterparts. Table 5.2 summarizes some of these survey data.

The difference here is not merely a matter of resources but of motivation and goals as well. U.S. movement organizations tend to be more pragmatic regardless of issue, focusing on making concrete political gains through conventional tactics such as lobbying, participating in electoral politics, and using the media as an arena of contest. German social movements, in contrast, often see themselves as countercultural in a broad way. They are more likely to focus on building small local groups in which transforming the identity of participants is at least as important as incremental changes in policy. They may lack not only the skill but also the desire to do the kind of work that makes them professionals in the media arena (Schreiber, Grunwald, and Hagemann-White 1994).

Gabi Kruk, an activist with the Women's Health Collective in Frankfurt am Main, describes the publicity work that they do as being "in the form of giving lectures and workshops. When one of us is invited to speak on this or that theme. I think that's our form of doing public relations work." When queried if they take the initiative or wait to be invited, she said "it goes both ways. We list in our program that we are available for lectures and workshops but we also just get invitations. . . . That doesn't mean that we wouldn't like to do other things, but simply that for us – publicity work in the form of putting out advertisements or things like that – we don't have the financial means to consider it. It's something we would think about, but only if we had the money first" (Interview, January 1996). Although she later says that the goal of the organization is "working for emancipatory enlightenment" (*emanzipatorische Aufklärungsarbeit*), this is not something that she conceptualizes as reaching a mass public through systematic mailings or sympathetic media coverage. A largely face-to-face, consciousness-raising group style of work appears to appeal to her and other women's movement activists more than working with the media does.

Anti-abortion movement organizations are somewhat more inclined to do energetic public relations. Benno Hofschulte of SOS Leben, also in Frankfurt, speaks proudly of the mailing list of 20,000 names that he has assembled and defines his goal as "bringing the right to life of the unborn more into the public discussion." And, he says, "that is something we have also accomplished. Not us alone . . . but other groups that were also active in politics saw themselves supported in our work, because we were always everywhere." But he sees his successes as coming in collecting donations through mailings that support more mailings, not in work with the mass media, who he says "use practically none of the press releases from Right-to-Life groups" (Interview, January 1996). Dr. Wolfgang Furch, a gynecologist who heads the evangelical Baptist group, ProVita, concurs that his group has had little success in gaining access to the mass media. When he has gotten into the press at all, it has been "as an expert, getting letters to the editor published, in church-related publications" (Interview, January 1996).

This general tendency for U.S. social movement groups to work actively to get their point of view into the newspapers manifests itself in our survey data. U.S. movement organizations cultivate their ties with journalists and try to gain standing in a way that German movement organizations rarely do. As Table 5.2 indicates, only one-fourth (24%) of German movement organizations say that they have staff members with media experience compared to two-thirds (64%) of U.S. movement organizations. Less than one-third (29%) of German groups say that they actively work to influence the abortion debate in the national media, compared to 86% of the U.S. groups.

In Germany, the movement groups who adopt a more U.S. style of fund-raising, mass-mailing, and press releases are more likely to be the anti-abortion groups. However, they are not any more successful than the Pro movement groups in gaining access to the mass media forum. Their standing in the content analysis data is virtually nonexistent (looking only at the nonstate sector, 2.3% of the German utterances are from anti-abortion groups compared to 2.1% from pro-abortion-rights movement speakers). In the United States, these groups provide 15% and 22% of the utterances from nonstate speakers, respectively.[39]

Thus, there are conspicuous differences in how U.S. groups are funded, the types of public relations work that they do, and the success they have in gaining access to the media when compared to German movement groups. A different attitude toward the type of group that they should be and the goals that they should pursue explains something of the difference in the type of production structure they command and the work they invest in gaining the attention of the public. But it is not the only feature explaining the greater presence of U.S. movement groups in the media. Even those German groups that try hard to gain access find themselves with "no open doors there," in the words of Dr. Furch. Why this is so is a question to which we will return in later chapters.

Proposition 5.4. *Church groups in Germany, particularly the Catholic Church, have higher standing than in the United States.*

Overall, the differences in standing do not appear dramatic, with German church groups scoring 12% compared to 9% in the United

---

[39] Note that this apparent imbalance between the sides disappears when Catholic Church spokespersons advocating the Anti position are added in to the Anti side.

States. However, the dominance of state and party actors obscures the advantage that German church groups have when one removes these speakers from the analysis. Here, the German churches' share of the total number of utterances rises to almost half (45%) compared to only 15% in the United States. Among church groups, it is the Catholic Church that dominates in both countries (66% of utterances by church speakers in Germany and 70% in the United States). Over time, church groups have lost some of their standing relative to other competitors (parties in Germany and social movements in the United States).

Most German Protestants are represented by a single church, the German Lutheran (Evangelical) Church, and, like the Catholic Church, it maintains a central national office and has spokespersons who regularly deal with the press. By contrast, U.S. Protestantism is divided and diverse, and no single organization can speak for a significant proportion of the Protestant churches. In addition, a strong, religiously oriented anti-abortion movement in the United States often speaks for Protestant evangelicals. The Roman Catholic Church is centrally governed in both countries and has a strong commitment to articulating a point of view on the abortion issue. We explore these differences in more detail in Chapter Eight, when we consider the representation of religious claims on the abortion issue.

Proposition 5.5. *Individuals are much more likely to receive standing in the United States than in Germany.*

A variety of individuals receive standing in the abortion discourse. Many of them are presented as "experts" who, while they may have an organizational affiliation (with a university or research institute, for example), make clear that they are speaking for themselves only. But there are a variety of other categories as well, mainly in the United States: television and film celebrities, plaintiffs and defendants in court cases, and persons in the street who are participating or witnessing some abortion-related event. These various types of individual speakers have an overall standing of 18% in the United States (with only half of them experts) and only 8% in Germany (with 88% of them experts).

This difference most likely reflects different journalistic norms and practices in the two countries. Donsbach (1993) surveyed German and U.S. journalists, asking them about the interviews that they conducted while working on their most recent assignment. Almost half (49%) of the U.S. journalists reported conducting interviews with eyewitnesses, compared to less than one-third (32%) in Germany.

While experts themselves provide about the same proportion of all utterances in Germany (7%) and the United States (9%), the notable difference is that expertise is nearly the only way that a German speaker without organizational backing can have a voice in the media forum. In the United States individuals of more diverse sorts are quoted as often as experts. What it means for such nonorganizationally supported speakers to have a voice in the discourse is an issue that we return to in more detail in Chapter Eleven.

In sum, our comparative analysis of standing in abortion discourse in Germany and the United States has revealed a number of striking differences between the two countries. State and party actors tend to dominate standing in Germany, marginalizing most civil society actors. The major exception is provided by church groups, particularly the Catholic Church, which has a much higher standing in Germany. In contrast, civil society actors generally have a much higher standing in the United States. This is especially true for social movement speakers on both sides of the abortion debate.

THE MAJOR PLAYERS IN CIVIL SOCIETY

In Germany, as we have already seen, outside of state and party actors, church groups account for almost half of the standing of civil society actors. The remaining standing is spread among a variety of small groups, none of which emerge as major players in the abortion arena. Therefore, rather than describing any of these groups, we simply point to the fact that both the feminist movement and the pro-life movement each consist of a plethora of minor groups even when, as with some pro-life organizations, they exist as organizations at the national level.

But the 2% cumulative standing for movement organizations in Germany contrasts with a robust 23% in the United States. We now look more closely at who these major civil society actors are in the United States and how their standing has changed over time. Examining standing by individual organizations, we find that there are seven groups with scores of 50 or more utterances over the entire sample period; after that, there is a sharp falloff in standing, with no other organization above 25. We will focus here on these seven major players, reserving discussion of other groups at relevant points in later chapters.

ANTI-ABORTION GROUPS

The three major players on the anti-abortion side are the Catholic Church, the National Right to Life Committee, and – for a short period – Operation Rescue. Mobilization in opposition to abortion reform began in the 1960s with the Catholic Church leading the way (Byrnes and Segers 1992). While our data show that there was more dispersal among the church spokespersons in the early days, increasingly the primary voice became the National Conference of Catholic Bishops, and especially its Secretariat for Pro-Life Activities. Blanchard (1994, p. 61) quotes *The New York Times* (of June 14, 1992) characterizing this actor as "the broadest, best organized and most powerful group, [according to] people on both sides of the issue."

While the Catholic Church led all others in standing through the late 1980s, in recent years it has dropped to fifth place, while the National Right to Life Committee (NRLC) has assumed the leading role as spokesperson for the anti-abortion movement. The emergence of the NRLC represents a conscious effort on the part of the church to broaden the anti-abortion coalition. As early as 1966, Bishop James McHugh of the Catholic Family Life Bureau invited a small number of already active abortion opponents to join him in an informal nondenominational body that he called the National Right-to-Life Committee. This group held its first national meeting in 1970, with about 70 participants (Segers 1992). After *Roe v. Wade* in 1973 the NRLC was encouraged to become independent and ecumenical. Granberg (1981) indicates that it was 72% Catholic at the time of his writing, but by the 1990s it had become an organization that attempts to unite Catholic and Protestant evangelical constitutents as well as nonreligious pro-life constituents in a broad anti-abortion coalition.[40]

The third major anti-abortion player, Operation Rescue, had a brief, meteoric career. Founded in 1987, it emerged on the national scene in 1988 with its campaign of mass blockades of clinics, leading to many arrests of demonstrators. From 1988 through 1990, it led all other civil society actors in standing on the abortion issue, but it declined rapidly during the 1990s. Williams and Blackburn (1996) interviewed Operation Rescue supporters and found them more united in their commitment to the nonviolent, direct action tactic, "provided that it was carried

---

[40] The NRLC has also added other issues to its primary focus on abortion, especially euthanasia, but takes no position on contraception or prayer in the schools, issues that are more likely to divide than unite its religious constituencies.

out in a spirit of faith, Christian love, and compassion," than to any distinctive view of abortion. "The issue is a symbol for wider concerns, although exactly what those wider concerns entail remains only partially shared" (Williams and Blackburn 1996, p. 183).

The escalation of anti-abortion violence to include the murder of physicians who performed abortions seems to have undermined the standing of Operation Rescue, in spite of its attempts to disassociate itself from such actions. We quote below from our 1997 interview with Executive Director Flip Benham:

> Benham: When Michael Griffin shot Dr. Gunn in Pensacola, Florida, everybody abhorred that. We couldn't believe that it happened. It was terrible.
>
> Interviewer: Can you think of any examples where the media implied that Operation Rescue – was Operation Rescue mentioned?
>
> Benham: Phil Donahue. Overt. Teddy Kennedy even said that "Operation Rescue is calling people out." We've got a suit with him right now in Massachusetts over that. But they did it all the time.

In Benham's view, Operation Rescue's high standing in the mass media did not lead to a fair presentation of its message. Hence, he defines the loss of standing as not really meaningful and argues that standing is not necessary for the organization to accomplish its mission.

ABORTION RIGHTS GROUPS

The four major players on the other side are Planned Parenthood, the American Civil Liberties Union (ACLU), NARAL, and NOW (National Organization for Women). Planned Parenthood emerged out of the complicated birth control movement of the 1920s and 1930s. Margaret Sanger founded the New York Birth Control League in 1916, a rival to the already existing National Birth Control League (see Burns 2002). The two organizations eventually merged in 1938 to form the Birth Control Federation of America. In 1942, this federation renamed itself the Planned Parenthood Federation of America.

Initially, the birth control movement promoted the legalization and availability of contraception, largely emphasizing women's own decisionmaking about childbearing. However, under assault from anti-obscenity campaigners such as Anthony Comstock, Sanger led her organization into defensive alliances with doctors who stressed eugenic themes. Linda Gordon (1977) argues that Planned Parenthood was increasingly captive to medical and upper-middle-class interests, and the organization's understanding of the issue shifted from affirming birth control (by women) to supporting population control (by doctors and politicians).

As the abortion reform movement gathered momentum in the 1960s, typically organized around getting states to adopt the ALI model law, Planned Parenthood emerged as the leading spokesperson. As a major provider of abortions in its free-standing health clinics, it has remained among the major players through the entire period of our study. In 1969, it was joined by a second player, a newly formed organization with the acronym NARAL[41] (for National Association for the Repeal of Abortion Laws), calling for more than the ALI model law provided. NARAL demanded women's right to make the decision on their own rather than merely extending the discretion of doctors and hospital committees. NARAL quickly gained standing as a major player and has kept this standing throughout the entire sample period.

The claim for repeal rather than reform was supported, with some controversy, by the emerging second wave of the women's movement. The National Organization for Women (NOW), founded in 1966, mobilized both younger activists at the local level and older women who were already engaged in establishment politics, aiming explicitly to use the federal courts as well as local political organizing to defend women's rights. Its decision to support abortion rights was controversial during its early years (Freeman 1975; Friedan 1976). As the women's movement grew, NOW's general standing increased rapidly, and, in the period 1973–1975, immediately after *Roe v. Wade*, it led all other abortion rights groups in standing and was second only to the Catholic Church among civil society actors. Nevertheless, abortion rights were not the highest priority issue for NOW compared to such issues as education and employment discrimination and the Equal Rights Amendment. After 1975, it no longer led in standing among the spokespersons for abortion rights but still remained one of the major players through the rest of the years in our sample.

The final abortion rights player, the American Civil Liberties Union (ACLU), only emerged as a player on the abortion issue after *Roe*, with

---

[41] After *Roe v. Wade*, the same acronym was used, but it stood for the National Abortion Rights Action League and after 1993 to the National Abortion and Reproductive Rights Action League.

its creation of a Reproductive Freedom Project. The organization had filed an *amicus curiae* brief on *Roe v. Wade* and its companion case, *Doe v. Bolton*. The Reproductive Freedom Project created a continuing organizational focus on the issue and the ACLU has remained consistently high in standing since then.

It is worth underlining the fact that of these four major players, only NOW is an explicitly feminist organization. Unlike Germany, where the only social movement organizations engaged in the abortion issue are specifically feminist, the U.S. social movements that champion the abortion rights cause are considerably more diverse. NARAL, while a single-issue organization, clearly has roots in the women's movement also. But the other two major players, the ACLU and Planned Parenthood, have different roots – in the birth and population control movements and in concern about individual rights and freedom from state interference. We could expect them therefore to use their standing to present different preferred frames on the abortion issue.

CONCLUSION

We have seen that different types of actors have standing in the two countries. In Germany, state and party actors dominate the debate, with only church actors having major standing among civil society actors. This high standing given to formal institutions, particularly parties and legislative actors, is not just an outgrowth of the German media's focus on the legislative arena or on time periods when legislation is pending. While it is characteristic of Germany at all times, party and legislative dominance grew substantially from the first to the second round of reform, until standing on the abortion issue became virtually their exclusive property. In the United States, party actors as such are insignificant while civil society actors, and especially social movement actors, have a major standing. In the United States it is social movement actors whose standing has grown over time, becoming the equal of state actors in standing on this issue. Among the civil society actors, there are seven organizations who emerge as major players.

Standing means being quoted directly or indirectly, and this is undoubtedly a help in getting one's preferred framing of the issue conveyed through the mass media. But it is no guarantee. One may be quoted selectively, only on strategic rather than substantive issues, or too briefly to convey a complex but less familiar frame. Furthermore, a group may have its preferred frame presented by journalists or by other actors, even if it never has the chance to be the presenter. In the next chapter we will turn to our second major outcome measure to examine the relative strength of competing abortion frames in the two countries and show how this, too, has changed over time.

CHAPTER SIX

Framing

Frames are central organizing ideas that provide coherence to a designated set of idea elements. They should not be conflated with policy positions. It is important to understand that in both countries, policy debates are actively carried on among participants who disagree on the best policies but nonetheless share a frame for asking questions. Other actors may agree on policy but frame the problem that the policy addresses in very different ways.

If the abortion question is framed as "how can the state protect human life before birth?" one can answer that question by advocating draconian legal punishments to deter abortion. But, alternatively, one can advocate state incentives to the pregnant woman to carry the fetus to term plus public health measures to improve the health of both the pregnant woman and the fetus. Although these policy approaches differ, they are both answers tailored to a specific framing of what the abortion issue is about.

They entirely ignore a different question, "Do limitations on a pregnant individual infringe on the right to control one's own body that all citizens hold?" Here, too, answers may differ considerably. One may stress the limits on her freedom imposed by the presence of another human life, or argue about the self-defense rights of a woman against an undesired invader,[42] or defend the right to terminate a pregnancy as analogous to seeking any other sort of medical care.

The issues highlighted in the first discussion take for granted the presence of an "unborn baby" and government responsibility for it. The second discussion assumes that individuals normally have control over

---

[42] See McDonagh (1996). For the general issue of self-determination as a frame, see Bordo (1995).

their bodies, but it does not highlight the economic and social constraints on health and welfare that limit such "control."

These two very different kinds of policy debates, operating with different frames, are not just a hypothetical example. They reflect some of the major differences in framing found in Germany and the United States today. This chapter looks at the variety of frames in which questions about abortion are asked and answered. It then examines the distribution of frames within each overall policy position – that is, which frames are most prominent in each country among advocates of more restrictive policies and less restrictive policies on abortion – and how the pattern of framing has changed over time in each country. Finally, we argue that the different constitutional court interpretations of abortion in each country have shaped the subsequent framing contest, but more strongly in Germany than in the United States.

FRAMES ON ABORTION

We grouped the hundreds of different idea elements that we coded into eight frames, admittedly still a lot for the reader to keep in mind. To make it a little easier, the frames can be grouped into four *rights* frames (*Fetal Life, Balancing, Women's Rights,* and *Individual and State*) and four others (*Social Morality, Effects on Society, Pragmatic Consequences,* and *Social Justice*).

Within any particular frame – for example, *Fetal Life* – ideas may be pro, anti, or neutral in their policy implications. "Life begins at conception" supports an Anti policy direction, "Life begins at birth" supports a Pro policy direction, and "the real issue is when life begins" is neutral. But usually there is a predominant direction in which this frame is used and that it can be said to favor – for example, anti-abortion in the case of the *Fetal Life* frame.[43] We present these frames in the text through a short sketch of typical ideas in that frame's predominant policy direction.[44] Remember, the actual frames are more

---

[43] We coded all three directions for all frames, and at different points in the analysis we will indicate whether we are discussing just the predominant direction, all of the ideas in a frame, or a specific cluster of ideas that is not necessarily limited to a single frame.

[44] In cases where the predominant policy direction is different in the two countries, we present a neutral version, or the predominant version in the country where it is more common.

inclusive, containing neutral and rebuttal ideas as well as additional ones supporting the predominant policy direction.

RIGHTS FRAMES

Fetal Life (Anti Direction): The fundamental issue is the sacredness of human life. The fetus is an unborn child and abortion is, whatever the mitigating circumstances may be, the taking of a human life. There is a real conflict when the continuation of a pregnancy really threatens the life of the mother, but this is not an issue in the overwhelming majority of unwanted pregnancies.

Balancing (Neutral Direction): The issue is about finding the proper balance between two rights in conflict: the rights of the fetus and the rights of the pregnant woman to self-determination. The rights of the fetus increase with fetal viability, so that the proper balance shifts during different stages of a pregnancy. But neither right is absolute and must always be weighed against another equally legitimate right.

Women's Rights (Pro Direction): The issue is about the most fundamental right of a woman to control her own body to determine whether or when she will have a child. Reproductive rights are basic since they affect both the right and opportunity to participate in the workplace and political life more generally. This is a fundamental feminist issue. The woman who will have primary responsibility for raising a child should be the one who decides whether or not to have one.

Individual and State (Pro Direction): The issue is about the intrusion of the state into the private lives of its citizens. Whether or not to have an abortion is a decision that involves private matters between the pregnant woman and her physician, family, and trusted personal counselors. The government has no business being involved.[45]

OTHER FRAMES

Social Morality (Anti Direction): The issue is symptomatic of the moral fabric of our society. Christian morality is unambiguous and ignoring it on this issue reflects a broader moral permissiveness and secular humanism on many other issues as well. How we

---

[45] This frame is very close to the "freedom of choice" rhetorical strategy discussed by Condit (1990).

treat unborn children is a fundamental statement on whether we govern ourselves by a broader moral vision.

Effects on Society (Neutral Direction): Abortion is something that deeply divides opinions. It is an intrinsically undecidable issue in which compromise is called for. The best position on abortion is one that ends the conflict. No ideal solution is ever going to be found. Social peace is more important than the content of any substantive decision.

Pragmatic Consequences (Pro Direction): The issue is the effect of criminalizing abortion by not making it legally available. The social consequence of legal restriction is to force women with unwanted pregnancies into obtaining abortions under conditions that greatly increase their health risks, both physical and psychological. Ultimately, one must judge social policies by their costs and benefits, and attempts to limit abortion, however well intended, do not reduce abortions but merely raise their social cost.[46]

Social Justice (Pro Direction): The issue is whether the costs and burdens of our abortion policies fall more heavily on the poor than on the well-off. The ability of a woman with an unwanted pregnancy to decide whether or not to have an abortion should not depend on her social location. It is unfair to have a system in which affluent women have a choice and poor women do not.

These capsule versions are a device for conveying the frames intuitively. The labels are, in the end, only a shorthand for a cluster of specific ideas. Table 6.1 supplements the presentation in the text, dividing each frame by policy direction and indicating the most prominent Pro and Anti ideas by which it is actually displayed in Germany and the United States.

OVERALL FRAME PROMINENCE

We begin our analysis by examining the relative prominence of the eight frames in the nearly 12,000 idea elements coded in the United States and nearly 7,000 coded in Germany. Table 6.2 presents the results, broken down by whether, within each frame, the idea elements are Pro, Anti, or Neutral on abortion policy.

---

[46] This frame is very close to what Burns (2002) in *The Moral Veto* calls a "medical/humanitarian" frame.

Table 6.1. *Summary of Abortion Frames*

Pro policy direction	Label	Anti policy direction
Fetus not fully human **Science** says fetus not life **Constitution** says fetus not life **Displace concern for born child, woman** *Enlist women's help to protect fetus*	Fetal Life	Protecting life is the issue *Social value of fetal life* Fetus is a baby/child **Abortion is murder** *Constitution says fetus is life* *Fetus has legal rights*
Women take priority before certain time **Rape & incest justify abortion** *Infant suffering/handicap justifes it* *Social need/econ circs justify abortion*	Balancing	OK only to save mothers life *Family need is a pretext* *Fetus should have priority* *Counseling put fetus first* Justifies acts to protect fetus
Women's self-determination **Women's absolute self determination** *Women's limited self-determination* Abortion is a constitutional right *Less restriction = respect for women* **Limits oppress women, feminist issue**	Women's Rights (Women's Self- Determination)	**Devalues motherhood, sacrifice** **Prohibition in wom's interests** **Protect women from abortion industry** *Protect women from coercion* Abortion not women's/feminist issue *Ignores fathers' rights*
Privacy from state, for women & family **Doctor–patient privacy** Separation of church & state Pro-choice is majority view *Prohibition just makes women criminals*	Individual and State (Individual Rights)	Public funding inappropriate **Religious freedom requires noncompliance** States rights to be antiabortion *State obligated to regulate morality* *Government should make society moral* Abortion is not private

Table 6.1.   *Continued*

Pro policy direction	Label	Anti policy direction
Religious people differ in views of it **Anti-abortion stance is hypocrisy** *Women choose it for major reasons* Abortion is morally neutral health care *Abortion should not be stigmatized*	Social Morality	**Abortion is simply wrong** **Indicates an immoral society** Christian morality unambiguous Morally unlike contraception Implications for sexual morality
Abortion for population control Abortion for dealing with poverty **Abortion for family planning** Anti-abortion means anti-contraception *Abortion a symbol of modernity* Part of modern health & reproduction technology	Effects on Society	**Permissive laws uncivilized** Not needed for population control Not a means to control poverty Inappropriate targeting of minorities Anti control of reproduction **Stop runaway medicine**
Horror stories, claim illegal abortion harms **Legal abortion good for womn's health** Limits are burdensome *Limits are ineffective, lead to illegal* *Reduce abortion with permissive laws*	Pragmatic Consequences	*Can't reduce without criminal law* Teens need help of parents Regulation helpful, not too much Legal abortion dangerous *Not right to weigh costs/benefits*
Limits unjust to doctors **Affordability, justice for poor** Funding limits specifically unjust *East–west issues* *Geographic injustices*	Social Justice	**Not discriminatory** No violation of constitutional rights **No real inequality in access**

Note: **bold = equally prominent in both;** *italic = more typical in Germany;* normal = used more in US.

Table 6.2. *Overall Distribution of Frames by Country*

Frame	United States	Germany
Fetal Life	**15.7%**	**25.4%**
Pro	1.8%	2.5%
Neutral	2.4%	.6%
Anti	11.5%	22.3%
Balancing	**10.9%**	**18.7%**
Pro	4.5%	4.4%
Neutral	2.5%	6.7%
Anti	2.9%	7.6%
Women's Rights	**8.5%**	**11.7%**
Pro	6.9%	9.0%
Neutral	.1%	.3%
Anti	1.5%	2.4%
Individual and State	**24.4%**	**13.9%**
Pro	14.4%	3.8%
Neutral	3.0%	4.7%
Anti	7.0%	5.4%
Social Morality	**15.4%**	**15.8%**
Pro	4.0%	2.0%
Neutral	5.0%	8.3%
Anti	6.4%	5.5%
Effects on Society	**11.5%**	**2.2%**
Pro	4.7%	1.1%
Neutral	5.5%	.7%
Anti	1.3%	.4%
Pragmatic Consequences	**8.8%**	**9.4%**
Pro	5.9%	5.9%
Neutral	.3%	1.5%
Anti	2.6%	2.0%
Social Justice	**5.8%**	**3.1%**
Pro	5.3%	2.9%
Neutral	.2%	.1%
Anti	.3%	.1%
All Idea Elements	**100%**	**100%**
Pro	47.5%	31.6%
Neutral	19.0%	22.9%
Anti	33.5%	45.7%
	n = 11,686	*n* = 6867

Again, we organize our discussion of these results around a series of propositions:

Proposition 6.1. *With respect to policy direction, Anti idea elements have a 3 to 2 edge in German discourse while Pro idea elements enjoy a similar advantage in the United States.*

Both countries show a decided tilt in framing that offers a rhetorical advantage to one side over the other in this conflict, but the direction of this tilt differs. Overall, more of the framing ideas in Germany favor the restrictive, anti-abortion position and more U.S. ideas advantage the pro-choice, abortion rights side. As Table 6.2 indicates, 46% of all framing ideas coded in the German newspapers favored the Anti side, compared to only 32% that favored the Pro side. In the United States, 48% of the ideas favored the Pro side and 34% gave the rhetorical advantage to the Anti side.

Proposition 6.2. *The Fetal Life frame is most prominent in Germany while the Individual and State frame is most prominent in U.S. discourse.*

In Germany, the Fetal Life frame accounts for just over one-quarter of all framing ideas that are expressed. In both countries, the policy tendency within this frame overwhelmingly favors more restrictions. The second most common frame in Germany, Balancing, presents abortion as a matter of finding some balance between the rights of the fetus and the rights of women. This not only assumes a conflict between these two rights, but also that some compromise or trade-off is possible and desirable.

In Germany, this balance is struck more often in the direction of more restrictive policies (about 8% of all ideas) compared to only 4% that favor a balance through less restrictive policies. In the United States, the direction is reversed. If we combine the Fetal Life frame with these other ideas that frame abortion as a matter of balancing rights in the direction of more restrictive policies, the tendency for German discourse to frame abortion in terms of protecting human life is even more pronounced. Almost one-third (30%) of all German ideas express the issue in terms of fetal life or balancing in favor of fetal life, compared to less than 15% of U.S. ideas.

In contrast, the single most prominent frame in the U.S. discourse is the Individual and State, accounting for almost one-quarter (24%) of all U.S. ideas expressed. This frame, while more often used in terms that advantage a Pro position (14% vs. 7% Anti), is much less skewed to one side than the Fetal Life frame.

As we discussed in Chapter Four, the "state" has different connotations in Germany and the United States. The dominant U.S. perspective views the state distrustfully, in terms of interference and the potential illegitimacy of state action. The dominant German perspective views the state as a force for good in social life, with specific responsibilities to both the fetus and the woman that it needs to meet. The German framing of abortion assumes a view of the state as legitimately a *welfare* state. Debates occur within a range that assumes that a state is able to "help" as well as, or instead of, "punishing" its citizens. This "help rather than punish" formulation is an especially important idea for those who wish to see abortion decriminalized, but it advocates a far more active role for the state in regard to abortion than most U.S. abortion rights speakers would accept as legitimate. We will explore this point further when we examine the issue of social justice in Chapter Nine.

Proposition 6.3. *No one frame dominates the U.S. discourse to the extent that the Fetal Life frame does in Germany.*

The 22% of all German ideas that claim that the fetus is human life are not nearly matched by any other single-directional framing in that country, and the one frame that is most frequent for supporting the other policy side in Germany (Women's Self-Determination) makes up only 9% of all ideas. In the United States, the gap between the most common Pro frame, Individual and State (14%), and the most common Anti frame, Fetal Life (12%), is considerably smaller. Thus the U.S. discourse is more of an even debate between contending, incompatible frames, while the German discourse gravitates to a dominant Fetal Life frame for the issue.

The centrality of the Fetal Life frame was evident among activists that we interviewed as well, and they suggested that there was a tendency for this to become even more dominant in recent years. For example, one anti-abortion-movement leader (Benno Hofschulte, *SOS-Leben*) argued that:

In the *Bundestag* [in the 1991–1992 debates] people spoke exclusively or only about the unborn child or unborn person and even talked about killing – not as before about whatever lump of cells or berrylike cells, that – well, that is, with the connotation that there is not a real person there. That has changed radically, the discussion has changed. . . . Even Mrs. Süßmuth, who is an intense if not to say radical supporter of abortion, because she is always on about the rights of women – even she spoke of the "unborn human child," even though she continued to plead for abortion (Interview, January 1996).

Dr. Rudolf Hammerschmidt of the German Catholic Bishops Conference was similarly convinced of the growing hegemony of the Fetal Life frame:

Those who want some sort of liberalization today have to justify themselves, because it is now uncontested that it is a matter of life. Of an irreplaceable life that has no qualitative jump to make but is simply developing, and when it is born continues to develop. . . . That is, we have to credit ourselves with a success. Today it is in the public consciousness that this is no clump of cells, but rather an unborn life [Interview, January 1996].

Nor is this merely wishful thinking. We can see the influence reflected in the words of Dr. Hertha Engelhardt, of the German Women's Law Association, one of the organizations created in the first wave of feminism. In characterizing the group's position, she argues:

One can't protect the embryo against the will of the woman, and we believe that our position does not violate the protection of life. We have just allowed the protection of unborn life for a certain period to step back behind the will of the woman [Interview, January, 1996].

The German pro-abortion-rights use of the Fetal Life frame is heavily concentrated in the specific argument that Dr. Engelhardt advances: The woman should be enlisted in cooperating to save the life of the fetus (29% of the Pro ideas within this frame use this very specific claim). This particular idea virtually never appears in U.S. pro-abortion-rights discourse.

Proposition 6.4. *German discourse is more "rights" oriented than U.S. discourse.*

The four rights frames collectively define what one might call a "rights" discourse. About two-fifths (41%) of U.S. ideas fall outside these rights-oriented frames, while only 30% of German ideas are outside of them. Some alert readers may notice that since we are comparing clusters of ideas as a share of the total, having more ideas in one frame necessarily reduces the relative share of others, allowing differences in the relative prominence of other frames to muddy the comparison. However, the same conclusion is reached if we use an absolute rate per utterance measure: In every 100 German utterances there are an average of 137 framing ideas in the four rights frames (74 of which are Anti, 38 Pro, and 24 Neutral) while in 100 U.S. utterances there are 103 ideas-based in rights (40 Anti, 49 Pro, and 14 Neutral) on average. In contrast, there are an average of 59 nonrights framing ideas per 100 utterances in Germany and 74 per 100 utterances in the United States.[47]

In the four rights-based frames there is a small difference in favor of German discourse including more neutral, balancing ideas. German rights ideas that are coded as neutral appear 24 times per 100 utterances compared to a rate of 14 per 100 in the United States, but even with these excluded, the rate of using Pro and Anti versions of rights talk remains higher in Germany.

Some of the difference in *relative* shares of rights ideas between the two countries is also accounted for by the much greater prominence of the Effects on Society frame (about 12% in the United States versus 2% in Germany). About half of the ideas expressed within this frame are neutral with regard to a position on abortion. Abortion in the United States is much more often being framed as something problematic for U.S. society without indicating what policies should be followed to resolve it, but positive and negative social implications are also drawn more often in the U.S. discourse. Given the less violent nature of the conflict in Germany over this issue, this is not surprising. There is little difference on the shares devoted to other frames by all speakers on average, though there are specific differences by position that we will explore more closely later in this chapter.

The Social Justice frame appears more often in the United States than in Germany (6% to 3%), but this frame is infrequent in both countries. It is striking how little the problem of differential access to medically safe abortion by class figures in the way that abortion is framed in either country. Even when issues of social justice are raised they are likely to be put in terms other than class. How, when, and by whom the issue of

---

[47] Based on utterances that contain any framing, all speakers including journalists are included.

social justice is raised is one that we will take up again when looking at the role of political parties and the left–right continuum in German and U.S. politics in Chapter Nine.

In sum, our findings suggest that U.S. abortion discourse shows less agreement on what fundamental values the abortion issue is about than does the German discourse. Even though they may differ sharply on what policy they support, there is considerable agreement among German speakers that the issue is human life and its protection. This agreement is lacking in the U.S. case.

These results should give pause to those who have argued that the apparently greater rancor of the U.S. abortion debate is due to the prevalence of a discourse about competing rights, providing what Tribe (1990) has called a "clash of absolutes." Surprisingly, it is the German way of talking about the question, more than the U.S. one, that tends to frame abortion as about fundamental and irreconcilable claims for the rights of the fetus or the self-determination of women.

Glendon (1989), in an oft-cited argument specifically comparing the United States to Germany, has suggested that the ill-advised "intervention" of the U.S. Supreme Court in *Roe v. Wade* stimulated a rights discourse that has made the abortion conflict less tractable and subject to compromise. This argument, it appears, rests on a faulty assumption.[48]

U.S. abortion discourse is less strongly dominated by frames about rights than is Germany. But when the issue is framed in terms of rights in the United States, there is less consensus about which rights are central. The German discourse is different, not because it focuses on easier, more pragmatic issues outside the domain of core values and rights but because the Fetal Life frame is its dominant frame for rights talk.

ANTI-ABORTION FRAMES

In this and the following section, we compare how abortion is framed by speakers on the same side of the policy debate in each country. Anti speakers are those who express a predominance of ideas favoring more restrictions or the need to preserve current ones; Pro speakers are those

---

[48] There is a second faulty assumption as well. As Chapter Two discussed, the German Constitutional Court also acted to overturn a legislative decision. Glendon uses the contrast between legislative dominance in Germany and court dominance in the United States to explain the difference in the course of the conflict, but the contrast is, at best, highly problematic.

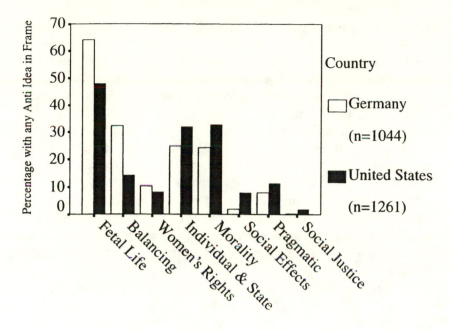

Frames

Figure 6.1. Anti-abortion frames by country. (Note: Only framing speakers whose ideas are all, or mostly, anti in direction are included.)

who express a predominance of ideas favoring fewer restrictions or none at all, or who oppose adding additional ones.

Proposition 6.5. *German Anti speakers are much more likely than their U.S. counterparts to use the Fetal Life and Balancing frames.*

Figure 6.1 shows the percentage of Anti speakers who include ideas from each of the eight frames.[49] The most striking differences are the much greater use of Fetal Life and Balancing by German speakers. Almost two-thirds (64%) of German speakers use the Fetal Life frame, compared to slightly under half (48%) of U.S. speakers. About one-third (32%) of the German speakers use the Balancing frame to argue for greater emphasis on fetal rights while only 14% of U.S. Anti speakers use this frame. German anti-abortion speakers are more literally "pro-life" than their U.S. counterparts – that is, they more narrowly

---

[49] Note that these percentages add up to more than 100% because speakers often include multiple ideas.

focus on the issue of fetal life. Here is further evidence for the dominance of this frame in German discourse.

There are often subtle differences in the expression of the same frame in the two countries by speakers favoring the same position. One-quarter of German anti-abortion speakers and about one-third (32%) of U.S. Anti speakers use the Individual and State frame. More than two-thirds of these German speakers use it by arguing that the state has a specific obligation to regulate morality and to act to make society more moral. U.S. anti-abortion speakers almost never make such a claim, arguing instead that the government should not interfere by funding abortion, that regulating abortion is a matter in which individual states have rights vis-a-vis the federal government, and that abortion is not a private matter. U.S. Anti speakers typically assert a more limited role for the state, even when they are urging it to restrict abortion.

U.S. Anti speakers are also more likely to include ideas about Social Morality, which, along with the Fetal Life frame and arguments for a more limited role for the state, is one of the three core ideas in their overall framing of the issue. Unlike German Anti speakers, who are more than twice as likely to use Fetal Life than any other frame, U.S. Anti speakers frequently include ideas from the Social Morality frame, too. They are distinctively likely to argue that abortion has implications for sexual morality in general and should not be used for contraception, while German Anti speakers are not only less likely to use this frame at all, but also within it to simply be averring that abortion is a moral wrong, without offering any reason. For German Anti speakers, the Fetal Life frame provides all the reason they need for their position, while Anti speakers in the United States are explicitly connecting abortion to a broader moral stance, especially about sexuality.

PRO-ABORTION-RIGHTS FRAMES

Proposition 6.6. *While the Women's Self-Determination frame is the leading frame for German Pro speakers, the Individual and State frame is the leader for U.S. Pro speakers.*

Figure 6.2 shows the percentage of Pro speakers including ideas from the different frames. The most striking contrast is the relative strength of the Women's Self-Determination and Individual Rights frames. In Germany, Women's Self-Determination is the most prominent frame by

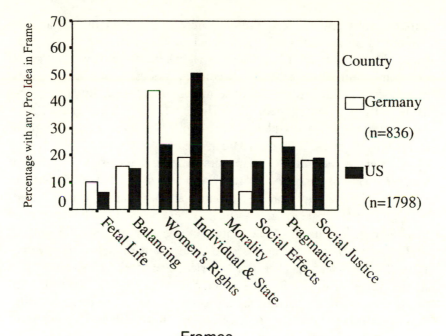

Frames

Figure 6.2. Pro-abortion-rights frames by country. (Note: Only framing speakers whose ideas are all, or mostly, pro in direction are included.)

far, with 44% of Pro speakers using it, compared to only 24% of U.S. Pro speakers. The Individual Rights frame is used by more than half (51%) of U.S. speakers, compared to less than one-fifth (19%) of German speakers.

The differences here are qualitative as well as quantitative. While both U.S. and German claims assert women's self-determination as a principle, German speakers are more likely to frame this principle as a limited one. The 1975 Constitutional Court decision can be read this way – as supporting a limited self-determination claim. As one Pro activist, Karen Schöler (*AWO*), put it, "the Court has affirmed this contradiction: protection of unborn life but also self-determination by women, so we can connect ourselves to that" (Interview, January 1996). U.S. claims about women's self-determination, by contrast, tend to specify the Constitution as securing women's right to decide and to point out the specific linkage of abortion with feminism as the basis for women's claims.

The U.S. emphasis on the gender-neutral Individual Rights frame over the gendered Women's Self Determination frame is at least in part self-conscious and tactical. Emily Tynes, a spokesperson for a pro-choice communications consortium, acknowledges that "all the [abortion rights] groups see it in a women's right's frame [but] when it plays out in terms of what's actually happening, it doesn't play out in terms of women's rights. It plays out in terms of constitutionality, or a piece of legislation invading people's bedrooms." She characterizes their media strategy as "really playing to basic U.S. values. And individual rights is at the top" [Interview, March 1998].

Another, smaller difference appears in the greater use that U.S. Pro speakers make of the Social Morality and Social Effects frames overall. Qualitatively, the ways that these frames are articulated in the United States differs from Germany as well. While some U.S. Pro speakers take the position that the Social Effect of abortion is a morally neutral matter of good, modern health care or a means of reducing poverty, virtually no German speakers do. American Pro speakers also rebut U.S. Anti arguments in the Social Morality frame by using this frame to argue that limiting abortion is connected to opposing contraception and by claiming that moral, religious people have different views about the wrongfulness of abortion, which are arguments more infrequently used in Germany. While U.S. Pro speakers who are using these frames are debating whether abortion is a moral wrong at all, this question appears to be largely treated as settled by both sides in the German discourse.

HOW COURT DECISIONS HAVE SHAPED THE DISCOURSE

The single most important factor accounting for the dominance of the Fetal Life frame in German discourse, we argue, is the 1975 decision of the German Constitutional Court overturning a liberalization of German abortion law by the *Bundestag*. The Court ruled that the abortion law violated the constitutional mandate for the state to protect human life. In Germany, more than one-third (36%) of the Anti ideas in the Fetal Life frame (and 18% of all Anti ideas) make specific reference to the constitutional or legal rights of the fetus. In contrast, only 10% of the U.S. Anti ideas within the Fetal Life frame (and only 3% of all Anti ideas) make such claims.

Even activists who were bitterly opposed to the constitutional interpretation conceded that it had a powerful impact on the discourse. Christina Schenk, one of the representatives of the PDS, the reformed communist party of former East Germany, in the unified German legislature averred:

> We were the only ones who came out and said that the Constitutional Court had covertly changed the constitution. No one else made that a theme. . . . Legal experts all had to concede that was true, but we tried to make that clear in our bill and also in our public relations work [that] the former basic understanding of the Basic Law was that to count as a person, as a human being – until now – [one counted] from the time of birth. But the Constitutional Court erased this . . . or tried to take the meaning out of it (Interview, May 1996).

The relative significance of the Fetal Life frame in Germany and the Individual and State frame in the United States can be traced back specifically to the ideas expressed by the highest courts in each country in their landmark decisions in the early 1970s. How important were these court decisions in shifting the frames in which abortion arguments are made by speakers on both sides of the issue? To what extent do differently formulated court decisions reflect underlying orientations and ideas in Germany and the United States that grow from their different histories, and to what extent do the court decisions themselves change the conditions in which all speakers look for ideas that can support their positions?

We see each constitutional court as both itself contributing to the framing of abortion in each country and also as reflecting legal precedents and historical traditions. Courts necessarily have to *interpret* their constitutions. The nature of the highest court's initial decision in either country was not considered self-evident or inevitable at the time it was reached.

The application of the constitutional principle of *Lebensschutz* (protection of life) to abortion is not obvious or automatic. The constitution does not specifically define when life begins, or single out fetuses as a form of human life that would fall under this mandate. Legal personhood in both countries, as Schenk pointed out earlier, is well established as beginning at birth. Thus it was unknown how the court would interpret this provision and if it would see it as applicable at all when the *Bundestag*'s Abortion Reform law of 1974 was referred to the Constitutional Court for review. Because the constitution also mandates that the state support the development of each human personality, advocates for less restrictive policies wanted the court to decide on the basis of women's rights to self-development and self-determination, and the balance to be struck between these two constitutional concerns was initially open.

Similarly, in the United States, the Supreme Court's decision in *Roe v. Wade* in 1973 was not easily predictable in advance. That the Court would look to provisions of the constitution that restricted state interference with individuals' control over their bodies, homes, and property – and extend the principle of privacy to cover women's decisions over their own bodies – was also a matter of some doubt. The Court decision in fact balanced the individual's right to privacy with the state's interest in public health by establishing a trimester system in which first one and then the other took precedence.

The U.S. Supreme Court decision also explicitly defined the matter of whether the fetus was a human life and when life begins as a matter of religious and philosophical controversy that the state should not attempt to answer. Thus, they chose not to rule on the specific question that the German Constitutional Court took on as its central concern. The U.S. Court thus decided that there was a fundamental disagreement over whether the fetus was a human person, while the German Court decided that this was not a matter of debate but of scientific fact and a matter of moral consensus.

In making these decisions, the courts of each country reflected and crystallized a historically grounded political tradition, but they also chose to downplay other concerns that might in principle have also been found in each constitution. While neither decision was inevitable, each was also consistent with law and tradition. Each decision also became the law of the land from that point forward.

Once each decision was announced, certain ways of talking and thinking about abortion became legally privileged and other ways that had existed previously became marginalized. For example, the frequency of debates about developmental stages in the United States (but not in Germany) reflects the trimester principle articulated by the U.S. Court. The German Court specifically disallowed such a stage-based law in overturning what the *Bundestag* had done and thus discouraged such discourse. Thus it is not surprising that the trimester distinction appears in only 2% of the Fetal Life framing ideas there, but in more than 15% of the Fetal Life ideas in the United States.

In the United States, the Court's decision led to a storm of controversy focused on amending the constitution and putting an explicit designation of the fetus as a human life in it, since the Supreme Court itself would not make that determination. In Germany, not only was there no precedent for amending the constitution in general, there also was no way to amend such a central and fundamental clause as the protection of life in particular. Furthermore, the *ex cathedra* nature of German high court decisions discussed in Chapter Four also helped to insulate the decision from subsequent challenge.

The opportunities for framing in both Germany and the United States were shifted by the court decisions of the 1970s, as Pro advocates in Germany and Anti advocates in the United States were faced with a steeper slope to climb. Just how much the change in discursive opportunity changed the discourse itself is the question to which we now turn. Given their different political histories and cultures, we would expect the discourses about abortion to differ in Germany and the United States even before the court decisions, but diverge to a far greater extent afterward.

We can see the courts' impact most clearly by establishing a cluster of specific ideas that were explicitly affirmed in the 1973 U.S. Court decision, ideas that have to do with privacy, individual rights, and developmental stage.[50] We similarly established a cluster of ideas that were central to the German Court decision in 1975, ideas that revolve around the fetus as a human life and the state's obligation to protect life.[51] In Figures 6.3 and 6.4, we compare the prominence of each cluster in both countries over time. In these charts, we use rates per 100 utterances by all speakers as our measure of prominence; hence, changes in the prominence of one idea are not related to the relative frequency with which speakers use other ideas, but instead show the absolute prominence of this set of ideas in the discourse.

Looking first at the ideas that the German Court privileged, largely revolving around state protection of the fetus as a human life, we see that they are used at a higher rate per utterance in Germany than in the United States even before either Constitutional Court acted. After the German Court delivered its decision, the rate in Germany actually dipped before then steadily rising to considerably higher levels than

---

[50] The full list of the ideas that we include in the U.S. constitutional cluster is found in the Methodological Appendix. The major ideas included are uncertainty as to when life begins, a right to privacy for the woman and her doctor, and the trimester system of evaluation.

[51] The full list of the ideas in the German constitutional cluster is in the Methodological Appendix, but the most frequent ideas are that the fetus is a human life, that the state has an obligation to protect life, and that the rights of the fetus take priority over those of the pregnant woman.

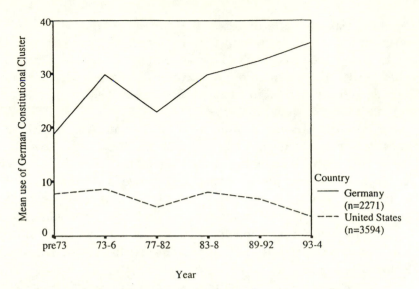

Figure 6.3. German constitutional cluster by country. (Note: Mean use of cluster is measured by rate per 100 utterances by framing speaker.)

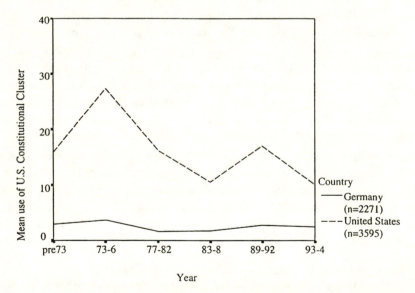

Figure 6.4. U.S. constitutional cluster by country. (Note: Mean use of cluster is measured by rate per 100 utterances of framing speaker.)

before the decision. The apparent dip may be an artifact of the shift away from the judicial and legislative arenas during a period when abortion discourse was sparse but, in any event, it proved to be only temporary. By 1993–1994, the specific ideas in the German Constitutional cluster appear at a rate of 35 per 100 utterances, higher than in any earlier period. Although these ideas are present in U.S. discourse, they never rise above a rate of 10 and never come close to the prominence that they have in Germany.

Turning to the ideas privileged by the U.S. Court, in Figure 6.4 we see that, as expected, they are more prominent in the United States than in Germany throughout the entire period. Indeed, the ideas of privacy and individual rights have negligible prominence in Germany and never rise or fall by any significant amount. More interestingly, and contrary to our expectation, these court-favored ideas do not show a pattern of becoming more prominent in the United States over time, but they are highest in and around the key court decisions of *Roe* and *Webster*. Over time, the absolute prominence of these privacy and individual rights ideas tends to decline.

The U.S. Court decision created a discursive opportunity favorable to these ideas, but they in fact do not become more prominent as ways of addressing the abortion issue over time. Instead, U.S. abortion discourse became more strongly contested, and the prominence of this privacy frame actually declined to its lowest point in the Reagan years. The U.S. constitutional cluster is never as prominent in the United States as the German one is in Germany, and it declines in significance in the U.S. discourse over time. The advocates of abortion rights in the United States do not enjoy a position in which the key constitutional ideas of the *Roe* decision become truly dominant in the way that the German Constitutional Court arguments are acknowledged and prominently included in the German discourse as a whole.

Looking at the whole range of individual ideas presented, we can see that the specific ideas that are advanced also respond to the parameters set by the courts in each country. Thus, U.S. arguments more often include claims about developmental stage than German ones do, and German arguments more often make reference to the grounds that women may have for seeking an abortion. The ideas that are offered also reflect the two different legal situations that the court decisions produced. The continuing criminalization of abortion in Germany set the agenda for claims of hypocrisy as well as for pragmatic, cost–benefit arguments for liberalization. In the United States, the legalization of abortion in 1973 provided the backdrop against which anti-abortion speakers made cost–benefit and social morality arguments for re-criminalization, ideas that are largely absent in German discourse.

Important as it is, the role of the respective Constitutional Court decisions is inadequate to explain all of the differences in political culture expressed in the abortion debate. The German focus on the moral role of the state and the U.S. emphasis on individual rights that is so evident in the respective discourses do not originate in the courts' decisions of the 1970s. The gendered framing of abortion rights in Germany and the dominance of individual rights arguments in the United States also seem to reflect more active choices by the players in the mass media arena. The less polarized use of the morality frame in Germany – seeing abortion as somewhat wrong and emphasizing alter-natives, including socio-economic alternatives, to abortion – may have more to do with welfare state politics and the more positive view of state action than with any particular court decision.

CONCLUSION

There are both striking and subtle differences in how abortion is framed in these two countries. Most obviously, the discourse in Germany is dominated by a single framing of the issue, Fetal Life, which is both the dominant idea around which Anti speakers orient their arguments and a much more prevalent frame than any of the Pro frames that are used by speakers on the other side. The rhetorical advantage lies quantita-tively and qualitatively on the Anti side, with more utterances coming from these speakers and with the dominance of a frame that is so markedly tilted in their advantage. German discourse is predominantly a literally "pro-life" discourse.

In the U.S. discourse, by contrast, even though Pro frames outnum-ber Anti frames overall, the preferred frame of the Pro side, Individual and State, both contains more counterarguments within it and is more evenly matched with the Fetal Life frame than any Pro frame is in Germany. American discourse is more conflictual, not because it uses more rights language, but because there is not the consensus in the United States that there is in Germany about *which* rights take priority. For speakers on both sides of the issue, individual rights arguments for limiting the state are notably stronger in the United States than in Germany, where the state is more likely to be seen as having a positive moral role.

Another striking difference is the framing of abortion as a matter of individual privacy by Pro speakers in the United States and as an issue of women's self-determination as women and mothers in Germany. Although there is certainly acknowledgment in the United States that abortion is something that directly affects women, American public discourse tends more to obscure than to emphasize this fact. U.S. Pro rights talk is about privacy and personal freedoms of individuals. German Pro rights talk is more about the well-being and entitlement to personal self-development of women, as women.

More subtle differences also emerge within the discourses of both sides. Anti speakers in the United States, lacking the rhetorical leverage that Fetal Life carries in Germany, also frame their arguments in terms of Social Morality and adopt the Individual and State frame to argue against state funding and for states' rights to limit or deny abortions. Although American Anti speakers would also claim to be "pro-life," the actual framing that they offer is more diverse than German Anti arguments.

German Pro speakers emphasize women's rights, but they also talk about the validity of women's reasons, the effects of pushing abortion underground, making women hypocrites and criminals, and not being able to reduce abortion without women's active support – issues that reflect the actual legal situation of continued criminalization and the prevalence of underground abortions, and which are therefore rarely mentioned in U.S. discourse. Instead, Pro speakers in the United States actively contest claims that abortion is a moral wrong and sometimes even cast it not as matter of morality but of health care. This debate about the morality of abortion is largely over already in Germany, where the claim that abortion is a matter of Fetal Life, and thus indisputably about moral wrongdoing, has become hegemonic.

The strength of Pro arguments in the United States and hegemony of the Fetal Life frame in Germany cannot be seen as mere expressions of pre-existing value commitments in each country, important as differences in thinking about welfare, privacy, and the moral role of the state undoubtedly were. In 1970, astute observers would not have been able to predict the way that the respective courts would decide the issue nor foresee when and how groups on both sides would contest these outcomes in the ensuing decades. The courts' choices of privacy in the United States and Fetal Life in Germany as the key framing ideas affected the way in which the debate developed in each country, but they did not determine it. Decisions of social actors, such as the Pro movements' emphasis on women's self-determination in Germany and on individual rights in the United States, also played an important role, as we will see in later chapters.

Overall, we conclude that the German Court's framing of the issue of abortion was more practically efficacious in shaping the direction of the overall debate as well as securing the prominence of the specific cluster of ideas that they affirmed than the Supreme Court was in the United States. Both countries experienced dramatic court interventions that overturned federal or state laws and articulated a set of principles that the court saw as defining the issue. But in Germany, this court-based framing became hegemonic in later years, while in the United States the court-based framing remained contested.

To understand just how – and by whom – the different ways of looking at abortion that we see in each country are being supported and contested, we turn in the following three chapters to three central ways of thinking and actors associated with them: (a) women and the arguments based on gender; (b) churches and the arguments based on morality; and (c) political parties and arguments grounded in a left–right continuum of social justice concerns.

Part III

Representing Different
Constituencies

This part explores the representation of the discursive interests of three major constituencies on the abortion issue. We examine who makes claims on behalf of each constituency – and their relative success in shaping abortion discourse. In Chapter Seven, we look at who attempts to represent women's claims. In both countries, there is an active women's movement that seeks to connect abortion rights to women's rights, but the movements differ in significant ways and have differential success. We examine both the voice that women have as speakers in the media discourse and the career of gendered frames sponsored by different mediators. We find that abortion is a more gender-polarized and gender-identified issue in Germany than in the United States, and has been from the very beginning of the period that we study.

Chapter Eight examines the nature of the religious constituency and the relative success of those promoting religious frames in shaping the abortion discourse. We particularly focus on the churches, active in both countries, and on the successful mobilization of the Christian Right constituency in the United States. U.S. speakers invoke religious pluralism and the diversity of moral values to legitimate choice, while German speakers assume a moral consensus from which they are more or less willing to countenance exceptions. There is also less ambivalence in Germany about the state as the guardian of morality and as a moral actor.

Chapter Nine considers the tradition of the left, a constituency that emphasizes inequality based on class, race, or ethnicity as well as gender and responds in terms of meeting needs and supporting autonomy for disadvantaged groups as well as making claims for social justice. We examine the impact of the would-be mediators of the left in shaping abortion discourse, focusing on the left–right continuum in politics and the alignment of political parties as representatives of "the disadvantaged." We look at the discursive obstacles that lead U.S. groups to back away from advocacy for the poor or for racial and ethnic minorities. In Germany, the framing of abortion as help for the needy, in this case pregnant women, also raises issues of state paternalism and women's autonomous decision making that are sources of controversy within the tradition of the left.

CHAPTER SEVEN

Representing Women's Claims

Since women are the only people who can experience the existential crisis of an unwanted pregnancy, it may seem self-evident that women have a special claim on the issue of abortion. Such claims, however, do not appear spontaneously and are not foreordained. Whether, when, and how gender claims are mobilized and made politically relevant is a matter of the discursive opportunities available, as well as the strategies and activities of specific actors in utilizing them. It may seem "natural" for women to have a distinctive position on abortion politics, but such positions grow from historically contingent mobilization processes that select gender as a relevant dimension for aggregating diverse interests and values (Solinger 1998).

Gender as a concept does not just mean women, or the social differences between women and men, but rather "gender is a constituitive element of social relationships based on perceived differences between the sexes and gender is a primary way of signifying relationships of power" (Scott 1986, p. 1067). To define men and women as categories of people with *different* understandings and interests means to minimize both the similarities between genders and the considerable variances within each. The meaning of gender is shaped by culture, time period, social location, and the nature of the issue.

Even when gender is, in fact, shaping experiences in major ways, it may not be recognized as a meaningful category and its significance may be socially ignored (as in the United States in the 1950s). Using language that emphasizes gender, whether talking about women or men, helps to constitute women and men as politically salient groups, just as *not* talking about gender can be a way of obscuring women's interests and political disempowerment as well as facilitating alliances on other grounds, such as race or class. Political choices are involved in constructing the categories of gender, investing them with social significance, and acknowledging their impact. We address the question of how closely women and abortion rights are linked as an illustration of this multifaceted and on-going process of constructing the specific political meaning of gender in particular times and places.

Our comparison between Germany and the United States highlights the contingency and variability in how gender enters the abortion debate. The political construction of abortion as an issue on which women have a special claim is a long-standing reality in Germany. German feminists took advantage of this discursive opportunity and mobilized strongly around abortion as a "women's issue." They have largely succeeded, we will show, in having abortion defined as a matter on which women in politics "naturally" have a special competence to speak. This success arose from and also has contributed to women's empowerment as a distinctive group that has different political interests than men.

By contrast, in the United States, women have neither claimed nor been granted such a privileged position. The framing of abortion as an individual privacy right has offered both opportunities and obstacles to feminist mobilization on this issue. The "pro-choice" coalition that has formed in the United States neither highlights "women" as a special interest nor advocates a distinctively feminist position. Even feminist groups bring women into the debate as "individuals" rather than as "women" with distinctive needs or perspectives. Women's organizing efforts in each country have moved in different directions and produced different kinds of political successes, for a variety of reasons that we explore in the following.

We begin our examination of how gender and abortion politics are connected with a brief overview of the standing that women hold in the media discourse. Although women are not the only people with gender, the absence of women's voices skews the ways in which gender can enter the debate. Since women are still marginalized in most political decision making, changes in women's standing in the media may both reflect and bring about shifts in gendered power relations.

We then show the sharply different degrees of gender polarization between male and female speakers in the two countries. We look at the differences in the prominence of a Women's Rights frame in media discourse in the two countries and how the gendering of abortion discourse has changed over time. We examine the interplay of discursive opportunity structure and the assets and activities of those who represent women's claims in the abortion arena to explain when and how women have gotten greater standing over time and to make sense of the differences in framing strategies. Overall, we see a political process unfolding that makes abortion unquestionably a "women's issue" in Germany but makes gender surprisingly irrelevant in shaping U.S. abortion discourse.

GENDER AND STANDING

The discursive opportunity structure has become increasingly favorable for women during the past 30 years. The mobilization of national women's movements into a range of issue-specific transnational movements created a climate in which gender has been increasingly acknowledged and legitimated as a meaningful political category (Berkovich 1999; Ferree and Gamson 1999). But opportunities need to be framed by participants, and one person's opportunity is another person's trap. The presence of an opportunity does not mean that it will necessarily be utilized. Hence we begin with the empirical questions: What is the standing of women as speakers in the mass media, and how has it changed?[52]

Proposition 7.1. *Women speakers have gained standing in both countries but much more so in Germany than in the United States.*

When the abortion issue emerged on the national political agenda in the late 1960s and early 1970s in both Germany and the United States, women were not the primary political actors. As Figure 7.1 shows, women in both countries were only a small fraction of all gendered speakers on abortion at the outset. In the earliest period, women made up only about 20% of U.S. speakers and about 30% of German. While U.S. women steadily increased their share of the media discourse, the rate of increase was slow, rising after 25 years to only about 40% of the total. German women's share of the discourse initially dropped, as the legislature took up the issue and the predominantly male legislators dominated the discourse. However, women's share then rose much more quickly in Germany than in the United States from the early 1980s, until women are half or more of the speakers in

---

[52] About one-third of the speakers are nongendered. These are mostly collective speakers (for example, organizations speaking through press releases). We omit these nongendered speakers from our analysis of standing but include their contributions when we analyze gender framing.

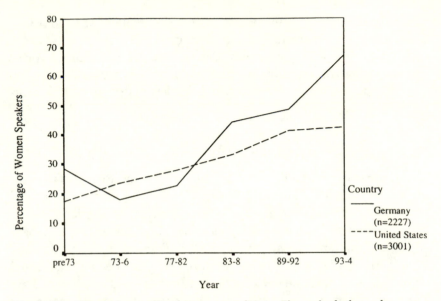

Figure 7.1. Women's standing by country. (Note: Figure includes only nonjournalist speakers with gender given.)

the German media from 1989 onward (and two-thirds in the most recent period).

In Germany, the increases in standing for women have been particularly striking among speakers who hold political office or represent a political party. Between the 1970s and the 1990s, the share of those speakers in state and party roles who were women rose dramatically in Germany but comparatively little in the United States. While less than 10% of U.S. state and party speakers on abortion were women in the early 1970s, this had climbed to just under 30% by the mid-1990s. Without any comparative data, this might seem a fairly substantial rise. Yet, in Germany over the same period, the proportion of women among state and party speakers rose from about 20% to about 70%.

In Chapter Four we saw how the political representation of women has increased much more rapidly and is greater in Germany than in the United States. These standing results reflect this increase, but the proportion of women among state and party speakers in Germany is also nearly three times as large as the proportion of women in the *Bundestag.* Women do somewhat better on standing in the United States, when one moves from the legislative arena to cultural, scientific, and other civil society arenas, including social movements, but women are not the

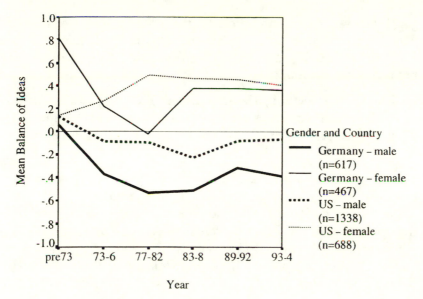

Figure 7.2. Gender and framing direction by country. (Note: Journalists and nonframing speakers were excluded.)

overwhelming majority of speakers in any of these areas as they have become among the state and party speakers in Germany.

GENDER POLARIZATION

Proposition 7.2. *The framing of the abortion issue is more gender-polarized in Germany than in the United States.*

From the very beginning in Germany, male and female speakers presented substantially different positions on abortion, as Figure 7.2 shows.[53] Women speakers start out strongly Pro while men are closely balanced between Pro and Anti utterances. Both groups' framing shifts first toward ideas more on the Anti side and then rebounds toward a more Pro rhetoric, but because the changes over time are similar in size and direction, the gender gap in favorability remains relatively constant. On average, across all periods, women speakers have a positive balance of .36 compared to a negative balance of −.29 for men – a very large

[53] Our measure here is the balance of Pro and Anti ideas where a score of 1.0 represents all Pro ideas, a score of −1 indicates all Anti ideas, and 0 represents equal numbers of both.

gap. When we asked Karin Schöler of the AWO (a social welfare organization associated with the Social Democrats) an open-ended question
about what "people" think about abortion, she challenged the very
premise of the question:

> "People" is something I would divide into men and women.
> That's very important to me. I can't say much about the men at
> all, even here in AWO. This is a topic for women (Interview,
> January 1996).

This framing of abortion as a fundamentally gendered issue accentu-
ates the relevance of gender for political mobilization.

For the United States, there is no difference in the pre-*Roe* period in
the favorability of the framing offered by women and men. Male and
female speakers on both sides offset each other and both genders come
out close to zero or balanced. In the immediate post-*Roe* period, a difference does emerge, with women speakers in the media on balance
framing abortion in a clearly Pro direction and men framing it slightly
on the Anti side. This gap increases further in the 1977–1982 period,
but then remains at about the same level for later periods. The gender
gap in framing in the United States is consistently smaller than in
Germany because U.S. men are less Anti in their choice of framing ideas
than German men; U.S. and German women in the second half of the
period are about equally Pro.[54]

The greater standing of women and greater gender polarization of
abortion framing in Germany compared to the United States identifies
abortion discursively in the mass media forum as being legitimately a
"women's issue" in Germany but does not make gender nearly as politically relevant in the United States.[55] In the following section we
examine just how gender enters into the framing of abortion and how
the increased presence of women in the discourse has changed the
overall way in which abortion is addressed in each country.

---

[54] Note that in any case these are elite opinions and selected by organizations and by
the media. They do not represent public opinion at large in either country, which
shows no significant effect for gender in positive or negative attitudes to restrictions
on abortion, although in polls women tend to ascribe more importance to abortion
as an issue (Cook, Jelen, and Wilcox 1992; Hertel and Russell 1999; Rattinger 1994;
Scott and Schuman 1988; Walker 1988).

[55] However, the gap in favorability between women and men media speakers may help
to explain why social scientists are repeatedly surprised to find that a comparable difference does not show up in polls.

FRAMING ABORTION AS A GENDER ISSUE

In the previous chapter we presented data supporting the proposition that Women's Rights is the leading frame for all German Pro speakers while Individual and State is the leader for U.S. Pro speakers. Indeed, in these countries the prominence of the two frames is reversed: the Women's Rights frame is used more than twice as often as the Individual and State frame in Germany and less than half as often in the United States. This result holds not only for Pro abortion rights speakers but for the discourse as a whole – the gender-specific framing of abortion as a *women's* right is more characteristic in Germany and the non-gender-specific framing of abortion as an *individual* right for a person of any gender is more typical of the United States. Thus we refer to the use of the Women's Rights frame as a "gendered" way of framing the issue and consider the use of the other three rights frames (Individual and State, Fetal Life, and Balancing) as "ungendered" rhetorics, not because they lack relevance to gender relations, but because they do not explicitly define women as a group with distinctive gender interests relative to men. Here we explore these results further by examining the frequency of the Women's Rights frame among all of these four rights frames over time and by the gender of the speaker.[56]

As Figure 7.3 shows, the gendering of the claim to abortion rights is relatively infrequent in the United States. Averaged across all time periods, the proportion of the four types of Pro or Neutral rights claims that U.S. women make that are gender-specific remain a minority (27% of the total) and are even less frequent among men (about 13% of their total). This contrasts sharply with Germany, where 53% of women's and even 20% of men's rights claims are explicitly gendered.

Proposition 7.3. *Women speakers are more likely to frame abortion as a women's issue in both countries, but the gendered framing is so much higher in Germany that, in recent years, German men are even more likely to use the gendered frame than are U.S. women.*[57]

---

[56] We exclude Anti versions of all four of these rights frames in the following analysis so as to not allow the hegemonic status of the Anti version of fetal life in Germany to obscure the results, but we include all speakers regardless of their dominant framing direction and all Neutral as well as Pro versions of these four frames.

[57] The organizational speakers and non-bylined journalists for which no gender can be coded look very much like the men of the same country.

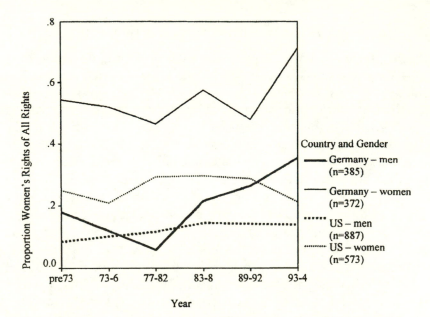

Figure 7.3. Women's rights frames by gender, country, and time period. (Note: All framing speakers with gender given. The proportion is the mean of Pro and Neutral women's rights frames as a proportion of Pro and Neutral Fetal Life, Balancing, Women's Rights, and Individual and State frames.)

Figure 7.3 examines change over time in gender frames as a proportion of all Pro and Neutral uses of rights frames (that is, Fetal Life, Balancing, Women's Rights, and Individual and State), regardless of the position of the speaker.[58] German women were highest in using the gendered frame from the beginning, with half or more of all their Pro or Neutral rights claims coming just from Women's Rights, and they have remained steadily high until the most recent period, where their usage of gendered claims about rights increases even further (to over 70%). There has always been a significant gender gap, but it has narrowed in recent years as German men also increased their use of this frame in the 1980s and 1990s (to over 30% of all their Pro or Neutral rights claims).

In the United States, women also use the gendered rights frame more than men, but the gender gap is considerably smaller and the overall

---

[58] The same pattern holds, though at a higher level, if we examine only the frames used by Pro speakers or consider only Pro versions of these frames.

use of the gendered frame is always lower than in Germany, never rising above 15% for men and 30% for women. If there is any change at all among American speakers, it is quite small, with U.S. women declining slightly in their use of gendered rather than nongendered rights language after a small increase in the late 1970s and early 1980s. The striking result is that, in spite of the sizeable gender gap in Germany, German men have overtaken U.S. women over time and are, in recent times, more likely to use the gendered frame on the abortion issue than are American women. As Rita Grieshaber, a spokesperson for the Alliance 90/Green Party, speculates: "For most men, the impression I get in discussion is that it has become clear that the woman has to decide one way or the other, because for many men it is also clear that they will participate very little if a kid comes" (Interview, January 1996).

These results indicate that the greater gender framing in Germany is not merely a function of the greatly increased standing of women as speakers. The increased gendered framing there is also reflected among males and nongendered speakers. But it also reflects a strategic choice by *women* speakers in the United States to play down the gender salience of the abortion issue. When we compared the documents of the major players on the Pro side – the ACLU, Planned Parenthood, NARAL, and NOW – the emphasis on individual rights rather than women's rights emerged clearly. The ACLU and Planned Parenthood were more likely to stress individual rights (44% of their leading ideas came from this frame) compared to NOW and NARAL (21% of their leading ideas did) but neither particularly stressed women's rights (approximately 10% of leading ideas), although both did emphasize the pragmatic dangers to women of restrictive laws.

As Emily Tynes of the Communications Consortium describes the way abortion rights groups chose their media strategy:

There are about eight values that are basically American values. . . . And so what you are really doing with that middle group, you are really playing to the basic American values. And individual rights is at the top. And so that's why, after all these years, and all the millions and millions of dollars of research, NARAL still sticks to messages about choice. People say "Oh, you need some new messages." But the thing is, that's the one that works. . . . That's why it doesn't change. That's how it plays itself out. . . . The individual rights frame gets more support. [Interviewer: In polls?] And with people, yeah. It's the message that resonates. There's lots of backlash against women and women's rights. (Interview, March 1998).

In fact, for those U.S. women who have a voice in the media, as for the abortion rights organizations in our survey, the dominant framing of abortion is as an individual right – one that reflects more general principles of privacy, freedom of religion, and personal liberty free of state interference that would apply to individuals regardless of gender. Comparing the preference just between Women's Rights and the Individual and State frames for those women speakers whose framing is on average pro-abortion-rights, in Germany three-quarters of their ideas take the gender-specific form and in the United States 62% take a *non*-gendered form.

The greater gendering of the issue in Germany is very visible even when we limit our comparison to only speakers from either specifically feminist or broader women's movement organizations. There are no differences in explicitly gendered framing between these two types of women's organizations in either country, but the German organizations of either type are twice as likely to use the Women's Rights frame as their U.S. counterparts. U.S. speakers representing abortion rights organizations that do not explicitly identify as feminist – such as the ACLU, NARAL, and Planned Parenthood – are even less likely to use gender-specific frames.

Feminist groups, like the Fund for a Feminist Majority, do emphasize that their position is "to fight for a women's absolute right to abortion. Women of all ages, all income levels. All races." But in this same interview, they conceded that they also are resigned to getting less attention to this aspect of the issue: "Media attention has just been very sporadic. . . . The attention on women's issues in general is never great" (Interview, September 1997).

Smaller, less mainstream groups in the United States see themselves as freer to challenge the dominant Individual and State frame that casts abortion as women's free choice. Rosemary Candelario, speaking for the decentralized, grassroots group, R2N2, which never succeeded in getting its voice into the media we sampled, sees its smallness as an advantage in pursuing its preferred frame:

Because we're not a national organization, we don't have to mince words. We don't have to necessarily be worried about stepping on toes. We don't have to be nice to the senator who helped us out . . . or all the different positions that a lot of people in D.C. get caught up in because it's the nature of the beast. So we're able to take a firm stand. I feel we can use the word "abortion" where other organizations might use "choice" (Interview, October 1997).

However, because such small and atypical groups are not granted the standing that the large Washington-based organizations have, their language has less chance to influence the overall shape of the discourse through the mass media.

The framing of rights as gender-specific or as a generic individual right both explains and reflects the priorities of the movements involved in advocating abortion rights. In Germany, the women's movement and feminist organizations lead the struggle against restrictive legislation. As advocates for abortion rights, women have gained standing particularly in the political parties, which, as we have seen, have considerable share of the overall media discourse. These women's groups in the parties and women speakers in the legislature appeal specifically to women and claim a gender-specific right. In the United States, abortion rights advocacy is shared by a broad coalition of feminist, civil liberties, and family-planning groups, and their agendas give less weight to the connection between abortion rights and gender. Women's standing in the U.S. media has grown on this issue over time, but not to the level now seen in Germany.

The relative gender-neutrality of rights discourse in the United States is double-edged. On the one hand, it gives women no privileged position from which to speak. On the other hand, it also affirms the interests and obligations of men to defend abortion rights as well and leads to less gender polarization on this issue. If U.S. women speakers are less powerful and prominent than German women speakers, they are also less isolated from the rest of the discourse.

The German abortion rights movement as a whole is self-consciously a *women's* movement, and this is also double-edged. Making this close connection between abortion rights and gender rights gives German women and women's movement organizations a particular claim on the discourse, as distinctively entitled by virtue of their gender to speak about abortion. German women have a strong political leadership role in the abortion debate, and they have exercised it effectively, gaining a political voice and even influencing other speakers to adopt their framing of abortion rights in gender-specific terms. The men, who continue to hold the major positions of authority in the parties, have deferred to women on this issue, at least in public.

On the other hand, the explicit gendering of the issue allows men to abdicate responsibility and tends to polarize the public discourse along gender lines. German men in state and party roles have increasingly withdrawn from the public debate, particularly from among the pro-abortion-rights speakers. German men who speak on the issue are more typically anti-abortion. And even those men who take a Pro position are less likely to advocate fewer restrictions as a matter of rights, but instead use the more pragmatic frames about the negative effects of restrictions.

MOBILIZING ON THE ABORTION ISSUE

Looking at the mobilization process on abortion helps to explain the previous results. In the United States, abortion reform efforts in the 1960s were often led by doctors and public health advocates, as Luker (1984) demonstrates in her study of California's early adoption of a more liberal law. The many grassroots feminist groups emerging in the late 1960s took up the challenge to abortion law in diverse ways. Feminist "raps" or speakouts on women's abortion experiences were part of this mobilization for repeal.

In one well-publicized incident in New York in 1969, the only woman officially invited to speak to the legislative commission considering abortion reform was a nun. A number of feminists "crashed" the hearing and insisted on being heard also. They spoke of illegal abortions that they had survived and about friends who had died from such procedures (Cisler 1970). Feminists in Chicago ran their own underground abortion service (known as "Jane") to insure that women had safe access to competent abortions (Kaplan 1995).

But as Burns' (2002) study of the pre-*Roe* abortion rights movement shows, feminists were by no means the only actors in bringing abortion out of the "century of silence" that had surrounded it. Indeed, the earliest campaigns focused on problems of birth defects and used middle-class women who could be presented as model wives and mothers to make their case to the public.[59] Some feminists are and were critical of *Roe v. Wade* for leaving women out of the picture. As Kim Gandy, Executive Vice-President of the National Organization for Women (NOW) put it:

[59] See, for example, Condit's (1990) discussion of the Sherri Finkbine case.

The basic *Roe versus Wade* decision was not a good decision, in my opinion, [it] was not a women's rights decision. It was a doctors' rights decision. . . . Justice Blackmun was the Mayo [Medical] Clinic's chief lawyer [before being appointed to the Supreme Court], and the decision that came out of him when you read it was very clearly a doctors' rights decision. I mean, it sort of mentioned women in passing, but it really was a non-interference with doctors (Interview, July 1997).

In contrast, Germany had a long history of political debate around §218, as we discussed in Chapter Two. Some of the middle-class women's groups that fought for suffrage in the 1910s also campaigned for elimination of this section from the criminal code in the 1920s and 1930s. In their eyes, the right to abortion was part of a general right of women to sexual self-determination that included destigmatizing women who gave birth out of wedlock, combating the international traffic in girls and women as prostitutes, and establishing the right of unmarried women to be self-supporting so that marriage could be a choice rather than a destiny (Allen 1985).

The socialist (SPD) and communist (KPD) parties of the Weimar era also made legal abortion a major issue, particularly for working-class women who could not afford children and had no access to the discreet care of private physicians who helped middle-class women limit their family size. Selective prosecution of physicians serving poor women was a *cause celebre* for socialist mobilization. Demonstrations and political theater kept the issue a lively topic of public debate until the Nazi rise to power ended all independent organizing.

After the war, issues of rape during the occupation and economic crisis were also raised, but the criminal code was not fundamentally changed. Issues of gender and self-determination for women in matters of abortion never entirely vanished from public discourse as they had in the United States for so many years. The German and U.S. mobilizations around the issue of abortion began in the late 1960s from very different starting points.

In the United States, the issue was a new one, and it was brought out of obscurity by doctors and legal reformers who were dealing with problems posed for middle-class women by the difficulties in obtaining safe abortions when birth control failed or birth defects loomed. Dealing with their own patients in these cases, doctors were in a legal limbo that they wanted resolved. Feminists added their voices to this chorus, but their claims for women's self-determination were initially visible only in local protest actions.

In Germany, when the issue of abortion returned to the political agenda in the early 1970s, the older legacy of gender politics was available to be mobilized. In the 1970s, feminist politics in West Germany was strongly associated with the call for removing §218 from the criminal code, a rallying cry that Alice Schwarzer continued to publicize though the feminist magazine, *Emma*. The legalization of abortion was clearly and early identified with women's rights in Germany, and feminist groups themselves supported the idea that abortion rights were central to their politics. "Mein Bauch gehört mir" ("my belly belongs to me") became a familiar feminist slogan. Feminists engaged in abortion rights proactively, as an issue that was important to their own self-definition.

While these different histories can explain some of the difference in initial polarization by gender before 1973, the women's movements in the two countries also developed in different directions overall, as described in Chapter Four. To summarize this earlier discussion, U.S. feminists have more organization, resources, and potential allies outside of the formal political structures of parties and legislatures, and German women with feminist inclinations have relatively more organization, resources, and allies within the parties than outside them.

Feminism is more differentiated from the women's movement in Germany, and feminist groups are much more decentralized. Because German feminists in the late 1960s and early 1970s resisted forming national organizations, the closest thing to a national leadership group for feminists on the abortion issue was the Federal Network for the Repeal of §218, a single-issue group with representatives from local feminist groups, but it received no standing in the elite newspapers studied here. The broader German women's movement is reflected in a variety of party-based organizations as well as by women's civic organizations, and on the abortion issue these broad constituency women's organizations in labor unions and social welfare achieved standing that feminist groups did not.

In the United States, national feminist groups take up a wide range of issues and have the potential for both cooperation and competition with other national interest groups, but they have no strong organizational base in the political parties as such. Coalitions that feminist groups have built with the broader-based women's movement, including in the latter such groups as the YWCA and the Girl Scouts, on issues such as the Equal Rights Amendment and employment discrimination, have not been evident on the abortion issue. Instead, on this issue, feminists join other national organizations that make the defense of abortion rights their central concern (for example, NARAL) or situate abortion as one of a number of fundamental constitutional rights to defend (e.g., the ACLU). These latter groups have a significant feminist presence within them, but they are not organizationally identified as feminist or as women's groups. As Jennifer Jackman of the Fund for a Feminist Majority pointed out:

> Most of the abortion rights groups in fact − while the leaders themselves are feminist − their mission, the organizational identity, they would be the first to say, they would not call themselves feminist organizations. Like NARAL, Alan Guttmacher, ACLU . . . I mean, they would define themselves as reproductive rights organizations (Interview, September 1997).

Some of these groups, such as the ACLU, also find themselves in conflict with feminist groups on other issues, such as regulating pornography and hate speech. Thus, while they form a working coalition on abortion they are not the same movement with a shared set of basic principles across issues to unite them.

On abortion, much strategy gets discussed and information shared in a "core group" that comprises both feminist and other reproductive rights organizations based in Washington. Like other U.S. interest groups, feminist organizations and reproductive rights groups raise money via mass-mailing, lobby candidates with paid staffers, and have media offices with regular relationships to journalists.

However, NOW is distinctively more a social movement organization than the other Washington-based groups because it retains an elected leadership that is directly accountable to the members, rather than the executive director and board of directors typical of lobbying organizations. This in NOW's own eyes accounts for its relative radicalism compared to other groups. NOW "pushes the envelope," continuing to fight on abortion issues that the coalition as a whole judges unwinnable and challenging language that does not seem feminist enough to them. As Kim Gandy tells it:

> There aren't enough groups talking about women and focusing the picture on women as opposed to women and their doctors and their children and their families and their communities and their

whatever. We just think somebody needs to be doing it. If nobody else is doing it, we do it, which is our way with anything (Interview, July 1997).

But even NOW, during an earlier period, was intent on keeping the abortion issue separate from the more general struggle for women's rights. Mansbridge (1986, p. 123) describes the ultimately unsuccessful battle to pass an Equal Rights Amendment (ERA) that ended in the 1980s and notes that "most NOW activists, and certainly the more conservative pro-ERA activists, consciously tried to keep the issues of abortion and ERA separate."

To further confound the relationship between feminism and abortion politics in the United States, consider Feminists for Life. This group offers an anti-abortion frame explicitly in the name of feminism. Serrin Foster, the spokesperson for this group, says that "we believe that no woman chooses abortion freely . . . that it is a last resort, that it's a reflection that there is a problem in society." She explains that many of her pro-life allies reject her perspective:

They hate the word feminism. [They say that] women were having abortions because they wanted to be free, you know, that it was the changing dynamics of the family structure that caused women to have abortions, and [we] were saying no, women were not having abortions because they want to be in control of their own lives and whatever . . . they were having abortions because women were abandoned by men and, in some cases, threatened and coerced by men into having abortions (Interview, July 1997).

Spokespeople for other U.S. feminist organizations challenge this group's claim to be feminist, but the logic of their position is supported by the separation between feminism and abortion rights that those other groups have observed.

No such anomalous group exists in Germany, nor is its appearance really conceivable given the predominant definition of what feminism means and the gendering of abortion rights. This does not mean that the frame offered by Feminists for Life is alien to German abortion politics. Quite the contrary. Feminists for Life argues that women often do not want abortions but are driven to them by pressure from others, especially men. Hence, restrictions on abortions can serve to protect women's interests. This is an argument frequently advanced by women in the German parties. The claims for women's self-determination that are core to a German feminist definition of the abortion issue are offered in a context in which mandatory counseling, a waiting period, social incentives in favor of childbearing, and other forms of government intervention on behalf of protecting the fetus as a human life are constitutionally mandated. Karin Schöler of the AWO describes how she, as a feminist, comes to terms with such restrictions:

> Consider the history of the AWO with §218, where it comes from, this struggle against §218. We oppose it. We want its elimination. At the same time, we want professionalization and to offer modern counseling, but we are restricted in our counseling by the legal rules. . . . The Court has affirmed this contradiction – protection of unborn life but also self-determination by women. So we can attach ourselves to that and say, "we can still carry out this counseling," and also do it in line with our conception of ourselves (Interview, January 1996).

Unlike American feminists, German feminist speakers combine claims to women's self-determination with arguments that women are the ones who have the most interest in protecting the life of the fetus, an emphasis on the social obstacles facing women who want to be mothers and the impossibility of forcing women to bear a child if they believe themselves incapable of facing this.

ORGANIZATIONAL DIFFERENCES

Our survey data on the spectrum of organizations involved in the abortion issue support this broad picture of the different gender politics in each country. On the one hand, the United States has a large and diverse abortion rights movement that overlaps only in part with the feminist movement; few other women's groups mobilize on abortion that are not specifically feminist organizations. On the other hand, in Germany there is a large and active women's movement institutionally separate from the autonomous feminist groups, even though both have been shaped by ideas about women's rights and roles that emerged in the 1970s. However, Germany largely lacks a distinct abortion rights movement; all of the groups in Table 7.1 that are placed in this category are groups directly involved in counseling.[60]

---

[60] Such as Pro Familia, which is similar to Planned Parenthood in providing sex education, contraception, and reproductive health services at its clinics, and AWO, a social welfare organization close to the Social Democratic Party.

Table 7.1. *Women's and Abortion-Rights Organizations by Country*

Type of group and country (n of organizations)	Feminist		Women's movement		Abortion rights/ family planning		All other organizations	
	Germany 12	US 7	Germany 15	US 4	Germany 9	US 22	Germany 58	US 22
% active in educating women on reproductive health/rights	55%	33%	27%	75%	67%	82%	13% (55)	14%
% that seek to influence women as means	58%	14%	40%	0%	22%	9%	5%	9%
% true that women should play more dominant role	91%	57%	79%	75%	89%	59%	27%	18%
% members share concern with women	92%	86%	80%	75%	33%	52%	2%	14%
% completely woman oriented (index)	82%	43%	73%	50%	33%	18%	2%	5%
Mean % women members (& n reporting)	99% (11)	93% (5)	91% (15)	90% (4)	73% (6)	65% (11)	36% (49)	51% (15)
Mean resource level	1.7	4.4 (6)	2.4 (12)	3.4	3.7	4.1 (19)	3.4 (50)	4.3 (19)
Number of individual members	292	51,300	123,000	156,000	1,080	25,776	1,067,000	854,000
(n groups reporting)	(9)	(7)	(10)	(4)	(6)	(19)	(38)	(16)

Note: All *n* are within one of the values reported in the first row except those cells that have the *n* in parentheses.

148

Proposition 7.4. *The feminist movement on the abortion issue is small and resource-poor in Germany compared to the United States.*

In terms of both resource levels and numbers of members, German feminist organizations are tiny, whether compared to other German organizations or to U.S. feminist groups. The largest among them are the two least typical – the Women's Law Association (with 2000 members) and the UFV (with 500 members).[61] This reflects the general commitment among West German feminists to local, nonhierarchical grassroots organizations as the ideal type. The Federal Network for Repeal of §218, the only national group, reports a membership of 40, even though it clearly could reach more women through local groups (themselves reporting memberships of 10–20 on average). U.S. feminist groups include both small local groups and large national organizations such as NOW (270,000 members) and the Feminist Majority (70,000 members). Even "small" U.S. feminist groups such as R2N2 (1000 members) or the New York chapter of NOW (3000 members) are more substantial than the largest German feminist organizations.

Proposition 7.5. *A broader women's movement in Germany represents women's claims on abortion and is comparable in size and resources to U.S. feminist organizations; a broader women's movement in the United States exists but is largely unmobilized on the abortion issue.*

At the national level, the SPD women's organization, the *AsF*, has roughly as many members as NOW (240,000 vs. 270,000) and takes similarly broad (albeit less radical) women's rights positions on multiple policy questions. Given the relative size of the two countries, this suggests that the women's movement in its broader form reaches proportionally more German women than do national feminist organizations in the United States, but such organizations are neither autonomous nor necessarily feminist in orientation. In the United States broad women's organizations, such as the YWCA or League of Women Voters, were essentially invisible in the media as speakers on the abortion issue.

---

[61] The numbers that we give for membership are those reported in our survey. The UFV had several thousand members in its prime in 1990–1991, but only a few hundred afterwards (Hampele-Ulrich 2000).

Proposition 7.6. *German abortion-rights groups are much more likely than their U.S. counterparts to define their constituency in terms of gender.*

First, German feminist organizations differ from U.S. feminist groups in their more exclusive orientation toward women. As Table 7.1 shows, even self-described feminist organizations in the United States invite participation by men who are "for women," though most of their membership is, in practice, female. Only 2 of 11 U.S. organizations that are self-defined as feminist or are part of a wider women's movement report an exclusively female membership, while in Germany 21 of 27 such groups say that they are exclusively female.

U.S. feminist groups are also less likely to agree that they are directing their efforts to influencing women in particular. Only one in seven U.S. groups makes this claim compared to most (8 of 12) of the German feminist groups that we surveyed. The U.S. groups are also less likely to agree strongly that their goal is to give women a more dominant voice in policy decisions about abortion (57%, versus 91% in Germany).

The centrality of gender as an organizing category for abortion politics in Germany is also evident among nonfeminist groups. It is especially striking that even the family planning/abortion rights groups in Germany are more likely to say that they are trying to give women in particular more influence (eight of nine agree). This figure is higher than even feminist organizations in the United States, where only 57% (four of seven) agree. Constructing an overall index of woman-orientation in terms of the groups' strategies and priorities, we find that both feminist and women's movement organizations in Germany are very strongly woman-oriented (82% and 73%, respectively), compared to 43% and 50% for the same type of groups in the United States.

The reluctance of U.S. abortion rights groups to identify with women as a special constituency is also apparent in their refusal to even give an estimate of the percentage of their membership that is female. Approximately half of the abortion rights groups in the survey simply skipped that question (even though most estimated the total number of individual members and probably did have some idea of the gender breakdown). In the United States, among those estimating their gender composition, abortion rights groups are only slightly higher in the percentage of female members than are all other organizations. Abortion rights groups are only a little more likely than other organizations to define their members' shared concerns as being about women (46%, versus 33% for other groups).

In Germany, by contrast, family planning groups do see women as their special constituency. Abortion counseling and family planning organizations report levels of female membership that are twice as high on average than other groups (73% vs. 36%) and are much more likely to see a concern with women and women's issues as what unites them (33%, versus only 2% of other organizations).

In sum, the explicit use of gender as a principle for building coalitions or defining members' common concerns plays a less central political role in U.S. than in German mobilization on abortion. Feminist groups in both countries do define the issue of abortion as a concern specifically for women and do use Women's Rights to frame this concern, but they do so less strongly and exclusively in the United States than in Germany. Women's groups are both more important in the overall mix in Germany and are more strongly oriented to defining women as a target group with perspectives and concerns that are different from those of men than their U.S. counterparts.

Feminist groups in the United States work in coalition with reproductive rights groups, rather than other organizations of women, and share a strategy of emphasizing non-gender-specific *individual* rights. Working within the party system, German women's groups have obtained more voice for women overall in the media than women in the United States have gained. They name women as the constituency that they represent, and they define their goals as gaining more influence for women in particular. Gender is thus a defining political category for organizing to support abortion rights in Germany to a greater extent than it is in the United States.

CONCLUSION

The connection drawn between abortion and gender is not inherent in the nature of the issue but is politically constructed in ways that vary sharply from country to country and over time. Naming gender as a specific interest that divides women from men necessarily minimizes the commonalities and overlaps between the genders, just as failing to name gender obscures the differences in women's and men's experiences and the common interests that women may share. In Germany, the media's discourse about abortion was more gender-polarized from the

start, reflecting both the long-term history of this issue and the immediate and unambivalent mobilization of feminists around abortion in
the late 1960s and early 1970s.

Within this opportunity structure, social movements make choices.
The continued development of the abortion issue in gender-specific
terms in Germany reflects a particular discursive strategy. Although the
feminist movement as such remains small and local and has a dimin-
ishing voice in the media over time, the leadership of the abortion rights
cause has been taken up by the wider women's movement, especially
women mobilized in the parties. Women in state and party roles have
gained increasing voice and legitimacy in public discourse about abortion over time, as both women and men see women as having the most
right to speak on something that is so "obviously" a distinctive women's
concern.

Abortion has become identified as a "women's issue" in Germany,
and women's influence on the discourse is evident not only in their own
increased standing on this issue but also in the increasing probability
that men and other speakers will also speak about abortion as a gender-
specific right. As we noted earlier, German men are now more likely to
speak of abortion rights in gender-specific terms than even American
women are. This does not necessarily mean that German women or
feminists have won the substantive rights that they seek, but they have
been brought into the negotiations around what compromise is acceptable via their role in the parties. Women speakers are seen – and see
themselves – as representing a specific women's constituency with distinctive interests. At the same time, however, the differences between
women's and men's voices in the media are highlighted, since those
German men who do get quoted in the media are not likely to be pro-
abortion-rights at all. While, as we have seen in earlier chapters, there
is more controversy between Pro and Anti frames in the United States,
there is more polarization between women's and men's organizations
and framing in Germany.

The U.S. separation of women's rights and abortion as distinct political issues has been less effective in helping women to gain a voice in
the media and has left most women's organizations (as distinct from
specifically feminist groups) unmobilized in support of abortion rights.
U.S. men, unlike German men, have a legitimate place in reproductive
rights organizations and are well-represented in coalitions on this issue.

U.S. media discourse does not present abortion as something on
which women as a group have a position that is distinguishable from

that of men or as a distinctive constituency on the issue – even though U.S. women speakers are in fact more pro-choice and more likely to use a Women's Rights frame than are U.S. men. Feminist efforts to empha-size the gendered nature of the issue receive less attention in the media when they occur. But they and their allies in reproductive rights orga-nizations generally prefer not to appeal specifically to women or frame the issue in gender terms in the first place. In the U.S. context, all acknowledge, appealing to individual rights is "what works." Although American women speakers have gained less standing on the abortion issue than German women have, they are also more likely to be joined in the media by men who are taking a pro-abortion-rights position. By not framing abortion as an issue that is specifically "about" gender, U.S. abortion discourse separates it from feminism and women, both for better and for worse.

We return to the gendering of abortion discourse in Chapter Nine in the context of discussing how the tradition of the left becomes repre-sented in abortion discourse. German abortion discourse is not only more explicitly gendered but gendered in a qualitatively different way than U.S. discourse. But first we turn, in the next chapter, to the repre-sentation of religious claims.

CHAPTER EIGHT

Representing Religious Claims

Every human being is a precious child of God, a brother or sister, of every other human being. . . . In this human family, the strong have a greater obligation to protect and defend the lives and rights of vulnerable persons who cannot defend themselves.

(Pamphlet, National Right to Life Committee)

Abortion can be a moral, ethical, and religiously responsible decision. . . . As religious people, we yearn for a just society – one that celebrates and honors the whole realm of human experience; one in which faith is not a rigid structure of ideas to be imposed and protected, but an active trust – in God, and in women and their families to make wise decisions according to their conscience.

(Pamphlet, Religious Coalition for Reproductive Choice, formerly Religious Coalition for Abortion Rights)

For Christian reasons, we want to protect life and accompany the woman, support the woman, in her decision-making, for or against the child, as much the one as the other. We want to be her conversational partner in the situation and through the decision-making process, help her come to a decision that even when she looks back on it is something she can bear.

(Ana-Maria Mathé, *Diakonisches Werk*,[62] Interview, April 1996)

---

[62] A social service agency affiliated with the Lutheran Church.

> That the state has an obligation to protect human life
> is neither a question for a political coalition nor the
> object of a compromise. Party political considerations
> should have no place here. What counts here is the
> voice of God, saying "thou shalt not kill!"
>
> (Friedrich Wetter, German Catholic Church
> spokesman, *SZ*, 9/17/1990)

Numerous citizens in many countries understand many political and social issues through the prism of a larger, transcendental belief system that is rooted in religion or spirituality. These religious master frames come in many varieties, from evangelical born-again Baptists, to mainstream Lutherans, to observant Jews, to Islamic fundamentalists, to justice-seeking Quakers, to dutiful Catholics, to New Age spiritualists. Furthermore, the application of any particular religious master frame to a position on any given issue is a complex and often contentious interpretive process, within religious groups as well as between them. Hence, one should begin by assuming that those who use a religious perspective will not all think the same way. Assume instead that on most issues there will be advocates of different positions competing as spokespersons for the religious.

Borrowing Berger's (1969) metaphor, various religious communities live under the same "sacred canopy." A *sacred canopy* renders a particular lifestyle or political order transcendently legitimate, an embodiment of the ultimate nature of things. Heinz (1983, p. 144), in developing the idea, describes it as clothing a political order or movement "with divine sanction."

The contest over the meaning and course of the American story is a contest over whose sacred canopy shall prevail. There are recurring attempts to topple one system of meaning and erect another in its place. For worldview construction and maintenance, religion is always available with its power to legitimize. When symbols are interpreted or experienced as religious, they gain a larger resonance.

Sacred canopies are especially likely when an issue engages existential events such as birth and death. Even those who are not themselves part of a religious constituency are more likely to grant religious claims political legitimacy on such issues. Abortion is in the heartland of religious territory.

In this chapter we first focus on the groups that invoke a sacred canopy for making claims about abortion and the nature of their religious frames. We then explore the standing achieved by different types of religious speakers. In Germany, churches are the major actors while in the United States, social movements, especially but not exclusively on the anti-abortion side, are important spokespersons for a religious perspective. We look at how the anti-abortion movement relates to the churches and the discursive strategy of the major players. We then look at the extent to which the preferred frames of different religious speakers have shaped the discourse more widely. We conclude that the Catholic Church has been generally successful in having its preferred Fetal Life frame accepted in Germany, while in the United States there is less consensus in framing among religious speakers and the use of any sacred canopy is itself a more contentious issue.

CHURCHES AND MOVEMENT GROUPS

In Chapter Four we discussed the complicated terrain on which competing carriers of religious frames must compete. To summarize, religion and politics are less separated institutionally in Germany than in the United States, but culturally they are more separated. The institutional separation means that gaining standing on political issues is more difficult for formal religious organizations in the United States. But the religious constituency is larger in the United States, and this creates a greater discursive opportunity for religious frames.

GERMANY

The major players offering religious frames are the Catholic Church, the Lutheran Church, and the Christian parties (CDU/CSU). While there are German evangelicals, they are a much smaller part of the religious constituency than in the United States. However, within the Catholic Church in Germany, as in the United States, there are groups with different moral and political positions on abortion that they articulate in religious language.

The major spokespersons for a Catholic constituency are the German Bishops' Conference and the *Katholikenrat* (Catholic Council), a national lay organization. In addition, groups such as the Catholic Women's Association of Germany (KFD) and the Central Committee of German Catholics (ZDK) have democratically elected leadership among the laity and may take positions that are distinct from those of the official church.

The sharpest differences among German Catholics have emerged in the wake of the post-unification abortion law that requires pro-life counseling of the pregnant woman, after which she receives a certificate that allows her to obtain an abortion should she so decide. In the Vatican's view, by participating in this counseling process, the church is complicit in the process of women obtaining abortions. Hence, the Vatican directed the German Catholic Bishops' Conference to discontinue its participation in providing such counseling, which ended the public, internal wrangling among the bishops about its appropriateness, even though one bishop, Franz Kamphaus of Limburg, has defied the pope and continues to offer officially sponsored counseling and certificates.

In most jurisdictions, however, Catholic lay groups have mobilized outside the formal structures of the church to continue to provide counseling to women seeking abortions. The lay-led foundation, Donum Vitae, that now runs these centers is close to but not officially part of the Catholic Church and thus is without access to its tax dollars. There is also a religiously based anti-abortion mobilization made up of grassroots groups operating outside of the mainstream churches. Some of these groups are connected in the Network of Christian Right-to-Life Groups and others work independently. Some of the leading activists are evangelical Baptists (for example, Pro Vita) and others Catholic (for example, SOS *Leben*), but they work outside the formal framework of these churches, while the Catholic Church itself offers a set of anti-abortion programs and mobilizes for protest demonstrations (a regular "say yes to life" march as well as other actions). Finally, there are professional organizations that are closely allied to the churches and that do take active anti-abortion positions, such as Lawyers for Life and Doctors for Life. These single-issue groups are largely but not officially Catholic, and there is some overlap in leadership between these groups and the Catholic Council.

The German Lutheran Synod (EKD) speaks for the Protestant constituency. Its social services arm (the *Diakonisches Werk*) remains an important provider of pre-abortion counseling and certification of need documents, as the Catholic social services agency, *Caritas*, was before the Vatican ended this role in 1999. The Lutheran approach, although it affirms that the fetus is "unborn life" and favors reducing abortions, is generally perceived as "pro-choice" in rejecting the use of absolute legal prohibitions and punishments.

As Bishop Martin Kruse said in a formal statement on behalf of the Lutheran Church in 1990, "all efforts to protect unborn life in the womb must be directed to doing so with the woman and not against her. In no way, including through the law, can the protection of unborn life be coerced" (*FAZ*, 8/25/90). As he further argued, while "the self-determination of a woman reaches its boundaries at the right to life of a child, a woman cannot be forced to bear a pregnancy to term," so the state can only "discourage" and not block actual abortions from taking place, legally or illegally (*SZ*, 6/21/91). Rather than prohibiting abortion, the Protestant position favors moral education of individuals to "develop a pro-life consciousness" while leaving the legal decision up to the woman. As an official statement of the Lutheran Church in 1976 emphasized, "Improved protection of unborn life is most likely to be expected not from changes in the law but from the formation of consciences and the political provision of social support measures."

Women with unwanted pregnancies will continue to seek abortions, they argue, and criminalizing abortion will not prevent it but will merely drive it underground. Helping women in such situations is more Christian than trying to enforce morality by punishing them. Ana-Maria Mathé of *Diakonisches Werk*, articulating the difference between her organization and others, notes that her organization is "more open as to outcome really. We see ourselves as in a *process* and don't try at any cost to get something across against the woman. That also just doesn't work" (Interview, April 1996).

Although this is in part a difference about the more effective means of reducing abortion, this different framing by the German Catholic and Protestant churches also reflects a different understanding of the role of the individual and the state. Catholics tend to see the state as needing to make people act morally, regardless of their own wishes, while Lutherans put more emphasis on the individual's own conscience. The Lutheran Church does participate jointly in what was originally only a Catholic "Week for Life" of public demonstrations against abortion, but they see their role as "taking off some of the edge" of the tone expressed in these actions, according to their central office (Interview, Thomas Krüger, January 1996).

However, their position could hardly be called supportive of abortion, even in the early stage. The official 1990 statement of the Lutheran Church on abortion begins with the assertion that "The right to life is a fundamental human right. It is the job of the law to be concerned about the protection of unborn life. The criminal code should also serve the purpose of protecting human life." In the process of German unification, Bishop Kruse also condemns the East German practice of allowing abortions in the first trimester without legal obstacles as being "inconsistent with the fundamental convictions of Christian faith and of the church" (*FAZ*, 8/25/90).

Thus, the official position of the German Lutheran Church accepts the frame that the fetus is a human life and that abortion is a moral wrong. But it encourages the state to allow women to make the decision about what is the "lesser evil," offering help in terms of social services and pro-life-oriented counseling. It does not support the use of the law to punish women who choose abortion after thoughtful and informed consideration in situations of "unresolvable conflict" in the early stages of a pregnancy. As a political policy position, this is a pro-choice stand, but it is also one that accepts the framing of the abortion issue as being about the "protection of unborn life." As Bishop Kruse avers, "It is beyond debate that unborn life deserves and needs protection. The controversy is really only about how this protection is best achieved" (*FAZ*, 8/25/90). This supports the claim by the German Constitutional Court that there is a "consensus." At least under the sacred canopy, there is no debate in Germany about the moral status of the fetus as being a life that the state has an obligation to protect.

Institutionally, the Catholic and Protestant Churches of Germany have been seen as closer to the CDU/CSU coalition than to any of the other political parties. The idea that these major parties are specifically Christian in orientation and speak with a "Christian" voice is not seen as infringing on either a separation of church and state or an underlying religious pluralism of society. "The 'C' in our party name allows us no twisting and turning," suggests Willi Stumpf, CSU county leader (*SZ*, 7/5/74). Archbishop Meissner, speaking for the German Catholic Bishops' Conference, criticizes the failure of the CDU/CSU coalition government to make support for restrictive abortion laws a party line issue. They "no longer deserve the 'C' in their name" (*SZ*, 6/15/92). Günther Gillesen, in an editorial in the *FAZ*, defines the abortion issue as "a test of the validity of the 'C' in their name" (2/20/86).

The sacred canopy is thus easily carried into party politics, where the "Christian" parties are expected to take an explicitly Christian position, and where the institutional strength of the two main churches is used to define what this position can and should be. This does not exclude debate over the specific policies supported to realize these values, but there is little disagreement in this public space over what "Christian values" are or whether one particular party has a mandate to represent them.

This institutional access means that the use of a sacred canopy to frame the fetus as unborn life is not a matter of controversial "interference" but a routine aspect of German social politics. Statements such as that of Joseph Cardinal Hoeffner (*SZ*, 4/7/72) that "Believing Catholics may not vote for politicians who do not guarantee the untouchability of the human life of the unborn child" are not considered inappropriate meddling in politics and do not bring forth the chorus of criticism that similar statements from U.S. Catholic bishops have unleashed.

UNITED STATES

U.S. religious speakers do not share a consensus on the moral status of the fetus as a person. Protestant churches are heterogeneous in their framing. One major division is between the mainstream or liberal denominations (Lutheran, Methodist, Episcopalian, Presbyterian, Congregational, and Unitarian) and the more fundamentalist and evangelical ones (Southern Baptist Convention, Assembly of God, Churches of Christ, and others). The former denominations often join with Jewish organizations and other broad interreligious groups, such as the National Council of Churches, to affirm the diversity of moral judgments possible for abortion.

They draw on those aspects of religion that emphasize tolerance and acceptance of difference, the equal personhood of women, and the separation of church and state. The very fact that abortion decisions represent a woman's relationship with God is a reason why the state should stay out of the decision-making process. Unlike the position of the German Lutheran Church, these groups treat the claim that the fetus should be considered a person as the doctrine of a particular religion, not a consensual belief.

As early as 1967, the Protestant Council of the City of New York took the position that "The sanctity of human life is of paramount concern to both Christians and Jews [but] . . . those who share this concern for human life . . . may sincerely differ on the point at which life begins" (*NYT*, 2/25/67). U.S. Protestant speakers from this tradition defend abortion as a possible moral choice and defend women as moral decision-makers. A formal statement of the Presbyterian Church in 1983 affirmed that "Abortion is not only a right but sometimes an act of faithfulness before God" (*LAT*, 1/26/85).

The insistence by one religious player that its view should be enshrined in law becomes, for some, an issue of religious freedom. Carroll Cannon of the Disciples of Christ notes that "To establish a national law which has its roots in established religion deprives all of religious freedom" (*LAT*, 5/23/75). Bishop Paul Moore of the Episcopal church similarly argued that "To abridge the right of abortion [is] to abridge freedom of religion" (*NYT*, 1/22/83).

Outside of formal church groups, the Religious Coalition for Abortion Rights (RCAR) and Catholics for a Free Choice (CFFC) represent this religious frame as well. Both organizations participate actively in coalitions with nonreligious abortion rights groups. As Evans (1997) shows, the framing of abortion by the RCAR has shifted over time in response to a changing discourse. Founded in 1973 by mainline Protestant and Reform Jewish congregations, the RCAR was the descendent of the Clergy Consultation Service on Abortion, which had helped women to locate safe abortions in the pre-*Roe* years.

Before *Roe*, they framed their support for legal abortion in terms of protecting women's health as their moral duty. Between 1973 and 1980, the RCAR's emphasis shifted to religious pluralism, with the Catholic Church depicted as attempting to make its own doctrine override that of others. After 1980, with a stronger and more visible Protestant anti-abortion movement to counter, their argument shifted again. Women were capable, they emphasized, of making their own "wise and responsible" moral decisions and that, under some circumstances, "abortion can be a moral choice" for them (Evans 1997).

The sacred canopy of the Religious Coalition emphasizes a religious commitment rooted in social justice concerns, extending beyond abortion to a broader series of reproductive issues. The name change to the Religious Coalition for Reproductive Choice reflects this broadening as the organization has evolved. The current mission statement notes that "Because women of color are disproportionately affected by restrictive laws and policies, the Coalition places particular emphasis on developing broad-based participation and leadership."

Catholics for a Free Choice (CFFC) was founded in 1972, shortly before *Roe*, but did not become active until after the decision. It is best viewed as part of a movement within what Cuneo (1989) calls a "progressive" or "social justice" Catholic constituency. He describes this imagined community as a "religious mentality – a way of thinking about Church and world – as much as it is an organized movement for change." The progressive strand within the Catholic Church is itself divided between those who see a "seamless garment" of "life-affirming" issues, including opposition to abortion, the death penalty, euthanasia, war, nuclear weapons, and welfare cutbacks, and those who stress the moral responsibility of the individual (Kelly 1992; Segers 1992).

The sacred canopy evident in the documents of Catholics for a Free Choice emphasizes that church teachings "affirm both the right and responsibility of a Catholic to follow his or her conscience on moral matters." Like the Religious Coalition, they argue that "abortion can be a moral choice. Women can be trusted to make decisions that support the well-being of their children, families, and society, and that enhance their own integrity and health," and that the "Catholic social justice tradition calls us to stand with the poor and other disadvantaged groups. Poor women are entitled to non-discriminatory public funding for childbearing and for their reproductive health, including abortion and family planning."

In short, CFFC and the religious coalition share the same religious abortion rights frame, one that is also found in mainstream Protestant and Reform Jewish denominations. But the particular religious constituency for whom they attempt to speak is also part of the tradition of the left discussed later in Chapter Nine.

The more conservative Protestant denominations, often called "evangelical," are now strongly opposed to abortion and increasingly inclined to call on the state to enforce their moral code. They too have struggled against the initial perception that opposition to legal abortion rested solely in Catholic doctrine. As one Right-to-Life activist suggested in 1972, "We have to reach more people of Protestant persuasion so we don't get clobbered again and again by the charge that this movement is the Catholic Church attempting to foist its ideas on the community" (*NYT*, 8/20/72).

Into the mid-1970s, Protestant evangelicals were politically quiescent and divided in party loyalty. They hardly looked like the source of a significant conservative social movement. Indeed, as Oldfield (1996, p. 3) observed, "When Americans thought of religiously based political activism, the images that came to mind were likely to be those of figures on the left: Martin Luther King, Jr., or antiwar priests such as Daniel Berrigan."

The emergence of the Christian Right as a significant social movement in the late 1970s caught most observers by surprise. But as Curt Young of the Christian Action Council observed in 1980, "Evangelical Protestants have always been against abortion, but now we are taking our opposition out of the church and into the public domain because, like other religious groups, we realize we have a social as well as individual mission" (*NYT*, 6/30/80). Evangelicals, buoyed by the use of broadcast media and their active local congregations, grew in size and political significance. A best guess on contemporary size puts the evangelical constituency at 20% of the U.S. population (Oldfield 1996, p. 97). The Christian Right organizational field is both a set of movement organizations and religious interest groups and, since the 1980s, also a major faction of the Republican Party.

In the early 1980s, three major organizations were the principal movement carriers: the Moral Majority, the Christian Voice, and the Religious Roundtable. By the late 1980s, with the rise of the Christian Coalition under the leadership of Pat Robertson and Ralph Reed, Christian Right activism became more and more directed at influence within the Republican Party. Christian Right influence in state and local Republican Party organizations grew to a point that *Campaigns and Elections* magazine estimated in 1994 that it was dominant in 18 state parties and a substantial force in 13 more. The Republican Party depended on the movement's ability to mobilize evangelical voters, and the movement depended on the party to form the broader-based coalitions that it needed to influence public policies on the issues that most concerned it. But as our data on standing make clear, Christian Right organizations have remained behind the scenes, rarely speaking to the media directly on the abortion issue.

The sacred canopy of the Christian Right is defined especially by what it opposes: the secularization of public life and the impact of this secularization on public education, the church, the mass media, and the family "The fear that animates movement members," writes Oldfield (1996, p. 217), quoting Christian Right activist, Gary Bauer, "is that their children will . . . be 'peeled away, seduced by the popular culture.'" Green et al. (1996) describe a variety of battles over abortion, school prayer, textbooks, and gay civil rights as aspects of a larger struggle to reclaim what are seen as traditional values. Abortion is central and often stands as a representative of them all.

Abortion and reproductive rights take on an additional significance here – beyond beliefs about the sacredness of life. Opposing abortion is part of the movement's affirmation of distinctive gender roles, opposition to feminism, and opposition to sex outside of marriage (Ginsberg 1989; Luker 1984). Unwanted pregnancies are not simply about the life of a future child but also about sexual permissiveness and the wages of sin. The abortion issue is the critical battleground in the defense of traditional family values, upholding "a model of the family capable of resisting secular pressures and transmitting evangelical values to the next generation" (Oldfield 1996, p. 68).

As we saw in Chapter Five, the three major players on the anti-abortion side in terms of media standing are the National Right to Life Committee (NRLC), the Catholic Church, and – for a short period – Operation Rescue.[63] All of them offer sacred canopies on abortion but, for various reasons both strategic and ideological, none of them offer the broader Christian Right master frame described previously.

Mobilization in opposition to abortion began in the United States in the late 1960s, with the Catholic Church leading the way. While there was dispersal among the church spokespersons in the early days, increasingly the primary voice became the National Conference of Catholic Bishops, and especially its Secretariat for Pro-Life Activities. While the Catholic Church led all other civil society actors in standing through the late 1980s, in recent years it has dropped to fifth place, while the NRLC has assumed the role of leading spokesperson for the anti-abortion movement.

For many Catholics who are inclined to more liberal positions on social welfare, their religious frame takes the form of what the late Joseph Cardinal Bernardin called the "seamless garment" of concern for life in all its forms (Kelly 1992). This ecumenical religious frame emphasizes the sacredness of life, including fetal life, and takes up issues of euthanasia, the death penalty, and compassionate care for the disabled. It does not emphasize the abortion issue as an exemplar of the broader set of issues in the Christian Right master frame, and it may even be in some conflict with them.

As *The New York Times* reported in 1997, then-Archbishop Bernardin, who was the president of the U.S. Council of Catholic Bishops, "set forth the most comprehensive anti-abortion program yet proposed by the American hierarchy. But in doing so, he called for church initiatives in the fields of employment, housing, health care

[63] Our survey of organizations asked about the five groups seen as most influential – a broader concept than media standing that includes less publicly visible policy influence. With 47 organizations responding, the NRLC led the way among religious speakers with 21 mentions, followed by the Christian Coalition with 16, and Operation Rescue with 11. The Catholic Church is listed by only 8 respondents, less than 20%. In contrast, the two churches in Germany were named as among the five most important actors 77 times among the 83 organizations responding to the question.

and welfare reform as 'a concrete test of the seriousness of our commitment to the basic human right to life'" (*NYT*, 8/17/77). This stance is in direct conflict with that of fiscal conservatives in the Republican Party, with whom the Christian Right was building political alliances (Kelly 1992).

To some extent, the U.S. Catholic Church acknowledges the lack of consensus in U.S. society about the moral status of the fetus. On the obligation to protect the life of the fetus, Bernardin said: "Science cannot establish when the soul is infused in the fetus and human personhood begins. But it is because we do not know precisely when this happens that the life process at all stages of prenatal development must be protected. We must treat the fetus as a human person from the moment of conception or risk the taking of a human life" (*NYT*, 9/28/84). This acknowledgement that there is no clear consensus on whether the fetus is a human life does not imply anything less than total opposition to abortion. As a statement from the Catholic Church (*LAT*, 4/15/91) affirmed: "The issue of abortion is not even subject to debate. Abortion is impermissible. End of discussion."

The sacred canopy offered by the NRLC is not distinctively Catholic, or even Christian, but represents a more general, ecumenical religious frame emphasizing the sacredness of life, including fetal life. They hope to attract persons of any religious persuasion who share their moral concerns, so they neither echo broader Christian Right denunciations of secularization nor support the welfare measures that the "seamless garment" approach would entail. Except for euthanasia, they do not link abortion to other policy issues.

Operation Rescue appears closer to the Christian Right. Operation Rescue members, Blanchard (1994) reports, are predominantly Protestant fundamentalists. Its most prominent spokesperson in the early 1990s was Randall Terry, who attacked the "godless, hedonistic, sexually perverted mind-set of today" (Terry 1988). Williams and Blackburn (1996, p. 173), in their detailed analysis of his book, note the Christian Right theme of how "reliance on human-centered values has usurped the legitimate authority of God over the nation." However, they interviewed Operation Rescue supporters and activists and found them heterogeneous in their response to this theme. They concluded that Operation Rescue is basically "a coalition of persons centered around a single issue, abortion. The issue is a symbol for wider concerns, although exactly what those wider concerns entail remains only partially shared" (1996, p. 183).

In sum, the spokespersons for religious framings of the abortion issue in the United States share no consensus on the Fetal Life frame. German Lutherans, unlike their mainstream Protestant counterparts in the United States, accept the framing of the fetus as a human life from conception. Both German Lutherans and a broad coalition of U.S. mainstream Protestant churches, dissident Catholics, Reform Jews, and religiously based pro-choice movement organizations support a less restrictive legal approach. The official bodies of the Catholic Church in both countries as well as fundamentalist Protestant denominations and organizations of the Christian Right actively work for legal restrictions or total prohibition.

The Christian Right in the United States is noteworthy for linking its opposition to abortion to a deeper challenge to what it perceives as "secular humanism" in U.S. culture and what its opponents value as the "American Way" of separation of church and state. Its linkage of anti-abortion arguments with wider claims to political relevance for a specific worldview, as well as its efforts to build an alliance with the Republican Party, are contested, not only by those who advocate abortion rights but also by those Catholics who use a "seamless garment" rhetoric to support more generous welfare measures and oppose the death penalty.

Since all U.S. claims to control the sacred canopy are controversial, all efforts to claim a consensus meet with opposition. Uses of the institutional power of the churches to support any political party or candidate are particularly hotly debated. Even Catholic Bishop John Malone was quick to "remind members of the hierarchy that they are pledged to avoid taking positions 'for or against political candidates'" when N.Y. Archbishop John O'Connor said that he did not see "how a Catholic in good conscience could vote for a candidate who explicitly supports abortion" (*NYT*, 8/10/84).

Individual faith, rather than institutional influence, is seen as the only way in which religion is legitimately allowed into the American political arena. The Catholic Church's efforts in the 1980s to pressure prominent Democratic Catholic politicians such as Mario Cuomo and Geraldine Ferraro quickly became controversies over the role of the church in politics rather than over the fetus's right to life. Since the separation of church and state is foreign to German thinking about religion, the policy role of the churches, especially the Catholic Church, is less controversial and more strongly institutionalized in Germany.

Table 8.1.   *Relative Standing of Religious Speakers by Country*

Percent of all religious speakers	Germany	United States
Churches[a]	**93%**	**45%**
Catholic	64%	32%
Protestant (mainstream)	25%	4%
Other	5%	10%
Anti abortion groups	**7%**	**52%**
NRLC	—	17%
Operation Rescue	—	11%
Other	—	23%
Pro abortion rights groups	**0%**	**3%**[b]
N^c =	420	750

[a] Includes affiliated social service agencies and theologians.
[b] Includes the Religious Coalition for Abortion Rights and Catholics for Free Choice.
[c] Of all speakers with religious organizational identification, both offering framing and not.

This analysis, we suggest, explains the following findings on standing by type of religious group in the two countries.

STANDING BY TYPE OF RELIGIOUS GROUP

Proposition 8.1.   *Official church groups dominate media standing among religious groups in Germany but are a minority of religious speakers in the United States.*

As Table 8.1 indicates, in Germany, 93% of religious speakers are speaking for the Catholic or Lutheran churches, with the Catholic Church predominating by more than 2 to 1. Each of these two large denominations has a central body that can and does speak for the church, and they believe that they have a responsibility to do so on the abortion issue. As Dr. Rudolf Hammerschmidt, spokesperson for the German Catholic Bishops' Conference, put it:

> It says in the Bible, "You must be the salt of the earth." You should be a challenge to what goes on in the world and that's a problem for our work with the media. We can't just conform . . . but what

we can do, naturally, is to use every means open to us to represent our position and that also includes public relations. . . . The Church is obliged to participate in shaping the world (Interview, January 1996).

Even when the churches do not take a position on a particular issue, mainstream German journalists will customarily seek their views. The national conventions of both churches are treated as newsworthy events, and discussions of abortion at these meetings as well as formal pronouncements by these two church bodies are widely reported.

However, the various anti-abortion social movement organizations active at the grassroots in Germany hardly make it into the media at all. For example, SOS Leben (SOS Life) is a grassroots anti-abortion group that runs on private donations and is primarily oriented to public relations work. It puts out newsletters with a circulation of about 20,000, subsidizes the printing of brochures for other pro-life groups, and once bought TV time to advertise their sale of the U.S. produced anti-abortion film *The Silent Scream*. The leader of the group, Benno Hofschulte, argues that "the right-to-life movement finds no open doors with the media. . . . The newspapers take practically no press releases from the right-to-life groups." After discussing how successful their TV ads for *The Silent Scream* had been when they were shown, he complains that all of the TV stations, even the private ones, now refuse to run the ads, claiming that "they are not allowed [by law] to run any political, religious or ideological advertisements – that is, ads with a political ideology or source, and they [the stations] decided it was religious or ideological. So that was the end of that" (Interview, January 1996).

When discussing the ten or so similar small groups of right-to-life advocates active in the Frankfurt area, he notes that they all are saying "We have to get into the media, we have to get into the media, [but it just doesn't happen] no matter how many press releases you distribute." Although he keeps a file of all of the times that his group has been mentioned in the press anywhere, he also notes that "It's the smallest file of the year" (Interview, January 1996). Other German anti-abortion groups outside the official church organizations also complain about how invisible they are. Their complaints are certainly supported by our data. In the 25 years of our sample, only 28 anti-abortion movement speakers appeared in these newspapers.

In contrast, official church groups account for less than half (45%) of religious speakers in the United States, less than the share (52%) captured by anti-abortion movement groups, led by the NRLC and Operation Rescue. Pro-abortion-rights groups that invoke a sacred canopy are considerably more rare (about 3%) but do not complain of media ignoring their presence. In the absence of any one unified Protestant alternative to the Catholic Bishops' stance on abortion, U.S. journalists occasionally use religious pro-abortion-rights movement speakers to balance the pronouncements of the Catholic Bishops, and to indicate what they perceive to be the reality of multiple views of morality among religious people.

In sum, the U.S. media are more open to social movement organizations that have a religious basis than are the German media, while the official churches have a dominating position in German newspapers. This is exactly what we would expect from the lesser institutional separation of church and state in Germany.

Our survey of organizations shows that the differences in media attention to different types of organization are also reflected in different perceptions of the fairness and openness of the media expressed by different types of religious speakers.

Proposition 8.2. *Church groups in Germany are less likely to see the mass media as hostile to them than are anti-abortion movement groups, even though they engage in fewer proactive efforts to gain media coverage; the differences between these types of groups are smaller and more mixed in the United States.*

Anti-abortion movement groups in both countries as well as church groups in the United States are more likely to see the media as biased against them than German churches do. Movement groups in both countries typically see the media as being untrustworthy but, while most U.S. movement groups reject the statement that the media is not interested in what they have to say, only 21% of German anti-abortion groups reject this statement.

The lack of media success of German anti-abortion groups is not for want of trying. As Table 8.2 shows, they are more likely to contact journalists, send out press releases, and hold conferences than are German church groups. The perceived lack of media interest in what they have to say is supported by our data on standing. U.S. religious organizations, including both church and movement groups, are much more

Table 8.2.   *Media Relations by Type of Anti-Abortion Group and Country*

Type of Organization[a]	Germany		United States	
	Churches[c]	Movements	Churches	Movements
Perceived Interest and Bias[b]				
Media biased against us	47%	93%	75%	100%
Media are untrustworthy	21%	64%	25%	67%
Media not interested in				
what we have to say	21%	57%	40%	31%
Activity[d]				
Contacted journalists	3.3	4.4	6.0	6.8
Issued press releases	2.7	5.0	5.0	8.4
Held press conferences	1.2	1.4	2.4	4.8
$n =$	19	14	5[e]	12

[a] Anti abortion groups only.   [b] % true or somewhat true.
[c] Includes affiliated social service agencies.
[d] Mean number of times per group in the past two years.
[e] Because of missing data, the *n* for the first two items is 4 rather than 5.

proactive in their media work than their German counterparts, but it is the U.S. movement groups that particularly benefit.

This pattern of media responsiveness supports the argument that German church groups have a strongly institutionalized presence in the media that allows them to be widely quoted without much active effort on their own part. In the United States, anti-abortion movement speakers have high standing but are very energetic in seeking out such coverage, while their German counterparts are unsuccessful in spite of their making more effort than church groups.[64] Hence, the institutionalized churches in Germany and both churches and movement groups in the United States are the religious actors with enough standing to make a difference in shaping the abortion debate.

Standing, however, represents opportunity, and, for strategic reasons, these actors may or may not emphasize the religious dimension of the abortion issue in their mass media efforts. One may decide to save the religious canopy for the faithful while muting it in presentations to a general audience. Hence, we now turn to the content of the frames that

[64] As we noted in the previous chapter, they also make more efforts than feminist groups but with a similar lack of standing as a result.

religious speakers are presenting, asking how different their framing of the issue is in comparison to nonreligious speakers.

RELIGIOUS FRAMES IN THE MEDIA

We begin by examining the direction of framing by different types of speakers, using the balance of Pro and Anti ideas where a score of 1.0 represents all Pro ideas, a score of −1 indicates all Anti ideas, and 0 represents equal numbers of both. We saw in Chapter Six that, overall, Anti ideas have a 3 to 2 edge in German discourse, while Pro idea elements enjoy a similar advantage in the United States. We therefore focus here on the relative position of different types of speakers in the two countries rather than on their absolute levels.

Proposition 8.3a. *Religious speakers are much more anti-abortion than nonreligious speakers in both countries.*

Proposition 8.3b. *Catholic speakers are more anti-abortion than Protestant speakers in both countries. The gap disappears in Germany during the low discourse period, when abortion is not on the state agenda and lessens in the United States during the same time period.*

Figure 8.1 shows, not surprisingly, that religious speakers are on balance more anti-abortion. Across all time periods, German Catholic speakers average −.73, with U.S. Catholic speakers not far behind at −.60. This drops to −.65 if we drop Catholics for a Free Choice from the Catholic category. German Protestant speakers score considerably less Anti with −.31 while U.S. Protestant speakers come close to being completely balanced at −.07. Other religious speakers (not shown in Figure 8.1), such as interdenominational groups, theologians not identified with a specific religion, and U.S. Jewish groups, are strongly Pro in the United States (+.37) and Anti in Germany (−.26).

Figure 8.1 reveals some interesting changes over time in the Catholic/Protestant gap.[65] Before 1977 in the United States, Catholic speakers were overwhelmingly anti-abortion in the ideas they expressed, while Protestant speakers were on balance Pro and were indistinguishable from nonreligious speakers. This huge gap

---

[65] Because using our usual six time periods would leave the number of speakers too small in some periods or some groups to compare, we drop to only three time periods here.

United States

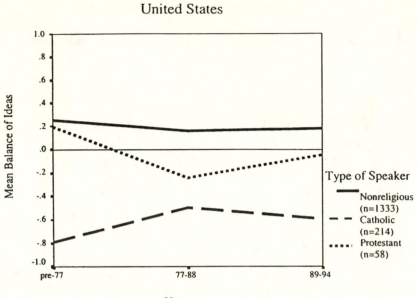

Germany

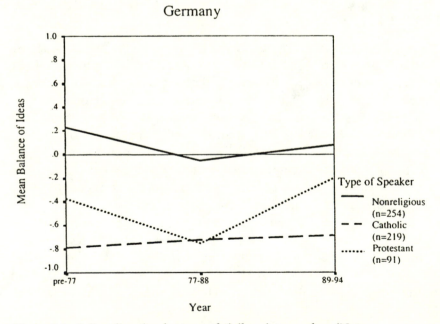

Figure 8.1. Policy direction by type of civil society speaker. (Note: Journalists, state, party, and nonframing speakers are excluded.)

substantially disappeared in the middle period. With the mobilization of the Christian Right, Protestant voices in the media tipped from a Pro to an Anti position. At the same time, more Pro ideas were being heard from Catholic speakers, whether dissident nuns and laity or Catholics for a Free Choice, also helping to close the denominational gap. The gap widened again in the most recent period, as Protestants moved back toward a balance of Pro and Anti ideas.

In Germany, by contrast, the Protestant/Catholic gap was much smaller than it was in the United States in the early years, disappeared during the low discourse period as Protestant speakers became more strongly Anti, and reappeared as German Protestant speakers swung back and became less anti-abortion in recent years. Religious freedom as an argument for not regulating abortion appears largely irrelevant in Germany, where the gap between the two major churches has, until recently, been so low.[66] At the same time, the gap between Protestant speakers and nonreligious speakers is considerably greater in Germany than in the United States in all three time periods.

THE FETAL LIFE FRAME

We showed in Chapter Six that while U.S. discourse is more of an even debate between contending frames, the Fetal Life frame is dominant in German discourse with no close competitor. The prominence of this frame was much higher from the beginning but has become even greater over time, with no comparable increase in its prevalence in the United States. We can gain insight into the reasons for this difference by examining the types of speakers who are most likely to be using the Fetal Life frame.

> **Proposition 8.4a.** *Religious speakers are more likely to use the* Fetal Life *frame than nonreligious speakers in both countries, but the gap between them is much greater in Germany.*
>
> **Proposition 8.4b.** *In Germany, Catholic speakers were much more likely to use the Fetal Life frame than Protestant speakers, but the gap has virtually disappeared in recent years.*

---

[66] The single German speaker most likely to use the word "conscience" in framing the issue is Rita Süßmuth, the most outspokenly feminist member of the CDU. Her framing of the issue as a "decision of conscience" for the woman was an influential part of the proposal for pro-life counseling but no criminal sanctions for women in the first trimester that eventually became law.

Proposition 8.4c. *In the United States, a substantial Catholic/Protes-*
tant gap in the early years actually reversed itself during the middle
years, with Protestant speakers more likely to use the Fetal Life frame;
the original gap reemerged in recent years but in reduced form.

In Germany, as Figure 8.2 indicates, over 70% of Catholic speakers
included at least one Fetal Life claim in their framing, and this
has changed little over the years. The change and overall increase
came from the Protestant speakers. In the first wave of the abortion
debate, slightly over 40% of them used the Fetal Life frame, a figure that
is much closer to nonreligious speakers than to Catholics. In the abortion debate of the early 1990s, German Protestants were virtually indistinguishable from Catholics, with over 60% of them using the Fetal Life
frame.[67] There is little change in the use of this frame by nonreligious
speakers.

In the United States, even Catholic speakers were considerably less
likely to use the Fetal Life frame than their German counterparts. In the
early years before 1977, less than 20% of Protestant speakers used this
frame – less than nonreligious speakers – while its use by Catholic
speakers was at its highest point.

The effort to de-Catholicize the anti-abortion position is reflected in
the reversal of the Catholic/Protestant gap in the middle period. First,
the Catholic Church seemed sensitive to the charge that it was attempting to impose its own religious doctrine on the rest of society. It made
conscious efforts to broaden the base of the anti-abortion effort by
sponsoring the National Right to Life Committee with its more ecumenical approach. Catholic speakers reflect this effort in their substantial drop in using the Fetal Life frame in their public statements directed
at a general audience, without in any way lessening their opposition to
abortion.

At the same time, the Christian Right mobilization of the evangelical Protestant constituency led to a sharp increase in the use of the Fetal
Life frame by Protestant speakers. The result of these two trends is the
development of a sizable and surprising reverse gap in which 20% more
Protestant speakers use this frame than do Catholic speakers.

In the pragmatic era of the Christian Coalition after 1989, the
spokespersons for the Christian Right have followed the Catholic path
toward a lower profile. None of the major figures such as Pat Robertson, Ralph Reed, or Jerry Falwell are prominent spokespersons on the

---

[67] As we noted earlier, this frame convergence does not mean policy convergence.

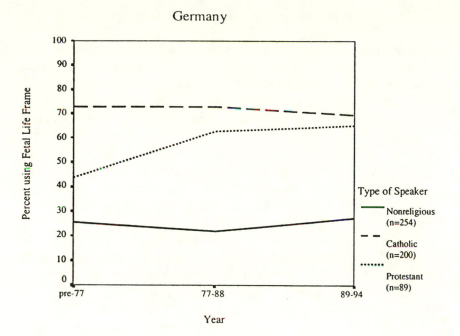

Germany

Percent using Fetal Life Frame

Type of Speaker

—— Nonreligious
(n=254)

– – Catholic
(n=200)

········ Protestant
(n=89)

United States

Percent using Fetal Life Frame

Type of Speaker

—— Nonreligious
(n=1333)

– – Catholic
(n=213)

········ Protestant
(n=58)

Figure 8.2. Fetal Life frame by type of civil society speaker. (Note:
Journalists, state and party speakers are excluded. Anti-abortion ideas only.)

abortion issue, nor do they strive to be. They seem comfortable with allowing the National Right to Life Committee and other religiously unaffiliated grassroots anti-abortion groups to speak for them on this issue. Other identifiable Protestant speakers are pro-choice, and the framing offered by all Protestant speakers overall is fairly balanced. Consequently, identifiable Protestant speakers are again indistinguishable from nonreligious speakers in their low use of the Fetal Life frame. It would appear that the greater cultural resonance of religious frames in the United States applies only when the sacred canopy is broad enough to include all religions and is not associated with any particular one.

Unlike in Germany, where the Fetal Life frame is endorsed by the court and institutionalized in the law, U.S. speakers using the frame are doing so without such support. In Germany, although Protestant speakers are different from the Catholic speakers in their overall framing of abortion, they have become similarly outspoken in their endorsement of the Fetal Life frame, which an absolute majority of both Catholic and Protestant speakers include. In the United States, even the Catholic Church, which remains strongly and distinctively anti-abortion in its utterances on balance, is nonetheless more likely to use some other ideas than Fetal Life to make its case, and decreases the share of all of its ideas that are in this frame over time.

Although the Catholic Church is a transnational organization with a common position on abortion set in Rome, Catholic discourse appearing in the media also reflects national differences in discursive opportunity structures, particularly for its favored Fetal Life frame. In the U.S. context, where the moral status of the fetus is disputed, claims made in these terms can be portrayed as basing public policy on a religious doctrine, violating religious freedom, and infringing on the separation of church and state. While in Germany the courts' endorsement of the fetus as a human life has led Protestant speakers to echo the dominant Catholic use of this frame in the years after the court decision, in the U.S. even Catholic speakers – who always used it less than German Catholic speakers – have come to downplay this framing even more after the U.S. Supreme Court rejected it.

CONCLUSION

The Catholic Church in Germany has been quite successful in shaping abortion discourse. Its speakers are quoted twice as often as Protestant speakers in our media sample, and their preferred Fetal Life frame has become the dominant frame in contemporary abortion discourse. Protestant speakers have so increased their use of this frame that, in spite of continued policy differences, there are no longer significant differences in its use by Catholic and Lutheran speakers.

In the United States, the story is more complicated. The separation of church and state, both institutionally and as a normative principle, produced a discursive strategy by anti-abortion advocates to de-Catholicize the issue. This effort has been successful, abetted by two interacting factors: (1) the desire of the Catholic Church to take a lower profile on the issue by supporting broader ecumenical groups such as the National Right to Life Committee as political spokespersons for their policy positions; and (2) the rise of an important movement among evangelical Protestants taking up the right-to-life cause.

This strategy has had certain nonobvious consequences for the framing contest over abortion. The Fetal Life frame – which runs the danger of being seen as a specifically Catholic doctrine – has a less frequent and decreasing usage among U.S. religious speakers. The greater appeal of religious frames in U.S. culture that we described earlier needs further specification. It is true only if the religious frame is ecumenical and interdenominational but not true if it is associated with any particular religion. Like U.S. political parties, the sacred canopy that works best is a big tent.

A second consequence of the ecumenical strategy came as a surprise to us. We looked for and expected to find a significant influence of the Christian Right in shaping abortion discourse. The Christian Coalition, with all its influence on the Republican Party and the centrality of the abortion issue to its adherents, has virtually no standing as a speaker on the abortion issue in our sample. Furthermore, there is no evidence that its specific master frame about secular humanism has become more dominant in religious frames on abortion in the mass media.[68] Nonetheless, we do see the indirect impact of Christian Right mobilization indirectly in the sharp movement of Protestant speakers in the 1980s toward more anti-abortion framing in general and a greater use of Fetal Life frames in particular.

[68] Anti arguments from the Social Effects and Social Morality frames are more common among anti-abortion speakers in civil society in the United States (where 46% included them) than in Germany (where 29% included them). But, if anything, their use declines among anti-abortion speakers in the United States in more recent years.

Our initial reaction to this nonresult was to think that the Christian Right had written off *The New York Times* and *The Los Angeles Times* as impenetrable bastions of secular humanism. Perhaps we would find different results in states where the Christian Right was a significant presence. Hence, we conducted a separate small study of two regional newspapers, selecting a comparably drawn sample of abortion-related articles from both the *Birmingham Post Herald* (Alabama) and the *Richmond Times Dispatch* (Virginia) for the periods after the *Webster* (1989) and *Casey* (1992) decisions. But we found no greater standing nor Christian Right themes in the abortion coverage of these two papers either. It appears that for media-directed speech, at least, the pragmatic, ecumenical religious strategy of building a broader anti-abortion movement in the United States has led to jettisoning those discursive elements that are not shared among religious constituents and are, therefore, potentially divisive.

The combination of (a) the strategic desire to seek wider support for anti-abortion policies than would be found by casting them in either specifically Catholic or specifically Christian Right terms, (b) the separation of the party system in the United States from institutionalized religion, and (c) the explicit rejection by the U.S. Supreme Court of the idea that there is a consensus on when life begins together makes the invocation of institutional religion a liability rather than an asset in the United States. In Germany, the institutional power of organized religion can be invoked much more easily. Not only is the German media more open to such large, nationally organized formal organizations, but there is a common ground in the Fetal Life frame that both churches comfortably share.

U.S. religious speakers therefore have to mobilize more diffuse and individual cultural commitments to religious worldviews, and on this discursive terrain the idea that the individual's conscience is the final arbiter has an advantage. While Americans are less secular than Germans, the cultural religiosity of U.S. society is available to be and has been mobilized by both sides of the abortion debate. It may even be that this diversity in the religious meanings given to abortion, along with the seriousness with which Americans take their religious beliefs, rather than any use of the language of rights, is what makes the U.S. debate so difficult to resolve.

CHAPTER NINE

Representing the Tradition of the Left

Choice requires the elimination of racism and economic discrimination, so all groups can make
parenting decisions equally unrestricted by concerns
for economic survival and quality of life. (Pamphlet,
Boston R2N2)

218 ist ein Paragraph, der immer nur die Armen
traf. [218 is a clause, that on the poor, exerts its
claws. More literally: §218 is a legal clause that
always has only affected the poor.] (chant by feminist
protesters, 1970).

Social issues were and are raised by both the political left and right.
However, whereas the right tended to consider the problems of poverty
essentially as a matter of private and state charity, the left claimed social
justice as a right. Hence, the imagined community of potential supporters of justice claims can be found in what Flacks (1988) calls "the
tradition of the left":

Radical democracy, populism, socialism, communism, syndical-
ism, anarcho-communism, pacifism – all of these are labels for
ideologies and organized political forces that, despite their mani-
fold differences and mutual hostilities, have espoused a common
idea. . . . It is useful to label all forces . . . that have sought to
democratize politics, institutions, or culture and have sought to
encourage relatively powerless groups to intervene in history as
the "tradition of the left" (1988, p. 7).

Flacks does not use the concepts of collective identity or imagined community to discuss the adherents of this tradition, but he is clearly thinking in such terms. While he pays attention to the mediators – the organizations of the political left that aim at political power – he also emphasizes the tradition as "an intellectual and cultural current, constituted by artists, writers, teachers, and other cultural workers, who have engaged in concerted critique of established conditions, institutions, and values . . ." (1988, p. 187).

Flacks' tradition of the left is an imagined community with historical continuity that is capable of periodic renewal, a "we" that provides an important and continuing identity to those who consider themselves part of it. Defined by its concerns with the inclusion and empowerment of relatively powerless groups, it is a significant part of the justice constituency in both Germany and the United States, with carriers both inside and outside political parties.

Feminists have had a complicated and ambivalent relationship with the left. This tradition of the left has, at times, been indifferent or even hostile to women's claims for inclusion as anything other than the wives and mothers of working men. Feminists have sometimes been indifferent or even hostile to the claims of less privileged women. Hence, gender and class politics have been fraught with tensions and contradictions.

As we saw in Chapter Four, the tradition of the left gets played out differently in Germany and the United States. Germany has more than a century of battles between an organized left that speaks in the name of "the workers" and a right that speaks for the bourgeoisie. These struggles have established class as a meaningful political principle to organize contemporary political parties and issues. Class as a fault line is not absent in the United States and has been important during various historical periods, but it is a controversial rather than a "natural" framing for discussions of specific issues. Class is a dominant theme in German political culture but a countertheme in U.S. discourse, where race and gender have also been highly visible divisions. Class politics are institutionalized in German political parties, while parties in the United States are not aligned explicitly on a single axis of left and right, but instead combine class interests with varying concerns about racial equality and "traditional family values."

Beyond the privileging of certain dimensions of justice discourse, there is an even more fundamental cultural difference. Injustice claims based on group differences are culturally suspect in the United States, while they seem natural and legitimate in Germany (see Roller 2000). In the dominant U.S. discourse, the assertion of injustices based on structural inequalities must contend with a culturally normative response that asserts that we are individuals and implicitly denies the relevance of social location and group differences. The classic understanding of liberalism as favoring meritocracy, individual choice, and personal freedoms, while largely ignoring differences in social location and rejecting state interventions, is a fundamental theme in U.S. political culture.

In the dominant German discourse, the state is viewed as having responsibilities to address structural inequality. Describing itself as a "social market economy," Germany accepts the idea of being a welfare state as a good thing and organizes programs to address the special needs of identifiable groups. Individualism and autonomy are counterthemes in Germany that are raised to critique the political status quo. Conversely, recognition of group-based disadvantage and the fairness of need-specific interventions are themes in Germany but are counterthemes raised by challengers in the United States. This, then, is the complicated playing field on which claims on behalf of the justice constituency must make their way.

In order to address the varying dimensions of the understanding of social justice that characterize German and U.S. political culture, we define what a "left" perspective on abortion might entail and then use these dimensions to look at three distinct issues. First we consider claims of social injustice that address the way in which abortion law unfairly impacts the disadvantaged.[69] We then consider the relative balance between responding to social needs and emphasizing individual autonomy in each country and how this has changed in both. Finally we examine how political parties carry these diverse meanings of "left" into politics and who and what gets neglected when they do.

---

[69] In this chapter we analyze only those speakers whose overall framing in an article is either Pro or Neutral. While, as we note below, there are occasional social justice arguments offered by Anti speakers, they are both rare and of a sufficiently different nature that including them would only muddy the interpretation of our findings.

SOCIAL JUSTICE, AUTONOMY AND NEED AS LEFT THEMES

Justice for the Poor

One indisputably important aspect of the left critique of abortion law is the argument that it affects women of different races and classes unequally. Differential impact on the poor was the traditional charge leveled by the socialist parties of Weimar Germany against abortion law in the 1920s, and this concern was explicitly addressed by legislatures and courts in both countries during the period that we studied, albeit with different outcomes.

In Germany, the Constitutional Court in 1975 specifically considered a situation of "social necessity" to be a legitimate ground for a legal abortion, and it drew on a century of debates about abortion carried on largely in class terms to affirm that it would be "insupportable" (*unzumutbar*) to demand that a poor woman sacrifice herself and her living children to provide for yet another mouth. As Chief Justice Ernst Benda, writing on behalf of the Court, argued at the time, "when the lawmaker exempts genuine conflicts of this sort from the coverage of criminal law, he does not violate his obligation to protect life. . . . It is expected that he will offer counseling and help with the goal of reminding the pregnant woman of her fundamental duty to respect the life of the unborn and, especially in cases of social need, of supporting her with practical assistance."

The reformulation of German policy in 1992 similarly preserved a principle of justice for the poor, although shifting the rationale slightly toward a language of equal rights. The Constitutional Court majority affirmed that women on welfare had the right to have an abortion paid for by the state even though private health insurance was no longer allowed to cover the cost for more affluent women. The Court held that the poorest women would be deprived of their actual rights if the state refused to make them realizable in practice.

In the United States, by contrast, Justice Powell, accepting the constitutionality of the individual states blocking Medicaid payments for the poorest women, wrote on behalf of the Supreme Court majority that "we are certainly not unsympathetic to the plight of an indigent woman who desires an abortion, but the Constitution does not provide judicial remedies for every social and economic ill" (*Maher v. Roe, 432 U.S. 464*). Asked whether he thought this decision was fair to the poor, President Carter, a Democrat, said "Well, you know, there are many things in life that are not fair, that wealthy people can afford and poor people can't. But I don't believe that the federal government should take action to make these opportunities exactly equal, particularly when there is a moral factor involved" (quoted in *LAT*, 7/20/77). The idea here seems to be that it is more acceptable for the state to try to shape the morality of the poor than to limit the moral choices of the affluent, but it is not necessary for the state to try to meet poor people's specific needs or equalize their ability to exercise their rights.

As the *NYT* editorialized in 1980, "since poverty is not the government's fault, it is not the government's duty to help women pay. The majority [of the Court] finds that they have a choice – just like wealthier women. Anatole France would understand. Rich and poor women have the right to pay for their own abortions" (*NYT*, 7/1/80). The image of sleeping under bridges evoked by this quote guides German social policy in quite the opposite direction from that in the United States. Shaped as it is by a tradition of concern over class, German abortion law is evaluated by its practical impact on the poor, not merely by the formal rights that it offers to the individual.

AUTONOMY

The rights of the individual and personal autonomy, themes in U.S. discourse, are a second element in considering what social justice entails. For the German new left, ideas of individual self-development and freedom from stifling social norms and traditions were central to their critique of the political status quo. Particularly for women, who were bound to conventional roles as dependent wives and mothers in the rhetoric and policies of both the socialist and the Christian parties, constitutional promises of equal rights seemed hollow without the liberty to freely determine their own life course (Böttger 1990; Moeller 1993).

The classical liberal ideal of a freely self-determining individual was not absent in Germany (indeed, it was represented in the small classic-liberal party, the FDP), but it posed a challenge to an established left that was more inclined to prescribe what was best for society in terms of the social responsibilities of the state and the special needs of groups. Thus women's rights were limited by their family role (for example, by giving legal status only to the male breadwinner, and in barring women from keeping their own name in marriage). Women's needs were to be met by policies protecting her in her role as a wife and mother (for example, through dependents' benefits added to the male breadwinners' pay and maternity benefits for both married and unmarried women).

The dominance of class over gender politics in Germany helped secure rights for male workers, and the welfare state provided women of all classes with benefits that were not enjoyed in the United States. But it offered women fewer protections from discrimination or rights as citizens with independent agency. As Orloff (1993) argues, full political rights of citizenship, not only entitlements to assistance, are important claims for the left to extend to women.

The rise of the new left in the 1970s, as well as the emergence of feminist claims to self-determination as full citizens in the body politic, challenged the conventional left on these grounds. The new left asserted that individual self-determination – not only social benefits – was part of what "the left" should fight for. Its advocates were not only feminists within the SPD and other parties but the new Green Party, which addressed this new left constituency. Abortion, an issue that was central to German feminist claims for autonomy, as we saw in Chapter Seven, offered a discursive context for the contest between old left and new left ideas about justice and rights.

WOMEN IN NEED

The claim that women are a group with special needs that require special help and protection is also within the tradition of the left, albeit not limited to that tradition. Seeing women as particularly vulnerable and victimized provided the rationale for a variety of social measures introduced by the left in the early part of this century in both countries. Special protections for women on the job (commonly called "protective legislation") were fought for by the left in both Germany and the United States. These laws were intended to restrain employers from exploiting women and children, who were seen as too weak to fight back on their own via collective bargaining. Although these laws have been rolled back in both countries, there is a well-established tradition on the left of seeing all women as in need of special help and protection from the state. The welfare state tradition is a concrete manifestation of this moral obligation to care for the needy.

Some feminists, writing within the tradition of the left, have pointed out the problems of emphasizing women as self-determining individuals in the context of male-defined models of work, family, and citizenship. Women carry a disproportionate responsibility for the care-taking work of society, including the labor of bearing and rearing children, and to treat women as "just like men" ignores the special costs that this work imposes on women. Moreover, in a society in which women are often dependent on male wages and exposed to male violence, the state has an affirmative responsibility to protect women (Petchesky 1984).

The argument that women need special help and protection is controversial and subject to left feminist critiques, drawing on the autonomy and justice themes. The new left's emphasis on self-determination and autonomy supports a critique of the welfare state as infantilizing the poor, especially poor women. Fraser (1989) argues that when the state defines the needs of the poor (or of women) on their behalf, it converts constituents into clients. A "clientelistic" discourse privileges the state's view (or that of private social welfare agencies) of what people need over their own self-definition of their needs.

Other critics emphasize women as an oppressed or subordinated group analogous to a subordinated class or ethnic group. From this perspective, welfare state measures can be seen as a form of social control that perpetuates social inequalities in power and resources (see Piven and Cloward 1971). In these critiques, a need-based discourse divorced from issues of social power and individual self-determination is viewed as giving the state too strong a role in defining and administering what clients need rather than what citizens want. Hence, many in the imagined community of the left see such a need-based discourse as a threat to democracy through its failure to recognize the needy as citizens with rights.

In sum, we have identified three different kinds of claims that are present in the tradition of the left but play out quite differently in the two countries. The social justice theme is the most central, explicit, and unambiguous claim. This theme of fairness to the poor is institutionalized in German abortion law but has been explicitly rejected as a basis for abortion policy in the United States.

Both the claim of self-determination and autonomy, associated with the new left, and the claim of special needs, associated with welfare state socialism, are also arguments that draw on the living tradition of the left. Each of these claims, however, can also be used to exclude or control the needy and has its critics as well as its supporters on the left.

In the following analysis we show how autonomy claims in the United States and a state-centered definition of needs in Germany both recognize and obscure claims for social justice. Each dominant framing of the discourse relegates different alternative voices on the left to the margins and makes the needs of different groups of women harder to acknowledge. We trace the relative significance of all of these three themes through the abortion discourse.

THE SOCIAL INJUSTICE THEME

We measured each of the three themes by a specific cluster of ideas. The social injustice cluster is a subset of the ideas in the Social Justice frame described in Chapter Six, including only Pro or Neutral claims of unfairness based on social location.[70] The overall use of this cluster is almost identical in the two countries, with about 14% of Pro and Neutral speakers using one or more ideas from it.

There are some differences in how frequently injustice claims emphasize economic hardship. In Germany, claims about affordability or hardship for the poor are only slightly more common than those emphasizing geographical or other noneconomic differences. In the United States, economic injustice claims are more than eight times as likely as geographical or other injustice claims. These differences appear to reflect policy differences in the two countries – with government supporting the cost of legal abortions for poor women in Germany and not providing support in the United States.

Proposition 9.1. *Social injustice framing is comparatively rare and at about the same level in Germany and the United States.*

Figure 9.1 shows the prominence of the social injustice cluster over time in the two countries among Pro and Neutral speakers. If we include Anti speakers as well, the trends are the same, but the overall prominence drops to less than 10% in both countries. The peaks come when issues of funding and access are on the policy agenda. In Germany, the first peak came early, before "social necessity" was established as one of four legitimate justifications for abortion. The second peak came in the early 1980s, at a time when the Christian Democrats established the *Stiftung "Hilfe für Mutter und Kind"* (Foundation to Help Mother and Child) to offer additional support for poor pregnant women.

For German speakers, the issue of fairness to the poor, which was adopted by the Court as a principle, is no longer in dispute. Conservative Christian voices in Germany are uniformly willing to advocate social assistance to poor women as part of a pro-life position. As an

---

[70] This excludes, for example, claims of unfairness to doctors or other health professionals.

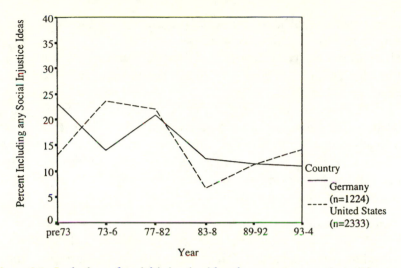

Figure 9.1. Inclusion of social injustice ideas by country over time. (Note: Only pro and neutral framing speakers are included.)

unnamed speaker from the Central Committee of German Catholics, a lay organization, stressed, "Comprehensive measures for counseling and help must make it possible for affected women to say yes to the life of her child. Economic and social need in pregnancy cannot be permitted to be a motive for the killing of unborn life" (*FAZ*, 3/26/73).[71]

In the United States, social injustice claims were most prominent during the period when the Hyde Amendment was introduced, debated, and passed in Congress and upheld in the Supreme Court. There was a rebound during the 1993–1994 period when anti-abortion violence was reducing access geographically.

Not all support for legal abortion for the poor comes from the left. Indeed, sometimes it is based on the claim that abortion is cheaper than supporting children on welfare. We found 156 cases of such claims in the United States (compared to only 27 in Germany). A *New York Times* editorial, for example, noted that "it costs the taxpayers many times more for poor women to have children and add them to the welfare rolls than to have elective abortions which might enable the women to

---

[71] Sentiment and practice do not always correspond. A study conducted by the Max Planck Institute in Freiburg of the 851 legal cases brought against women for illegal abortions between 1977 and 1985 found that more than one-half of the accused had the lowest level of education (*Hauptschule* or *Sonderschule*), and their average income was only 600 DM per month.

enter or remain in the job market" (*NYT*, 2/18/72). Or, David Tread-well, an opinion columnist, asks the rhetorical question, "Are you willing to pay the costs, in terms of Medicaid and social welfare pro-grams for children of poor women who might otherwise seek abor-tion?" (*LAT*, 4/29/92).

Finding themselves uncomfortable with arguments for supporting abortions for the poor based on social costs rather than social justice, some advocates of abortion rights have withdrawn from raising issues of hardships for poor women. In addition, by 1983, defeating the Hyde Amendment seemed to be a lost cause. As Emily Tynes of the Com-munications Consortium put it, with a tinge of regret:

> [We] could put all the money in the world into it, at [that] par-ticular time, and [we] would not be able to win back Medicaid funding for abortions. . . . There have always been groups at the table who argued the moral position. Yeah, we can't win but we shouldn't give up [the fight for] Medicaid funding. . . . [The abor-tion rights movement] lost the moral high ground in terms of the women's movement by not also being an advocate [for funding for the poor] (Interview, March 1998).

In sum, the low overall use and general decline of social justice framing in both Germany and the United States, while similar on the surface, reflect different underlying dynamics. In Germany, the decline reflects a victory for this framing. Poor women are seen as having a special claim on the welfare state. However, the state's power to grant or withhold a certification of neediness is increasingly viewed on the left as an infringement on women's autonomy. Karin Schöler of the AWO, for example, criticizes the kind of help and social support that the Foundation to Help Mother and Child offers poor women "because there is no claim of rights being made there, but instead, disempower-ment" (Interview, January 1996). The controversial issue in Germany in the tradition of the left is whether the welfare state approach to abortions is truly an acceptable alternative to women's own self-determination of whether they are able to and want to rear a child.

In the United States, the decline of the social injustice cluster reflects defeat and strategic withdrawal from a losing fight. The lack of support for welfare programs in general and the danger that arguments for sup-porting abortions for poor women might be appropriated to control and limit their childbearing have made it a discouraging and danger-ous discursive strategy. Finally, during the 1980s, when *Roe v. Wade* appeared to hang by a thread and all legal access to abortion was threatened, fighting for the cause of equal access for the poor seemed a luxury that the abortion rights movement could ill afford.[72]

SOCIAL NEED VERSUS AUTONOMY AS THEMES

We constructed a cluster of idea elements around the definition of women as a group that is vulnerable and in special need of help and protection from the state and civil society. We also included in this *social needs* cluster those ideas that, without emphasizing gender, presented abortion as a matter of social needs that the state should address through increases in social benefits for childbearing, adoption programs, or other help for children and parents.

To some critics from the left, the social needs cluster is a form of "judicial-administrative-therapeutic" rhetoric in which the power of the state overrides the voices of those who are directly affected in defining what is best for their "needy" clients (see Fraser 1989). Some German feminists, for example, denounced incentive plans for childbearing as "birth bonuses" (*Gebärprämie*) that intrinsically insulted a woman's own ability to decide if she wanted a child or not. Thus, to affirm women as needing state protection is sometimes criticized from within the tradition of the left as undervaluing autonomy.

Hence, we contrast the social needs cluster with an *autonomy* cluster.[73] The autonomy cluster draws on specific pro-abortion-rights ideas from the Women's Rights and Individual and State frames described in Chapter Six. This autonomy cluster, especially in the United States, is criticized from within the tradition of the left for failing to recognize that a woman's "choice" of an abortion may often reflect a lack of the practical means to pursue alternatives (Petchesky 1984).

There is, then, a potential tension between the social needs and autonomy themes. An exclusive emphasis on either one leaves the speaker vulnerable to a well-developed critique for neglecting the

---

[72] There was evidence in virtually all of the interviews, however, that feminist and pro-choice organizations were sensitive to the criticisms of racism and colorblindness raised particularly by women of color, and that this affected their own thinking about what the "moral high ground" was on the issue, even if they felt incapable of taking it.

[73] The list of all specific ideas included in these clusters is provided in the Methodological Appendix.

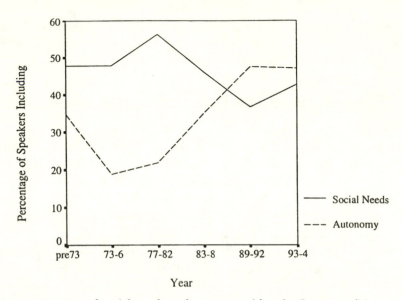

Figure 9.2a. Use of social needs and autonomy ideas in Germany. (Note: *n* = 1224. Only Pro and Neutral framing speakers are included.)

other. Hence, our analysis will focus on the relative strength of the two clusters and their balance over time in Germany and the United States.

Proposition 9.2a. *The social needs cluster is consistently high in Germany while it began fairly high in the United States but has steadily declined.*

Proposition 9.2b. *Except for the earliest period, the autonomy cluster receives substantially more prominence than the needs cluster in the United States. In Germany, autonomy was once far behind needs, but in recent years it has surpassed it.*

Both of these clusters appear at consistently higher absolute levels in both countries than does the injustice cluster examined earlier. In Germany, as Figure 9.2a shows, initially about half of Pro and Neutral speakers included one or more ideas from the social needs cluster, and this figure never falls below 35%. The autonomy cluster is initially much less prominent, but it rises dramatically in the 1980s. In the second round of reform, it becomes even more prominent than social needs. Both are commonly included by speakers in the 1989–1994 period, with 32% of German Pro speakers emphasizing autonomy claims, 23% emphasizing need claims, and 15% including both.

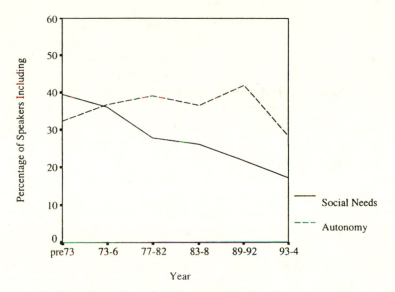

Figure 9.2b. Use of social needs and autonomy ideas in the United States. (Note: $n = 2328$. Only Pro and Neutral framing speakers are included.)

In the United States, as **Figure 9.2b** shows, the social needs cluster is initially almost as prominent as it is in Germany, but its trajectory is quite different. The use of this cluster declines precipitously, falling to around 20% by 1993–1994. Its use in the pre-*Roe* years reflects the "doctor-oriented" discourse of that period. Pro and Neutral speakers in the media were drawn especially from doctors and social service agencies[74] and particularly addressed women's deaths from illegal abortions and doctors' rights to make decisions about what was best for their patients (Luker 1984). In the immediate post-*Roe* period, 1973–1976, autonomy and need arguments were roughly balanced, with 35% of speakers including each cluster. After that, U.S. abortion discourse was much more about autonomy than about protection and need. By the 1989–1994 period, only 11% of U.S. Pro speakers used the needs cluster, 28% used the autonomy cluster, and 10% combined both. This means that German Pro speakers were almost twice as likely to include a neediness argument than Americans were (38% vs. 21%) as well as more likely to include autonomy claims (47% vs. 38%) in this recent period.

[74] They were 20–30% of all Pro and Neutral speakers in the early 1970s but about one-half that proportion in later years.

In both countries, there is a marked trend over time toward framing abortion as being about autonomy more than about helping and protecting those in need, but the trends occur, we argue, for different reasons. In the United States, the priority given to autonomy reflects classic liberalism applied to women as citizens on the same basis as men – with the impetus for such application coming from the second wave of the women's movement. The steady decline in attention paid to social need, alone or in combination with autonomy arguments, tends to exclude attention to the distinctive needs and concerns that make women economically vulnerable, emotionally exploited, and subject to most of the burdens of child care.

In Germany, in the legislative debate in 1973–1976 and even more markedly in the period after the Court decision, German discourse heavily favored need over autonomy. Hans Jochen Vogel, head of the SPD's Justice Ministry in the 1970s, put it strongly: "That everyone is the free master of his own body [sic] – such individualistic justifications offered by middle class feminists for the elimination of punishment for abortion are completely alien to us" (*FAZ*, 9/7/79). The SPD campaign in the 1990s for decriminalization was also characterized by the slogan "help don't punish" the pregnant woman. A welfare state response to social need was a well-institutionalized theme. However, beginning in the mid-1980s, well before the *Bundestag* returned to the abortion issue, but as the German new left emerged as a political force, there was a shift toward a greater emphasis on autonomy. In the second round of debate, the discourse as a whole actually favored autonomy over need as a frame for Pro arguments.

The rising prominence of the autonomy cluster represents a shift in the idea of what abortion represents to the left. The new left vision of autonomy is increasingly recognized in old left (socialist party) abortion discourse while, at the same time, new left speakers increasingly acknowledge women as a group with special needs. Autonomy and need concerns intertwine in the idea that women, not the courts or legislature, are the final arbiters of their social needs. As Inge Wettig-Danielmeyer, a leader of the SPD's women's organization, the AsF, argued, "a woman can only be helped by recognizing the ultimate responsibility is hers in situations of conflict" (*FAZ*, 7/15/91). In spite of this new emphasis on autonomy among Pro speakers, the legislative framework for abortion in Germany continues to frame it as a matter of helping the needy. The abortion reform law of 1992 is officially titled "Help for Pregnant Women and Families" and subtitled "Law for the protection of preborn/developing life, for the encouragement of a child-friendly society, for help with conflict pregnancies, and for the regulation of pregnancy terminations."

For the cross-party coalition of women legislators whose bill finally passed, self-determination did not mean full decisional autonomy for women. It meant that only the pregnant woman herself could tell if the problems facing her were so great that it would be intolerable (*unzumutbar*) to have the child, but it required the state to intervene in her decision-making process (by demanding that she undergo counseling that encourages childbirth).

According to the new law, requiring her to convince someone else of her "social necessity," as the earlier law did, infringes on her self-determination of what her needs are, but necessity rather than choice remains the discursive context for her decision. Several of the women legislators argued that "no woman would have an abortion if she could avoid it." Or, as another group of legislators put it, "the legal disapproval of abortion must find its expression in criminal law. A termination of pregnancy can only be permitted when the pregnant woman finds herself in a situation that makes the continuation of the pregnancy intolerable for her. This question of whether it is intolerable is one that only the pregnant woman herself can answer" (*FAZ*, 11/27/91). The new law did not really offer full autonomy but prevented the state from stepping in to prosecute a woman for her abortions if it did not agree that she was needy enough, thus adding a degree of autonomy in the context of a need-based definition of abortion law.

For German speakers, autonomy is presented in a discourse in which social justice, women's social needs, and the state's moral obligation to offer social support to the needy are taken for granted and institutionalized in the law governing abortion. In the United States, this context of social support is absent, and autonomy themes are often decoupled from justice and needs, in spite of the efforts of movement organizations to broaden the rhetoric of "choice" to include a broader vision of "reproductive rights."

In both countries, as a result, the parameters of the debate place certain women outside of the mainstream. Women who are not as free in their social circumstances as the U.S. discourse of autonomy assumes are "abandoned in their crisis" to make a decision, as the German women legislators charged. A number of anti-abortion groups in the United States attempt to address these women – including American Victims of Abortion, Birthright, Project Rachel, and Feminists for Life.

Olivia Gans, Director of American Victims of Abortion, notes how a legal right to abortion "does not create a compassionate society, nor does it solve the problems of poverty, neglect or lack of opportunities for women" (1989, p. 10).

Of course, other women do feel free to choose or not choose an abortion. Such women, who are often assumed to be the norm in U.S. Pro discourse, are hardly visible in German discourse. In the most recent round of reforms, claims on behalf of women as full moral agents who might freely choose an abortion for good reasons came mainly from East Germany, both before and after it was merged into the Federal Republic. A generation of living under a system of legal abortion in the first trimester produced a widespread belief that women were able to evaluate their own needs and come to a responsible decision without the state intervening to "protect life." But this was not a perspective welcomed by the mainstream of West German feminism (Maleck-Lewy and Ferree 2000; Wuerth 1996), nor did it receive much coverage in the *FAZ* and *SZ*.

In sum, the interplay of autonomy and need language has, over time, created a different mainstream and a different marginalized position in Pro discourse in each country. The nearly invisible alternative on the left in Germany is one that affirms women's self-determination without state intervention – the repeal of §218 that earlier feminists once imagined possible. The nearly invisible alternative on the left in the United States is one that calls not only for practical access to abortion for poor women, but also imagines a strong set of state measures that would financially support all women, married or unmarried, who wanted to have children and would defend them from physical and emotional threats from boyfriends, husbands, and even their parents.

While each of these discursively marginalized positions exists within the social movement sector, neither is much present in the media, and the media in both countries would no doubt consider their absence justified since their claims would be judged politically unobtainable. What is so striking is that in each case this "impossibility" is realized in the other country.

POLITICAL PARTIES AS CARRIERS OF LEFT THEMES

Particular political parties, especially in Germany, are the major carriers of the tradition of the left. On abortion, they can choose to emphasize any of the three themes discussed in the previous section, or some

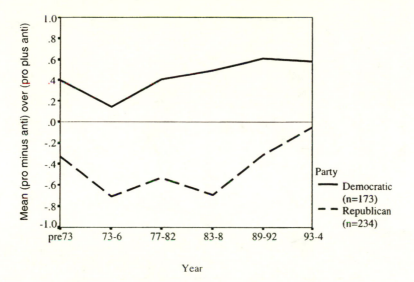

Figure 9.3a. Abortion positions for party speakers in the United States. (Note: Only framing speakers are included.)

combination of them. Which parties emphasize which themes, and does this change over time? To answer this, we have selected for our analysis all speakers who are identified with a political party, regardless of whether they are speaking for the party in some official capacity. Before we look at how these party-identified speakers frame abortion, we examine the Pro or Anti direction of the ideas that they offer, using the measure of balance introduced earlier.[75]

> **Proposition 9.3.** *Party speakers have clearly differentiated positions on abortion in both countries.*

In the United States, as we indicated earlier, distinctive party plat-form positions on abortion did not really become established until the late 1970s. But as Figure 9.3a shows, if we look at what party-identified speakers at all levels of government were actually saying, the differences between Republicans and Democrats were as sharp in the early days as they were in the mid-1990s. The gap was greatest during the 1980s and narrowed somewhat as Republican speakers moved toward something close to balance by 1993–1994.

[75] The measure is the balance of Pro and Anti ideas, where a score of 1.0 represents all Pro ideas, a score of −1.0 indicates all Anti-ideas, and 0 represents equal numbers of both.

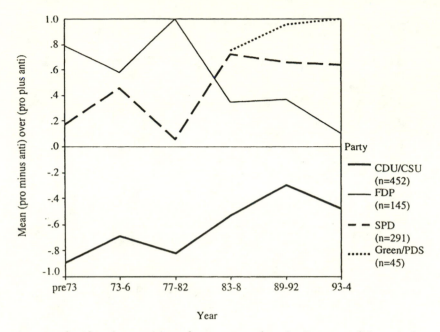

Figure 9.3b. Abortion positions for party speakers in Germany. (Note: Only framing speakers are included.)

The situation in Germany, where there are more than just two parties, is more complex. As Figure 9.3b indicates, party positions are not as stable or consistent as the established left–right continuum might lead one to expect. The Christian Union parties (CDU/CSU) are clearly distinct from the others and consistently favor anti-abortion ideas, although to a lesser degree in recent years. In the 1970s' round of reform and immediately afterward, the classic liberal Free Democrats (FDP) were considerably more supportive of an abortion rights position than were the Social Democrats (SPD), the traditional representative of the moderate left.

In the early 1980s, the Green Party entered the political scene, positioning itself to the left of the SPD, but with its roots in the "autonomous" new left.[76] The Green Party began to embrace feminism and to compete with the older parties on these terms. Not surprisingly, the ideas that they offered strongly supported abortion rights. Compe-

---

[76] The term frequently used for the new left in Germany is the *Autonomen*, or autonomous.

tition with the Greens may help to account for the sharp movement in a Pro direction by SPD speakers since 1982. By the 1990s, the German parties were again neatly aligned on abortion along the conventional left–right continuum.

To get a better sense of what was going on, we examine how the four pro-abortion-rights parties[77] utilized the three themes in the tradition of the left. We focus on Pro and Neutral party speakers who use one or more ideas from any of the three clusters. To highlight their relative emphasis on autonomy, we constructed a measure of the relative balance between the autonomy cluster and the two "social problem" themes of need and injustice combined. In this social problem/autonomy balance measure, a positive score means relatively more ideas from the social problem clusters and a negative score means relatively more from the autonomy cluster.

Proposition 9.4. *With the exception of the FDP in Germany, all Pro parties have moved in the direction of increasing emphasis on autonomy compared to social needs.*

Figure 9.4 shows that in the United States, after the initial period,[78] the Democrats have moved from an emphasis on needs and injustice to a strong emphasis on autonomy. The Social Democrats in Germany, although they started from an initial position with much more emphasis on needs and justice, have moved to a relative balance. The parties more allied with progressive social movements have also moved to a much greater emphasis on autonomy.

The liberal FDP follows a different course. Their speakers, initially the most supportive of abortion rights, began with a heavy emphasis on autonomy that sharply distinguished them from SPD speakers. But from 1977 on, they moved toward more emphasis on the social need and justice themes until, in the most recent period, they put relatively less emphasis on autonomy than does the SPD. In this regard, they look like the mirror image of the U.S. Democratic Party, for their balance swung away from autonomy alone, the classic liberal position of freedom to choose, toward a greater discursive acknowledgment of social circumstances that limit women's actual choices, while the U.S.

---

[77] The Democrats in the United States and the FDP, the SDP, and the Alliance90/Green Party in Germany. After 1990, we also group PDS speakers with the Greens.

[78] To insure that we had a sample of sufficient size for meaningful analysis, we collapsed the six time periods into three in this analysis.

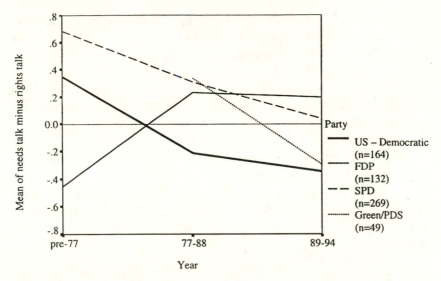

Figure 9.4. Social problems/autonomy balance among Pro party speakers. (Note: Only Pro and Neutral framing speakers are included.)

Democrats swung from an emphasis on fixing a social problem toward a freedom of choice position.

The parties more allied with progressive social movements are now the main carriers of the autonomy theme in Germany. During the debate in the 1990s, the Alliance90/Green coalition and the PDS/Left list in the *Bundestag* supported the abolition of §218, affirming a women's absolute right to make a decision in the first trimester. Other Pro party speakers emphasized women's self-determination "within the constitution," meaning in such a way that the overall priority given to protecting fetal life could still be assured.

Overall, the dominant U.S. framing of abortion by supporters of abortion rights is solely as a matter of individual autonomy without much attention to either social needs or justice. Democratic Party speakers, potential carriers of a left perspective, did little or nothing to challenge this definition from 1977 onward. The social context in which choice is exercised became virtually invisible. While in the early round of abortion reform in the 1970s, Democratic party speakers were almost as likely as SPD speakers to address women as victims of social circumstances, the balance swung strongly to the autonomy side in later years. This outcome has to be seen not only as a matter of the existence of a stronger welfare-state ethic in Germany, but also of a *change* in political discourse in the United States toward a more exclusive focus on individual choice alone.

In contrast, the social injustice cluster increased in Germany among both the Greens and the Free Democrats (FDP), the leading advocates of autonomy during the most recent period. For the FDP, fewer than 5% of their speakers included ideas from the social justice cluster in the period up to 1977, compared to over 20% in the 1990s. This does not mean, however, that the FDP suddenly discovered class inequity. The ideas that their speakers tended to use were mainly about unfairness to women in the former East Germany, and this was true for the Green and PDS parties on the left as well.

Nevertheless, it underlines one of the principal differences between countries emphasized in this chapter: *While the autonomy theme tends to stand alone in the United States, it is accompanied by justice or needs discourse in Germany.* German spokespersons for pro-abortion-rights parties, most of whom are now women, as we saw in Chapter Seven, include women's self-determination as a rhetoric of legitimation for abortion reform. Women Pro speakers in Germany are more likely than Pro men to use the language of autonomy and self-determination, drawing it especially from the Women's Rights frame. But unlike their U.S. counterparts, they also pay greater attention to advocating state interventions to meet social needs and to assure equal practical access at the same time. These are claims that in Germany, unlike in the United States, find resonance in legal decisions as well.

CONCLUSION

The definition of what "the left" stands for with regard to abortion is neither simple nor unidimensional. The imagined community of those who identify with the left has cast abortion variously as a matter of the inalienable rights of citizens to control their most private lives, the state's responsibility to care for and protect the needy, and social justice for those who face structural inequalities. In practice, each of these themes has shifted over time in both countries, but for different reasons and with differing results. In both countries, themes of structural inequality in access to legal abortion have become relatively less signif-icant, but only in Germany has access for the poor been institutional-ized through state subsidies for the neediest women.

In both countries, themes of autonomy and self-determination have flourished with the rise of feminism and the new left, but only in the

United States has this emphasis on autonomy been institutionalized in a way that bars the state from manipulative or coercive interventions. In both countries, the parties traditionally associated with the left have moved away from a discourse that was predominantly about need and protection for women and families, but the shift in Germany was premised on a legal and policy context in which the existence of supportive measures (*flankierende Massnahmen*) for women and children already surrounded the prohibitions and mandates of the law.

Moreover, both countries use a discourse of autonomy in a way that limits its actual applicability and places some women and their experiences in a marginalized position vis-a-vis the discourse as a whole. Those German women who continue to insist on no state intervention in their decisions about pregnancy (that is, the outright repeal of §218), and those American women who are confronting socially oppressive conditions that force them into abortions that they do not want, find themselves largely excluded from the discourse and attention of the left as well. In neither country is social justice in its fullest sense either espoused or realized.

Part IV

The Quality of Abortion Discourse

In the previous three chapters we looked at various outcomes in media discourse and addressed which actors were competing and with what success in shaping these outcomes. We showed how their discursive strategies were themselves influenced by the contours of the complicated playing field on which they competed – the discursive opportunity structure – as well as by strategic choices that they made to position themselves in this field. Part of the problem faced by all of these actors was discursively to construct a constituency for themselves – women, the religious, the left – as well as to address this constructed public in ways that would advance the policy positions that they favored. In both Germany and the United States, the abortion debate has changed in character over time as different groups have achieved more standing and certain ideas have come to be more or less favored than others.

Using the concept of a discursive opportunity structure, we suggested that the chances for different groups and points of views to be heard were structured differently in each country. The institutionalized position of the parties and the churches, the state-centered coverage of news events, the language of the high court's constitutional decision, and the formal organizations and cultural traditions associated with class and gender politics all combine to give systematic advantages to certain speakers and ways of framing abortion in Germany. Similarly, we found that the suspicion of the state, the dominance of interest group politics over formal parties, traditions of religious pluralism, and the privacy-centered language of the Supreme Court provided advantages to a very different constellation of voices in the United States.

Yet the story that we have already told is not just one of "path-dependency," where history sets each nation on a different path that simply unrolls before it. In each country we have also found important points where shifts occur and options change because of the interventions of various social actors, both inside and outside of formal political institutions. Women's mobilizations in both Germany and the United States changed the course of the discourse in each country, although not in the same way in each. Religious speakers mobilized in different institutional settings and shifted their framing to better match the opportunities available to them. The balance between autonomy and need-based claims about what abortion means for those interested in social justice has been changed over time, both within the parties of the left and in the discourses of both countries as a whole.

This first story that we have told is thus a story about the shape that conflicting cultural and institutional forces and mobilized political actors have given to abortion discourse in each country. The empirical outcome of the struggle among all of these speakers in Germany has been to create a discourse that revolves around the protection of fetal life and, to a secondary degree and in a subordinate sense, the self-determination of women. In the United States the struggle has resulted in more of a stalemate of contending, equally balanced discursive forces centered around the problematic relation between the individual and the state. The individual is largely seen by both sides as free from the social forces that shape opportunity and oppression, whether through poverty or gender, and the state is viewed with suspicion regarding social welfare and religion.

In looking at these various outcomes in media discourse, we addressed which actors were competing and with what success, and we offered explanations of their strategies and their achievements. But the empirical picture of democratic practices by which actors contest the framing of issues in the public sphere is only half of the picture.

In our second story, we turn to normative questions beginning with the central one: What qualities in the public sphere do we need to nurture and sustain democratic public life? This is a particularly important question to ask relative to the abortion debate, since thoughtful observers in the United States have frequently come to the discouraging conclusion that this issue more than any other illustrates the failure of democracy to grapple effectively with really tough questions or to create a space in which practical solutions to contested issues can be found (Hunter 1994; Tribe 1990).

The answer to this question clearly depends on the theory of democratic politics with which one begins. In Chapter Ten, we mine different theoretical traditions for their normative criteria about what are desirable qualities in the forum that concerns us here: the mass media. In some cases, different traditions point to similar or overlapping criteria; in other cases, there are theoretical controversies and a lack of normative consensus.

In Chapter Eleven we attempt to operationalize these normative criteria, applying them to the abortion discourse. We then compare German and American discourse on how closely the different criteria are achieved and whether there are any visible trends over time in how well they are met. Where there is a lack of normative consensus on the desirability of a criterion, we leave the reader to judge whether meeting it is for better or worse.

Finally, in Chapter Twelve, we look at what the participants and journalists involved in the abortion issue have to say about the quality of discourse. Here, our data on actor observations come from the survey of organizations and interviews with organizational spokespersons. Our data on journalist observations come from our interviews with journalists who covered the abortion issue and the meta-discourse commentary of journalists that appeared in our newspaper sample.

CHAPTER TEN

Normative Criteria for the Public Sphere

What qualities should the public sphere have to nurture and sustain a vigorous democratic public life? More specifically, who should be participating and on what occasions? What should be the form and content of their contributions to public discourse? How should the actors communicate with each other? What are the desirable outcomes if the process is working as it should? These are normative questions that have been important issues in political theory for many years. Classical theorists such as Rousseau, Locke, and Mill provide certain broad parameters in which answers can be sought; contemporary political theory develops the answers in more detail. There is a close link between theories of the public sphere and democratic theory more generally. Democratic theory focuses on accountability and responsiveness in the decision-making process; theories of the public sphere focus on the role of public communication in facilitating or hindering this process.

We review four traditions of democratic theory in this chapter, mining them for the answers that they suggest for mass media discourse in "actually existing democracies."[79] We regard our categorization as a convenient organizing tool for attempting to identify normative criteria that play a significant role within and across perspectives. A number of writers overlap traditions or make shifts over time, so we consider their ideas wherever it seems most convenient. Often we will find different traditions calling attention to similar criteria, and sometimes there are different emphases among theorists that we are grouping together and calling a tradition. The boundaries do not really matter

---

[79] Fraser (1997) uses the phrase to distinguish normative theories based on nonutopian and achievable assumptions.

for our purpose of unpacking the normative criteria for mass media discourse that they collectively imply.

We label the four traditions as representative liberal, participatory liberal, discursive, and constructionist. In each of the traditions sketched in the following sections we attempt to highlight the ideas that we see as being shared – thus defining a tradition – and to highlight the specific normative criteria that each perspective would endorse and emphasize. At the end of this chapter we summarize these criteria in terms of *who* should speak, the content (*what*), the style (*how*), and the *outcomes* that are sought (or feared).

REPRESENTATIVE LIBERAL THEORY

We group a range of theories under this rubric. At one end are those who take a strongly elitist and conservative stance – the "school of democratic elitism," as Bachrach (1967) calls it. At this end, theorists so much fear the participation of "the rabble" in democratic politics that they wish to see filters and barriers erected to diminish the citizen's role. At the other end are writers who want a strong and well-functioning public sphere, but they see its role as strengthening a system of formal representation that secures the real basis of democracy. We focus particularly on theories that accept the desirability of a public sphere but one in which general public participation is limited and largely indirect.

One can trace the roots of representative liberal theory back to John Stuart Mill (1861) and such skeptical commentators on popular democracy and the French revolution as Edmund Burke (1790). Schumpeter's *Capitalism, Socialism, and Democracy* (1942) is a classic modern articulation. More contemporary exemplars include Anthony Downs' *An Economic Theory of Democracy* (1957) and William Kornhauser's *The Politics of Mass Society* (1960).

This tradition shares the assumption that ultimate authority in society rests with the citizenry. Citizens need policy-makers who are ultimately accountable to them, but they do not need to participate in public discourse on policy issues. Not only do they not need to, but public life is actually better off if they don't. This is the "realist" school of democracy – the belief that ordinary citizens are poorly informed, have no serious interest in public affairs, and are generally ill-equipped for political participation. Hence, it is both natural and desirable for citizens to be passive, quiescent, and limited in their political participation in a well-functioning, party-led democracy.

For representative liberal theorists, the citizen's main role is to choose periodically which among competing teams of would-be office-holders will exercise public authority. Some would argue that such voting should be the only role, while others would accept some limited direct participation in public discourse as completely appropriate, though not so important that it demands active encouragement by the media. If the media is doing its job, citizens will be encouraged to vote, and the media will provide enough information about the parties and candidates so that citizens can choose intelligently among them. If citizens are dissatisfied with what they are getting, they can vote the rascals out. In the interim between elections, officials need to respond to problems that are technically complex, and most people have neither the inclination nor the ability to master the issues involved.

From this perspective, an important criterion of good public discourse is its *transparency*. It should reveal what citizens need to know about the workings of their government, the parties that aggregate and represent their interests, and the office-holders that they have elected to make policy on their behalf. Inclusion is important, not in the sense of giving ordinary citizens a chance to be heard, but in the sense that their representatives should have the time and space to present their contrasting positions fully and accurately.

Inclusion should depend on having a legitimate representative to articulate one's preferred frame in a public forum. Those citizens who feel that their views are insufficiently represented have the political obligation to use the representative process being offered. Without their own representative at the table, their preferred frames will, appropriately, be largely disregarded. This is normatively legitimate, since such views are, at best, irrelevant in practice and, at worst, potentially dangerous.

We will call this standard *elite dominance*. The public sphere, according to representative liberalism, should reflect the public's representatives. The larger and more representative the party or organization, the more voice it has earned in the media, and the more powerful it should be in shaping decisions. This suggests a criterion of *proportionality* – that is, media standing and the amount of coverage of the frames of different actors should be more or less proportional to their share of the electoral vote for parties, or to membership size for relevant civil society actors. Thus, government officials, major party spokespersons, and large formal organizations that can credibly claim to represent the interests of a substantial portion of the population should dominate the public sphere.

To expect citizens to be actively engaged in public life is seen by advocates of this view as at best wishful thinking, what Baker (1998) in summarizing this theory characterizes as "romantic but idle fantasy." At worst, encouraging such engagement obstructs and complicates the problems of democratic governance by politicizing and oversimplifying complex problems that require skilled leadership and technical expertise. The media can play a positive role in assuring transparency – for example, exposure of corruption and incompetence and providing the public with reliable information about what is actually happening. But they can also play a negative role if they give too much voice to those who misunderstand, oversimplify, or distort issues to serve their own personal agendas.

The media should encourage a dialogue among the informed, and most citizens are not well-informed enough to contribute. There are exceptions – citizens defined as "experts," either on the political process in general or on the substantive matter under discussion. This criterion of representative liberalism, *expertise*, emphasizes its value in informing the people's representatives in making wise decisions, rather than in informing the public.

Ideally, experts should not be stakeholders in the conflict, but disinterested and without any political agenda. From this position, they can dispassionately advise. Representative liberal theorists are realistic enough to recognize that, in conflict situations, opposing sides will often have their own technical experts. This only enhances the value of independent experts who have no political axe to grind. Experts should play a particularly strong role in defining the issues before they reach the stage at which decisions need to be reached.

In some versions, journalists themselves should play the role of dispassionate experts. From their inside knowledge of the political process and their research on the substantive issues, journalists acquire expertise that they should share with decision-makers and attentive publics. As advisors to decision-makers in their commentary, journalists are expected to take a position on the issues at stake and so guide officials toward more knowledgeable choices. Editorial opinion should reflect what journalists, as experts, think is right and need not be either representative or neutral.

When it comes to evaluating the *content* of public discourse, the operant metaphor for representative liberalism is the free marketplace of ideas. Restrictions on content are inherently suspect. The criterion of proportionality legitimately excludes those ideas held by small minorities, but this does not exclude them on substantive grounds. Whether or not any content is too extreme to be permitted is a matter for debate.

In Germany, groups or ideas that are judged to be "hostile to the constitution" (*verfassungsfeindlich*) are formally excluded, and denial of the Holocaust, the use of Nazi symbols, and the advocacy of Nazi views are legally prohibited. In the United States, no ideas are formally excluded, but the "specter of communism" was used to allow both government and private actors to suppress and punish advocates of socialist ideas throughout most of the twentieth century.[80] But even the exclusion of "anti-democratic" ideas is problematic for representative liberal theorists, and not clearly normative.

This openness to a range of ideas does not extend to a range of styles of expression. On the *how* question, the prescribed form of communication is *detachment* – a rejection of the expression of emotion. To betray emotions through one's facial expression or body language suggests that one's arguments are driven by them rather than by cool reason.

> In a democratic society, reasonable decisions are preferable to unreasonable ones; considered thought leads to the former, emotions to the latter; therefore, deliberation is preferable to visceral reaction as a basis for democratic decision-making. [This view] prescribes that citizens are to approach the subject of politics with temperate consideration and objective analysis, that is, to use their heads when making judgments about public affairs. Conversely, people are not to react emotionally to political phenomena. A democracy in which citizens evaluate politics affectively, to use the current language of social psychology, presumably leaves much to be desired. (Kulinski et al. 1991, p. 1).

In this view, emotion and reason are defined as inherently contradictory. As a result, all impassioned appeals are inherently suspect.

Representative liberalism endorses a normative standard of *civility*, that is, a way of speaking politically that does not inflame passion or

---

[80] Consider the legal prosecution of Wobblies, deportations of communist and socialists, and various formal and informal blacklists (Schultz and Schultz 1989).

permit *ad hominem* attacks on other speakers. It is not the same as detachment since civility is perfectly consistent with the expression of positive emotions such as empathy, but it dovetails nicely with detachment. Detachment focuses on one's emotional relationship to one's own ideas, while civility is about how one treats the ideas of those who disagree.

Because there is no universal standard by which we can resolve normative disagreements, others have a right to their contrary opinions. This implies respectful disagreement and the avoidance of verbal attacks on others. Speakers can say anything they want, but they ought to avoid saying it in a deliberately offensive and provocative way and be prepared to defend it against reasoned argument.

Representatives are elected to decide for the people, and once a decision is reached, there is no further need for debate. Representative liberal theory endorses a norm of *closure* – a time at which all concerned can agree that the matter has been decided and the system moves on. The public sphere should be full of discourse on a subject in the period leading up to a decision, but once a decision is reached, the media should move on to other issues on which decisions are still pending. The model is that of an election: The winner and loser alike acknowledge their respective positions, the winner takes a place in the system, the loser concedes graciously, and the contest is set aside until the next appropriate time for a decision comes around. It is enough that the discussion has taken place in a public and informed manner, and a majority of legitimate, accountable representatives have decided on a particular policy. Even if no decision can be reached, closure is desirable lest endless and irreconcilable debates ensue.

In sum, representative liberal theory endorses the following criteria: *elite dominance, transparency, proportionality, expertise, a free marketplace of ideas, detachment, civility,* and *closure.* A public sphere designed to produce wise decisions by accountable representatives best serves the needs of democracy.

PARTICIPATORY LIBERAL THEORY

The common thread in participatory liberal theories is the desirability of maximizing the participation of citizens in the public decisions that affect their lives. To do this, they should, to the extent feasible, be active participants in the public sphere as part of an ongoing process. With roots in Rousseau's preference for direct democracy over representative democracy, writers in this tradition often share a distrust of institutional barriers and mediating structures that make participation indirect and difficult. While Hirst (1994) refers to this as an "associative democracy," Barber (1984, p. 151) calls his version "strong democracy":

> Strong democracy is defined by politics in the participatory mode: literally it is self-government by citizens rather than representative government in the name of citizens. Active citizens govern themselves directly here, not necessarily at every level and in every instance, but frequently enough and in particular when basic policies are being decided and when significant power is deployed. Self government is carried on through institutions designed to facilitate ongoing civic participation in agenda-setting, deliberation, legislation, and policy implementation (in the form of "common work").

In a complex modern democracy, no one expects or desires that all citizens spend all of their time discussing public affairs and directly deciding on public policies. Inevitably, there must be delegation to mediators who aggregate and articulate one's discursive interests in the public sphere. But this implies a particular relationship between these mediators and the citizens on behalf of whom they speak. Michels (1911) described how even social democratic parties with ideological beliefs in participatory democracy became staff-driven rather than member-driven. While Michels himself never used the phrase, others characterized his argument as an "iron law of oligarchy." The iron law, it turns out, is more conditional than Michels recognized in his argument; still, the tendency toward oligarchy is common enough (Rucht 1999).

In the participatory liberal tradition, organizations with active forms of member participation and a leadership that is accountable to members are more desirable mediators than those who are only nominally accountable to members. More centralized and bureaucratic organizations with a division of labor can be accountable. Indeed, some degree of centralization and bureaucratization may serve the wider goal of effectively mobilizing large numbers of citizens to act politically on their own behalf, rather than merely delegating their political interests to others (Mansbridge 1980; Staggenborg, 1991).

Furthermore, participation in public discourse is an ongoing process, and the participation of these grassroots actors should be continuous – not simply something that occurs periodically during election campaigns or only at the beginning of the decision process. Writers in this tradition typically share with the discursive and constructionist traditions discussed in the following pages the belief that preferences and abilities for judging public issues emerge in the process of public deliberation. Participation transforms individuals into public citizens. In this view, political interests are not given a priori by the descriptive characteristics of people, but produced in the political process. To quote Barber (1984, p. 151) again:

> In place of a search for a pre-political independent ground or for an immutable rational plan, strong democracy relies on participation in an evolving problem-solving community that creates public ends where there were none before by means of its own activity. . . . In such communities, public ends are neither extrapolated from absolutes nor "discovered" in a preexisting "hidden consensus." They are literally forged through the act of public participation, created through common deliberation and common action and the effect that deliberation and action have on interests, which change shape and direction when subjected to these participatory processes.

Popular inclusion, as we label this criterion, has implications for media content. As Dahlgren (1991, pp. 2 and 11) puts it, the public sphere should provide "the institutional sites where popular political will should take form and citizens should be able to constitute themselves as active agents in the political process. . . . The goal is to establish structures of broadcasting in the public interest . . . which optimize diversity in terms of information, viewpoints and forms of expression, and which foster full and active citizenship." Similarly, Curran (1991, p. 30) argues that "The basic requirement of a democratic media system should be . . . that it represents all significant interests in society. It should facilitate their participation in the public domain, enable them to contribute to public debate and have an input in the framing of public policy." Or, in the hopeful words of Carey (1987, p. 14), citizens will "reawaken when they are addressed as a conversational partner and are encouraged [by the media] to join the talk rather than sit passively as spectators before a discussion conducted by journalists and [political] experts."

Popular inclusion does not simply demand a passive nonexclusion nor encourage only a top-down transparency for governmental action. It places normative demands on the media to seek out and actively facilitate the inclusion of diverse speakers and interests. In addition to the voices of member-driven organizations, the voices of ordinary citizens ought to be present. Formal credentials should not be a prerequisite for participation; the participatory liberal tradition rejects the norm of *expertise* that representative liberals endorse.

The argument that public participation transforms individuals into engaged citizens implies that the media content should encourage *empowerment*. This requires that media discourse address a major impediment to political engagement. As John Gaventa (1980) argues, people often do not rise up to challenge even decisions that are contrary to their own interests because one of the "hidden aspects" of political power is its ability to obscure real lines of cleavage and conflict in a society.

Participatory liberalism thus draws on a long and rich history of social and political conflict theories, including many social movement theories, to suggest that social inequality is typically reproduced by a variety of social, political, and cultural practices. To challenge such entrenched inequalities, people need to be actively mobilized to recognize and act on their own interests. From this perspective, therefore, social movements have a positive role to play in mobilizing individuals – especially those who are socially and politically disadvantaged – to develop and act on political commitments. Since engagement in politics is itself a spur to developing political awareness, media discourse that facilitates such mobilization is desirable.

Some advocates of the participatory liberal tradition extend the criterion of empowerment to reject the norm of *civility*, at least as representative liberal theory interprets it. Polemical speech acts or symbols that capture the emotional loading of public issues as well as their cognitive content can play a very important mobilizing role. Kennedy (1998, p. 85), for example, criticizes what he calls the "civility movement":

> The civility movement is deeply at odds with what an invigorated liberalism requires: intellectual clarity; an insistence upon grappling with the substance of controversies; and a willingness to fight loudly, openly, militantly, even rudely for policies and values that will increase freedom, equality, and happiness in America and around the world.

Style, in this view, is intertwined with empowerment. Speech that mobilizes people to participate places them in a position in which their awareness of the complexity of politics can grow through their participation in the political process itself. Thus even "emotional" slogans such as "abortion takes an innocent life" or "my belly belongs to me" should directly foster a more inclusive public sphere and indirectly lead, through greater participation, to a more politically competent and knowledgeable public.

Other participatory liberal theorists are more skeptical of this mobilization path and are wary about what an ill-informed and slogan-driven participation may produce. Barber (1996, p. 8), for example, in calling for a more deliberative process, echoes the discursive tradition:

> The public voice is deliberative, which means it is critically reflective as well as self-reflective; it must be able to withstand reiteration, critical cross-examination, and the test of time – which guarantees a certain distance and dispassion. Like all deliberative voices, the public voice is dialectical: it transcends contraries without surrendering their distinctiveness.

Thus, while participatory liberal theorists cannot be said to endorse slogans and polemics as a means of discourse, they do not reject such styles of expression out of hand. The normative criterion here is a *range of communicative styles*. Whatever frames or points of view are most entrenched and taken-for-granted should be challenged by ideas that call the taken-for-granted into question. Opponents of the political status quo have a normative role in challenging established elites and dominant ideologies. Appropriate forms of discourse do not preclude civility and deliberativeness but do not necessarily require it.

Writers in this tradition also tend to be suspicious of calls for closure, seeing in such demands a means of pushing enduring structural conflicts of interest off the political table. Social movements can and should play an important role in agenda-setting, calling public attention to issues that the established parties and elites would prefer to see ignored, and even intervene in the process of policy implementation. The ability of social movements to continue to press their agenda in the public sphere is an alternative source of political power for them, and it allows the alternative frames that they advance to enter into debates with official power-holders. Critical theorists in the participatory liberal tradition see social conflict stemming from structural inequality as ongoing; hence, the fear here is of premature closure and pseudoconsensus, not of endless debate.

"Good deliberation," writes Mansbridge (1996, p. 47), "will have opened areas of agreement and will have clarified the remaining areas of conflict." Mansbridge even suggests that those who lose in any specific decision have a particular responsibility to continue to articulate the alternative, a "loser speaks" norm that specifically rejects closure without a normatively achieved consensus to back it up. The mere exercise of majority power in making a decision, she argues, does not legitimate the silencing of the minority. Given the inequalities in political power in all "actually existing" democracies, minority voices and political outsiders are essential to a well-functioning public sphere.

In sum, participatory liberal theory is a critical perspective on democracy that particularly stresses the benefits of active engagement in politics both for the citizen as an individual and for the system as a whole. It endorses *popular inclusion, empowerment, a range of communicative styles*, and *avoidance of premature closure*. It rejects or is ambivalent about such criteria as *expertise, detachment*, and *civility*. Since the role of public discourse in this view is to mobilize participation among ordinary people, not merely to help elites decide, it is dubious about criteria that may have the consequence (perhaps unintended) of discouraging and excluding popular participation.

DISCURSIVE THEORY

The line between participatory liberal and discursive theories is not easy to draw, especially regarding who should be included in the public sphere. *Popular inclusion* is equally embraced by both traditions. As Cohen (1989, p. 17) puts it, "The notion of a deliberative democracy is rooted in the intuitive ideal of a democratic association in which justification of the terms and conditions of association proceeds through public argument and reasoning among equal citizens."

Jürgen Habermas, the most commanding figure in this tradition, accepts the fact that decisions on public affairs are normally made at the political center – by government agencies, parliaments, courts, and political parties. For routine decisions, it is reasonable and acceptable if these are made without extensive public discussion. But when important normative questions are at stake, it is crucial that the discussion not be limited to actors at the center of the political system. On such issues, a well-functioning public sphere should simultaneously include actors from the *periphery* as well – that is, civil society actors including especially grassroots organizations.

Within this periphery, Habermas makes a distinction between autonomous (*autochtone*) actors, characterized by a mode of association tied to the "lifeworld" of the citizens, and power-regulated (*vermachtete*) actors, characterized by formal bureaucratic relations of hierarchy.[81] The autonomous actors, by which Habermas basically means small, nonbureaucratically organized grassroots associations with little or no division of labor, are minimally mediated and closer to personal, everyday experience.

Habermas assumes that such associations will take a particular organizational form, noting that "with their informal, multiply differentiated and networked communication processes, they form the true periphery" (1992, p. 431). In this regard, his standard for what "counts" as a grassroots organization is much narrower than the participatory liberal perspective, which values groups that actively bring their members into politics regardless of their specific form of organization. For Habermas, the organizational form is important because of its contribution to the deliberative process – the less bureaucratic, centralized form serves to carry political discussion into the lifeworld of the members.[82]

Autonomous groups have a special role in the public sphere, and their inclusion is vital. These associations, Habermas writes (1989, p. 474):

> are the knots in a communication net constructed among autonomous publics. Such associations are specialists in creating and spreading practical convictions. They specialize in discovering issues of relevance to the entire society, contributing to possible solutions, interpreting values, producing good rationales and discrediting others.

Habermas assumes that these autonomous actors communicate in a different way. They are free from the burden of making decisions and

---

[81] As Habermas uses the term, "lifeworld" is in the realm of communicative action, in contrast to systems run by power or money. The lifeworld, if intact and not colonized by other systems, secures cultural reproduction, social integration, and socialization (Habermas 1984, Vol. II).

[82] In practice, the distinction may simply reflect differences in how real social movements are structured in the United States and Germany. As we saw in Chapter Five, social movement organizations in the United States are typically larger and have more of a division of labor, including a media relations division or specialist, while German social movements, being organizationally decentralized and nonbureaucratic, come closer to Habermas' ideal type.

from the constraints of organizational maintenance. This allows them, in contrast to other actors, to deliberate more freely; they can more easily take the viewpoint of other actors and respect the better arguments (Habermas 1989, p. 474).

Several years before Habermas' *Structural Transformation of the Public Sphere* first appeared in German, C. Wright Mills (1956, pp. 303–304) seems to have anticipated some of the central themes of the discursive tradition:

> In a public, as we may understand the term, 1) virtually as many people express opinions as receive them. 2) public communications are so organized that there is a chance immediately and effectively to answer back any opinion expressed in public. Opinion formed by such discussion 3) readily finds an outlet in effective action . . . 4) authoritative institutions do not penetrate the public, which is thus more or less autonomous.

Criteria concerning the style and content of public communication are at the heart of the discursive tradition. The ultimate goal is a public sphere in which better ideas prevail over weaker ones because of the strength of these ideas rather than the strength of their proponents. The normative ideal in the Habermas version is embodied in the concept of an "ideal speech situation." He insists that it is more than simply an abstract ideal that should guide practice without ever being fully achieved. It is being realized, at least in part, whenever one starts to argue in order to convince others rather than simply commanding, negotiating, suggesting a compromise, or in other ways abandoning the effort to persuade.

Gutmann and Thompson's (1996) "deliberative democracy" suggests a similar set of normative standards. Citizens must be able to transcend their narrow interest to consider what can be reasonably justified to people who disagree with them:

> Deliberation can clarify the nature of a moral conflict, helping to distinguish among the moral, the amoral, and the immoral, and between compatible and incompatible values. Citizens are more likely to recognize what is at stake in a dispute if they employ moral reasoning in trying to resolve it. Deliberation helps sort out self-interested claims from public-spirited ones (p. 43).

For the better argument to be decisive, it should not matter who is making the argument. Differences in external status or power among speakers should be bracketed – that is, put aside and ignored. There must be mutual and reciprocal recognition of each by all as autonomous, rational subjects whose claims will be accepted if supported by valid arguments. If this process is constrained by political or economic force or manipulation, or some arguments are disallowed, then participants are not taking the arguments of others seriously – and the conditions of an ideal speech situation are not being met. Thus, *popular inclusion* in the discursive tradition is justified in part by its ability to foster *deliberativeness*, the more theoretically central criterion.

Other criteria on the how and what of good public communication also flow from deliberativeness. *Civility* and *mutual respect* are required. In an ideal deliberative process, one seeks agreement when it is possible and maintains mutual respect when it is not. Mutual respect is a form of agreeing to disagree, but it demands more than simply tolerance. "It requires a favorable attitude toward, and constructive interaction with the persons with whom one disagrees" (Gutmann and Thompson 1996, p. 79).

Communitarians such as Amitai Etzioni (1996, pp. 104–105) offer similar rules of engagement for what he calls "values talk." The normative standards should "reflect the tenet that one should act on the recognition that the conflicting parties are members of one and the same community; hence, they should fight, as the saying goes, with one hand tied behind their back." These standards lead him to such specific rules as: The participants should not "demonize" one another or depict those with whom they disagree as "satanic" or "treasonous." Another rule is "not to affront the deepest moral commitments of the other groups. The assumption is that each group is committed to some particular values that are sacrosanct to it, values which must be particularly respected by others; as well as some dark moments in its history upon which members prefer not to dwell. . . . Self-restraint in these matters . . . enhances the processes that underlie moral dialogue."[83]

---

[83] All of these strands of discursive democratic theory share an underlying assumption – that the participants are part of the same moral community, sharing basic values. They assume that all of the participants deserve respect, but what of those participants who repudiate the shared values or whose ideas are not worthy of respect? Once one acknowledges that there is a boundary defining what content is included or excluded in a mutually respectful discourse, one can see that this is often contested and not consensual. Suppose that one believes that a doctor who performs an abortion is a murderer, or that a person who murders a receptionist in a women's health clinic is outside of the moral community? Then it hardly makes sense to extend mutual respect to those who defend such people. It turns out that most issues with

In addition to mutual respect, the participants in public discourse should demonstrate their readiness for *dialogue*. Dialogue, in the Habermas version, implies a discourse in which claims and assertions are backed by reasoned, understandable arguments. This implies a willingness to entertain the arguments of those who disagree. Dialogue-oriented speakers take account of the arguments of others, include some of their valid points in further refining and developing their own position, provide a full account of their reasoning and justifications so that others in turn may attend to them, and actively rebut rather than ignore ideas that they view as invalid.

Hunter (1994, p. 239) argues that the right to participate in the public sphere should be balanced and limited by a corresponding responsibility to speak appropriately:

> First, those who claim the right to dissent should assume the responsibility to debate. . . . Second, those who claim the right to criticize should assume the responsibility to comprehend. . . . Third, those who claim the right to influence should accept the responsibility not to inflame. . . . Fourth, those who claim the right to participate should accept the responsibility to persuade.

The normative standards of dialogue, civility, and mutual respect combine to promote a positive value on consensus-seeking speech. Interestingly, Guttman and Thompson (1996, p. 89) explicitly apply their model of deliberative democracy to abortion discourse:

> Accommodation calls on citizens to try to minimize the range of their public disagreement by promoting policies on which their principles converge, even if they would otherwise place those policies significantly lower on their own list of political priorities. Thus, pro-choice advocates may think that publicly funded programs that help unwed mothers care for their own children are less important than pro-life proponents do, but the pro-choice advocates should join in actively promoting these programs and other policies that are similarly consistent with the principles they share with opponents. By trying to maximize political agreement

a strong moral component involve ambiguity about who is or is not in the same moral community. Different frames give different answers and draw the boundaries of who should be extended mutual respect in different ways. The applicability of this normative standard of mutual respect depends on and assumes a consensus about the boundaries of inclusion that often does not exist in practice.

in these ways, citizens do not end serious moral conflict, but they affirm that they accept significant parts of the substantive morality of their fellow citizens to whom they may find themselves deeply opposed in other respects.

Guttman and Thompson (1996, p. 360) contrast the normative standards of deliberative democracy with a discourse that

> encourages the practice of impugning the motives of one's opponents instead of assessing the merits of their positions. . . . When the "imputation of bad motive" dominates an institutional culture, citizens do not reason together so much as they reason against one another. They reflexively attack persons instead of policies, looking for what is behind policies rather than what is in them. In a culture where moral disagreement turns so readily into general distrust, citizens are not disposed to think and act in a reciprocal frame of mind. A reciprocal perspective is important not only to enable citizens to resolve disagreement but also to enable them to learn to live with it.

The practices that they impugn are often associated with the actual mobilizing efforts of social movements that, as participatory liberal theory points out, may need to heighten contrast between positions, emphasize threats to strongly held values, and discredit the trustworthiness of government in order to encourage people to see their own political actions as necessary and efficacious.

It is worth noting that Guttman and Thompson make repeated efforts to define the boundaries of what is acceptable discursive practice more broadly than in the Habermas version. "We do not assume," they assert (1996, p. 4), "that politics should be a realm where the logical syllogism rules." They argue, for example, that deliberation can be "consistent with impassioned and immoderate speech. First, even extreme non-deliberative methods may be justified as necessary steps to deliberation. . . . Second, deliberation itself does not always have to take the form of a reasoned argument of the kind that philosophers are inclined to favor" (1996, p. 136).

Their standards of *civility* are relatively weak in comparison to those of representative liberalism. They do not demand that a priority be given to logic over emotion. They concede that their "politics of mutual respect is not always pretty . . . Citizens may find it necessary to take extreme and even offensive stands. . . . These strategies may be justified when, for example, they are required to gain attention for a legitimate position that would otherwise be ignored, and thereby to promote mutual respect in the long term" (Guttman and Thompson 1996, p. 90). Here they show recognition of the potential conflict between the norm of popular inclusiveness and the norms of deliberativeness and civility – a tension that we will examine more thoroughly later in reviewing the constructionist theory.

The civic or public journalism movement in the United States draws much of its inspiration from this discursive tradition. Lambeth (1998, p. 27), in an essay discussing civic journalism as democratic practice, suggests that if it were "to require a philosophical patron saint, Habermas . . . would appear to be a logical nominee." Haas (1999, p. 356) elaborates on this point. Habermas, she argues, implies that "the primary responsibility of journalists should be to *facilitate* [emphasis in original] public deliberations aimed at reaching rational-critical public opinions that are autonomous vis-à-vis the private sphere and the state." Or, to quote Rosen (1994, p. 376), one of the major articulators of the civic journalism project, journalists should "focus on citizens as actors within rather than as spectators to [the democratic process]."

The discursive democratic tradition assumes that an ideally conducted public discourse should produce a gradual consensus over time. People are encouraged to think in terms of the collective good rather than their private good and search for areas of agreement in an atmosphere of mutual respect. If consensus is ever possible, these conditions should produce it, since conditions such as these promote an atmosphere designed for conflict resolution. At a minimum, a good public discourse should produce a working consensus – enough of an agreement on the general direction of public policy to remove it from the public agenda.

While this tradition shares with representative liberalism a belief in the positive normative value of *closure*, it assumes that achieving a consensus is both desirable and attainable, at least in the ideal case. Only under these conditions does closure after a decision make sense:

> According to the perspective of discourse theory, majority opinion must maintain an internal link to the praxis of argumentation. . . . A majority rule should only be formed in a way that its content can be considered as a rationally motivated but fallible result of a temporarily finished discussion about the right direction to solve a given problem (Habermas 1992, p. 42).

In sum, the discursive tradition shares the value of *popular inclusion* with participatory liberalism but, unlike that tradition, views this as a means to a more deliberative public sphere rather than as an end in itself. Inclusion of speakers from the periphery should contribute to an active dialogue between center and periphery and foster more deliberative speech. *Deliberativeness* is the core value of this perspective, and it involves recognizing, incorporating, and rebutting the arguments of others – *dialogue* and *mutual respect* – as well as justifying one's own. *Civility* and *closure* are also values that this tradition shares with representative liberalism, but these norms are interpreted more loosely: Civility is not tantamount to emotional detachment, nor is closure desirable if consensus has not been achieved.

CONSTRUCTIONIST THEORY

Writers in this tradition share a critical approach, questioning existing arrangements and categories to see if they conceal hidden inequalities. This body of theory is indebted to Michel Foucault in identifying discourse as the practices of power diffused outside formal political institutions, making use of seemingly neutral categories of knowledge and expertise to control others as well as to construct the self as a political actor.

Many of the most active theorists in this tradition such as Nancy Fraser, Seyla Benhabib, and Iris Marion Young begin from feminist premises and develop their theories in part to explain and critique the marginality of women in politics. They point out that the very definition of "politics" situates it as a separate "sphere" apart from and in some ways "naturally" opposed to private life. From this perspective, the sharp boundary drawn between "politics" and everything else that happens in life serves to obscure the continuities of power relations across these domains and is itself, therefore, a discursive use of power.

On the question of who should participate and when, they share the strong normative value placed on *popular inclusion*. Many would go so far as to privilege those who are marginalized in society, since they can offer the "double vision" of those who are "outsiders within" the system (Collins 1991; Smith 1990). Indeed, inclusion is at the heart of this tradition, and those who represent it are especially wary of theories that celebrate practices about how one should communicate that may conflict with the inclusion norm.

This emphasis on those who are marginalized from the core institutions of formal politics stresses how ordinary people are actually engaging in politics in diverse arenas of their lives – by what they buy, wear, eat, or use to travel. Hence, it is appropriate for the media to seek out and validate the politics of everyday life as well. While the participatory liberal tradition wants grassroots actors to mobilize and speak to the media in the media's terms, the constructionist tradition wants the media to step out of its routines for dealing with the powerful and actively seek out other perspectives at the grassroots. Benhabib (1992, pp. 86–87), for example, is critical of the way in which participation is understood in the Republican civic virtue tradition, contrasting it with:

> a conception of participation which emphasizes the determination of norms of action through the practical debate of all affected by them. . . . This modernist understanding of participation yields a novel conception of public space. Public space is not understood agonistically as a space of competition for acclaim and immortality among a political elite; it is viewed democratically as the creation of procedures whereby those affected by general social norms and collective political decisions can have a say in their formulation, stipulation, and adoption. . . . Democratization in contemporary societies can be viewed as the increase and growth of autonomous public spheres among participants.

Constructionists challenge the desirability of a single public sphere, preferring the idea of multiple independent public spheres. Dialogue in a single public sphere is not necessarily as desirable as autonomous and separate cultural domains, or "free spaces" in which individuals may speak together supportively and develop their identities free of the conformity pressures of the mainstream. Although the issues are framed somewhat differently, the constructionist tradition shares the high value placed on *empowerment.*

How the *popular inclusion* criteria applies to general audience mass media, and the type of elite-oriented newspapers that we consider here, is less clear. As we interpret this tradition, it shares the priority of high inclusion for grassroots, *autochtone* actors, who introduce knowledge drawn from the lifeworld, perhaps on even a broader range of "routine" decisions than Habermas would include. It also shares with the participatory liberal and discursive traditions the inclusion of social movements and ordinary citizens. However, unlike the participatory liberal tradition, which sees public discourse as a resource for mobilizing individuals to join a separate "political" sphere, this constructionist tradition sees the political as spilling across the artificial boundary between public and private.

Families, cultural activities, and even lifestyles are political in the sense of having power relations woven through them. One of the tasks of critical theory, Fraser (1989) argues, should be to expose ways in which the labeling of some issues and interests as "private" limits the range of problems, and of approaches to problems, that can be widely contested in contemporary societies. Because politics resonate throughout an individual's "private" life, a good public discourse would include individual speakers who would name and exemplify such connections for others. This tradition thus actively rejects the representative liberal criterion of *expertise*.

Cohen (1995, pp. 79–80) applies this argument to the abortion issue:

> Every modern feminist movement has explicitly attempted to reshape the universe of discourse so that women's voices could be heard, women's concerns perceived, women's identities reconstructed, and the traditional conceptions of women's roles, bodies, and identities, as well as the male dominant supported by it, undermined . . . The abortion issue encompassed all of these concerns. It quickly became apparent that this issue threw down the gauntlet to the traditional universe of discourse because it signified a fundamental change and the demand of "control over our own bodies" expressed more than a desire for equal rights. [It] symbolized a demand for autonomy regarding self-formative processes, for self-determination, and for bodily integrity; in short, for the right for women to decide for themselves who they want to be including whether and when they choose to become mothers.

With regard to content and style, constructionists do not devalue deliberation and formal argument in discourse, but they are concerned that unexamined assumptions about how discourse should be conducted may, intentionally or inadvertently, limit who participates. While public discourse should be conducted by public rules, these norms need scrutiny lest they return women's concerns and voices to the "backyard" of politics (Holland-Cunz 1994). More specifically, if cultural norms of how discourse should be conducted differ by social location, then these norms have the potential to silence those who habitually use alternative modes. The issue here is not the inability of some groups to provide rational arguments for their beliefs, but that narrative and other preferred modes may be unfairly devalued and the "impartiality" of technical expert discourse may conceal an unacknowledged political agenda.

This is a central theme in constructionist and feminist readings of Habermas. Fraser (1995), in her discussion of Habermas' arguments on "the colonization of the lifeworld by systems" in welfare state capitalism, notes that the key to an emancipatory outcome lies in the replacement of normatively secured contexts of interaction by communicatively achieved ones. Normatively secured forms of action are "actions coordinated on the basis of a conventional, prereflective, taken-for-granted consensus about values and ends, consensus rooted in the precritical internalization of socialization and cultural tradition." In contrast, communicatively achieved actions are "coordinated on the basis of explicit, reflectively achieved consensus, consensus reached by unconstrained discussion under condition of freedom, equality, and fairness" (Fraser 1995, p. 28, drawing on Habermas 1984). From this vantage point, the norms of deliberativeness that Habermas advances as well as the standards of civility that representative liberals offer are both seen as too limited in that they reflect conventional rather than inclusively forged standards.

The tendency to forget the socially constructed nature of such categories as public and private – that is, to treat them as natural categories describing the world – blinds us to their potential for exclusion. Indeed, Habermas has conceded this point.[84] Public and private spheres have a gendered subtext in which the public realm is a male sphere and its norms and practices reflect this in subtle (and often not so subtle) ways to exclude "feminine" modes of participation. The norms and practices governing policy discourse privilege certain forms of presentation over others, and thus selectively disempower certain categories of speakers.

In particular, the normative standards regarding policy discourse derive from specific institutional contexts in Western society – in particular, parliaments and courts. As Young (1996, p. 123) observes, "Their institutional forms, rules, and rhetorical styles have defined the

---

[84] "Empirically, I've learned most from the criticisms that point to the exclusionary mechanisms of the public sphere, liberal or postliberal.... An analysis of the exclusionary aspects of established public spheres is particularly revealing..., the critique of that which has been excluded from the public sphere and from my analysis too: gender, ethnicity, class, popular culture" (Habermas 1992, p. 466).

meaning of reason itself in the modern world." Claims of universality are made, but the norms of deliberation are culturally specific and often operate as forms of power that silence or devalue the speech of some people.

> The norms of deliberation privilege speech that is dispassionate and disembodied. They tend to presuppose an opposition between mind and body, reason and emotion. They tend falsely to identify objectivity with calm and absence of emotional expression.... These differences of speech privilege correlate with other differences of social privilege. The speech culture of white, middle class men tends to be more controlled, without significant gesture and expression of emotion. The speech culture of women and racial minorities ... tends to be more excited and embodied, more valuing the expression of emotion, the use of figurative language, modulation in tone of voice, and wide gesture (Young 1996, p. 124).

Young calls her model of a broader normative standard "communicative" to distinguish it from the narrower "deliberative" model. She makes an especially strong case for the importance of *narrative* as an appropriate and desirable form of policy discourse. "Narrative," she writes, "fosters understanding across ... difference without making those who are different symmetrical." It reveals experiences based on social locations that cannot be shared fully by those who are differently situated. She offers the example of wheelchair-users making claims on university resources. "A primary way they make their case will be through telling stories of their physical, temporal, social, and emotional obstacles" (Young 1996, p. 131).

Storytelling promotes empathy across different social locations. Similarly, Sanders (1992) points out that narrative complements arguments, while tending to be more egalitarian since everyone is an expert on their own experiential knowledge. Thus the positive criterion for the content and style of a good public sphere that this perspective offers is the inclusion of narratives that directly bridge the lifeworld and the sphere of formal politics, undercutting both the separation between these spheres and the power relations that produce and maintain that separation (Smith 1987, 1999).

Style of public expression is also a matter of class, as the distinction between the bourgeois public sphere and the plebian one suggests. Constructionists worry that the original insight about the exclusionary character of the bourgeois public sphere becomes lost in allowing elements of rhetorical style to determine the definition of rational-deliberative discourse. Ryan reminds us that, in the nineteenth century, "American citizens enacted publicness in an active, raucous, contentious, and unbounded style of debate that defied literary standards of rational and critical discourse," and that "Those most remote from public authorities and governmental institutions and least versed in their language sometimes resort to shrill tones, civil disobedience, and even violent acts in order to make themselves heard" (1992, pp. 264, 285–286).

Civility in discourse is a matter of socially secured agreements to conform to the local culture, and such local and specific cultures are deeply imbued with power. What is normal in public discussion in some places is rude in others; and what is considered a normal way of showing respect in some venues seems mannered and arid in others. Constructionists remind us that in identifying normative criteria about deliberative discourse we must be careful to attend to different dimensions of power, including those that act discursively to restrict content and participation through the limits that they place on acceptable style.

Like critical theorists in the participatory liberal tradition, constructionist writers fear premature closure and false consensus. Gould (1996, p. 74) argues that the emphasis on consensus as a desirable outcome in the Habermas model "does not value but aims to override difference." Mouffe (1996, p. 248) echoes the point: "To negate the ineradicable character of antagonism and aim at a universal rational consensus – that is the real threat to democracy." In their search for a model that revels in the diversity and pluralism of actually existing democracies, constructionists broaden the type of desirable outcomes beyond the ability to produce policy outcomes.

Meehan (1995, p. 17), using the concept of an ideal speech situation as her starting point, asks how it might be broadened to accommodate "a feminism truly committed to a plurality of perspectives arising from differences." The ideal that she suggests is "an arena for exploring, comparing, and working not towards consensus, but towards building a community in which we work together to develop solutions to concrete problems which will allow the diversity of our beliefs and values to be served." Consensus, in this tradition, is not always desirable, and it always requires critical analysis in evaluating it.

Conversational constraint is a similarly flawed concept in this analysis, resting as it does on the principle of "dialogic neutrality." This principle, as Ackerman (1989, p. 11) develops it, requires that "no reason advanced within a discourse of legitimation can be a good reason if it requires the power-holder to assert that his conception of the good is better than that asserted by his fellow citizens, or that regardless of his conception of the good, he is intrinsically superior to one or more of his fellow citizens." Benhabib (1992, p. 84) argues that this principle

> is too restrictive and frozen in application to the dynamics of power struggles in actual political processes. A public life conducted according to the principle of liberal dialogic neutrality . . . would restrict the scope of public conversation in a way that would be inimical to the interests of oppressed groups. All struggles against oppression in the modern world begin by redefining what had previously been considered private, nonpublic, and nonpolitical issues as matters of public concern, as issues of justice, as sites of power that need discursive legitimation.

Conversational constraint and pseudoconsensus can work against the outcome of public discourse that is most important here: furthering the process of building a discursive community that allows a diversity of beliefs and values to be served.

In sum, the constructionist view of a well-functioning public sphere begins by questioning the separateness of the public sphere at all. Public discourse should question the boundaries of "the political" by a strong norm of *popular inclusion*, particularly incorporating socially marginalized individuals and social movements that can both name and exemplify the linkages between public action and private life. The norm of *expertise* is rejected explicitly, and the standards of *deliberativeness* and *civility* are qualified by subjecting them to critiques based on higher values of popular inclusion and *empowerment*.

Rather than *dialogue* and formal argumentation, constructionists particularly value *narrative* as a characteristic of content and style that challenges both the diffuse power relations of daily life and the concentrated power of disembodied formal political institutions by revealing the connections between them. Legitimating the language of the lifeworld in discourse privileges the experiential knowledge of ordinary citizens and contributes to their empowerment. Finally, *closure* after a decision is suspect since it can so easily suppress the diversity of expression that vitalizes democracy.

Table 10.1   *Normative Criteria in Democratic Theory*

Theory	Who	What and How	Outcome
Representative Liberal	Elite dominance Expertise Proportionality	Free marketplace of ideas Transparency Detachment Civility	Closure
Participatory Liberal	Popular inclusion	Empowerment Range of communicative styles	Avoidance of premature closure
Discursive	Popular inclusion	Deliberativeness Dialogue Mutual respect Civility	Closure contingent on consensus
Constructionist	Privilege the periphery/ oppressed	Empowerment Narrative	Avoidance of premature closure

CONCLUSION

We summarize this excursion through democratic theories of the public sphere by grouping the criteria suggested into three broad categories: Who should be included, what is the ideal style and content, and what should happen if the process works as it should? For some criteria, there are advocates and those who are indifferent, but virtually no dissenting voices. For others, there is significant challenge to the normative standard. We hope to clarify the nature of the disagreements by distinguishing criteria that are sometimes conflated. Table 10.1 summarizes the differences among the four traditions.

On the who question, the representative liberal tradition stands alone in valuing *elite dominance* over stronger and more active versions of *popular inclusion*. The representative liberal tradition positively values *expertise*, while constructionists suspect it as a way of managing discourse to maintain existing relations of dominance and subordination. The other two traditions are essentially indifferent to the extent to which experts are included, as long as their participation does not displace that of ordinary individuals, speaking from the lifeworld.

Representative liberal theory suggests a criterion on how public discourse space should be allocated: *proportionality*. It should be distributed proportional to voting strength or size of representation. Discursive theory suggests that it should be divided among actors in the center and periphery. The participatory liberal tradition is vague on this question, but constructionists emphasize the perspective of the "outsider within" as particularly valuable. Thus it should be given special attention and represented even more than mere proportionality would suggest (Leidner 1993).

On the content of the discourse, none of these traditions would defend a priori restrictions. For the representative liberal tradition, the discourse should make visible to the public what its representatives are doing so that they can be held accountable – the criterion that we have labeled *transparency*. Other traditions do not reject this but emphasize its insufficiency.

There are major disagreements, however, on the *empowerment* criterion. For the participatory liberal theory, it is a central responsibility of public discourse to engage citizens in public life. For the constructionist tradition, empowerment is equally central and even more broadly interpreted, while it is less emphasized but implicit in the discursive tradition. However, it is explicitly rejected by the representative liberal theory as a normative criterion for public discourse.

There are also major differences on the how question. The representative liberal tradition calls for a strong form of *civility* and *emotional detachment* as the proper form of communication. The discursive tradition endorses a weaker variant of civility, emphasizing *mutual respect* but not necessarily detachment. The other traditions are not opposed to civility but emphasize its potential conflict with *popular inclusion* and *empowerment*, on which they place a higher value.

Deliberativeness, the highest value in discursive theory, includes the criterion of *dialogue*, a process in which one provides fully developed arguments for one's own position and takes seriously and responds to the arguments of others. The participatory liberal theory does not reject dialogue but calls for a *range of communicative styles* to promote empowerment, a higher value. Similarly, the constructionist theory does not reject dialogue but is wary that emphasizing it can delegitimize other forms. In particular, it can delegitimize *narratives* of personal experience and other preferred forms of communication in the lifeworld, thereby silencing women and other culturally excluded groups.

Finally, on the outcome question, the representative liberal tradition places the strongest value on *closure*. Discursive theories also value closure but contingent on it arising from a consensus that has emerged through a deliberative process. The other traditions are more concerned with *avoiding premature closure*. The participatory liberals fear an imposed closure by the powerful that serves to silence the less powerful. The constructionists fear an imposed closure that suppresses diversity, a continuing source of vitality for a democracy.

In the following chapter we operationalize the previous criteria using abortion discourse. We then examine how well they are met in Germany and the United States and how much this has changed over time.

CHAPTER ELEVEN

Measuring the Quality of Discourse

In this chapter we analyze empirically the three sets of questions raised in the previous chapter – who speaks, how and what they communicate, and what is the outcome of the discourse – to compare the extent to which the normative criteria of the different theoretical traditions are met in Germany and the United States.

THE INCLUSION ISSUE

Who speaks? We have already operationalized this with the concept of standing and have largely answered it in Chapter Five (summarized in Table 5.1). State and party actors are 75% of the speakers in Germany compared to 40% in the United States. The residual 25% in Germany is given over mainly to the Catholic and Lutheran churches and to experts, with a negligible 2% going to Pro and Anti movement organizations. The discourse focuses heavily on legislative and judicial actions, keeping citizens well informed about what their representatives are doing. This discourse looks very much like what the representative liberal model would consider ideal.

In the United States, in contrast, state and party actors are a minority and Pro and Anti movement organizations make up about one-quarter of all speakers. The U.S. newspapers are three times as likely as German newspapers to quote individuals who are not spokespersons for anyone but themselves. U.S. discourse is slightly higher in including experts (6%, versus 4% in Germany), but experts are practically the only individuals who are quoted in Germany. They are only 40% of the individuals with standing in the United States. These results all suggest that the German discourse comes closer to meeting the elite dominance norm of representative liberalism while the United States better accords with the norm of popular inclusion that is valued in the other traditions.

Our earlier results do not address the criterion of *proportionality*. In the United States this criterion is difficult to evaluate, since the legislative and executive branches are separately elected and may have different majorities, and because considerable debate focuses on state rather than federal action. The standard of representation to which the share of the discourse might be compared is thus not obvious. In the United States, polling data are sometimes used to set the criterion of what "most Americans" think, but just what survey question is to be used or how the distribution of answers are to be read is contested by both sides. The absence of a persuasive standard of just what is to be represented proportionally, we argue, is part of what gives journalists in the United States more responsibility for creating their own norms of balance, an issue to which we return in the next chapter.

This issue of a standard of representation is not so amorphous in Germany, where the parliamentary system connects the executive with the legislative majority and where abortion is regulated legally at the federal level. Does German discourse, which meets the elite dominance criteria so well, also meet the proportionality criterion? The various parties appear to think so. For example, Christina Schenk, *Bundestag* Representative from the PDS, pondering a question on mass media work, notes that:

> A differentiated depiction of our position – that's rare. One has to say that this coverage [of the abortion issue] . . . is apparently driven by the presumed role and significance of the parties. So the Conservatives have, let's say, ten lines and then the SPD gets five and then the PDS, you're glad if you get more than a line, you know (Interview, May 1996).

Table 11.1 largely supports the assumption of proportionality, but only if *both* the legislative share of seats and which party is governing are taken into account. There is a clear advantage in standing for the dominant governing party – the SPD in the early years and the CDU/CSU after 1980. In addition, there is a rough proportionality here, with the two major parties who hold between 84% and 92% of the seats in parliament commanding between 75% and 100% of all standing given to party-identified actors.

But there are also some variations from this trend. The FDP, which is typically the junior partner in coalition with either the CDU/CSU or

Table 11.1. *Proportionality of Bundestag Seats and Media Standing by Legislative Period*

Legislative period	1972	1976	1980	1983	1987	1990
CDU/CSU						
Standing	39.3	35.3	58.8	62	51.9	51.7
Seats	45.4	49.0	45.5	49	44.8	48.2
(net)	(−6.1)	(−13.7)	(13.3)	(13)	(7.1)	(3.5)
SPD						
Standing	49.0	49.1	41.2	15.0	23.2	22.5
Seats	46.4	43.1	43.9	38.8	37.3	36.1
(net)	(2.6)	(6.0)	(−2.7)	(−23.8)	(−14.1)	(−13.6)
FDP						
Standing	11.7	15.6	0	19.0	15.7	20.9
Seats	8.3	7.9	10.6	4.8	9.4	11.9
(net)	(3.4)	(7.7)	(−10.6)	(14.2)	(6.3)	(9.0)
Greens						
Standing				4.0	9.2	5[a]
Seats				5.4	8.4	1.2
(net)				(−1.4)	(0.8)	
PDS						
Standing						5[a]
Seats						2.6

[a] Since in this legislative session the only Green representatives that were seated were those representing districts from the former GDR, and thus actually the pre-electoral coalition formed among Green, feminist and citizens' movements, we computed standing for the PDS and Green/Alliance90 combined. Thus, the net disadvantage is not computed.

the SPD, gets considerably more standing than its share of the vote or its position in government would explain. For example, in the heat of the postunification round of reform in the legistative period beginning in 1990, the FDP was overrepresented in its standing to a greater degree than were the Christian Union parties.[85] The distinctiveness of the FDP's position on abortion, which was discussed in Chapter Nine, and

[85] The one period in which the FDP fails to get standing is 1980–83, when the total amount of discourse is at its lowest point.

Table 11.2. *Center and Periphery in U.S. and German Articles*

Speaker types included	Germany	United States
Only political center	60%	27%
Center and periphery	26%	44%
Only periphery	15%	29%
Number of articles	712[a]	1124

[a] In sampling German articles, we used a lower length threshold than for U.S. articles. These very short "news in brief" German articles were excluded from this analysis to make sure that we were comparing articles of similar minimum length in the two countries.

its possible role in breaking a coalition and thus bringing down a government, both appear to give it more standing in the eyes of journalists than strict proportionality would demand. But overall, the proportionality criterion of the representative liberal theory appears to be met quite well in Germany.

The Habermas version of discursive theory suggests that discourse should simultaneously include both actors from the political center – state and party speakers – and those from the periphery, especially grassroots, autonomous actors. We can address this criterion directly by looking at the spectrum of speakers included in a single article. We treat speakers who represent any branch of government (executive, legislative, or judicial) or any political party as speaking for the center, and those representing formal associations and social movements or simply speaking for themselves alone as constituting the periphery. Rather than counting the number of speakers of each type, as we did in Chapter Five, here in Table 11.2 we look at how articles as units are constructed to include speakers of both types or only one type.

A majority of the articles in Germany (60%) include only state and party speakers, while less than half that number (26%) includes both types simultaneously. In the United States, in contrast, about one-quarter (27%) contain only speakers from the political center while close to half (44%) have both types in the same article. Since there are more speakers from social movements and other groups and associations in civil society in the United States than in Germany, it is not surprising that there are fewer articles using only speakers from the center in Germany and more from the periphery in the United States. What is surprising here is the much greater proportion of articles in the United States that put both types of speakers together in the same article. This can be read as a kind of implicit dialogue between center and periphery that occurs within individual articles, or simply as a less sharp distinction between the types of sources that journalists rely on for covering substantively different content. Whichever interpretation one favors, on this criterion, U.S. discourse clearly comes closer to meeting the Habermas ideal type than does German discourse.

On the issue of inclusion, our results are quite clear. Again, German media discourse fits the criteria emphasized by representative liberal theory quite well. U.S. discourse fits the criteria of *popular inclusion* emphasized by the other three traditions much better than does German discourse. Additionally, U.S. newspapers bring both center and periphery together in the same articles, which is at least a precondition for dialogue between them.

CONTENT AND STYLE

In this section we concentrate on the question of how people should speak and what should be communicated.

EMPOWERMENT

Participatory liberal and constructionist theories stress *empowerment*. We define this as the extent to which the mass media provide support and encouragement of a sense that, by acting together, grassroots constituencies can influence the policies and conditions that affect their daily life. This is difficult to operationalize, and we resort to two indirect measures of it.

Our first measure of empowerment looks at the proportion that social movement actors are of all actors in civil society.[86] By restricting the arena in which we look for empowerment to just civil society, we are already taking into account the stronger dominance of state and party actors in Germany than in the United States and therefore not simply measuring inclusion again. But a larger share, and especially an increasing share, of all civil society speakers who are coming from social movements should be an indication not only of greater mobilization

---

[86] We are also excluding journalists themselves from this calculation.

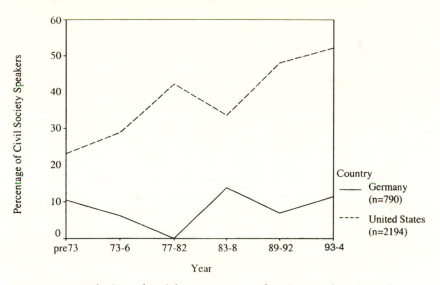

Figure 11.1. Inclusion of social movements as framing speakers in civil society. (Note: Noncivil society speakers were excluded.)

and activity by such groups but also the legitimacy that they have to participate in shaping the discourse. Thus we also restrict this measure, unlike our indicators of standing in Chapter Five, to just those speakers who are actively framing the discourse.

As we see clearly in Figure 11.1, the proportion of social movement speakers who are both allowed to and willing to participate in saying what abortion is about is always higher in the United States than it is in Germany, but it also climbs relatively steadily in the United States while not changing very much in Germany at all. The share of social movement speakers more than doubles in the United States, from just over 20% to over 50%, while it hovers more or less around 10% in Germany through this entire period. More of the substantive content of the discourse about abortion is coming from social movement speakers in the United States, which suggests that they are more empowered to participate, and are becoming more so over time.

Our second measure of empowerment looks specifically for language that asserts the political rights of the speakers themselves. To focus on the language of empowerment means to focus on just those speakers who are claiming more rights to self-determination, which, as we saw earlier, women in both Germany and the United States are doing. Looking at the extent to which these claims to personal self-

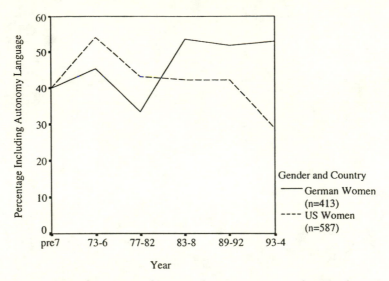

Figure 11.2. Use of autonomy language by women Pro and Neutral speakers. (Note: Only Pro and Neutral speakers are included and journalists are excluded.)

determination (whether in the gendered form typical in Germany or the nongendered form prevalent in the United States) are increasing or decreasing among women speakers is another way to see if the discourse is empowering. As Figure 11.2 indicates, the results on this measure are somewhat mixed.

Both German and American women who are Pro or Neutral on balance are fairly likely to include some of the language of autonomy at all times, and the differences in levels of use are not very great between the two countries. In the United States, however, the high point of such discourse comes in the immediate post-*Roe* period and declines, although not very steeply, thereafter. German women who are taking a Pro or Neutral position are more likely to include some reference to autonomy and self-determination in the later rather than earlier years of the debate. These women speakers in Germany are, as we saw in Chapter Seven, predominantly speaking as representatives of the state and the parties.

Thus there is an indication of increasing empowerment for women in Germany that is particularly focused on women who are now empowered to speak in more formal roles in the center of the polity.

Those women who are not in these formal institutional roles, however, always speak the language of self-determination to a greater extent than these political insiders do, and while the number of cases is small, they do not show any increase in autonomy language over time.

Overall, our measures suggest that the discourse about abortion in the United States fits the criteria of empowerment when looking at social movements and civil society, but that German discourse fits the criteria of empowerment for those who do succeed in gaining entry into the polity. Neither discourse can be said to fit or fail to meet this criterion across the board.

CIVILITY

Representative liberalism and, to a lesser extent, discursive theory emphasize the value of *civility*. Our operationalization of this criterion focuses on the use of "hot button" language, that is, words that are likely to outrage opponents such as accusations of murder, persecution, or barbarity.[87] It turns out that there are no significant differences between Germany and the United States in the use of such language in these very respectable newspapers. Overall, only 5% of German speakers use such language while very slightly fewer (4%) speakers use it in the United States. Our data suggest some decline in incivility over time. It is at its lowest level in Germany after 1989 and virtually absent from the discourse after 1992. In the United States, it was only relatively high in the period before 1973 and has remained at quite low levels since then, never exceeding 4%.

This result says nothing, of course, about the kind of incivility that may occur when abortion-rights activists, escorting pregnant women to health clinics, confront anti-abortion demonstrators face to face. Nor does it say anything about what happens in tabloids or on talk shows or in private communications. Incivility, at least as it appears in these elite newspapers, is comparatively rare. As we will see in the next chapter, this may be a norm that journalists feel an obligation to uphold in what they choose to publish. However, it is also the case that the impact of incivility is felt more strongly than its quantitative share of the total discourse would suggest. The issue of the journalists' role in how norms of civility are met is an issue that we pursue further in the next chapter.

---

[87] Details are provided in the Methodological Appendix.

Table 11.3. *Dialogic Structure of Articles by Country*

Composition of Articles	Germany	United States
One direction only	75%	58%
Only Anti[a]	38%	19%
Only Pro[b]	29%	35%
Only Neutral	8%	4%
Both Directions	25%	42%
N =	744	1190

Note: German "news in brief" articles were excluded as well as nonframing speakers.

[a] Some articles may also include Neutral speakers.
[b] Some articles may also include Neutral speakers.

DIALOGUE

Discursive theories are united by their emphasis on the criterion of *dialogue*. A dialogic process is one in which the participants provide fully developed arguments for their own position and take seriously and respond to the arguments of others. We used multiple operationalizations of this process in examining our data.

One variable, *dialogic structure*, measures the presence of speakers with opposing views in the same article. This is, at best, a measure of potential dialogue, and the extent to which it is realized depends on whether in such a forum speakers are actually any more likely to engage with each other's arguments. They are simply sharing the same space in a newspaper article. Table 11.3 shows the composition of articles in terms of dialogic structure.

By this measure, United States articles are much more likely to have a dialogic structure (42%) than German articles (25%). The articles that include only one side reflect the general tilt that we have described earlier – toward including just the anti-abortion side in Germany and just the pro-abortion-rights side in the United States. In both Germany and the United States, articles that contain both core and periphery speakers are also much more likely to use the more dialogic structure of having both Pro and Anti speakers in the same article. Thus, 37% of German articles with mixed sources include both points of view, compared to only 20% of articles that are based just on speakers from the political core, and 61% of U.S. mixed source articles do compared to only 33% of those based on these core speakers. The inclusiveness of sources therefore appears to have a positive impact on the inclusiveness of diversity of arguments in articles in both countries.[88]

Our more direct measures of dialogue look at what speakers actually say. The *rebuttals* variable defines utterances as dialogic when they refer to and argue against ideas that they oppose. Arguments that "the fetus is not a human person" or "women have no right to decide" or "abortion cannot be treated as a private matter" are all grouped together as rebuttal ideas.[89] We measured the use of rebuttals in three ways: (a) by speakers as a rate per 100 utterances, (b) by the percentage of speakers who use at least one rebuttal argument, and (c) by the average number of rebuttal arguments per article.

Germany is considerably higher than the United States on the first rebuttal measure, rate per utterance. For every 100 utterances in Germany, there are 31 specific rebuttals of opposing ideas, compared to 24 in the United States. If we look instead at the percent of speakers in both countries who include at least one rebuttal argument, the German advantage disappears (29% versus 28% in the United States). Apparently, German speakers are not more likely to include any rebuttal at all, but they do use more rebuttal arguments on average than do U.S. speakers.[90] And, if we change our unit of analysis to the article, we find that there is no difference by country as a whole: Both U.S. and German articles average 1.31 rebuttal arguments. If there is an overall advantage for one country or the other on the rebuttal variable, it is too slight to appear consistently using similar measures to detect it.

However, the absence of a difference between countries in the aggregate obscures the extent to which a dialogic article structure (one that puts Pro and Anti speakers in the same article) contributes to greater dialogue in terms of what speakers say and how they say it. Table 11.4

---

[88] But as this comparison makes clear, the placing of Pro and Anti speakers in the same articles is something that all U.S articles, not just those that bring in speakers from the political periphery, are more likely to do than the German ones. The greater use of opposing speakers in the structure of U.S. articles is not merely an artifact of the different types of sources used in each country.

[89] See the Methodological Appendix for a full list.

[90] In both countries, those speakers who include both Pro and Anti frames in their utterances are much more likely to be including a rebuttal (51% of U.S. speakers and 56% of German speakers of this type do, compared to about 23% of other speakers). Recognition of the arguments of the other side is clearly part of the preconditions for contesting their validity, and thus inclusion of both Pro and Anti arguments by a speaker is also a measure of engaging in what Habermas would recognize as real dialogue. Such recognition is never very high (just under 20% of speakers in both countries meet this criterion).

Table 11.4. *Rebuttal Rate and Incivility by Country and Dialogic Structure of Articles*

	Germany	United States
Rebuttals per article[a]	1.31	1.31
With both Pro & Anti speakers	2.23	1.80
All others with framing	1.01	.96
Percent of articles with any incivility[b]	10%	10%
With both Pro & Anti speakers	13.7%	12.5%
All others with framing	8.7%	8.5%

Note: German "news in brief" articles were excluded.
[a] Rate of rebuttal ideas per article, for all articles with framing speakers (Germany $n = 744$, U.S. $n = 1189$ articles).
[b] Percentage of articles with any framing speakers in which any speaker includes any "hot button" language (Germany $n = 744$, U.S. $n = 1189$ articles).

compares articles in both countries that either do or do not have a dialogic structure in terms of their discursive quality. As we can easily see there, articles that do put opposing speakers together are richer in direct rebuttals as well as higher in incivility in both countries.

As we already saw, the dialogic structure is one that is more prevalent in the United States, and it also is more likely when both core and periphery speakers are being included in the same article. Thus the "debate" type article, which U.S. journalistic practices support, is also one that on average promotes some interaction, both positive and negative, between speakers representing contending perspectives. Whether this is a true dialogue in the Habermasian sense is more dubious. A third measure of discursive quality, whether speakers recognize the arguments of the other by including ideas drawn from the other side in their own speech, even without endorsing these ideas, shows only small differences and in the opposite direction.[91]

Regardless of which of the three measures of rebuttals we take as our indicator of dialogue, the results of examining variation over time are striking. In Germany, dialogue is always highest during the period in which the issue is off the state agenda and state and party actors yield

[91] This would also make sense in a debatelike article, since the presence of the opposite side in the article makes it less necessary for the journalist to quote the speakers' references to what they are opposing.

Table 11.5. *Rebuttal Rate and Incivility by Co-Presence of Center and Periphery and Country*

	Germany	United States
Rebuttals per article[a]	1.39	1.35
Center only	1.28	1.04
Periphery only	1.40	1.33
Both	1.61	1.54
Percent of articles with incivility[b]	10%	10%
Center only	7.5%	4.9%
Periphery only	11.7%	11.2%
Both	15.3%	12.1%

Note: German "news in brief" articles were excluded.

[a] Rate of rebuttal ideas per article for all articles with framing speakers (Germany $n = 638$, U.S. $n = 1088$).

[b] Percentage of articles with any framing speakers in which any speaker includes any "hot button" language (Germany $n = 638$, U.S. $n = 1088$).

the stage somewhat to civil society actors. Ironically, dialogue is apparently highest in Germany precisely when no decision is pending! For the United States, while the dialogic structure of articles actually increases over time, all three measures of inclusion of rebuttal show a small but consistent decline over the same period, and these declines are a bit more marked in the late 1980s and early 1990s than in earlier periods. The contribution of a debate-type structure to fostering an actual debate between speakers, at least as measured by the use of direct rebuttals of their arguments, therefore has become much smaller as the debate has dragged on in the United States.

Habermas also argues that the simultaneous presence of speakers from the center and the periphery will improve the deliberativeness of the discourse. We can test this by dividing the articles with two or more speakers into those that include only one type of speaker or both. In Table 11.5 we compare the deliberativeness in articles of different types in the two countries in regard to rebuttal arguments, using the rate per article. The Habermas hypothesis finds some support. Rebuttal ideas are highest in both countries when articles include speakers from both the center and periphery and lowest when only speakers from the center are included.

By contrast, however, the level of incivility, measured as the inclusion of any of hot button language in an article, is highest when actors from the periphery are included, alone or with actors from the core. This is especially true in Germany, where the relatively few articles that include speakers from both the core and the periphery have comparatively high levels of incivility. Looking to the characteristics of the speakers who use uncivil speech helps to explain this finding, since this language disproportionately comes from Anti speakers (14% of all German Catholic speakers and 8% of U.S. pro-life movement speakers include at least one hot button idea).[92] When we look at these particular articles, the speaker using such uncivil rhetoric is often being combined with legislative or governmental speakers who are decrying the use of such inflammatory language.

The strongest effect of combining speakers from the center and periphery in the same article, however, is to construct a context in which both Pro and Anti ideas are represented in the same space. In both Germany and the United States articles that have speakers from both the center and the periphery are much more likely to also be the articles that include both Pro and Anti speakers. These are also the articles that include proportionally more rebuttals and more incivility. Thus dialogue, if not civility, appears to be fostered by the inclusion of both the core and periphery together.

NARRATIVES

The constructionist tradition emphasizes the criterion of personal *narratives* as a form of discourse – as a way of bridging the world of individual experience and discourse on public policy. We did not code articles specifically for the presence of personal narratives, so our analysis here is less systematic and more qualitative. The use of narrative is clearly more normative for U.S. journalists than for their German counterparts. It is common for U.S. journalists to provide personal profiles of activists, considering them outside of their public roles.

---

[92] There are 207 German Catholic speakers and 282 American pro-life speakers, which makes a sufficiently large set of speakers to compare. Only 8% of German pro-life movement speakers include such uncivil language, but the low number of such speakers ($n = 23$) makes any comparison of percentages suspect. However, the number of U.S. Catholic speakers ($n = 207$) is great enough to suggest that hot button language is less frequently used by these speakers (5% include it) than by their German counterparts.

The Los Angeles Times, for example, featured a long profile of Faye Wattleton, the president of Planned Parenthood, emphasizing her religious background as the daughter and granddaughter of fundamentalist ministers. The story describes her experiences as a graduate student in nursing witnessing a 17-year-old young woman dying after a botched abortion in the days before it was legal. Her personal life is treated as relevant, including her time-bind in raising her 11-year-old daughter alone, after a divorce.

Similarly, Kate Michelman, the director of NARAL, is profiled in a 1989 *Los Angeles Times* article by Karen Tumulty. Again her personal life is treated as a central part of the narrative – her Catholic background, including nine years of Catholic school, and her desertion by her husband, leaving her with three young children. Most importantly, the story includes her own difficult decision (in 1969) to have an abortion when she realized that she was pregnant with a fourth child and at a loss to how she would support the three children she already had (11/10/89).

The political point of the story comes in her discovery that the difficult decision was not her decision to make. She had to convince a panel of doctors that she had never met before, "relating the most intimate, humiliating details of her private life. And, in one final indignity, she had to get written permission from the man who had walked out on her." "One of the most important decisions of my life was out of my hands," Michelman recalls. "I finally understood how little control women really had over their own lives" (11/10/89).

In an attempt to gain some idea of the frequency of such personal narratives, we examined the 46 U.S. articles in the final year of our data analysis, 1994. We found that 13% of them contained such personal narratives, providing details of private experiences and using them to draw political conclusions.

The German journalistic norms for elite newspapers would make such details of one's private life off limits and inappropriate. To get some evidence on this, we systematically examined the articles from 1973 and 1988, looking for narrative elements. In 1973, the focus of coverage was on discussions of abortion reform in the *Bundestag*, but the main arena was broader in 1988. In particular, it included the controversial prosecutions for illegal abortions in Memmingen, described in Chapter Two.

We found very little that could be considered personal narrative, even in the broadest possible definition. There was not a single article in 1973 in which women appeared as speakers discussing their experiences with abortion, the law, or their family situations. If there was any reference to the lifeworld at all, it was indirect and mediated through the voice of experts. One article in the *FAZ* gave voice to a male scientist who reported the social and demographic profile of women using counseling services without any women ever being quoted directly (*FAZ*, 7/11/73).

The 1988 picture was similar, even though the prosecutions in Memmingen provided a potential hook for consideration of the experiences of women. The prosecutions focused on the alleged abuse of the social necessity indication for granting an abortion. By U.S. media norms, one would have expected some stories about individual women who had been threatened with or actually prosecuted for illegal abortions. Instead, there were few references to the actual situation of women, and they were filtered through the voice of an expert. In one article in the *FAZ* on the Memmingen case, a male social worker was cited: "Among further possible motives for seeking an abortion, the social worker named the feeling among very young women that they were not yet mature enough to raise a child or the fear of unmarried mothers that they would lose their jobs and be relegated to welfare" (*FAZ*, 9/21/88). These same comments by the social worker were also carried in an article in the *SZ*.

The *SZ* also included an article citing counselors at a pregnancy counseling clinic: "According to the experience of the counselors, the majority of the women who come to them do want to have the child. But they face massive pressure from their environment. They expect no support from their parents, partner, employer" (*SZ*, 1/30/80). Again, such women themselves were not interviewed. And even in this period of heightened concern over what social justifications for abortion meant in practice, these three articles were the only ones in which women's experiences with this rule were treated as newsworthy.

Even by the loosest definition of establishing a connection between the lifeworld and the domain of formal political policy, there were only two additional articles that might be included from the 221 that we reviewed. In each of these, a politically active person was described in more personal terms. In one case, a CDU male legislator was described in a subordinate clause as the father of six children (*SZ*, 9/17/88). In the other, it was reported that "the (CDU Party) convention was also impressed by the delegate from Baden-Württemberg, who introduced herself as the mother of six children and called on the delegates not to produce unrest in the discussion of this important issue by demanding more stringent laws, but to have patience and wait for a change in conscience" (*FAZ*, 6/15/88). This latter article at least transmited the speaker's own effort to use her lifeworld experience to create credibility for her political claims.

In sum, regarding *narrative* as a criterion for a good public discourse, the German abortion discussion in elite newspapers failed to even come close. The lifeworld is far removed from these pages, and even in situations where some minimal attention to life experience was given, it was mediated through experts' and journalists' interpretations. Even representative liberals might express some concern over how little evidence was presented to the public about how policies were being implemented and what costs and benefits these implementations brought at a personal level. Clearly, the constructionist standard of narrative is better met in the United States. Personal narratives, so much a normal part of U.S. media discourse on abortion, are virtually nonexistent in German elite newspapers.

To summarize our results, U.S. media discourse is somewhat better on the criterion of *empowerment* for ordinary people, either as nonexperts or representatives of social movements, but the German discourse offers self-determination as a language of empowerment that women in public office have particularly turned to their advantage. Still, neither country seems particularly high. There is no clear edge for either country on *civility*, nor does it appear that including actors on the periphery in either country contributes to improving the level.

Our results on *dialogue* present a mixed picture. German speakers have a higher rate of rebuttals per utterance, but there is no difference in the percentage of speakers who include at least one rebuttal argument or in rebuttals per article. The co-presence of speakers from both the core and the periphery, which is more typical in the United States, contributes to dialogic structure. This structure in turn is associated with increasing both the rate of rebuttals per article and the inclusion of incivility in both countries. The positive effect of a dialogic structure on fostering more direct rebuttals declines over time in the United States, regardless of the measure that we use, and, likewise, the use of rebuttals is highest in Germany when the issue is not being debated in the legislature and overall media attention is low. Debate-type structures do seem to foster some dialogue, but more so in Germany, where they are rarer, and less so in the United States, especially in more recent years.

The differences seem clearest on the *narrative* criterion emphasized by constructionists with U.S. journalists including personal stories as a routine part of their coverage and German journalists avoiding it with very rare exceptions. On the criteria of content and style, U.S. discourse most clearly has an edge on constructionist criteria and, less clearly, on participatory liberal criteria. Representative liberals would tend to find the low levels of incivility in elite newspapers in both countries reassuring, but they would favor the formal style of argumentation found in Germany over the more narrative style that is typical of the United States. By our measures, both countries fail to foster real dialogue in critical periods, and neither country has a clear-cut advantage in meeting the criteria set by discursive theory.

THE CLOSURE ISSUE

We operationalize the criterion of *closure* as a sharp drop in the volume of public discourse following authoritative action by state actors. We already know from earlier chapters that this very much fits the wavelike pattern of German discourse. Following legislative and judicial actions in the mid 1970s and early 1990s, the total amount of abortion discourse in these newspapers sharply declines. U.S. abortion discourse does not decline significantly in the aftermath of *Roe v. Wade* and remains relatively high throughout most of the period, reaching a peak in 1989 with the *Webster* decision. But even after *Webster*, there was only a modest decline. Clearly, German discourse meets this representative liberal criterion better than the United States.

It is more difficult to assess whether German discourse meets the criterion of discursive theory that closure should flow from a deliberatively achieved consensus. We use *focusing* as our measure of consensus. Focusing measures whether the discourse is converging on particular ways of framing the issue, which is reflected in declining heterogeneity over time in the distribution of the eight basic frames described in Chapter Five. The flatter the distribution among frames, the higher the overall pattern scores on the heterogeneity index.[93] The lower the heterogeneity index, the more the discourse is focused.

Figure 11.3 provides the results over time for the discourse as a whole and within the sets of ideas favoring a Pro or Anti position. We ask, has

---

[93] This index is based on the Herfindahl-Hirschmann index (*h*-index) of industrial concentration. For a discussion of this index, see Taagepera and Ray (1977). The *h*-index is exactly the same as the *aw*-index (Lieberson 1969).

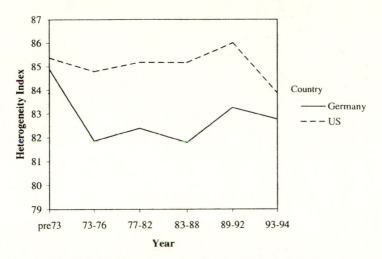

Figure 11.3a. Focusing of framing over time by country (all frames).

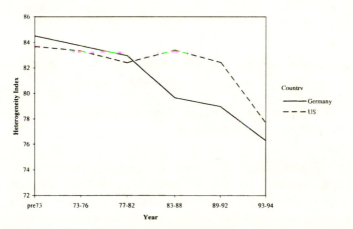

Figure 11.3b. Focusing of framing over time by country (Pro frames).

the discourse as a whole become more focused, and has each camp become more focused? The overall index is slightly higher for the United States (that is, there is less focus on particular frames than in Germany) and there is no evidence here for convergence over time.[94]

---

[94] The one exception to this generalization is Germany at the time of the first Constitutional Court decision. Between the first period (1970–1972) and 1973–1976, when the decision was reached and responded to by the *Bundestag*, there was a noticeable drop in heterogeneity that was evident not within the separate camps but between them, as seen in the figure that combines both groups of speakers.

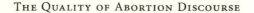

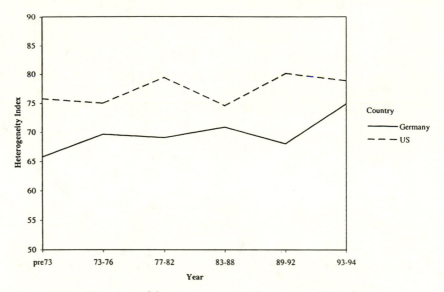

Figure 11.3c. Focusing of framing over time by country (Anti frames).

Within camps, there is some indication of increasing focus on the Pro side, especially in Germany, where the index is significantly lower during the last half of the period. In the United States, there is increasing focus only in the most recent time period. Anti-abortion ideas fail to decline on the heterogeneity index in either country and show some tendency to increase.

In sum, there is little evidence here of increased consensus as measured by the focusing variable. Thus we conclude that the closure shown in Germany by the considerable drop in the amount of coverage given to the issue after a decision does not seem to reflect a greater level of focus or consensus on what is important. The more stringent criterion of closure only after a consensus does not seem to be met.

There is less closure in U.S. discourse, but public opinion data suggest that there may be more popular consensus than appears in public discourse. Hunter and Bowman (1994) review the polls available at the time, emphasizing the ambivalence about abortion that most people feel. These data suggest an uneasy consensus that abortion should be permitted but discouraged. Expressed as a policy position, this is captured by the oft-repeated assertion of spokespersons for the Clinton administration that "abortion should be safe, legal, and rare." Many U.S. speakers in our data did not in fact speak in absolute terms about rights, as we saw back in Chapter Six, but about a range of moral and practical considerations for individuals and for society as a whole.

Those who do see irreconcilable principles at stake do continue to resist closure and want to keep the abortion issue on the public agenda. For these advocates on both sides in both countries, there is no desire for closure evident in their speech. However, there are more venues available in the United States than in Germany to raise the issue as a formal political decision and more attention given by the media to speakers other than formal decision-makers. Both of these discursive opportunities allow the issue to remain more open for coverage in the public forum in the United States and to sink more readily from sight in Germany. Additionally, the U.S. Supreme Court's *Webster* decision in 1989 has kept the issue open for continuing debate in two ways. First, by allowing states to require restrictions that do not place an "undue burden" on the choice of the pregnant woman, they have shifted the battleground even more than before to the 50 state legislatures. Second, the "undue burden" standard has yet to be fully explicated by federal and state courts. While the ambiguity provides an impetus to continuing struggle, the ability of organizations engaged in this struggle to draw media attention to specific cases in which some explicated standard needs to be applied, and to bring such cases to a multitude of state and federal courts, also helps to keep the nature of this standard open to discussion and revision.

CONCLUSION

We have been able to measure and systematically analyze many of the criteria discussed in the previous chapter, including *inclusion, expertise, proportionality, empowerment, dialogue, civility,* and *closure*. We did not code our materials for the presence of *narrative*, but we assessed the frequency of story-telling using sample years and emphasized the qualitative differences between Germany and the United States on this variable. We did not measure directly such criteria as *free marketplace of ideas, transparency, emotional detachment, and mutual respect,* but we have our shared judgments on these based on our immersion in the discourse.

REPRESENTATIVE LIBERAL THEORY

In most respects, German discourse meets the criteria very well. It is dominated by accountable state and party actors, supplemented by experts and representatives of the Catholic and Lutheran churches. It is carried on with little incivility. Not all ideas appear, of course. There are no voices, for example, calling for compulsory abortions for "life that is not worthy of life." But within a broad range, the sponsors of different policies are given free reign to offer the most persuasive arguments that they can muster and do so.

The discourse provides extensive and detailed accounts and commentary on what the people's representatives are doing in both countries. Anyone who takes the time to read the abortion stories in these four newspapers will be extremely well informed on what is going on in the decision-making process. It also meets the standard of proportionality, if an allowance is made for overrepresentation of the party that is in power at the time. The media gives the parties roughly the amount of standing that their share of seats in the *Bundestag* would warrant, although it gives somewhat more attention to the ideologically distinctive and politically critical FDP than its share of the votes alone would earn for it.

The focus of the coverage is, however, only on passing a law, not actually enforcing it. In Germany, one would have little sense of how these policies operate in the various *Länder* where they are implemented. Although there were hundreds of criminal prosecutions for illegal abortions in the period covered in our study, there were no stories told about the specifics of the individual cases that led to the woman's decision to seek an illegal abortion or to the state's decision to prosecute. On this aspect of transparency, German discourse fails to meet the representative liberal standard.

Finally, German discourse provides just the kind of closure that is advocated by this tradition. Authoritative decisions should provide a clear signal that this discussion is completed and public discourse should move on to other topics. With minor exceptions, then, German media discourse is a good approximation of the representative liberal ideal.

PARTICIPATORY LIBERAL THEORY

U.S. discourse comes much closer than German discourse in meeting the criteria emphasized by this tradition. Civil society actors, including grassroots organizations and ordinary people, are given a lot of standing, in later years just as much as the people's elected representatives. The social movements that represent an engaged citizenry grow also as a proportion of voices in civil society and become more influential in framing the issue, not merely achieving standing on their own. Being included in the same articles as speakers from the core, speakers from social movements in the United States have apparently gained legitimacy as "players" in the political process. The result that is least consistent with the notion of empowerment is the small decline in the language of self-determination among U.S. women advocates of abortion rights. Government decisions do not force an artificial end to efforts by mobilized citizen groups to achieve policies that they consider better. Advocates of this tradition should have few complaints about the quality of U.S. abortion discourse, relative to the German debate.

DISCURSIVE THEORY

The answer to which country best fits the criteria of the discursive theory is more complicated. On the issues of inclusion, U.S. discourse is clearly a better fit. It does better in providing a balance of center and periphery, providing much more standing for civil society actors, especially grassroots ones.

On the issue of deliberativeness, the evidence is ambiguous, with no clear-cut advantage for either country. On dialogue, in particular, different measures show slight advantages for one country or the other or no difference. If there is a difference in the amount of dialogue between countries, it is not robust enough to show up consistently. Incivility is not very high in either country, nor does it increase over time as some have charged. The debatelike structure that the American press favors, in which both sides appear in the same article, contributes to more dialogue in the form of direct rebuttals of the other side, but it does so less than in Germany, where this structure is rarer, and it does so less effectively over time.

The closure that German discourse provides does not flow from a deliberatively achieved consensus and, hence, is not the closure that the model envisions. But the ongoing U.S. discourse does not fit this standard any better since it shows little tendency to produce a consensus that should lead to voluntary closure. The absence of a tendency toward consensus is a failure of the deliberative process in both countries, but one that is more visible in the United States because coverage continues more.

CONSTRUCTIONIST THEORY

U.S. discourse comes much closer than German discourse in meeting the criteria emphasized by this tradition. The criteria that it shares with the participatory liberal tradition – popular inclusion, empowerment, and the avoidance of premature closure – are better met in the United States. U.S. discourse also is stronger on overcoming the artificial distinction between the public and private realms, and in legitimizing the language of the lifeworld and experiential knowledge through personal narratives. Rather than a focus on elected representatives and formal passage of laws, U.S. discourse particularly offers a transparency to the lifeworld via narratives that are often based on court cases applying the law and underlining the personal consequences of decisions.

In the next chapter we look at what participants and journalists involved in the abortion issue say about the quality of the discourse and the extent to which they apply any of these diverse criteria emphasized by the different variants of democratic theory.

CHAPTER TWELVE

Metatalk

Here we examine metatalk – discourse about discourse. What do participants see when they step back and observe the very discourse that they are involved in shaping? Their subjective view of media coverage of the abortion issue has its own reality, especially when it is widely shared.

We have observations from two different kinds of participants here: journalists and spokespersons for advocacy organizations. Journalists in our newspaper samples often write about the discourse, both in news accounts and commentaries. We have culled their observations looking for implied standards of quality. In addition, we have interviews with a small number of American and German journalists who have frequently written on one or more aspects of the abortion issue for the newspapers in our sample. The interviews solicit their observations on the abortion discourse and on how they and their colleagues have performed. Advocates are sometimes quoted in the media, commenting on the discourse rather than on abortion per se. In addition, we have their responses to interviews that focus on their perceptions of the media.

Metatalk examines a discourse with an implicit set of normative standards – that is, it praises or condemns from the standpoint of some often-unstated ideal that is used to assess what is observed. We examine two questions here: (a) What are the similarities and differences in the normative standards in Germany and the United States? and (b) To what extent are these normative standards congruent with the criteria from democratic theory discussed in the last two chapters?

COMMON STANDARDS

Some normative standards are shared even though those who comment on them may see them as being met in different ways and to different degrees. We begin our examination by looking at the discursive norms that are most similar and gradually turn to areas of greater difference.

ACCURACY

As a general norm, the desirability of accuracy is completely shared in the two countries. Journalists and their sources should get their facts straight and the discourse should be free of inaccuracy and misinformation. They should write so that they can be understood clearly. But there are subtle and important differences in how these norms are translated into journalistic practice.

German journalists, for example, tend to rely more on press handouts and do less independent research (see Köcher 1986). A failure to carry out independent research and "fact-checking," then, might be regarded as sloppy reporting in the United States while the same performance probably would be less harshly criticized in Germany. Accuracy in reporting includes the choice of credible sources. Credibility is not only a judgment about accuracy but also a judgment about what credentials should give one standing. We have already seen that institutional position is much more important than experiential knowledge in defining credibility for German journalists.

Even factual accuracy rests on institutionally defined validators of claims about the world. When there is high consensus on the institutional validators, such as official bodies of physicians on medical claims, the competent journalist provides "factual accuracy" by honoring their claims. When there are competing validators, journalists have a problem, and the norms that they apply in making judgments are a reflection of the different cultural and journalistic validation norms in their respective countries.

Once one accepts the idea that journalists, through their reporting practices, bestow *facticity* on claims about the world, it is easy to understand their concern with the credibility of sources (see Tuchman 1978). The most frequently cited criticism of journalistic accuracy and competence involves the reporting of factual claims as having been validated by "appropriate" sources when they have not been. The idea of checking "facts" typically means finding additional, more persuasive, validators for claims made by advocates.

In our interviews, some U.S. journalists took their profession to task for its reporting of claims related to a procedure generally referred to as "partial birth abortion."[95] Karen Tumulty, a former staff writer for *The Los Angeles Times* and currently the congressional correspondent for *Time Magazine*, notes that "It was about a year into the debate before someone went and looked at how often is this procedure happening and under what circumstances. That is the first question everybody should have asked and they should not have accepted either side's version of the truth. I mean, that is not how we handle other issues" (Interview, May 1998). "Facticity" here means finding additional sources – disinterested hospital administrators or medical associations who have kept systematic statistics and are, therefore, credible validators of factual claims for the journalists themselves, no less than for their readers.

Advocates also know that journalists value accuracy and attribute their successes with the media in part to their credibility. Frances Kissling, of Catholics for a Free Choice, for example, explains her group's media standing as follows: "One, we never lie. A reporter knows that the information we give them is accurate, that they are not gonna get caught because they use something that we gave them. That's one important piece" (Interview, May 1997).

Wanda Franz, of the National Right to Life Committee, also acknowledges that providing accurate information to journalists is critical to their standing as the primary spokesman for the "pro-life movement, which is what we are. And I think they also found out that they get accurate information . . . so our people are real essential." She argues that "there are reporters out there who really do their best to report accurately – to the point where you don't have any idea what their position on abortion is." At the same time, she complains that her organization's view of reality is not treated as fact by many journalists: "I think there is a certain level of regard with which, especially Washington-based journalists hold NRLC, but you don't see it translated into accurate reporting necessarily" (Interview, May 1997).

Helen Alvare, spokeswoman for the National Council of Catholic Bishops, on the abortion issue, blames the media for what she sees as

---

[95] The problem of finding neutral language asserts itself again here. This term is used by anti-abortion advocates but has no clear medical definition. It refers to at least some uses of a medical procedure called "intact dilation and extraction," but this term, preferred by abortion rights advocates, is not generally understood by the audience and violates the norm of writing to be understood. The anti-abortion advocates have succeeded in this naming contest by making their label the clearest and most effective way of communicating to the general reader.

inadequate fact-checking: "I would also like to see less of the too-ready acceptance of statements about statistics or claims made in a particular debate, without investigation behind it. The partial birth debate was the paradigm example of that, but it only revealed what has always been true . . . too little investigation is done about claims being made" (Interview, July 1997).

Because German journalists rely more on institutionalized sources and less on their own news-gathering routines and fact-checking, the issue of accuracy does not appear to be as salient for them or for their sources. It was not raised by advocates as either a means to improve their access to the media or as a criticism of what the media did report.

CIVILITY AND MUTUAL RESPECT

This is a strong theme in the journalist commentary in both countries. In Germany, there are some interesting differences between our two newspapers. While they share the same standards, different actors draw their ire for violating them, in predictable fashion.

The more conservative *FAZ* directs its editorial complaints mainly against feminists and other abortion rights supporters (73%, $N = 15$). The more liberal *SZ* finds abortion opponents, especially the Catholic Church, to be the primary norm violators (65%, $N = 26$). Both papers also criticize advocates close to their own position in the political spectrum but in milder terms. The *FAZ*, for example, does criticize the Catholic Church but less harshly than the *SZ*.

"Respect for the conscientious earnestness of opposing opinions" is how the *FAZ* (4/27/74) articulates this principle of mutual respect. One should not treat those who disagree with one as enemies but as part of the same moral community. And nothing seems to violate this more clearly than the invocation of Holocaust imagery in the discussion of abortion.

When the Bishop of Münster compared the abortion reform efforts of German legislators to the Nazi euthanasia program, the *SZ* called it "an outrageous insult – to the politicians, to the women, and to the Nazi's victims – and this in the name of the Church, which wishes to be taken seriously in its statements in the abortion debate" (5/26/92). When the Archbishop of Fulda used the term "holocaust of children" in a speech on abortion, the *SZ* labeled it an "evil term" and called it the "height of verbal escalation" and a "libel" (7/25/88). When a Bavarian official made a comment that, while the Nazis killed Jews, abortion involves killing babies and was worse because it involved "killing one's own," the comment was quoted six different times as journalists deplored it and various sources issued statements condemning it.

Equating abortion with child murder draws similar criticism as a violation of norms of discourse. In 1988, several Catholic bishops instigated a campaign to toll church bells as an admonition against abortion. The *SZ* found it especially disconcerting that these "bells against dialogue" will be tolled on December 28th, the day the Church commemorates the children of Bethlehem murdered by King Herod.

> The Bishops must be aware that with their campaign, they are contributing to further polarization within the Church and society. It is inevitable that all those who consider §218 in its current version to be acceptable or at least tolerable will be morally marginalized. Rather than seeking dialogue, and thus standing up for unborn life, with their provocative tolling the Church leaders are presumably putting off precisely those on whom they would have to rely in order to change something (12/27/89).

Ultimately, in response to such criticism, a majority of the bishops voted to discontinue the campaign, "because it was open to misinterpretation, because too many had experienced it as an accusation rather than a warning" (Interview with Rudolf Hammerschmidt, spokesperson for the German Bishop's Conference, August 1996).

We asked German journalists whether the opposing sides "treated each other in a civilized way and with respect." Friedrich Fromme (*FAZ*) commented that "It was a debate dominated by mutual respect although there were, naturally, exceptions. These exceptions were hardly noticed, however, because there was an overarching consensus that the debate would be carried on with mutual respect" (Interview, March 2000). Günter Bannas (*FAZ*) had a similar view: "With some exceptions, the debate was handled with respect . . . Overall, one could say there was respect, people respected each other and did not claim that, on the one hand, women should go back to the kitchen or, on the other side, that people wanted more dead embryos" (Interview, March 2000). Stephan-Andreas Casdorff (*SZ*) provides examples where words or actions cross the boundaries of legitimate debate:

> Every effort to present a political opponent as a criminal is wicked. But, on the other side, tough arguments are quite appropriate. Politics is not a choral society full of harmony. If I want to change something in society, then I have to be able to stand the battle.

There are people who legitimately but passionately advocate their positions. . . . Conflict is appropriate – one has to be able to endure that – but always with an effort to find a solution. . . . When the right-to-lifers appeared at the CDU convention, or when anyone who was for liberalization was accused of killing babies, that was hitting below the belt (Interview, March 2000).

One sees, in the United States, similar calls for civility from the very beginning of the abortion debate. By 1967, an active movement for the reform of state abortion laws had emerged, especially in New York state, where a bill had been introduced to broaden a law that allowed abortions only when necessary to save the life of the mother. The bill would have allowed abortions in cases where the infant would be born with severe handicaps or where there was substantial risk that the woman's physical or mental health would be impaired by continuing the pregnancy.

One article, focusing on the debate in the New York legislature, reported comments by an opponent of the bill that allowing the abortion of "potentially defective children" was like the "elimination of defective Jewish persons" by Nazi Germany. Since the bill's sponsor, Albert Blumenthal, and several active supporters of reform were Jewish, the remarks were predictably explosive. *The New York Times* article (3/9/67) quotes one supporter, Joseph Kottler, "his voice shaking with anger," as saying he was "deeply shocked that supporters of the abortion reform bill had been compared to Nazis."

New York State's eight Catholic bishops issued a pastoral letter, read at masses throughout the state, urging Catholics to "do all in your power to prevent direct attack upon the lives of unborn children." *A New York Times* article focused on a response to this letter and other statements by Catholic Church spokesmen equating abortion with murder and genocide. The responding organizations included the Protestant Council of the City of New York and three Jewish organizations.

In a fitting symbol of ecumenism, the Rev. Norman Vincent Peale of the Protestant Council read the statement at a press conference held at the Union of American Hebrew Congregations. "We do not feel," the group complained, "that the cause of ecumenism is best served by attributing to us the advocacy of murder and genocide." Calling for respect for each other's differences, they pointed to their shared concern for the sanctity of human life even though they may disagree "on the point at which life begins and the conditions under which it is theologically or socially allowable to end it" (*NYT*, 2/25/67). This call for civility and mutual respect in conducting a dialogue on abortion also claimed that the Catholic bishops and legislative opponents of reform overstepped the bounds. The statement emphasized that they were not asking the bishops to change their views on abortion but "we do wish them to respect our beliefs based on our religious traditions and our consciences." They called for "better methods of communication . . . for dialogue about our differences."

A 1971 article indicates again the early presence of the civility issue. This time it was the Boston Archbishop, Humberto Medeiros, who precipitated the charges by calling the abortion reform bills recently passed by New York and other states as instituting a "new barbarism." The Reverend Robert West of the Unitarian Universalist Association criticized the archbishop for "hurling epithets such as 'barbarian'" and regretted that opponents of abortion had "been reduced to frantic and fanatic name-calling." Other religious leaders also were quoted as complaining about "the particular way" in which the archbishop expressed his opinion. These were, in effect, claims that the rules of civil discourse have been violated. Note how easily the characterization of liberalized abortion laws as barbarism became transmuted into calling those who supported such reform barbarians.

Painting opponents as undeserving of moral respect is the danger to which accusations of incivility point, and the violence that punctuates the American debate on abortion is often laid at the feet of those who use inflammatory language, particularly the anti-abortion movement. The groups in the movement that we interviewed unanimously rejected these charges, and instead pointed to individuals who are given a forum in less respectable news outlets, such as talk shows. For example, Flip Benham of Operation Rescue, referring to Paul Hill, a supporter of violence who later shot a doctor himself, says,

He's not with any organization. He's just a guy that says that Michael Griffin [the man who shot Dr. Gunn] . . . [that] what he did was right. And now Phil Donahue says "Ah ha!! Saying just what I want. To paint these people as –" And so [Paul Hill] pours gasoline on this fire and whooomp. And he's on every radio and TV talk show speaking for the pro-life movement. He was never a leader in the pro-life movement. Nobody ever *heard* of this guy and now the media finds him, digs him up. And now he's saying "Yup. It's all right. It's the way we gotta do it. We gotta go shoot abortionists." Well, nothing could be further from the truth. (Interview, June 1997)

Whether because the more legitimate movement organizations to which these newspapers give standing rarely use inflammatory speech or because these newspapers are careful about transmitting it, there is no evidence in our data to support any link between acts of violence, which increased in the early 1990s, and incivility, which occured with equal, but low, frequency, throughout the debate.[96] Uncivil speech is also not distinctive to the United States, and the relatively rare instances that we did identify in both countries were invariably surrounded by calls from journalists and others for a return to a more respectful way of dealing with differences of opinion.

Frances Kissling, of Catholics for a Free Choice (CFFC), commented that "civil discourse on this issue is really important and is sorely lacking. [pause] Sorely lacking." But her remarks remind us that standards for what constitutes civil public expression are different in the United States and Europe. The food fight journalism of American talk shows does not play well with European audiences, she suggests. "They don't like that in Europe. They want civil discourse. Even I am too aggressive sometimes on British television, on British radio – and they scold me. Then I behave myself" (Interview, May 1997).

At the same time, she also described a dramatic action (the baptism on the church steps of a baby whom the bishop had refused to allow local priests to baptize because the mother was an abortion rights advocate) as a useful strategy, distinguishing provocation and mobilizing language from attacks on others: "We still believe in being provocative and do so . . . And, I mean I think this speaks also to generally how the issue does or doesn't get covered, not just for CFFC but for other organizations. I'm still pretty willing to say the outrageous not just for the sake of saying the outrageous but because it makes sense" (Interview, May 1997).

The type of provocations to which she referred were clearly judged more harshly in Germany than in the United States, whether this be bell-tolling or any other demonstrative action by either side.

---

[96] It appears in fact very slightly higher in the beginning years rather than later ones, but the differences are small. Note also that incivility in the mass media forum is entirely a different matter than calls for violence within a segment of the social movement's own media, be these books such as Michael Bray's *A Time To Kill* (Advocates for Life Ministries 1994) or Web sites.

DIALOGUE

For many observers, civility and mutual respect are important because they create the necessary conditions for a genuine dialogue in which participants who disagree listen to each other and address each other's concerns. What observers sometimes see instead is a dialogue in which people are not engaging each other. It is not so much a dialogue of the deaf as one in which participants are saying, "I hear your answer but you are asking the wrong question."

"These discussions are going around in circles," complained the *SZ* (4/26/73), "not least because the participants have a predilection for countering one another's arguments with arguments that come from quite different levels of the issue and are thus at cross purposes. If, for instance, one person says, 'After the egg cell has been fertilized we are dealing with independent life,' then another will retort: 'Section 218 should be done away with because rich women go to England anyway.'" Although the writer did not use our language of framing, he clearly expressed how discussants talk past each other when they are using different frames.

In a 1991 *Los Angeles Times* article, Elizabeth Mehren described a forum held at Boston College, characterized as "a decidedly Catholic institution," bringing together Helen Alvare, the director and chief spokesperson for the Secretariat of Pro-Life Activities of the National Conference of Catholic Bishops, and Frances Kissling, the president of Catholics for a Free Choice. Although Kissling is a half-generation older, the two women had much in common to begin a dialogue. Alvare is a lawyer who specialized in commercial litigation before taking her present job and was pursuing a doctorate in theology at Catholic University as well. Kissling as a teenager entered a convent, intending to become a nun, but left before taking her vows. In spite of clear disagreement, they were not likely to regard their antagonist as outside of their own moral community.

Yet neither woman remembered the occasion with any fondness, nor was there any likelihood that either would want to repeat it. Alvare challenged the authenticity of the Catholic nature of Catholics for a Free Choice and resisted providing the kind of legitimacy that the Boston College forum provided. Kissling was skeptical about the ability of such debates to promote any genuine dialogue. Alvare directly denied any potential for dialogue with CFFC: "A conversation presumes an encounter, and encounter presumes the possibility for openness to the others' ideas. And on our part we are not open to the idea of killing and we never will be. And so, what's the point?" (Interview, July 1997).

While journalists typically blame the participants for producing a shouting match instead of a genuine deliberative process, advocacy groups from across the spectrum see the problem as inherent in media practices. Media norms pit one side against the other and emphasize conflict, avoiding the voices of moderation and reason within the movement. Journalists, in this view, play the role of a *tertius gaudens*, the third party who gains by the fight of others. The gain, in this case, is through creating a polarized pseudo-dialogue of dramatic conflict to sell newspapers.

Carol Campbell, speaking for the National Abortion Federation, described her feeling of "just being forced into this forum of 'us against them,' and I really hate that! You know how diplomatic I try to stay and I see the sides to every issue" (Interview, August 1997). Darrel Figuera, of Planned Parenthood, voiced a similar frustration. "Now it has to be that if you go on, then they have a Gary Bauer [from the conservative Family Research Council] on as well. We'll no longer participate because it just sets up a debate situation. You never get anywhere. You don't get to say what you came on to say and you're just responding to all the charges the other side is hurling at you, because that's all that they ever do" (Interview, October 1997). Jay Heavner of the Religious Coalition for Reproductive Choice echoed this response. The media, he suggested, "want to have a really hot and heavy debate with sparks flying" (Interview, June 1997).

Opponents of abortion have similar complaints against the media. "It seems to be basic journalism that you really try to paint black and white because grey is not really that interesting," suggested Serrin Foster of Feminists for Life. "The business of the media is to paint polar opposites, [not] to create solutions."

In sum, there is a good deal of consensus among advocates that we are often provided with a pseudo-dialogue rather than the genuine one that we should have, but journalists and advocates generally point the finger of blame for this sorry state at each other.

CLOSURE

Journalists in both countries seem to share the belief that issues have a natural life cycle and that public discourse about them should move toward some sort of resolution. Talk has gone on too long when it simply goes around in circles, with the same arguments being repeated constantly. Journalist metatalk takes on a tone of weariness.

But consider the following: Calls for ending a discussion are never politically neutral. Silence favors the status quo. In the period before *Roe* in the United States, public silence favored the continuation of state laws in which abortion was typically illegal except to protect the life of the pregnant woman. Breaking the silence was part of a strategy of abortion reform. After *Roe*, a call to end the debate is a call to accept the new status quo of legalized abortion and favors supporters of abortion rights in the United States, while in Germany calls for ending public debate favor those who accept the restrictions imposed in the status quo. Keeping the issue from falling off the U.S. public agenda is part of a strategy to end or restrict legalized abortions, while Germans with interests in both more or less regulation would want to try to keep the issue visible. Calls for closure, then, can reflect discomfort that the issue is being discussed at all and comfort with the status quo rather than weariness with a discourse that has gone on too long.

In Germany, it is especially striking how early in the process the calls for closure came. During the first wave of abortion reform, an expert commission was created and in 1970 a group of legal experts proposed alternatives to §218. The majority suggested the legalization of abortion in the first trimester after a counseling process (the *Fristenlösung*); the minority suggested legalization only under specific circumstances, (*Indikationslösung*). In addition, the German Women's Law Association (*Juristinnenbund*) proposed a very liberal reform with "almost total absence of prosecution" at around the same time.

Even before the commission had held its first hearings, the value of public discourse on the issue was being called into question. Similar claims were made in 1973 and 1974, before the *Bundestag* had reached a decision. There was no implication that the *Bundestag* discussion should follow a free and open debate in which all sides have a full opportunity to present their views in the period before a decision is reached. This is premature closure even by representative liberal standards. When the *FAZ* said in July 1990 that "There were no new arguments and the old ones have been stated a hundred times over" (*FAZ*, 7/2/90), it is helpful to know that they also commented in April 1974 that "no new insights" could be discerned (*FAZ*, 4/26/74).

Journalists for the less conservative *SZ* were more positive in their assessment of the discourse. We asked Heidrun Graupner (*SZ*) whether she felt that there was a learning process in the debate or whether it had gotten redundant and run out of gas. "I'd be inclined to say there was a learning process," she responded. "Even in comparison to other public debates?" we asked. "Perhaps in comparison to the debate in the 70s with the slogan, 'My belly belongs to me.' In comparison to that, the arguments have gotten more differentiated and complex" (Interview, February 2000).

Graupner's observations suggest a consensus-driven closure but activists' observations suggest more resignation than consensus. Karen Schöler of the Federal AWO[97] agreed that there is diminished conflict and intensity in the discourse and reduced public interest. When asked why, she responded:

> Resignation is something I perceive among women, who say "we can't do more, we've tried for so long, and now we have to come to terms." The counselors, the counselees, and also the public have all come to terms with the new law, that's my thesis. There is no more strength left, and also an inner resignation, we can't do anything (Interview, January 1996).

Given the support for pre-decision closure, it is not surprising that the call for post-decision closure is even stronger. German journalists, more than their American counterparts, are likely to use the Constitutional Court decision or a legislative act as the marker that an issue has been dealt with and that further talk is beside the point. While this is often implicit rather than stated, a writer in *FAZ* articulated it very clearly:

> A court judgment has the task of making peace. Opinions can differ just as much as on whether the decision is completely right, as they can anyway of what is "right" and what is "just." The dispute cannot, however, continue unceasingly. The verdict of the Constitutional Court must be accepted, even if the judges of this court are fallible human beings. (2/25/75)

The call for closure and the tone of weariness is also quite pronounced in the metatalk of American journalists, although it does not appear as early in the process. In 1990, David Shaw of the *Los Angeles Times* wrote a four-part series on "Abortion and the Media." In prepar-

---

[97] *Arbeiterwohlfahrt* [Workers' Welfare], a welfare and counseling organization affiliated with the SPD and the trade unions.

ing it, he interviewed a number of high-ranking media executives and discussed with them their coverage of the abortion issue.

Many expressed the wish that the issue would simply go away. Paul Friedman, executive producer of ABC's *World News Tonight*, told Shaw that he was "stunned the way this intensely personal issue has taken over the public debate. I'm profoundly tired of the story. As a citizen, I just resent the fact that it is taking so much time and attention away from other issues that are so critical." Joseph Lelyveld, managing editor of *The New York Times*, told Shaw that "The ethical debate, while intense, seems to me kind of frozen: most people have heard it." Henry Muller, managing editor of *Time*, complained to Shaw about the "constantly repeated points of view," leading him to conclude that "I don't find a whole lot in the media that's very enlightening on this issue."[98]

None of the media executives whom Shaw interviewed saw their own personal views about the issue as a reason to reduce their coverage, although it led them to search for a fresh angle. The abortion issue seemed to annoy them because it was a "stale" issue that kept going on and on past its time, never really becoming dormant and never really getting resolved. The women journalists we interviewed, however, were not as apt to think that the abortion issue was boring or a distraction from more critical issues. Advocates for changing the status quo were also especially likely to resist calls for closure. As Orrin Hatch, a leader of anti-abortion forces in Congress, asserted, "This is not an exercise in futility . . . The women's suffrage issue took 93 years to resolve. We've [abortion debaters] only been at this 10 years [since *Roe v. Wade*]" (*NYT*, 7/1/83).

Advocates, while continuing to view the issue as important and unresolved, recognized the weariness and desire for closure around them. Helen Alvare, speaking for the National Conference of Catholic Bishops, noted the letters to Catholic newspapers saying, "I'm tired of hearing about this. Why are we spending so much time on that?" Jay Heavner, of the Religious Coalition for Reproductive Choice, noted that "the media is as tired of talking about this issue as everyone else. I think there is just a lot of frustration, that people just are tired of talking about it

[98] In our data, the specific framing ideas that say that any solution is better than a continuing conflict or that the better policy solution is one that is more likely to end the conflict or that the conflict is intrinsically unresolvable are all disproportionately found in the journalists' own utterances. It may be part of the institutional interest of the media itself to seek closure for "old" issues to have more space for "novelty."

– when the 'it' is abortion." And Rosemary Candelario of the *Abortion Access Project* of the *Reproductive Rights National Network* (R2N2) suggested that "there is almost a moratorium on abortion coverage." Advocates recognize the "staleness" of the abortion issue for journalists but see the challenge as moving the discourse in a new direction – but with no consensus, of course, on what that fresh direction should be.

DIVERGENT STANDARDS

We have argued that a number of common standards play out differently in the two countries in important ways, but there are two others that are more striking for how they differentiate the normative standards being applied by participant observers in Germany and the United States.

RATIONAL ARGUMENTATION VERSUS NARRATIVES WITH LESSONS

American and German journalists are sending different messages to their readers about *how* people should express themselves. To be sure, they all believe that contributors ought to explain what they mean in comprehensible terms.

For German journalists, this seems to imply that they themselves at least should be able to understand what is meant. A commentator in the *SZ*, for example, took the Constitutional Court to task for voicing its opinion in language that is "difficult for both citizens and politicians. Rather than judging in the name of the people, they have judged in atrocious legalese" (6/01/93).

But such complaints are rare compared to those who object to a style that emphasizes emotions and passion rather than detachment and rational argumentation. The use of political symbolism through such devices as metaphors, catchphrases, and visual symbols seems to violate such norms almost independently of their content. Such political expression seems especially likely to provoke vehement censure for "bad taste."[99]

The *SZ* complained about the organized activity of "various, usually fairly young women's groups" against the Constitutional Court decision

---

[99] Note that we are talking about the normative standards of two newspapers directed at political elites. The popular press in Germany (most notably, *Bild*, a Hamburg-based tabloid) and certainly the alternative press (the *taz*, a left-alternative daily newspaper based in Berlin) do not necessarily share this definition of what constitutes bad taste.

in 1975. "The protest is of the usual type: Demonstrations, leaflets, banners, collections of signatures with self-accusations or with the declaration that one will continue to contravene the regulations in the future. The bad taste in the event appears boundless" (2/18/75).

Sometimes such symbolic politics is seen as going even beyond bad taste to violate norms of civil discourse. The *FAZ* was especially offended by an item in the newsletter of the Young Democrats in North Rhine-Westphalia, who titled their lampoon, "Maria, if you had had an abortion, we would have been spared the Pope." "This is more than nasty bad taste," complained the *FAZ* (11/10/79).

In 1974, during the period in which abortion reform was being debated in the *Bundestag* and other public forums, the German television magazine show, *Panorama*, prepared a story on where and how illegal abortions were then taking place, focusing on a doctor who was doing them (and whose identity would be disguised). The *SZ* accused *Panorama* of "sensationalizing the issue" (*SZ*, 3/13/74). In the face of such criticism, and despite outrage over "censorship" by feminists and other pro-abortion-rights groups, the show was cancelled by the state-run television station that had proposed to run it.

Emotion, in this metatalk, is treated as in opposition to rationality, particularly as it is expressed in "unbridled passion." Hot emotion is the enemy of cool reason. The discussion of abortion "has become stuck in the jungle of principles and emotions" and "it is time to pull the debate back out into coolness, into pragmatism." The "emotions and dogmas" oppose a "rational consideration of the problem." Emotions are understandable on such an existential issue, but "only reason can respond appropriately . . . to changed realities" (*FAZ*, 7/30/71).

There are also reservations about this normative standard, even among mainstream German journalists. The criticism did not come up spontaneously, but we asked Heidrun Graupner of the *SZ* the following direct question: "Many say that the discussion about abortion is too abstract, because it is a discussion about general abstract values and lacks a relation to human beings. The concrete experience of abortions and pregnancies of those affected was said to be too little taken into account in the public debate. What do you think of this view?" Graupner, in her response, was surprisingly unequivocal: "It's true. I'd share that evaluation. It is an abstract debate, the debate was carried on most aggressively by those who understand the least about the reality: by men, by the abortion opponents among men" (Interview, February 2000).

This particular professional journalist does not sound that different from Rita Grieshaber, a leading German feminist and spokesperson for the Alliance '90/Green Party. Commenting on the debate in the *Bundestag*, she noted that "there were two types of negotiators – lawyers and feminist politicians. And the vocabulary, the world, the thinking about the problem – these were on two different continents . . . You can't really imagine how little [the lawyers] know about the situation of women or women's conflicts. It was really unbelievable." She went on to contrast the political coverage that concerned "who was winning or losing" with attention to "the substance of what comes out of the process." She argued that "Substantive interest in [abortion] in a normal daily newspaper is petty slight. There are few enough that have some expert interest in presenting the real substantive complexity of the problem the way that *Brigitte* [a widely read women's magazine] did, for example, which was really an excellent job. But there are few of that sort" (Interview, August 1996). The *Brigitte* coverage to which she referred gave space to women who discussed the meaning of abortion in their own lives and in the lives of women in general.

While one sees complaints from U.S. journalists about the "stridency" of the abortion debate, that call is more for greater civility than greater rationality. In fact, there is a strong theme that the discourse suffers from the fault identified by Graupner and Grieshaber – excessive abstraction and insufficient rootedness in the concrete reality of women with unwanted pregnancies.

Syndicated columnist Ellen Goodman expressed this theme most clearly in a 1983 opinion column. Goodman called for "a new vocabulary" to replace "the verbal war of attrition" in which "we've been stuck for a decade." The two groups have "lobbed names and accusations at each other across the public terrain." The problem in Goodman's view is that "the complex moral dilemmas of abortion end up straightjacketed by Constitution-speak. In the end, we can talk only about individual rights, the right to life and rights to privacy." The problem is that the abstract argument about principles that goes on in the legal system is "so removed from the argument that goes on in the mind of a woman faced with an unwanted pregnancy. The private struggle is less over rights than over responsibilities. It is less about conflicts with others than connections to them. It has less to do with the ability to carry a pregnancy for nine months than to care for a child for 18 years" (*LAT*, 1/21/83).

Apparently, even constitutional lawyers such as Lawrence Tribe agree about the curse of excessive abstraction. In the section of his 1990 book, *Abortion: The Clash of Absolutes*, excerpted by *The Los Angeles Times*, Tribe makes the point that the conflict is, for most people, internal within most of us rather than between opposing camps. The debate about principles creates invisible abstractions in which either the real woman or real fetus disappears, "reduced to ghostly anonymity."

Many who can readily envision the concrete humanity of a fetus, who hold its picture high and weep, barely see the woman who carries it and her human plight. To them, she becomes an all-but-invisible abstraction. Many others, who can readily envision the woman and her body, who cry out for her right to control her destiny, barely envision the fetus within that woman and do not imagine as real the life it might have been allowed to lead. For them, the life of the fetus becomes an equally invisible abstraction.

If detached and impersonal argumentation is the normative standard for German journalists, the ability to connect policy discourse with the lifeworld of the citizen offers a contrasting norm in the United States.[100] This is accomplished through the use of personal narratives, considered highly legitimate by American journalists. They see narratives as a way of reaching the audience in a way that abstract argument fails to do.

The endorsement of narrative comes with certain cautions. David Shaw concedes that "you are always more likely to get people to read your story if you can humanize and personalize it. But you have to be careful in the process not to trivialize and sensationalize it. It is easy to write horror stories about – whether it is back alley abortions or violent confrontations in an abortion clinic, and what has happened to people who have terminated or not terminated unwanted pregnancies. Since the bottom of this is about human beings, you have to include something about it. But I think you run the risk of sensationalizing it if you lose sight of the fact that we are talking about a serious public policy issue. You just have to strike a balance" (Interview, May 1998).

We asked journalists whether they thought citizens were getting what they needed from the media on the abortion issue. Linda Greenhouse

---

[100] For a fuller development of this argument, see Gamson (1999).

saw a problem in the event-driven nature of media coverage more generally as well as on abortion. This runs the danger of losing focus. "On the abortion issue, it is always important to keep the focus on what the issue is about, which is the lives of women and the quality of lives of women, in my opinion. I think this sometimes gets lost in the day to day reporting or the political rhetoric or the latest political wrinkle on the story" (Interview, June 1998).

Similarly, Karen Tumulty emphasized the importance of getting "beyond the professional advocates" and talking "to the women who are having abortions, and the doctors who are providing them, and the nurses who are sitting with these girls and these women." Noting that the statistical data on abortion are often not very good, this makes personal stories even more important. But to get beyond idiosyncrasies to valid patterns, "you just have to get enough of them, you have to keep going and get enough of them to satisfy yourself that you are getting the full picture" (Interview, May 1998).

Narrative also contributes to the emotional tone of the debate, allowing a legitimate focus on the pain and suffering of individuals that German media practices keep out of sight. Commenting on the showing of Bernard Nathanson's anti-abortion film, *The Silent Scream*, which suggests that a fetus suffers pain, Ann Taylor Allen asks in a 1985 *New York Times* op-ed:

> Why may Bernard Nathanson speak freely and publicly about his experience of abortion while I, his ex-patient, am ashamed, embarrassed, and afraid to speak? Why should a 12 week fetus be given a voice, even a "scream," while the woman in whose body it resides has no voice at all? I am writing in order to give that woman a voice and a name – my voice, my name. If women who support reproductive choice do not tell their stories, then the debate will be dominated by those who, in the name of political, religious or moral principle, ignore us and our needs and sometimes view us simply as containers for the next generation" (*NYT*, 5/22/85).

Thus U.S. newspapers offer a forum for personalizing the debate that can contribute to its moralistic and emotionally wrought tone as well as highlight the specifics of individual experience. Such deeply felt passion is also considered part of the "story" that a journalist is obliged to tell, and so space is provided for this and similar pleas inspired by both sides' commitments to their versions of truth-telling.

In sum, German newspapers hold up very different normative standards on the style and form of expression. Emotionally detached, disembodied argumentation is privileged and personal narratives are considered highly inappropriate by most observers and are largely nonexistent. In contrast, U.S. journalists see personal narratives as a way of helping citizens connect their own personal experiences with a policy debate and as a way of overcoming a discourse that can become unreal through too much abstract argumentation – and so they accept a level of emotionality in the discourse that German newspapers find highly problematic.

FAIRNESS

The theme of fairness, balance, and freedom from bias that is so prominent in the metatalk of American journalists is almost completely absent in German media commentary. Part of the explanation may lie in the relative dominance of the Fetal Life frame in Germany, making it seem "natural" rather than a journalistic choice. But the observance of proportionality – the allocation of space to reflect the share of party seats in the legislature and role in government – also works to remove fairness as an issue. If journalists follow this rule in allocating space and quoting sources, they are being fair by definition.

Fairness is not an issue to which German journalists appear to have given much thought. We asked Heidrun Graupner (*SZ*) whether she thought that all positions and interpretations were fairly represented. She answered, "As the debate continued a very long time, all positions were represented" (Interview, February 2000).

The use of institutionalized actors such as parties and churches as a reference point for discussions of fairness is well illustrated in our interview with Günther Bannas (*FAZ*). We asked him whether the position of the right-to-life social movement groups (*Lebenschützer*) should be represented in the media. He responded, "Not really. [The vehemently anti-abortion Cardinal] Dyba and the Right-to-Life groups were marginalized inside the Catholic Church and the CDU/CSU" (Interview, March 2000). If these larger institutionalized actors did not see fit to represent the views of some elements in their midst, this is reason enough for the media to ignore them.

Compared to their U.S. counterparts, German journalists seem much less concerned that their choice of language and labels might be biased. When we asked Stephan-Andreas Casdorff (*SZ*) whether he used the term "fetus" (*Foetus*) or "unborn life" (*ungeborenes Leben*), he answered,

"I can't remember exactly what I have written" (Interview, March 2000). Günther Bannas (*FAZ*) was similarly vague in his memory: "I don't believe I used the term 'fetus.' I guess I used 'unborn life' " (Interview, March 2000).

German journalists apparently also view an orientation to accepting the status quo as being unbiased. Bannas, for example, averred, "The language used does play a role. For example, we said we were not going to speak of 'abortion rights' as there is no right to abortion" (Interview, March 2000). Graupner, at the more liberal *SZ*, also accepted the status quo as framing the terms of the debate, saying "I used the terms somewhat interchangeably, at times unborn life, at times developing life, and adapted myself to the debate which was premised on unborn life"(Interview, February 2000). The hegemony of the Fetal Life frame thus, in a circular way, made journalists less concerned about representing any alternative frames in their own terms, which also made this frame more dominant.

While advocates generally tend to see bias toward their opponents but not themselves, even abortion rights supporters in Germany concede general fairness on the part of German mainstream media. Christina Schenk, spokesperson for the PDS (Party of Democratic Socialism), expressed the qualified nature of this judgment: "One has to say that in this coverage of the §218 discussion, this coverage is apparently driven by the presumed role and significance of the parties ... [For] the PDS, you're glad if you get more than a line, you know." When we asked her directly if the newspapers were "objective and fair," she answered "Yes, basically ... the big ones, *SZ*, *FR*, and even the *FAZ*. Insofar as one can talk somehow about fair treatment within the framework of this one-line paradigm in any sense. A position is simply not transmitted only in one line. It's really difficult" (Interview, August 1996). Rita Grieshaber of the Alliance '90/Green Party also acknowledged that "The largest, cross-regional newspapers have in general reported objectively. You can't say otherwise."

In Germany, legitimacy flows from the party mainstream and the legal status quo. Minority voices within the Catholic Church and all social movement representatives can be marginalized without calling the basic fairness of coverage into question. In the United States, in contrast, umbrella parties prefer to avoid comment rather than offer potentially controversial interpretations on issues such as abortion that divide their constituencies. No simple proportionality rule solves the problem of allocating space. Journalists themselves must make decisions on choice of sources and how much of what they say deserves quoting.

The issue of fairness or the lack of it is the dominant theme in the metatalk of U.S. journalists. Media bias was the central question in the series of articles on abortion discourse by David Shaw in *The Los Angeles Times*. Shaw presented it as a debate between anti-abortion groups who charge the media with a bias against them and editors and reporters who proclaim a special effort to be fair and balanced on the issue. A number of journalists, however, conceded that an unwitting and largely unconscious bias may exist. Abortion-rights groups sometimes complained about superficiality during this period but did not regard the media as biased against them and were generally happy with the treatment that they received. Shaw himself took the view that most papers, at the time of his writing, had an unintentional and unwitting bias against anti-abortion ideas and their advocates.

As usual, attempts to determine whether or not bias really exists lead into the dead end of having no consensual standard of what constitutes an unbiased account. This is brought home most clearly in Shaw's detailed account of *The Washington Post's* coverage of an April 1990 "Rally for Life" demonstration at the Washington monument. The *Post* relegated their story about the rally to the Metropolitan section and gave it only about half the space that *The New York Times* gave it. Did this lesser coverage, Shaw asked, reveal the *Post's* pro-abortion rights bias?

To answer the question, Shaw compared the *Post's* coverage to the rally a year earlier by abortion-rights forces that drew five stories in five days leading up to the event and multiple stories when the event occurred. But, having suggested their comparability in one breath, he undermined it in the next. "There is no question," Shaw conceded, "that the 1989 abortion-rights march was a more newsworthy event than the 1990 'Rally for Life'," and he went on to describe how the context was different in several respects to support his argument for noncomparability.

Shaw made much of the fact that the *Post's* managing editor, Leonard Downie, was himself highly critical of his own paper. Downie claimed to have been embarrassed by its undercoverage of the 1990 rally and said, "I really took them [the paper's metropolitan editors] to the woodshed." It was, in his view, an exception to the generally successful efforts of the *Post* to be "unusually conscious of trying to present both sides all the time."

The source of Downie's embarrassment was not the noncomparability with coverage of the 1989 abortion rights march but with being out of step with other mainstream media. The rally was treated as the lead story on the evening news of the three major television networks and received front-page coverage in *The New York Times*, *The Los Angeles Times*, *The Boston Globe*, and a number of other major newspapers. Bias here, it turns out, is a matter of not doing what everyone else seems to be doing. Ironically, the same standard applied to *The Washington Post*'s coverage of the Watergate burglary in June 1972 would have supported the Nixon's administration's charges of the *Post*'s anti-Nixon bias – in this case, for giving too much coverage to what other news outlets, including *The New York Times*, treated as a "third-rate burglary."

Shaw also made a case for an implicit pro-choice framing through the media's use of language. He accepted the criticism of Douglas Johnson, legislative director of the National Right to Life Committee, who pointed out that *The Washington Post*, "in discussing abortion as a matter of 'a women's reproductive rights,' adopts both the paradigm and the polemic of the abortion-rights lobby." Neither Johnson nor Shaw thus saw the Supreme Court's use of this language as legitimating journalists' own use of it, the way that journalists "adapting" to "the premises of the debate" is widely accepted as appropriate in Germany.

Earlier naming struggles were resolved in ways that generally left abortion rights supporters happier than their opponents. The human organism in the womb of a pregnant woman is generally called a "fetus" rather than a "baby" or, as is the custom in Germany, an "unborn child." "Fetus" appears to journalists as more neutral and value-free because of its status as a scientific, medical term, but there is no neutral term in this instance.

The term "unborn child" suggests continuity between pre-birth and post-birth and, hence, is the preference of abortion opponents; the term "fetus" emphasizes discontinuity and qualitative difference and, hence, is the preference of abortion rights advocates. The term "fetus," complained John Wilke, president of the National Right to Life Committee, sounds like a "nonhuman glob," and deprives his side of its "most powerful image" (*LAT*, 7/1/90). More recently, however, it is the proponents of abortion rights who complain about unfair language, particularly focusing on the widespread use of the term "partial birth abortion" discussed earlier.

All of these contests over language have made American journalists sensitive to their choice of labels in a way that few German journalists are. There is an especially striking example from our journalist interviews. Both Greenhouse and Tumulty, spontaneously and independently, made the same point about the terms "pregnant woman" and "mother." "I always used 'pregnant woman' rather than 'mother,'" Tumulty observed, "which is something I appreciate all the more since I have become a mother. It is not the same."

Greenhouse took up the same issue. "I sometimes see it [written] as the life of the 'mother,' the exception to save the life of the 'mother.' I am always careful to say the 'pregnant woman,' because I am a mother and I have been a pregnant woman and, in my opinion, there is a difference between the two." It is difficult to imagine journalists for the *SZ* or the *FAZ* paying attention to this difference and even more unlikely that they would draw on their personal experience to provide the authority for the distinction.

In spite of their best intentions, Shaw argued, journalists are unconsciously influenced by the pro-abortion-rights atmosphere in which they operate. Shaw quoted Richard Harwood, ombudsman for *The Washington Post*, who wondered "if we have our antennae raised as high" for the anti-abortion side. "*Post* journalists and editors," wrote Shaw, "like most journalists in other big-city news organizations, don't seem to have many friends or colleagues who oppose abortion." Their newspapers take pro-choice editorial positions and their Union – the American Newspaper Guild – officially endorses "freedom of choice in abortion decisions."

Advocacy groups, not surprisingly, share no consensus about media bias. For Flip Benham, of Operation Rescue, the heavily secular media is incapable of comprehending a belief system so different from their own. Benham had a good media story when he presided over the baptism of Norma McCorvey, the Jane Roe of *Roe v. Wade*. He provided it as an exclusive to ABC Network News because the reporter assigned to cover it, Peggy Weymeyer, "was a born-again Christian, and knew what was going on." But not her boss, Peter Jennings, who wanted to play it as a political shift. In Benham's view, this was a story about a change in a person's relation to God, *not* a political shift. "Peter Jennings could not see it," he explained. "Now you don't blame him. You don't say he is biased. You don't say 'that is a conspiracy, he doesn't want the truth out.' He just doesn't have a clue. That is the media" (Interview,

June 1997). Helen Alvare, from the National Council of Catholic Bishops, also described reporters as "clueless" when it comes to covering Catholic doctrine and so are more inclined to get "the political story" right but not understand or appreciate "the moral issue" (Interview, July 1997).

Some abortion rights supporters see the bias problem as embedded in the media system as a whole, not simply in the minds and practices of reporters. Kim Gandy, of the National Organization for Women (NOW), conceded that reporters on the beat tend to support abortion rights and women's rights more generally. The problem is that the people who own and run newspapers and television stations and the corporately owned networks have "a very strong bias against women's rights. . . . They tend to be certainly anti-feminist if not anti-women" (Interview, June 1997). And Rosemary Candelario of R2N2 saw a bias toward the middle of the road: "While the media isn't pro-life, they're real empathetic to the mainstream approach" (Interview, October 1997).

In the end, many of the advocacy groups simply lower their expectations, doing whatever they can to reduce their dependence on mainstream media. Wanda Franz of the National Right to Life Committee described the difficulty of getting their message to evangelical Protestants through the media. "We can't get them in that way. So we have to appeal to them ourselves because we know the normal channels aren't available to us. Because the media has closed us out" (Interview, May 1997). Kim Gandy of NOW, after giving a long string of specific examples of media unfairness to her organization including one within the previous 48 hours, noted, "That's the kind of thing that happens all the time. This happens constantly, constantly, constantly. It's really an ongoing frustration, but you can't use the media. You can't use the media. You have to do something else" (Interview, July 1997). Flip Benham of Operation Rescue emphasized media blindness more than hostility but drew the same conclusion: "Our point will never be brought across in the media. Our media is the streets" (Interview, June 1997).

What do we conclude from this metatalk on fairness? Germany has an institutional and procedural solution to the problem that does not depend on an assessment of content. The implicit normative standard is that, since the political parties can be arrayed on a left–right dimension with their strength determined by a popular vote, all the media need do to provide fairness is to provide the parties with voice proportional to their electoral share. Then, one adds to this mix other major institutional actors that have historically been spokespersons for recognized issue constituencies. On "moral" issues, this means the institutional churches, on economic issues, the trade unions, and so forth.

As a "woman's" issue, abortion is also represented by institutionally validated women speakers, namely, those within the political parties, rather than by the anti-institutional women's movement. Finally, when there is an institutional speaker with legitimacy to decide an issue, such as the Constitutional Court, its definition of the terms of the debate can be accepted without raising questions of fairness to those who would challenge this framing.

This procedural, institutional approach solves the problem of fairness for journalists, but it has the consequence of excluding noninstitutional actors from the discourse. In the case of abortion, this means especially that the voices of the autonomous women's movement are virtually nonexistent in the pages of the *FAZ* and *SZ*. Their slogans and calls for repeal of §218, everyone agrees, "are not heard any more." It also marginalizes the right-to-life movement and its most vehement supporters within the Catholic Church. Hence, the institutional solution for fairness directly conflicts with the normative criterion of inclusion emphasized by many democratic theories.

For the United States, the institutional solution is not really available on issues that do not fall neatly along party lines. Even though the political parties line up on different sides on abortion, neither wants to be a highly visible speaker on an issue that threatens to divide its various constituencies. In the face of ongoing calls to "overturn *Roe v. Wade*" from the anti-abortion movement, the Supreme Court's own language also fails to offer a generally accepted vocabulary. Lacking an institutional resolution, journalists and advocates look for a content-based standard of fairness. Since any content-based definition is frame-dependent, this solution can work only when there is a consensual or hegemonic frame. In the case of abortion in the United States, there are multiple frames, each embodying its own standard of fairness. Journalists therefore place speakers on both sides of any issue together, hoping to find fairness procedurally via the clash of their opposing arguments.

American journalists, then, are doomed to an endless quest for the holy grail of a frame-free standard of fairness that by its very nature is unattainable. The process, however, may be more conducive to meeting the normative criterion of including grassroots actors in the process.

We conclude this chapter by asking how these normative standards derived from the metatalk of participant observers relate to those derived from democratic theory.

DEMOCRATIC THEORY AND JOURNALIST NORMS

We have argued, in this review of U.S. and German metatalk, that the standards by which media quality is evaluated by journalists and advocates are partly shared, and partly divergent. The two countries share the standards of *accuracy, civility and mutual respect, dialogue*, and *closure* – but the meaning of these standards is culturally contingent in ways that we have tried to specify. They differ in the emphasis that they place on rational argumentation versus narrative and on the issue of fairness and bias. Presumably, these norms influence the behavior of journalists who try to meet them as best they can within the inevitable constraints of their job.

How do these norms help us to understand the results we found in Chapter Eleven? To review, in most respects German discourse meets the criteria of representative liberal theory very well. It is dominated by accountable state and party actors, supplemented by experts and representatives of the Catholic and Lutheran Churches. It is carried on with little incivility. Not all ideas appear, of course, but within a broad range the sponsors of different policies are given free reign to offer the most persuasive arguments that they can muster and do so.

The discourse provides extensive and detailed accounts and commentary on what the people's representatives are doing in both countries but with significant gaps in Germany on the implementation process. German discourse also generally meets the proportionality standard, if it is adjusted to give more weight to the party in government than its share of legislative seats alone would warrant. It deviates only in its treatment of the minor parties, by providing the FDP somewhat more and the more social-movement-based parties only slightly less coverage than their share of seats would predict. The norms espoused by journalists and shared by advocacy groups agree that this institutional focus is what they would call "fair." There is only sporadic criticism of this focus on "winning and losing" as obscuring the experiences and meanings of ordinary people.

Finally, German discourse provides just the kind of closure that is advocated by the Representative Liberal tradition even though calls for closure come earlier than might be expected. Authoritative decisions should provide a clear signal that this discussion is completed and public discourse should move on to other topics; and as we have seen, it does. With minor exceptions, then, German media discourse is a good approximation of the Representative Liberal ideal and judged to be appropriate according to these standards.

U.S. discourse comes much closer than German discourse in meeting the criteria emphasized by the participatory liberal tradition. Civil society actors, including grassroots organizations and ordinary people, are given considerable voice along with the people's representatives, and the social movement share of the framing offered expands over time, in the way that Participatory Liberal arguments for empowerment would value. This norm is strongly affirmed as part of journalists' responsibilities for truth-seeking and representation of significant points of view. There is allowance for, and even encouragement of, styles of expression that are considered bad taste or worse in Germany. Yet there is relatively little uncivil speech in either country, and no measurable tendency for the discourse to become more loaded with inflammatory language in recent years in the United States, even though citizen mobilization has expanded. This does not mean that no groups ever adopt language that would lead to excluding others from their moral community, but there is little to suggest that this kind of framing appears commonly in these newspapers. In fact, the frequency with which denunciations of such talk accompany the examples that do appear suggests that they are being used as examples of norm violation in order to affirm the value of civility rather than as being real exceptions to the rule.

With regard to closure, participatory liberals would also be more reassured in the United States that government decisions are not forcing an artificial end to efforts by mobilized citizen groups to achieve policies that they consider better. Overall, movements achieve a more regularized standing; active participation in framing by less institutionalized actors expands; more styles of discourse, including emotional ones, are included; and opportunities to critique the status quo and power-holders are kept more open in the U.S. media than in German newspapers. Participatory Liberals would approve.

The answer to which country best fits the criteria of discursive theory is more complicated. On the issues of inclusion, U.S. discourse is clearly a better fit. U.S. discourse clearly does better in providing a balance of center and periphery, providing much more standing for civil society actors, especially grassroots, autonomous ones. Actors from civil society directly encounter and debate the core institutional players in the same articles, leaving the institutional speakers, including the courts, in a less privileged position to define the terms of the debate. The language of the Supreme Court is still contested, while in Germany journalists use the language of the Constitutional Court as defining the "facts" for all sides.

The U.S. model of constructing articles to include speakers on both sides of an issue provides a structure for dialogue, and the speakers in these debates are more likely to be offering direct rebuttals, suggesting that there is at least some communication of what is at stake, even though there is no agreement on what that is. On the issue of deliberativeness, the evidence is ambiguous, with no clear advantage for either country. On dialogue, in particular, different measures show slight advantages for one country or the other or no difference. If there is a difference in the amount of dialogue between countries, it is not robust enough to show up consistently.

The closure that German discourse provides does not flow from a deliberatively arrived at consensus and, hence, is not the closure that the model envisions. But the ongoing U.S. discourse does not fit this discursive norm any better since it shows little tendency to produce a consensus that should lead to voluntary closure. The absence of a tendency toward consensus is a failure of the deliberative process in both countries, but one that is accentuated in the United States by the continuing movement of the conflict into different institutional and noninstitutional venues. This ongoing visibility of the abortion debate in the press has made the absence of closure more prominent and more troubling to U.S. journalists in recent years.

U.S discourse comes much closer than German discourse in meeting the criteria emphasized by the constructionist tradition. The criteria that it shares with the participatory liberal tradition – popular inclusion, empowerment, and the avoidance of premature closure – are better met in the United States. U.S. discourse is clearly stronger on overcoming the artificial distinction between the public and private realm, and in legitimizing the language of the lifeworld and experiential knowledge through personal narratives.

The analysis of participant standards for judging the media help us to understand these results in the following ways:

First, the different solutions to the fairness problem have different consequences for *inclusion*. The representative liberal criterion of *pro-*

portionality is implicit in the metatalk of German observers and is even accepted, albeit grudgingly, by spokespersons for the smaller parties who support abortion rights. The lack of metatalk about fairness in Germany allows the consequence of journalistic practice for the exclusion of less institutionalized, grassroots actors to go unmarked. It also directs attention away from coverage of the implementation of the law in practice, where party interests are less engaged.

In the United States, there is much greater sensitivity by journalists to accusations of unfairness. This sensitivity is kept alive by the hopeless quest for a frame-free standard that, in fact, keeps moving about as one examines media content through the lens of different frames. Journalistic uncertainty creates greater opportunities for the voices of grassroots actors to be heard, notwithstanding the advocates' own sense of being shut out or misrepresented. Hence, differences in U.S. and German understanding and practice on the fairness issue helps to explain the better fit of U.S. discourse with *popular inclusion* and German discourse with *elite dominance*.

Second, there is a close correspondence between the common themes in German and U.S. metatalk and the normative criteria of *deliberativeness* emphasized by discursive theory, and its components of *dialogue, mutual respect*, and *civility*. But there are substantial differences in Germany and the United States on the boundaries of civility. In particular, much of the symbolic politics and emotional speech practiced by grassroots movements is considered within bounds in the United States but out of bounds in Germany. This difference in the way that civility is defined has implications for the normative criterion of *inclusion* discussed earlier.

Third, the normative criterion of *empowerment* is not explicitly addressed; it is a nonissue in the metatalk of journalists in either country. It is implicit in some of the comments that advocates make but, given that the media fail on so many lesser standards, such as genuine dialogue, it would seem wildly utopian, in their view, to expect the mass media to provide this.

Fourth, the different emphasis on logical *argumentation* versus *narrative* as preferred forms of discourse has implications for *empowerment*. Each privileges different types of knowledge – in the one case role-derived expertise and in the other experiential knowledge. The latter tends to empower grassroots actors by validating their experiences as a claim to knowledge and to enable them by making it easier to connect their experiences with the language of policy discourse. This also has implications for the *inclusion* of such grassroots actors and ordinary citizens.

Fifth, there is a great desire for *closure* in the metatalk of journalists in both countries. It is very difficult to separate how much of this talk reflects discomfort with discussing the issue at all or agreement with the policies set by the legislature and courts, and how much of it reflects a reaction to the actual content of the discourse. The very early calls for closure, especially in the *FAZ*, suggest discomfort more than a policy agenda or a debate that has gone on too long. They suggest a normative standard of closure that would be premature even by representative liberal criteria.

Some German commentators suggest that the closure they observe reflects a degree of consensus as the competing sides make some effort to accommodate each other's arguments. But advocates for abortion rights suggest a closure born of resignation rather than one emerging from consensus. Nor do U.S. journalists, in their calls for closure, argue that the deliberative process has produced consensus but suggest, instead, that since it probably never will, discussion should move on to other topics anyway. Advocates of one or the other solution disagree, of course, and their continuing ability to move the conflict from the courts to the legislature to the streets and back again means that the newspapers will have to continue to follow their actions and to represent their still divergent perspectives.

In general, then, journalistic norms in Germany fit quite well with those emphasized by representative democratic theory – *elite domination, proportionality, detachment, civility,* and *closure.* There is some emphasis on the importance of *expertise* on this issue, and there are few but striking examples of inflammatory speech. The lack of coverage of the actual implementation of laws, including most cases of criminal prosecution, is a weakness in meeting the standard of *transparency,* and the early calls for *closure* seem to undermine the idea of a free marketplace of ideas, but these are minor and partial exceptions. Journalistic norms in both countries support the discursive criteria of *deliberativeness,* but there are not many observers who feel that this standard is being met in the discourse that they have observed. Nor would many claim that the *closure* that took place emerged from a genuine consensus.

Journalistic norms in the United States strongly support the constructionist endorsement of *narrative* and the constructionist version of *empowerment* – breaking down the sharp boundaries between public policy and the lifeworld and opening discursive opportunities. They actively foster *inclusion* and allow a wide range of symbolic and emotional speech without calling it uncivil, while also condemning particularly inflammatory remarks. But they do not explicitly endorse a participatory liberal standard of *empowerment* as a discourse that encourages political engagement by citizens as collective actors. Journalists complain about the absence of *closure*, but in the absence of consensus they also continue to follow the story and to give voice to both those who favor and those who oppose the status quo.

CHAPTER THIRTEEN

Lessons for Democracy and the Public Sphere

Understanding the complexities of discourse about abortion policy in Germany and the United States has been a challenge. We leave it to the reader to judge how well we have met it. Ultimately, we are interested in using this study of abortion as a tool for addressing a broader set of questions about democracy and the public sphere. These questions focus on the processes by which the practices of newspapers and the activities of groups and individuals, in and out of political institutions, interact to provide a public discourse about policy issues and the quality of the outcome that they produce, evaluated by several competing standards in normative democratic theory. In this concluding chapter, we review what we learned about the dynamics that generate a discourse about abortion and the nature of this discourse in both countries, focusing on the implications for political discourse more generally.

In our model, media discourse on any issue is shaped by more or less organized collective actors of different types who sponsor certain preferred frames. Their resources, connections, skills, and choices about framing strategy influence their standing and the relative prominence of their frames in the media. Organizational and strategic decisions can make a difference in the career of the frame that they sponsor in ways that are reflected in changing its prominence in the mass media forum.

The actors do not contest frames on a neutral or level arena, but on a complicated terrain. The playing field is uneven and littered with obstacles, some of which may impede certain actors more than others, and it changes over time as decisions are reached and policies put in place. Because the arena is different in each country, the availability and cost of any particular route to influence are not the same in both, even for actors that appear to be quite similar in each country (such as the

Catholic Church). To be effective, the strategic choices that actors make must take into account the features of this complicated landscape. We use the concept of a *discursive opportunity structure*, discussed in Chapter Four, as our label for this playing field.

One cannot really begin to compare the language and ideas that appear in the German and U.S. mass media forums without understanding the differences between arenas in the two countries. At an extreme, the field is wide open to some actors and some ideas in one country that are blocked or loaded with traps in the other country.

Take one example of this context – cultural norms about the welfare state. The idea that the state can be and should be a force for good in social life – that the state is a *welfare* state – is a consensual and taken-for-granted assumption in German political culture. Opponents of abortion more or less uniformly support a variety of state subsidies for raising children and special benefits targeted to the poor. In the United States, the welfare state is a politically contested idea with its supporters on the defensive; it is very far from being taken-for-granted. More importantly, many conservatives combine opposition to abortion with opposition to state support for raising children, especially for the poor. This leaves them vulnerable to charges of hypocrisy about their concern for unborn children and their lack of concern about those born into unpromising circumstances.

Only within this context can one decipher the quip by U.S. Congressman Barney Frank that "Right-to-lifers believe that life begins at conception and ends at birth." In the United States, it is likely to draw a wry smile from abortion rights supporters and a dirty look from opponents, but both sides understand the point. It is more likely to draw a puzzled look or blank stare from Europeans who tend to take for granted the embrace of the welfare state by abortion opponents. Moreover, this context has concrete policy ramifications that also become part of the discursive opportunity structure. In Germany, the Constitutional Court affirmed that the poorest women deserve welfare state support to guarantee them the same access to abortion that more affluent women can secure, while the U.S. Court specifically allowed access to be limited to those financially able to pay for it.

Both diffuse ideas and specific policy decisions shape the national arenas in different ways, tilting the ground toward different sides in various specific places and changing over time as actors attempt to restructure the very ground on which their contest takes place. In other words, the differences that we find between the two countries are not just because the game is different in each – as if the Germans were playing soccer and the Americans football. In both countries, the nature of the field on which the contest is to be carried out is not fixed and unchanging, and the rules of the games, as well as the points scored by each side, are being negotiated while the plays are already going on. Players enter and leave not by the call of some neutral referee who stands outside the field, but by the decisions of journalists who are themselves players with interests in the outcome. Although one would expect that such complications could only generate chaos, there are in fact understandable patterns in the outcomes that emerge.

THE INTERPLAY OF STRATEGY AND OPPORTUNITY

We believe that the various findings reported in earlier chapters about how two very different abortion discourses are generated in these two countries are best explained by the deliberate efforts of social actors to shape them. Actors choose the parts of the field in which they decide to play as well as the specific moves that they make in that space. Their efforts are limited by the opportunities and constraints of the arena in which they compete, as well as shaped by the actors' understanding of and responses to these conditions. We will organize our review of these findings around the components of the discursive opportunity structure discussed in Chapter Four.

LEGAL/JUDICIAL

The German Court, in accepting the status of the fetus as life as being uncontroversial and emphasizing the state's responsibility for the protection of life, gave a powerful advantage to those who framed the abortion issue in such terms. The U.S. Court, in emphasizing the right to privacy from state intrusion on individual rights and expanding the definition of privacy to include women's reproductive choices, gave a parallel advantage to this alternative frame. In making these decisions the courts in both countries could draw on different discursive resources: political suspicion of an active, interventionist state in the United States and heightened concern with the protection of life in post–Nazi Germany. In each case, the sponsors of a particular frame are able to claim constitutional sanction for their demands; their competitors face an uphill battle in promoting alternatives without such sanctions. This is a fundamental cause for the broad differences in framing that we identified in Chapter Five: the tilt toward Anti ideas, especially the Fetal

Life frame, in Germany and the tilt toward Pro ideas, especially the Individual Rights frame, in the United States. However, this aspect of the arena can change during the course of a framing contest, requiring nimbleness in devising and revising framing strategies.

We used the device of a *constitutional cluster* of ideas about abortion that had legal sanction – in this case, from court decisions – to measure this component. We found that, as expected, the cluster of idea elements used by the German Constitutional Court was more prominent in German media than in the U.S. media even before the Constitutional Court acted, but became even more prominent afterward. The U.S. constitutional cluster was, as expected, higher in the United States than in Germany throughout the sample period but, unexpectedly, did not gain in prominence over time. This nonchange underlines the limits of opportunity structure as an explanation. While the opportunity for frame prominence may well have been enhanced, U.S. abortion discourse became more strongly contested. The prominence of the constitutional cluster actually declined to its lowest point during the Reagan years.

The differences in the auras of the highest court in each country help to make sense of this result. The less visible nature of the process of appointment and the high confidence of Germans in their legal system make the German Court decisions appear as *ex cathedra*, the ultimate judgements of an abstract institution rather than the particular opinions of a specific group of men and women. U.S. Court decisions are more likely to appear as the contingent outcome of the group process of nine individuals rather than any kind of ultimate judgment. A parallel to U.S. calls to "overturn *Roe v. Wade*" is inconceivable in Germany, and a political strategy that would focus on shifting the composition of the court is not an available option for German social movements.

We suspect that what we found for abortion – that the legal/judicial component was more important in shaping media discourse in Germany than in the United States – would hold for other issues in the two countries as well. But this remains a hypothesis to be tested by others.

PARTY/STATE

We emphasized differences between Germany and the United States in the role of the state and political parties. More specifically, the positive view of a welfare state in Germany – that the state can be and should be a force for good in social life – contrasts with a contested and

distrustful discourse on the role of the state in the United States. Applied to the abortion issue, this helps to account for the prominence
in German discourse of the idea that the government should "help
rather than punish" women with an unwanted pregnancy and the
virtual absence of this idea in U.S. discourse. The shared assumption in
the United States that all state action is suspect allows Pro forces an
advantage in blocking state regulations on abortion and Anti forces a
comparable advantage in blocking state funding for the poor.

In addition to this difference on the role of the state, there is an
equally clear difference in the legitimacy and quasi-state role of political parties. German political parties have a constitutionally recognized
role in the formation of a government, with defined responsibilities and
rights that even include the granting of state subsidies. U.S. political
parties were viewed with suspicion by the framers of the U.S. Constitution and are weakly institutionalized; party discipline is weak, and the
desire to maintain unity often leads to the avoidance of statements on
issues that might provoke internal divisions. One result of this difference is the much higher standing of party and state actors on the issue
of abortion in Germany compared to the United States that we identified in Chapter Five.

While these differences may distinguish Germany from the United
States, they do not distinguish Germany from most other parliamentary democracies in the western hemisphere. Germany appears to be
typical in both the cultural acceptance of the welfare state and the quasi-
official role of political parties; the United States is the exception.
Hence, this state and party component should be highly relevant for
comparisons between the United States and a wide variety of other
countries.

Additionally, we have seen how the norms that the media employ to
decide who should have standing are different in the United States and
in Germany. The more institutionally oriented rules for who should be
sought out as sources by journalists further advantage state and party
speakers and tilt the playing field away from social movement speakers
of all stripes, who have to struggle much harder to be heard at all.

These differences are likely to shape many if not most other issues
as well. We should expect state speakers – and especially legislative
speakers – along with party spokespersons to dominate standing on
most issues in Germany and to be less prominent on most issues in the
United States. Very few issues offer sharper differences on party lines
than does abortion policy, and yet party spokespersons in the United

States are reluctant to speak "for the party." Two-party competition in this context produces rhetorical strategies in which both parties claim to seek the same things, often blurring real party differences in policy preferences. As we discuss later, this party dynamic affects the nature of the public sphere.

There is every reason, then, to expect that what we found for abortion will hold more generally – that the standing of civil society actors, especially social movement speakers, will be substantially higher in the United States than in Germany. In sum, the party/state component of the discursive opportunity structure facilitates standing for speakers from these sectors in Germany and retards it in the United States generally, and not just on the abortion issue.

GENDER

As we saw in Chapter Seven, abortion is much more explicitly defined as a "women's issue" in Germany than in the United States. Germany has a long political history of contention around §218. German feminists took advantage of this discursive opportunity and mobilized strongly around abortion as an issue. They have largely succeeded in having abortion defined as an issue on which women in politics "naturally" have a special competence to speak.

In contrast, abortion emerged as a political issue much later and in more medical terms in the United States, and reproductive rights were granted to a non-gender-specific individual, the "pregnant person" in the words of the Supreme Court.[101] This does not mean that gender relations are not at issue or gendered perspectives not in play in the United States, but that women and women's rights are not named as being at stake. In Germany they are, and have been for a century. This explicitness conveys some advantages to women in Germany, for example, in the gender of spokespersons for the political parties, who are now predominantly women, with a dramatic increase since the first wave of discourse in the mid-1970s (see Franz 1999). While women speakers have increased their share somewhat in the United States, there is greater gender balance among Pro advocates.

However, the close connection between abortion rights and women's rights in Germany has mixed consequences overall. It gives German women and women's organizations, not just feminist movement

---

[101] This was in the employment discrimination case, *Gilbert v. General Electric* in 1976, that spurred the passage of the Pregnancy Discrimination Act of 1978.

groups, a particular claim on the discourse, as distinctively entitled to speak about abortion by virtue of their gender. But it takes abortion off the agenda for men who might otherwise speak out in support of abortion rights and therefore tends to keep the discourse polarized along gender lines, with German differences between men and women who are visible players on abortion policy much greater than in the United States. This deprives German women of conspicuous support from male allies.

In the United States, framing of the abortion issue as a privacy right has also offered both opportunities and obstacles to the mobilization of women on this issue. A gender-specific claim of women's special entitlement to speak on abortion carries little weight in U.S. discourse. This is not merely a matter of lesser opportunity. Women themselves rely heavily on a nongendered Individual Rights frame in advocating for abortion rights; they haven't failed in making an explicitly gender claim but have not tried very hard to do so. By not framing abortion as something that is especially about gender, U.S. discourse separates it, for both better and worse, from the women's movement. Thus broad coalitions are evident between feminists and mixed-sex abortion rights groups, but not between feminists and other sorts of women's groups on the abortion issue.

German abortion discourse is not only more explicitly gendered than U.S. discourse but gendered in a different way, interacting with the welfare state differences discussed previously. German discourse is much more likely to focus on women with unwanted pregnancies as clients to be served by state and private human service agencies – to help, not punish. U.S. discourse is more likely to frame women as autonomous moral agents endowed with rights and responsibilities.[102] Operating from this starting point, German women have been able to shift the overall discourse in that country toward greater acknowledgement of women's self-determination, but U.S. women have not been able to achieve a comparable recognition of the social situations in which women are driven to seek abortions as being needs that the state should help to meet.

Finally, the gendered component requires that we attend to subtext as well as text – that is, to implicitly (and often unconsciously) gendered aspects of the discursive opportunity structure. The clearest example,

---

[102] See Ferree and Gamson (2002) for a fuller development and presentation of this argument.

in the case of abortion, is the ongoing contest over what are considered "public" and "private" matters. Public and private, as Fraser (1995) and others have argued, have a gendered subtext in which the "public" realm has traditionally been a male sphere, and its norms and practices reflect this.

Norms about appropriate public discourse may discount personal narratives, for example. Since the experience of an unwanted pregnancy is gender-specific, the discounting falls unequally on men and women. In the United States, the more fluid boundaries between public and private create discursive opportunities for women that do not exist in Germany, where the boundaries are sharper (Kalberg 1987a, 1987b). In sum, the gender component shapes opportunities through assumptions that, although not explicitly gendered, affect male and female speakers in different ways.

MORAL/RELIGIOUS

In comparing Germany and the United States on abortion, we were forced to confront a paradox. Institutionally, religion and politics are less separated in Germany than in the United States, but culturally they are more separated. This creates two quite complicated and contrasting playing fields for sponsors of sacred canopies.

These differences on the moral/religious component help to account for certain results. In Germany, churches give the Fetal Life frame a sacred canopy while their political partners in the Christian parties promote the same frame with less explicitly religious appeals to shared values on the sanctity of life. The Catholic Church enjoys a high proportion of the standing given to all civil society speakers. Protestant speakers come to echo Catholics in accepting the Fetal Life frame as the single standard of morality, a standard that the Constitutional Court institutionally affirmed.

In the United States, with its contrasting normative climate on the institutional separation of religion and politics, the diversity of moral judgments is a more central theme and religious organizations are more likely both to disagree among themselves and to defer to other, non-denominational actors in civil society to invoke a sacred canopy. Hence, we find the Catholic Church encouraging the National Right-to-Life Committee to speak for a broader religious constituency including both Catholics and Protestant evangelicals, while it withdraws to a somewhat less prominent role in an effort to de-Catholicize the opposition to abortion. The U.S. opportunity structure is friendlier to a religious framing, but only if it is ecumenical and interdenominational, not if it is associated with any particular religion or points to only one possible moral conclusion. It is also less friendly to church groups as the vehicle for public sponsorship of such frames.

One final aspect of the moral/religious component plays a special role in Germany – the image of Nazi Germany as a negative moral standard. Although Holocaust imagery also appears in the United States as a type of inflammatory speech (along with parallels to slavery), appeals to the sanctity of life have a special cultural and constitutional resonance in Germany less because of the sacred canopy of organized religion and the influence of the church on politics, and more because of the Nazi repudiation of this moral principle.

SOCIAL JUSTICE

We need to underline the fact that there *are* differences in access to legal abortion among women of different social locations in both countries. Whether these differences are trivial or significant enough to need to be addressed is a matter of framing. Hence, we need to explain the low overall use and general decline of social justice framing in both Germany and the United States.

While similar on the surface, we argue that the explanation reflects different underlying dynamics in the two countries. In Germany, the decline reflects a victory for this framing. Poor women are seen as having a special claim on the welfare state, but the state's power to grant or withhold a certification of neediness is increasingly viewed by abortion rights advocates as an infringement on women's autonomy.

In the United States, the decline of social justice framing reflects defeat and strategic withdrawal from a losing fight. The lack of support for welfare programs in general and the danger that arguments for supporting abortion for poor women might be appropriated to control and limit their childbearing have made it a discouraging discursive strategy. Given the generally more favorable arena for claims about individual privacy rights and the successes that the movement has had, plus the overall unfavorable terrain for raising class claims, why push this frame? This underlines again that the characteristics of the arena help to explain the choices of the players, but that only both together can explain the outcome.

We have defined the primary constituency for social justice claims as an imagined community called the "tradition of the left." But where this community stands on abortion is neither simple nor unidimensional.

Autonomy and need, as well as social justice themes, have an important place in this discourse. Those who make claims on behalf of this constituency can frame abortion variously as a matter of the inalienable rights of citizens to control their most private lives, the state's responsibility to care for and protect the needy, and social justice for those who face structural inequalities. In practice, each of these themes has shifted over time in both countries, but for different reasons and with differing results. In both countries, themes of structural inequality in access to legal abortion have become relatively less significant, but only in Germany has access for the poor been institutionalized through state subsidies for the neediest.

Mass Media

German journalists take for granted a public sphere dominated by political parties and the organizations closely associated with them such as churches and trade unions. In such a situation, the journalist does not need to play a very active role as an interpreter of meaning. The choice of sources, for example, is obvious and established by long-standing political convention.

In the United States, in contrast, these actors are weaker. Political parties are loose coalitions organized to compete for public office, not for expressing unified frames. As a result of this relative vacuum, the mass media become, Hallin and Mancini (1984) argue, *the* primary actor of the U.S. public sphere in providing political interpretation. Because of this enhanced role, certain journalistic conventions have developed in the United States that are unusual in Europe. These include a greater tendency to frame and interpret, and to use narrative structures and images.

On the abortion issue, we found mixed support for this hypothesis. We did find some tendency for U.S. coverage to include more personal narratives. However, we found negligible differences in the role of journalists in framing the issue. Journalists were 29% of the U.S. nonstate speakers, versus 28% of the German nonstate speakers who offered framing ideas.

If we find no solid support for this part of the Hallin and Mancini hypothesis, we find very strong support for a second journalistic convention that flows from these differences in the nature of the public sphere. Journalists face a very different situation in choosing sources. The vacuum left by the unwillingness of U.S. political parties to speak on the abortion issue led journalists to either fill the gap themselves or seek other interpreters, including a variety of civil society actors.

On the abortion issue, this greater opportunity clearly converted into higher standing for these civil society actors. Advocates for anti-abortion- or pro-abortion-rights movement organizations accounted for about a quarter of the speakers in the United States, compared to only 2% in Germany.

Whether this hypothesis – that advocacy organizations in the civil society occupy a niche in the U.S. public sphere that is filled by political parties in the German public sphere – is supported on other issues as well remains an empirical question. On the nuclear power issue, for example, anti-nuclear movement organizations in Germany played a major role (see Joppke 1993; Rucht 1994) but also chose to seek political representation in the form of a new political party, the Greens. Other political interests, such as environmentalism, consumer rights, feminism, and democratic reform, also invested in this party to a greater or lesser degree. To the extent that they do so, they are strategically choosing the party-centered route at the cost of building national advocacy organizations like those that throng to Washington, DC. This seems quite obviously true in contrasting the party-centered and advocacy-organization routes taken by feminists who wish to influence a wider range of policy outcomes, not just abortion policy, in the two countries and would suggest that the pattern we found on the abortion issue would also characterize other issues. However, because many contemporary issues, such as environmentalism, have less historical association with particular political parties than abortion does, the extent of party dominance may also be lesser for these issues as well.

Nonetheless, the sharp differences that we find between Germany and the United States in how parties and movements address the public on the abortion issue suggest that, both in terms of establishing political control over attention paid to other particular policy issues and in regard to meeting normative criteria of inclusiveness in public discourse, the relative roles of parties and movements in taking leadership roles in framing issues in the media is an important and understudied aspect of political representation in democracies.

QUALITY OF THE DISCOURSE FOR A DEMOCRATIC PUBLIC SPHERE

Different strands of democratic theory offer different images of an ideal public sphere or set of spheres. Many of these differences in norms about who should participate and what the process and outcome should look like stem from basic differences about the role of the democratic citizen. Schudson (1998), in looking at the historical evolution of the model citizen in the United States, contrasts the ideals of republican virtue, the citizen as loyal party member, the informed citizen, and the rights-regarding citizen.

We have emphasized the contrast between the relatively passive citizen of representative liberal theory and the more engaged and active citizen of other traditions. Representative liberal theory embraces what we have called *elite dominance*. Citizens need to be minimally informed to make sure that policy-makers are ultimately accountable to them and party loyalty will help their representatives to be more effective. But they do not need to participate in public discourse on issues.

In fact, they not only do not need to, but public life may be better off if they don't. This is the tradition of "democratic realism" – the belief that ordinary citizens are poorly informed about public affairs, have no serious interest in it, and are generally ill-equipped for political participation. Dissenting voices should not be excluded from the public sphere a priori, but their inclusion depends on their having a legitimate representative to articulate their views in public forums. Those who want to be represented have the political obligation to use the representative process. Without their own representatives at the table, their preferred frames will, appropriately, be ignored. This is normatively desirable, since outsiders' frames are, at best, irrelevant in practice and, at worst, potentially dangerous.

The other three traditions – participatory, discursive, and constructionist models – all emphasize what we have called *popular inclusiveness*. In contrast to democratic realism, public discourse can and should empower citizens, give them voice and agency, build community, and help them to act on behalf of their interests and values. The normative standard here is one of engaging citizens in the democratic process by encouraging their active participation in the public sphere. This standard is better met in U.S. discourse, where social movements do not merely enjoy greater standing but have grown in visibility and influence among all actors of civil society. Moreover, the individuals affected by decisions – not only women but their partners, parents, doctors, and friends – are sought out by journalists and included in their own words.

If the citizens in the participatory liberal tradition seem especially "rights regarding," "republican virtue" is still very much present in the discursive tradition. To convince others, one must appeal to common interests and values. The process itself tends to produce citizens who think in terms of the public good rather than merely their private interests. The deliberative process helps citizens to engage in politics as a community of action and not merely as individuals.

On the abortion issue, German discourse meets quite well the standard of elite dominance. U.S. discourse, with its broader inclusion of civil society actors, is much closer to meeting the standard of popular inclusiveness. With respect to the style and content of the discourse in the two countries, we find more modest differences. Speakers in both countries respect the norm of civility with a few notable exceptions. Differences in the overall proportion of statements oriented toward dialogue are relatively small.

Differences exist mainly in the greater structure of dialogue in U.S. articles and the extent to which the lifeworld of the ordinary citizen enters the public discussion. U.S. articles include speakers from both core and periphery together; construct articles to include both Pro and Anti speakers in the same space; give more standing to speakers who are not representing any institution or organization but themselves; and include more personal narratives drawing on the experiences of the people affected. Discourse that treats women with unwanted pregnancies as clients rather than as agents is more common in German discourse. In all of these respects, U.S. discourse is closer than German discourse to the normative model emphasized by discursive and feminist/constructionist traditions.

Finally, if we look at the extent to which abortion discourse in both countries has moved toward closure, there is a much sharper decline in total media coverage of the issue following legislative and judicial decisions in Germany than in the United States. This outcome is embraced by the representative liberal theory but treated more equivocally by other traditions. For the discursive theory, closure should follow the development of a genuine consensus or rapprochement among the contesting actors that arises from the discourse. In the absence of consensus, the disappearance of discourse may reflect satisfaction with the outcome, whatever it might be, but it may also reflect resignation and bowing to the inevitable among those who are unhappy with the resulting policies. Participatory liberal and constructionist traditions are even more suspicious of closure because it can so easily promote a silencing of losers in a still unresolved conflict. For better or worse, then, German discourse better reflects this representative liberal standard than does U.S. discourse.

One can also learn a lot about normative standards in any forum from the metatalk of participants and journalists when they make comments on the quality of discourse. On the abortion issue, we found both convergent and divergent standards in the two countries. The convergent standards involve concerns about accuracy and competence, civility, mutual respect, dialogue, and weariness about how long the topic has been a subject of public discourse with a general call for closure.

Even on these convergent standards, however, there are subtle but important differences. On civility, for example, German observers sometimes see breaches in remarks that would be considered standard in U.S. discourse (see Chapter Twelve). In both countries, the sources quoted should be credible, but this involves a judgment about what credentials make one qualified for standing. This is made differently in Germany and the United States; in Germany institutional roles and expertise are central, while U.S. journalists use a wider array of criteria.

Furthermore, the frequent claim in both countries that the debate has gone on too long may hide a subtle difference. Calls for ending a discussion are never politically neutral. Silence favors the status quo. Calls for ending discussion can be an indirect way of expressing the belief that we really shouldn't be spending so much time talking about this issue because it is trivial or inappropriate for public discussion altogether. This is suggested by how early, especially in Germany, such complaints are heard.

Rather than considering "rights talk" to be the source of the intractability of the U.S. debate to come to any end, our analysis suggests that use of the language of rights is even more frequent in Germany than in the United States but is more evenly balanced between the two sides in the United States than in Germany. The hegemony of the Fetal Life frame that we found in Germany, however, is not a consensus that allows a decision with which everyone is satisfied, but a tilted field on which social movements that disagree can find little traction to move their agenda. The differences that we found between Germany and the United States do not suggest that the 1976 Constitutional Court decision in Germany was less dramatic or effective an intervention than the U.S. *Roe v. Wade* decision was, but quite the contrary. The court in Germany remains less contested and more convincing in part because the elite-dominated model of media coverage allows journalists to withdraw attention from the issue once it has been made a law, leaving questions of implementation and impact on individuals out of the picture.

In the United States, the greater inclusion of social movements as well as other voices from the periphery, the variety of legislative and judicial venues into which policy struggles can be brought, and the media practice of combining institutional speakers and their critics from civil society in the same articles all contribute to sustaining a contentious discourse in the United States even after an institutional decision has been reached. The sharp declines in coverage after a legislative decision in Germany are not only possible because there is a single central political institution responsible for drawing a law that applies to all the federal states, but also because the German media does not focus on the implementation of the laws or seek out the individual voices of those who are affected by them to comment on what they mean.

U.S. and German metatalk also sends different messages about *how* people should express themselves. In Germany, there are many objections to a style that emphasizes emotions and passion rather than detachment and rational argumentation. For some players, especially those who are more marginalized from the core of political decision making in both countries, passionate protest is the best means open to them to make their concerns known. Both symbolic expression and emotional speech are ways of drawing attention to what might otherwise be ignored. Thus the greater openness of U.S. discourse to diverse styles of speech is not only a reflection of the more prominent roles that movement speakers play but a facilitating condition for such involvement.

Finally, the theme of fairness that is so prominent in U.S. metatalk is much less important in German metatalk on abortion. The difference, we have argued, reflects differences in the nature of the public sphere and should hold for metatalk on other issues as well. German journalists have an institutional and procedural solution to the problem of fairness that does not depend on an assessment of content. Since the political parties can be arrayed on a left–right dimension with their strength determined by a popular vote, all that the media need do to insure fairness is to provide the parties with a voice proportional to their electoral share. Then, one adds to this mix other major institutional actors that historically have been spokespersons for recognized issue constituencies.

For the United States, the institutional solution is not really available on most issues, especially abortion. Lacking a procedural resolution, journalists and advocates look for a standard of fairness that balances different views rather than different kinds of actors. But since any content-based definition is frame-dependent, this solution can work only when there is a hegemonic frame. In the case of abortion, there are multiple frames, each embodying its own standard of fairness. For advocates, fairness ultimately reduces to whether or not one's own frame is consistently present and accurately portrayed.

U.S. journalists, then, are doomed to an endless quest for the holy grail of a frame-free standard of fairness that is unattainable. The quest itself, however, is conducive to meeting the normative criterion of including grassroots actors in the process. The lack of metatalk about fairness in Germany means that the consequence of journalistic practice for the exclusion of less institutionalized, grassroots actors goes unnoticed. This exclusion is reinforced by defining civility in a way that often excludes the characteristic rhetorical style of these actors.

In the United States, there is a broad enough boundary of civility to accommodate this rhetorical style and a sensitivity by journalists to accusations of unfairness. This sensitivity is kept alive by the quest for a frame-free standard. Journalistic uncertainty creates greater opportunities for the voices of grassroots actors to be heard, notwithstanding the advocate's own sense of being shut out or misrepresented.

FINAL THOUGHTS

Claims are sometimes made that "globalization has made it increasingly necessary to break with the nation-state centered analysis. . . . Social structure is becoming transnationalized and . . . studies should be predicated on a paradigmatic shift in the focus of the nation-state as the basic unit of analysis to the global system as the appropriate unit" (Robinson 1998, p. 561). Like a number of scholars who have criticized the view of globalization as a uniform and all-encompassing process (for example, Held et al. 1999; Garrett 1997; Soskice 1999), we believe that our study of abortion discourse should give one pause about prematurely discarding nation-state–centered analyses.

Abortion discourse would seem to be a prime candidate for an issue on which global discourse exists. In particular, the existence of a transnational pro-life lobby and a transnational women's movement with a rich infrastructure would appear to provide strong carriers for such a discourse. As for the women's movement, however, we found that their transnational discourse is focused primarily on reproductive rights issues in the countries of the South, not those at the center of discussion in Germany and the United States (Ferree and Gamson 1999). For understanding discourse in the countries studied here, this transnational discourse was of little relevance.

While there is more transnational influence between Germany and the United States on the anti-abortion side, including the import of U.S. materials such as the film *The Silent Scream* and through organizations such as the Catholic Church that are institutionally represented in both countries, there are still remarkable differences in what is contested and what resonates in each country. *The Silent Scream* drew considerable attention in the United States, where a discourse of individual rights and a focus on the costs of implementation of a law on those affected by it made this film a particularly effective way of focusing attention on the fetus as a person who could have rights and be harmed.

But since the idea of the fetus as a person deserving the protection of the state is already the hegemonic frame for the German debate, there was neither a strong effect on mobilizing anti-abortion forces, nor a shift in terms of discourse, nor an uproar from advocates of abortion rights. The social movement organization that sponsored this film in Germany remains small and all but invisible in the media. The Catholic Church in Germany, as an institutional player with legitimacy from the Constitutional Court for its central claims, sees no such need to "de-Catholicize" anti-abortion claims as the U.S. Catholic Church does. Nor does it face rivals, such as Catholics for a Free Choice in the United States, that challenge its claim to speak for all Catholics on this issue.

Our concept of a discursive opportunity structure suggests that what is true for abortion is likely to be true on many issues. We are struck by how many of the components are rooted in the specific history, institutions, and culture of each country. There are so many basic national differences shaping the arena in different ways that they overwhelm the influence of globalization. It is difficult to see how the latter adds much to our understanding of the discursive opportunity structure or of the choices of the relevant players. A globalization argument suggests that the abortion discourse in Germany and the United States should have converged in the last few decades, but we see no evidence of this. Deeply rooted national cultures and institutions continue to shape the discourse on abortion and other issues.

In the end, the German discourse produced an uneasy compromise that is accepted, in some cases grudgingly, by most people, while in the United States the abortion debate goes on and is even marred by violence. One might be tempted to conclude that greater elite dominance and lesser popular inclusion in German discourse was responsible for this outcome by excluding "extremists" from the debate.

Much of our evidence contradicts this interpretation. The broader inclusion of grassroots and movement actors in U.S. discourse did not produce more "inflammatory" or "absolute" frames in the material that we analyzed, nor did incivility increase over time as violence did. The U.S. discourse did not produce calls to take up arms against one's opponents or to use other extrainstitutional means for bringing about change. Indeed, in interviews we heard how participation in the public sphere often put anti-abortion speakers in the position of moderating their rhetoric to reach a wider audience, and we saw evidence of speakers turning to more rather than less pragmatic frames. Social movement organizations in the United States took up incremental strategies and abandoned claims for changes that they thought desirable but unobtainable, whether a constitutional amendment barring all abortions, on the one side, or a national policy that supported financially women's choices to have children or not, on the other.

Anti-abortion violence was deplored and repudiated by almost all opponents of abortion as they attempted, not always successfully, to disassociate themselves from such acts.[103] It increased in the United States even as anti-abortion movement organizations moved toward incremental and pragmatic solutions, such as focusing on late-term abortions and consent rules for teenagers seeking abortions. In the end, anti-abortion violence in the United States seems to depend less on the nature and quality of discourse and more on the easy availability of guns to an angry handful who have no interest in participating in a truly public debate, civil or otherwise.

But the stories that are produced about public issues and the normative value of the ways in which such debate is carried out have implications for democracies that extend beyond calculating if they might contribute to violence in some way, whether we have been able to measure any such effects or not. Narrowing concern with public discourse to the issue of violence alone is seriously misleading. The mass

[103] This repudiation of violence appears to be virtually a precondition for inclusion in the array of actors who may be legitimately accorded voice in the mass media as a public arena. Although there are some individuals and groups on the anti-abortion side of the debate who do advocate violence (e.g., Michael Bray, convicted of conspiracy in the bombings of ten abortion clinics and the author of a book justifying killing providers that was published by Advocates for Life Ministries, and other groups such as Lambs of Christ and Life Enterprise Unlimited) these radical fringe groups do not receive standing in the mainstream newspapers that we studied.

media as a public arena may – or may not – offer a terrain on which ordinary people have an opportunity to participate as citizens in shaping public discourse about matters that concern them. Whether this is what we believe that democracy is and ought to be about is something that examining democratic theories should empower us all to decide for ourselves. When and how and to whom these two countries offer such opportunities is something that we hope we have been able to demonstrate.

Methodological Appendix

A copy of the complete codebook used in the content analysis, including detailed instructions to coders on how to handle ambiguous statements, is available at www.ssc.wisc.edu/abortionstudy. This Web site also includes additional data on our procedures for sampling articles, a complete list of the German and U.S. organizations surveyed, the questionnaire used in the survey of organizations, and some of the data sets used in our various analyses.

The brief appendix provided here, which complements our Chapter Three on methods, lists the spokespersons and journalists whom we interviewed. It also provides a short summary that the reader may use to gain a better idea of how we operationalized a number of key variables. But for a full exposition with examples, consult the Web site listed.

The following appendix has three main sections, outlining first the persons with whom we conducted interviews, then the main ideas that were represented in each of the eight frames in all three specific directions in the content analysis, and then the particular cross-frame clusters of ideas that were used to create other variables.

I. THE INTENSIVE INTERVIEWS

As described in Chapter Three, we completed interviews with spokespersons for selected U.S. and German organizations (aside from state agencies) who were involved, directly or indirectly, in shaping abortion discourse (for the selection criteria, see Chapter Three). We also interviewed a small number of journalists who frequently wrote on abortion for the newspapers in our sample. The complete list of interviewees is as follows:

PARTICIPANT INTERVIEWS BY COUNTRY

GERMANY (N = 23)

Anti-Abortion Groups

Dr. Wolfgang Furch, *Pro-Vita*
Margriet de Haan, *Catholic Women's Association*
Dr. Rudolf Hammerschmidt, *German Catholic Bishops Conference*
Christa Heinel, *Rahel* (Rachel)
Benno Hofschulte, *SOS-Leben Deutschland* (SOS-Life)
Renate Neuhierl, *Women's Union of the CSU*
Dr. Felix Raabe, *Central Committee of German Catholics*
Hartmut Steeb, *Union of Christian Pro Life Groups/Christian Alliance*

Pro-Abortion-Rights Groups

Joachim von Baross, *Pro Familia*, national level
Marion Buchner, *Pro Familia*, Augsburg
Dr. Hertha Engelbrecht, *Women's Law Association*
Rita Griesshaber, *Alliance90/Green Party*
Gabriel Kruk, *Women's Health Center*, Frankfurt am Main
Regina Linzbach, *Federal Network for the Abolition of §218*, Berlin
Vera Morgenstern, *ÖTV* (Public Employees Union)
Anne Neugebauer, *local group for abolition of §218*, Münster
Ingeburg Gruender-Schaefer, *AWO* (Worker's Welfare), Kassel
Christina Schenk, *PDS* (Party of Democratic Socialism)
Karen Schoeler, *AWO* (Worker's Welfare), national level

Other

Thomas Krueger, *Lutheran Church of Germany*
Ada-Maria Mathé, *Diakonisches Werk* (Lutheran Social Services), Hessen-Nassau
Annegret Wanka, *Working Group of State-Approved Counseling Services*, Munich
Dr. Inge Wolf, *Women Doctors' Association*

UNITED STATES (N = 20)

Anti-Abortion Groups

Helen Alvare, *National Conference of Catholic Bishops*
Flip Benham, *Operation Rescue*
Denise Ciocilonne, *National Life Center* (Birthright)
Serrin Foster, *Feminists for Life*

Wanda Franz, *National Right to Life Committee*
Scott Hogenson, *Republican National Committee*

Pro-Abortion-Rights Groups

Carol Campbell, *National Abortion Federation*
Rosemary Candelario, *Reproductive Rights National Network* (R2N2)
Charlotte Elliotson, Heather O'Neal, and Karen Steinam, *Population Council*
Darrel Figueroa, *Planned Parenthood*
Kim Gandy, *National Organization for Women* (NOW)
Jane Hull Harvey, *United Methodist Church*
Heather Hauck, *Coalition of Labor Union Women* (CLUW)
Jay Heavner, *Religious Coalition for Reproductive Choice* (formerly, Religious Coalition for Abortion Rights)
Jennifer Jackman, *Fund for a Feminist Majority*
Frances Kissling and John O'Brien, *Catholics for a Free Choice*
Lawrence Lader, *Abortion Rights Mobilization*
Robert and Jana, *Refuse and Resist*
Emily Tynes, *Communications Consortium Media Center*
Catherine Wineset, Louise Mellen, and Sheryl Cohen, *ACLU Reproductive Rights Project*

JOURNALISTS

GERMANY

Günther Bannas, *Frankfurter Allgemeine Zeitung*
Stephan-Andreas Casdorff, *Süddeutsche Zeitung*
Friedrich Fromme, *Frankfurter Allgemeine Zeitung*
Heidrun Graupner, *Süddeutsche Zeitung*

UNITED STATES

Linda Greenhouse, *The New York Times*
David Shaw, *The Los Angeles Times*
Karen Tumulty (former staff member, *The Los Angeles Times*) presently, Congressional correspondent for *Time Magazine.*

II. THE EIGHT MAJOR FRAMES AND THREE DIRECTIONS OF IDEA ELEMENTS

The following three tables summarize in greater detail the distribution of the idea elements (ies) across the eight frames that we discuss in Chapter

Six. Each table reports only the ideas that were actually used with any frequency in either country and shows the relative share of ideas in that particular direction in a given frame (that is, a "framelet") as well as their relative share of all of the ideas that were expressed or were conducive to supporting that particular direction for policy. Pro-abortion-rights ideas are those that favor less restrictions, anti-abortion ideas support prohibition or greater restrictiveness, and neutral ideas are those that are either not indicative of a direction or that indicate opposite directions in different countries. For example, seeing teenagers as being more in need of counseling than adults is an argument that would tend to support more restrictions in the United States but fewer in Germany.

PRO-CHOICE DIRECTION	Germany		United States	
Major ies within framelets (% of framelet accounted for by these ies)	% within framelet	% of all Pro	% within framelet	% of all Pro
Pro1	(71%)	**7.8**	(72%)	**3.8**
Fetus not fully human	14%	1.1	17%	0.6
Science says fetus not life	15%	1.2	20%	0.8
Constitution says fetus not life	5%	0.4	15%	0.6
Displaces concern for born child, woman (2 ies)	9%	0.7	18%	0.7
Enlist women's cooperation to protect fetus	29%	1.7	2%	0.1
Pro 2	(72%)	**13.9**	(73%)	**9.5**
Women take priority before a certain time	1%	0.1	17%	1.7
Rape & incest justify abortion	25%	3.5	37%	3.5
Infant suffering/handicap justifies abortion (3 ies)	30%	4.2	14%	1.4
Social need/economic circumstances justify abortion	16%	2.3	5%	0.5
Pro3	(68%)	**28.4**	(71%)	**14.5**
Women's self determination	8%	2.1	11%	1.6
Women's absolute self determination	18%	5.2	16%	2.3
Women's limited self determination	20%	5.7	4%	0.6

PRO-CHOICE DIRECTION	Germany		United States	
Major ies within framelets (% of framelet accounted for by these ies)	% within framelet	% of all Pro	% within framelet	% of all Pro
Abortion is a constitutional right	2%	0.6	15%	2.2
Less restrictions imply more respect for women	12%	3.4	3%	0.5
Limiting ab. oppresses women, feminist issue (4 ies)	8%	2.3	22%	3.3
Pro4	**(68%)**	**11.9**	**(64%)**	**30.4**
Privacy from state, for women & family (3 ies)	14%	1.6	26%	8.0
Doctor-patient privacy	11%	1.3	8%	2.5
Separation of church & state (5 ies)	16%	1.8	19%	5.8
Pro-choice is majority view	0	—	9%	2.7
Prohibition hypocrisy, only makes criminals (2 ies)	27%	3.2	2%	0.5
Pro5	**(80%)**	**6.4**	**(77%)**	**8.4**
Religious people differ in views of abortion	12%	0.7	31%	2.6
Antiabortion stance is hypocrisy	6%	0.4	13%	1.1
Women choose abortion for major reasons	25%	1.6	6%	0.5
Abortion morally neutral health care	2%	0.2	25%	2.1
Abortion should not be stigmatized	35%	2.2	2%	0.1
Pro6	**(81%)**	**3.6**	**(76%)**	**9.9**
Abortion for population control (4 ies)	20%	0.8	10%	0.8
Abortion for dealing with poverty (4 ies)	0	—	11%	1.1
Abortion for family planning (3 ies)	19%	0.7	11%	1.1
Anti-abortion means anti-contraception	0	—	15%	1.5

continued

PRO-CHOICE DIRECTION	Germany		United States	
Major ies within framelets (% of framelet accounted for by these ies)	% within framelet	% of all Pro	% within framelet	% of all Pro
Abortion a symbol of modernity	38%	1.4	8%	0.8
Abortion part of mod. health care, reprod. tech. (2 ies)	4%	0.1	21%	2.1
Pro7	(83%)	**18.6**	(76%)	**12.4**
Horror stories, claims illegal abortion harms (2 ies)	24%	4.5	33%	4.1
Legal abortion good for women's health	4%	0.6	11%	1.4
Limits are burdensome (8 ies)	4%	0.8	22%	2.8
Limits are ineffective, lead to illegal (2 ies)	35%	6.8	9%	1.1
Reduce abortion with permissive laws (2 ies)	16%	3.0	1%	0.1
Pro8	(83%)	**9.3**	(83%)	**11.1**
Limits unjust to doctors	0	—	14%	1.5
Affordability, justice for poor (3 ies)	32%	3.0	35%	3.8
Funding limits specifically unjust	2%	0.1	25%	2.7
East-west issues (5 ies)	23%	2.1	0	—
Geographic injustices	26%	2.5	9%	1.0

PRO-LIFE DIRECTION	Germany		United States	
Major ies within framelets	% within framelet	% of all Anti	% within framelet	% of all Anti
Anti1	(72%)	**48.8**	(68%)	**34.3**
Protecting life is the issue	3%	1.6	14%	4.9
Social value of fetal life	13%	6.3	6%	2.1
Fetus is a baby/child	4%	2.2	14%	4.6
Abortion is murder	16%	7.9	25%	8.6
Constitution says fetus is life	16%	7.9	3%	1.1
Fetus has legal rights	20%	9.8	7%	2.3

PRO-LIFE DIRECTION	Germany		United States	
Major ies within framelets (% of framelet)	% within framelet	% of all Anti	% within framelet	% of all Anti
Anti2	(88%)	**16.7**	(75%)	**8.7**
Abortion ok only to save mothers life	9%	1.4	44%	3.8
Family need is a pretext	21%	3.4	2%	0.1
Fetus should have priority	21%	3.4	12%	1.0
Counseling should put fetus first	37%	6.2	3%	0.3
Private action to protect fetus is justified	0	—	14%	1.2
Anti3	(94%)	**5.3**	(88%)	**4.4**
Abortion devalues motherhood/sacrifice (4 ies)	16%	0.9	8%	0.8
Prohibition is in women's interests	1%	0.1	9%	0.4
Protect women from abortion industry	17%	0.9	14%	0.6
Protect women from coercion	36%	1.9	19%	0.9
Abortion not women's/ feminist issue (3 ies)	17%	0.9	13%	0.6
Ignores fathers' rights	7%	0.4	25%	1.1
Anti4	(91%)	**11.9**	(61%)	**20.8**
Public funding inappropriate	7%	0.8	23%	4.7
Religious freedom requires noncompliance	18%	2.2	3%	0.7
States rights to be antiabortion	1%	0.1	16%	3.3
State obligation to regulate morality (4 ies)	40%	4.7	8%	1.6
Government should make society moral	19%	2.3	1%	0.2
Abortion is not private (4 ies)	6%	0.8	10%	2.0
Anti5	(81%)	**12.0**	(73%)	**19.2**
Abortion is simply wrong	44%	5.3	20%	3.8
Abortion indicates an immoral society	10%	1.2	7%	1.3

continued

PRO-LIFE DIRECTION	Germany		United States	
Major ies within framelets (% of framelet)	% within framelet	% of all Anti	% within framelet	% of all Anti
Christian morality is unambiguous	17%	2.0	26%	4.9
Morally unlike contraception	7%	0.9	11%	2.2
Implications for sexual morality (5 ies)	3%	0.3	9%	1.8
Anti6	(72%)	**0.8**	(88%)	**3.9**
Permissive laws uncivilized	28%	0.2	3%	0.1
Abortion not needed for pop control	8%	0.1	14%	0.5
Not a means to control poverty	0	—	17%	0.6
Inappropriate targeting of minorities	0	—	12%	0.5
Should not rationally control reproduction (3 ies)	16%	0.2	30%	1.3
Stop runaway medicine	20%	0.2	12%	0.5
Anti7	(92%)	**4.3**	(86%)	**7.7**
Can't reduce abortion w/o criminal law (2 ies)	41%	1.8	5%	0.4
Teens need help of restriction/ parents (2 ies)	0	—	27%	2.2
Regulations helpful, not excessive (4 ies)	2%	0.1	15%	1.2
Legal abortion dangerous, incl horror story (3 ies)	25%	1.1	38%	2.9
Not right to weigh costs/ benefits	24%	1.0	1%	0.1
Anti8	(100%)	**0.2**	(80%)	**1.0**
Not discriminatory, unjust to some (3 ies)	60%	0.1	30%	0.3
No violation of constitutional rights	0	—	28%	0.3
No real inequality in access	40%	0.1	22%	0.2

MIXED/NEUTRAL DIRECTION	Germany		United States	
Major ies within framelets (% of framelet)	% within framelet	% of all Neutral	% within framelet	% of all Neutral
Neutral1	(100%)	**2.4**	(92%)	**12.3**
Issue is when life begins	19%	0.4	33%	4.0
Protection depends on stage of development	65%	1.5	40%	4.9
Nature of fetus differs by stage	16%	0.4	19%	2.3
Neutral2	(90%)	**29.3**	(76%)	**13.2**
There is a conflict between fetus and woman	27%	8.0	13%	1.7
Abortion might sometimes be lesser evil	37%	10.8	8%	1.0
Individual or social ambivalence (4 ies)	4%	1.3	23%	4.8
Medical reasons are compelling (2 ies)	22%	6.4	33%	4.4
Neutral3	(100%)	**1.3**	(100%)	**0.7**
Issue is position of women in society	100%	1.3	100%	0.7
Neutral4	(89%)	**20.7**	(78%)	**15.8**
Issue is what state should do	4%	0.9	18%	2.9
Abortion should not be litmus test	0	—	16%	2.5
About democracy	2%	0.4	10%	1.6
Judicial decisions undemocratic	6%	1.3	15%	2.4
State morality should be in noncriminal law	76%	15.7	6%	0.1
Authority has spoken	1%	0.1	13%	2.1
Neutral5	(84%)	**36.5**	(56%)	**26.3**
Abortion is an issue of morality	9%	3.3	13%	3.3
Abortions should be fewer (2 ies)	19%	7.0	5%	1.4

continued

MIXED/NEUTRAL DIRECTION	Germany		United States	
Major ies within framelets (% of framelet)	% within framelet	% of all Neutral	% within framelet	% of all Neutral
People answer moral questions differently	3%	1.0	11%	2.9
Socioeconomic support is better than abortion	17%	6.2	5%	1.3
Sex ed. is better than abortion	21%	7.6	15%	4.0
Society, family should support woman (2 ies)	15%	5.3	6%	1.5
Neutral6	(87%)	**2.9**	(78%)	**28.8**
Issue is social impact of abortion	33%	1.0	3%	0.9
Society is divided by feelings on abortion	0	—	38%	10.8
Abortion is an intrinsically undecidable issue	33%	1.0	8%	2.4
Abortion conflict threatens social peace	6%	0.2	24%	7.1
Best position is one that ends conflict	15%	0.4	5%	1.4
Neutral7	(100%)	**6.5**	(100%)	**1.6**
Important to weigh costs and benefits	32%	2.1	57%	0.9
Support for women isn't enough	18%	1.1	0	—
Counseling helps women	50%	3.3	43%	0.7
Neutral8	(100%)	**0.4**	(100%)	**1.3**
Issue is social justice	100%	0.4	100%	1.3

III. IDEAS CODED IN SPECIFIC CROSS-FRAME CLUSTERS (SPANNING THE EIGHT MAJOR FRAMES)

In addition to the eight frames, we also grouped specific idea elements into special-purpose clusters that cut across the boundaries of frames and operationalized particular types or uses of discourse. The clusters used in the analyses reported in this book were those that operationalized the core ideas of the constitutional courts in each country (constitutional clusters), those that expressed certain ideas associated with traditions of the left (autonomy, social needs, and social justice clusters), and those that had certain discursive characteristics (inflammatory or "hot button" language, rebutting the claims of the other side). The specific idea elements coded into each of these clusters are as follows.

CONSTITUTIONAL CLUSTERS

GERMANY

112 – Protecting life is the highest social value, the most important issue.

114 – Fetus is unborn baby, child.

122 – Assertion that constitutional protection of life includes the fetus.

140 – Restrictions/limits on abortion are about protecting the developing life.

142 – The issue is to protect the lives of unborn children at all times and stages.

290 – A child's right to life takes precedence over the mother's right to self-determination.

291 – Counseling should be directed to the purpose of protecting life.

UNITED STATES

190 – The protection owed to the fetus varies with the stage of development.

192 – Nature of fetus differs depending on stage.

213 – Before a certain time, women's self determination takes priority over the fetus.

214 – Because of disagreement about when life begins, the woman has priority.

314 – A woman's right to decide is a fundamental right guaranteed by the constitution.

410 – Laws restricting abortion infringe on personal freedom.

411 – Families have a right to make contraceptive decisions, including the choice to abort, without government interference.

412 – The issue is about the privacy of individual women.

413 – The government should not intrude in the privacy of doctor/patient relationships.

433 – Federal mandates on abortion funding violate states or hospital rights.

456 – The state's role should be limited to providing reasonable safety standards.

AUTONOMY CLUSTER

184 – Women have no legal obligation to the fetus; people are not obliged to save others' lives.

210 – Assertion that women's rights have priority (no rationale given).

211 – The life of a fetus is less valuable than a woman's.

212 – Women have a right to self-defense; the fetus is threatening the woman's physical or psychological life.

213 – Before a certain time, women take priority over the fetus.

214 – Because of disagreement about when life begins, the woman has priority.

310 – Women have a right to self-determination.

311 – Women have an absolute right to control their bodies.

312 – Women should have the right to make certain decisions, but the right to decide has limits.

313 – No contraception is perfect, so women cannot control pregnancy without legal abortion.

314 – A woman's right to decide is a fundamental right guaranteed by the constitution.

320 – Less restriction on abortion implies respect for women as decision-makers.

321 – Offering women social incentives to bear children is demeaning.

322 – Counseling is a disrespectful and manipulative strategy.

340 – Limiting or prohibiting abortion oppresses women; abortion is an essential part of a feminist agenda.

341 – Abortion rights are a symbol of women's control over their lives and the right to participate in public life.

342 – Limits on abortion are part of a general anti-feminist agenda.

343 – Limits on abortion denigrate, stereotype, and demean women.

351 – Women who do not have the right to decide about abortion are not free to determine their lives in any other way.

352 – Women's economic opportunities depend on reproductive rights.

353 – Not all women are willing or able to be mothers.

354 – Women will never be able to achieve practical equality with men until they have control over if and when they get pregnant.

360 – The issue at stake is women's power.

361 – Abortion is, in general, a conflict between men and women over who has the power to decide.

362 – Giving husbands power to withhold consent for abortion is wronging women.

363 – Women will decide to have an abortion or not, regardless of whether it is legal.

410 – Laws restricting abortion infringe on personal freedom.

411 – Families have a right to make contraceptive decisions, including choice to abort, without government interference.

412 – The issue is about the privacy of individual women.

413 – The government should not intrude in the privacy of doctor/patient relationships.

414 – It is not appropriate for the government to address moral questions.

562 – Women choose abortion for their own major, responsible reasons.

597 – Abortion is one option for pregnant women, among other options.

635 – Opposition to abortion will necessarily lead to blocking access to contraception.

SOCIAL NEEDS CLUSTER

130 – Protecting fetal life is on the same level with protecting other vulnerable groups.

131 – Protecting fetal life is linked to protecting the elderly from right-to-die groups.

132 – Protecting fetal life is linked to protecting the handicapped.

136 – The best way to protect unborn life is to protect living women.

176 – Concern for the fetus displaces concern for women.

182 – The role of protecting unborn life belongs with nonstate agents (for example, family and church).

223 – Women are conflicted over the decision to abort, and threatening them with criminal law is the least suitable way to help them.

240 – Eugenic abortions protect children and families from suffering.

241 – Serious physical deformities are grounds for abortion.

242 – A mental handicap is grounds for abortion.

252 – Mothers' health needs outweigh fetal rights.

253 – Insuring the psychological health of women justifies abortion.

260 – There are life situations in which a woman cannot be expected to bear a child that she does not want.

261 – Family economic circumstances can justify having an abortion.

262 – Other family needs (such as care taking) outweigh the rights of the fetus.

291 – All counseling should have the purpose of persuading women away from having an abortion.

380 – Prohibiting abortion is in women's best interests.

381 – Women need to be protected from the abortion industry.

382 – Women need protection from being coerced into having abortions that they do not want.

383 – The true feminist position would be anti-abortion.

384 – Women are not competent to decide on their own about abortion.

455 – Laws about social welfare measures better express the moral concern of the state than criminal law does.

456 – The state's role should be limited to providing reasonable safety standards.

534 – Permissive abortion laws allow men to escape accountability.

570 – General claim that there are alternatives to abortion.

571 – Socio-economic support for women is an alternative to abortion.

573 – Promoting adoption is preferable to allowing abortion as a means of dealing with unwanted children.

580 – Society should show more solidarity and support to pregnant women and to mothers instead of complaining about the high number of abortions.

582 – Responsibility for the decision about abortion falls on the family, not individual woman.

583 – Responsibility for the decision about abortion falls on society, not the individual woman.

584 – Society should protect young women from illegal abortions.

592 – Abortion is just like other forms of birth control.

595 – Stigma placed on abortion only makes abortion harder on the woman than it already is.

596 – Unmarried mothers should not be stigmatized but helped.

610 – General claim that population control is the central issue.

611 – Abortion is a necessary means of restraining population growth.

615 – Making abortion more difficult will only serve to increase the birthrate; this is bad.

618 – If abortion is permitted, the birthrate will decline; this is bad.

622 – Abortion is a cheaper alternative to welfare and medical care for poor mothers and children than having and raising a baby.

623 – People who can't afford to raise children should not be allowed to have them.

630 – General, nonevaluative statements casting abortion as family planning.

631 – Family planning is the goal of abortion.

632 – Unwanted children will be future social problems (for example, child abuse, neglect, crime).

634 – Abortion prevents terrible social problems for pregnant teenagers.

674 – Knowledgeable, informed people (experts) are anti-abortion.

711 – Horror story of danger and trauma when obtaining an illegal, or restricted, abortion.

712 – Making abortions difficult to obtain makes them dangerous.

714 – Conflict over abortion (for example, protestors, waiting periods, etc.) increases the traumatic consequences of obtaining an abortion.

735 – Just prohibiting abortion is not enough.

751 – Women need a lot of help in reaching a decision about abortion.

752 – Teenagers who are considering abortion need guidance from their family.

753 – Major life decisions should be thought through carefully; waiting periods and counseling are good because they produce thoughtful decisions.

761 – Parental notification is required for other medical procedures, so abortion should be no exception.

771 – Horror stories of traumatic *legal* abortions.

772 – Abstract claims of danger (for example, personal or psychological trauma) from legal abortions.

774 – Legal abortions are not dangerous or harmful.

HOT BUTTON CLUSTER

115 – Abortion is murder.

116 – Abortion is mass murder.

133 – Implicit or explicit link between abortion and the Nazi Holocaust.

137 – Analogy with slavery (used to justify protection of the fetus).

311 – Women have an absolute right to control their bodies that it is immoral to infringe on.

462 – Abortion is evidence of the immorality of a government.

640 – Laws against, or restrictions on, abortion takes society back to the Middle Ages.

646 – It is ignorant and backward to be anti-abortion.

671 – Permissive abortion laws are uncivilized and primitive.

SOCIAL INJUSTICE CLUSTER

800 – The issue is fairness and justice to everyone equally.

810 – Justice and decency demand legal abortions.

811 – Criminal prosecution produces random punishment and haphazard enforcement.

820 – General emphasis on the affordability of abortion as a principle.

821 – Wealthy women have always had access to safe/legal abortions.

822 – Prohibition or regulation of abortion has the most impact on poor women.

823 – Financial restrictions on abortion (for example, restrictions on third-party payments) are a special burden on the poor.

831 – Minority women will especially suffer if abortions are illegal.

832 – Prohibition of abortion is especially unjust for immigrant women.

841 – Regulation of abortion is particularly unfair to East German Women.

842 – Regulation of abortion is unfair to all East Germans because it is a symbolic rejection of East Germany.

843 – New laws about abortion must be fair to both East and West Germans.

844 – It is unjust to allow East German women to obtain abortions without penalty when West German women will be punished for having an abortion.

851 – Rural women suffer a greater burden from restrictions on abortion.

852 – Young women suffer particularly from restrictions on abortion.

853 – Geographic injustices because of variation between states.

854 – Women with little education will suffer particularly from restrictions on abortion.

REBUTTAL CLUSTER

150 – General rejection of pro-life claims.

151 – Fetus is not yet fully human.

161 – The determination of when life begins is medically impossible.

162 – Constitutional protection of life does not cover the unborn fetus.

163 – Human rights language not intended to cover unborn fetus.

164 – The majority of people do not think that abortion is murder.

165 – Religions see fetuses differently, so no absolute definition of life is possible.

166 – Historical argument about abortion (for example, abortion has been legal for most of this country's history).

170 – All slippery slope arguments are inherently fallacious.

172 – Division drawn between the kind of life a fetus represents and any group of born persons.

173 – It trivializes the Holocaust and its deliberate evil to compare it to abortion.

174 – Consistency in pro-life position requires general pacifism and/or opposition to the death penalty.

175 – Concern with unborn children displaces concern with born children.

176 – Concern with fetuses displaces concern with women.

180 – It is not the state's role to protect unborn life.

182 – Role of protecting unborn life belongs with nonstate agents (for example, church, family).

183 – Definition of life does not per se offer legal personhood or protection.

184 – When life begins is irrelevant to the legal obligations that women have to the fetus.

270 – In deciding whether abortion is legal, the context of the pregnancy does not matter.

271 – Threats to the mother's health are a pretext.

272 – Eugenic claim is hypocritical because every child would prefer to be born.

273 – Eugenic claim is immoral.

274 – Eugenic claim is a pretext for doctors/state attempt to grab power over who should live or die.

276 – Family need and social necessity are pretexts.

278 – It is not legitimate to distinguish between wanted and unwanted children.

280 – There is no conflict between the fetus and the woman.

283 – There is no such thing as an unwanted child.

290 – Self-determination cannot override life; general priority of the fetus over the woman.

293 – No other rights or situations can reduce the rights of the fetus.

380 – Prohibiting abortion is in women's best interests.

381 – Women need protection from the abortion industry.

383 – The true feminist position would be anti-abortion.

384 – Women are not competent to decide on their own.

390 – General claim that abortion is not a special issue of women's.

391 – Abortion is not an issue of women's equality.

392 – Abortion is, or should be, irrelevant to the women's movement.

393 – Giving women alone the power to decide ignores the rights of the fathers.

394 – Women have no right to self-determination.

414 – It is not appropriate for the government to address moral questions.

470 – *Roe v. Wade* was wrong – abortion is not private.

471 – The decision to have an abortion is not a private decision.

472 – General denial of a right to privacy.

473 – It goes too far to put abortion under a right to privacy.

474 – Privacy/free speech is not absolute; it is limited by government funding.

480 – Church and state are not separate.

481 – Social justice analogy to legitimate church influence in abortion debate.

482 – Anti-separation of church and state on grounds of tradition or history.

484 – Abortion is not a matter of special interest to Christians.

490 – Abortion is not an issue of democracy, but of something else.

516 – It is morally impossible to support legal abortion if one personally opposes it.

523 – Abortion is not a morally neutral medical treatment.

524 – Abortion is not morally equivalent to contraception.

590 – Abortion is not a moral issue.

594 – There are not too many, or too frequent, abortions.

613 – Opposition to abortion is insensitive to population problems.

615 – Making abortion more difficult will only serve to increase the birthrate; this is bad.

618 – If abortion is permitted, the birthrate will decline; this is bad.

624 – Opposition to abortion is insensitive to poverty and hunger.

655 – Medicine/technology cannot resolve political problems and end social divisions.

672 – Modern medicine has eliminated the need for abortion.

681 – Rebuttal of argument that abortion is needed for population control.

682 – Abortion should not be used to control poverty.

683 – Permissive abortion laws are not good to poor, are targeted to minorities.

721 – The requirement for counseling creates an unnecessary burden.

722 – Waiting periods create an unnecessary burden.

723 – Barriers to funding create an unnecessary burden.

724 – Requirements for second opinions create an unnecessary burden.

725 – Parental consent is an unnecessary burden.

726 – Spousal consent is an unnecessary burden.

727 – Justification before a judge is an unnecessary burden.

728 – Legal burdens do not end abortion or lead to illegal, out of state, or out of country abortions.

730 – Restrictive or penal laws are ineffective ways to regulate abortions.

731 – There are more effective ways that the state could use to reduce the number of abortions than by prohibition or regulation.

732 – Prohibiting abortion does not prevent it; it just turns women into criminals.

734 – Laws cannot create the conditions that would make abortion unnecessary.

735 – Just prohibiting abortion is not enough.

740 – Noncriminal measures do not work.

741 – Supportive measures for women and children do not stop abortions.

742 – It is not possible to reduce the number of abortions without criminal laws.

750 – Regulation of abortion is helpful, not harmful, to women.

751 – Women need a lot of help in reaching a decision about abortion.

752 – Teenagers who are considering abortion need guidance from their family.

753 – Major life decisions should be thought through carefully; waiting periods and counseling are good because they produce thoughtful decisions.

760 – The burden of restricted abortions exists but is not excessive.

761 – Parental notification is required for other medical procedures, so abortion should be no exception.

762 – Burdens on adult women are manageable.

763 – The burden of spousal consent is necessary to be fair to men.

764 – Deaths from illegal abortions are exaggerated or false.

774 – Legal abortion is not proven to be emotionally or medically dangerous.

780 – It is inappropriate to consider costs and benefits when fundamental issues of right and wrong are at stake.

781 – Women are to blame for getting in risky situations.

782 – Two wrongs do not make a right.

860 – Inequality in access to abortion is not discriminatory.

861 – Inequality in access to abortion does not discriminate against the poor.

862 – Inequality in access to abortion does not discriminate against blacks.

863 – Inequality in access to abortion does not violate constitutional rights.

870 – There is no real inequality in access to abortion.

871 – Unequal access to abortion is not relevant in this particular case.

872 – It is fair for the government to not provide services or information.

References

Ackerman, Bruce. 1980. *Social Justice in the Liberal State*. New Haven, CT: Yale University Press.

1989. "Why Dialogue?" *Journal of Philosophy* 86: 5–22.

Alan Guttmacher Institute. 1999. *The Status of Major Abortion-related Laws and Policies in the States*. Washington, DC: Alan Guttmacher Institute.

Allen, Ann Taylor. 1985. "Mothers of the New Generation: Adele Schreiber, Helene Stöcker, and the Evolution of a German Idea of Motherhood." *Signs* 10: 418–438.

Anderson, Benedict. 1991. *Imagined Communities*. New York: Verso.

Arato, Andrew and Jean Cohen. 1992. *Civil Society and Political Theory*. Cambridge, MA: MIT Press.

Arendt, Hans-Jürgen. 1970. "Die Volksaktion gegen den Papstbrief und §218 im Frühjahr 1931 – eine demokratische Massenbewegung unter Führung der KPD," pp. 92–98 in *Wissenschaftliche Studien des Pädagogischen Institut Leipzig*, Vol. 1.

Aubert, Vilhelm. 1972. "Interessenkonflikt und Wertkonflikt," pp. 178–205 in Walter L. Bühl (ed), *Konflikt und Konfliktstrategie*. München: Nymphenburger Verlag.

Augstein, Renate. 1983. "Abtreibung," pp. 9–13 in Johanna Beyer, Franziska Lamott, and Birgit Meyer (eds), *Frauenlexikon. Stichworte zur Selbstbestimmung*. München: C.H. Beck.

Bachrach, Peter. 1967. *The Theory of Democratic Elitism: A Critique*. Boston: Little Brown.

Baker, C. Edwin. 1998. "The Media that Citizens Need." *University of Pennsylvania Law Review* 147: 317–407.

Barber, Benjamin R. 1984. *Strong Democracy: Participatory Politics for a New Age*. Berkeley: University of California Press.

Benhabib, Seyla (ed). 1996. *Democracy and Difference*. Princeton, NJ: Princeton University Press.

1992. "Models of Public Space," pp. 73–98 in Craig Calhoun (ed), *Habermas and the Public Sphere*. Cambridge, MA: MIT Press.

Bennett, W. Lance. 1975. *The Political Mind and the Political Environment*. Lexington, MA: D.C. Heath.

Berger, Peter L. 1969. *The Sacred Canopy*. Garden City, NY: Anchor Press.

Berkovich, Nitza. 1999. *From Motherhood to Citizenship: Women's Rights and International Organizations*. Baltimore, MD: Johns Hopkins University Press.

Billig, Werner. 2000. "Bundesverfassungsgericht," pp. 100–105 in Uwe Andersen and Wichard Woyke (eds), *Handwörterbuch des politischen Systems der Bundesrepublik Deutschland* (Fourth and revised edition). Bonn: Bundeszentrale für politische Bildung.

Blanchard, Dallas A. 1994. *The Anti-Abortion Movement and the Rise of the Religious Right.* New York: Twayne.

Bobbio, Norberto. 1997. *Left and Right: The Significance of a Political Distinction.* Chicago: University of Chicago Press.

Bordo, Susan. 1995. "Are Mothers Persons? Reproductive Rights and the Politics of Subjectivity," pp. 71–97 in *Unbearable Weight: Feminism, Western Culture and the Body.* Berkeley: University of California Press.

Böttger, Barbara. 1990. *Das Recht auf Gleichheit und Differenz: Elisabeth Selbert und das Kampf um Artikel 3.2 des Grundgesetzes.* Münster: Westfälisches Dampfboot.

Bray, Michael. 1994. *A Time to Kill.* Portland, OR: Advocates for Life Ministries

Bundesweite Koordination Frauen gegen den §218 (ed). 1991. *Vorsicht "Lebensschützer"! Die Macht der organisierten Abtreibungsgegner.* Hamburg: Konkret Literatur Verlag.

Burke, Edmund. 1993 (originally 1790). *Reflections on the Revolution in France.* Edited with introduction by L.G. Mitchell. New York: Oxford University Press.

Burns, Gene. 2002. *The Moral Veto: Stalemate and Change in American Debates over Contraception and Abortion.* New York: Cambridge University Press.

Byrnes, Timothy and Mary C. Segers, 1992. *The Catholic Church and the Politics of Abortion: A View from the States.* Boulder, CO: Westview.

Carbaugh, Donal. 1988. *Talking American: Cultural Discourse on DONAHUE.* Norwood, NJ: Ablex.

Carey, James. 1987. "The Press and Public Discourse." *The Center Magazine* 20: 4–16.

Chilton, Paul. 1987. "Metaphor, Euphemism, and the Militarization of Language." *Current Research on Peace and Violence.* 10: 7–19.

Cisler, Lucinda. 1970. "Unfinished Business: Birth Control and Women's Liberation," pp. 245–288 in Robin Morgan (ed), *Sisterhood is Powerful.* New York: Vintage.

Clemens, Elisabeth. 1997. *The People's Lobby: Organizational Innovation and the Rise of Interest Group Politics in the United States, 1890–1925.* Chicago: University of Chicago Press.

Cohen, Jean L. 1995. "Critical Social Theory and Feminist Critiques," pp. 57–90 in Johanna Meehan (ed), *Feminists Read Habermas.* New York and London: Routledge.

Cohen, Joshua. 1989. "Deliberation and Democratic Legitimacy," pp. 17–34 in Alan Hamlin and Philip Pettit (eds), *The Good Polity.* Cambridge, MA: Blackwell.

Collins, Patricia Hill. 1991. *Black Feminist Thought: Knowledge, Consciousness and the Politics of Empowerment.* New York: Routledge.

Condit, Celeste Michelle. 1990. *Decoding Abortion Rhetoric: Communicating Social Change.* Urbana and Chicago: University of Illinois Press.

Cook, Elisabeth A., Ted G. Jelen, and Clyde Wilcox. 1992. *Between Two Absolutes: Public Opinion and the Politics of Abortion.* Boulder, CO: Westview.

Croteau, David and William Hoynes. 1994. *By Invitation Only: How the Media Limit Political Debate.* Monroe, ME: Common Courage Press.

Cuneo, Michael W. 1989. *Catholics Against the Church.* Toronto: University of Toronto Press.

REFERENCES

Curran, James. 1991. "Rethinking the Media as a Public Sphere," pp. 27–57 in Peter Dahlgren and Colin Sparks (eds), *Communication and Citizenship: Journalism and the Public Sphere*. London: Routledge.

Czarnowski, Gabriele. 1997 "Herediary And Racial Welfare (Erb- und Rassenpflege): The Politics Of Sexuality And Reproduction In Nazi Germany." *Social Politics* 4(1): 114–135.

Dahlgren, Peter. 1991. "Introduction," pp. 1–24 in Peter Dahlgren and Colin Sparks (eds), *Communication and Citizenship: Journalism and the Public Sphere*. London: Routledge.

Dillon, Michele. 1993. "Argumentative Complexity of Abortion Discourse." *Public Opinion Quarterly* 57: 305–314.

Döbert, Rainer. 1996. "§218 vor dem Bundesverfassungsgericht. Verfahrenstheoretische Überlegungen zur sozialen Integration," pp. 327–370 in Wolfgang van den Daele and Friedhelm Neidhardt (eds), *Kommunikation und Entscheidung*. Jahrbuch des WZB 1996. Berlin: Edition Sigma.

Donsbach, Wolfgang. 1993. "Journalismus versus journalism: ein Vergleich zum Verhältnis von Medien und Politik in Deutschland und in den USA," pp. 283–315 in Wolfgang Donsbach, Otfried Jarren, Hans-Mathias Kepplinger and Barbara Pfetsch (eds), *Beziehungsspiele: Medien und Politik in der öffentlichen Diskussion*. Gütersloh: Bertelsmann.

Downs, Anthony. 1957. *An Economic Theory of Democracy*. New York: Harper and Row.

Esping-Anderson, Gösta. 1990. *The Three Worlds of Capitalism*. Cambridge: Polity Press.

Etzioni, Amitai. 1996. *The New Golden Rule*. New York: Basic Books.

Evans, John. 1997. "Multi-Organizational Fields and Social Movement Organization Frame Content: The Religious Pro-Choice Movement." *Sociological Inquiry* 67(4): 451–469.

Evans, Richard J. 1976. *The Feminist Movement in Germany, 1894–1933*. Beverly Hills, CA: Sage.

Ferree, Myra Marx. 1987. "Equality and Autonomy: Feminist Politics in the United States and West Germany," pp. 172–195 in Mary F. Katzenstein and Carol McClurg Mueller (eds), *Women's Movements in the US and Western Europe*. Philadelphia: Temple University Press.

1993. " 'The Rise and Fall of 'Mommy Politics': Feminism and German Unification." *Feminist Studies* 19(1): 89–115.

Ferree, Myra Marx and William A. Gamson. 1999. "The Gendering of Abortion Discourse," pp. 40–56 in Donatella della Porta, Hanspeter Kriesi, and Dieter Rucht (eds), *Social Movements in a Globalizing World*. New York: St. Martin's Press.

2002. "The Gendering of Governance and the Governance of Gender," in Barbara Hobson (ed), *Recognition Struggles*, forthcoming.

Ferree, Myra Marx and Silke Roth. 1998. "Gender, Class and the Interaction Among Social Movements: A Strike of West Berlin Daycare Workers." *Gender & Society* 12(6): 626–648.

Ferree, Myra Marx and Beth B. Hess. 2000. *Controversy and Coalition: The New Women's Movement across Three Decades of Change*. New York: Routledge.

Ferree, Myra Marx, Judith Lorber, and Beth Hess (eds). 1998. *Re-visioning Gender*. Beverly Hills, CA: Sage.

Flacks, Richard. 1988. *Making History: The Radical Tradition in American Life.* New York: Columbia University Press.

Francome, Colin, 1984: *Abortion Freedom. A Worldwide Movement.* London: Allen and Unwin.

Franz, Barbara. 1999. Öffentlichkeitsrhetorik. Der Bedeutungswandel von Selbstbestimmung im massenmedialen Diskurs um §218. Unpublished PhD Dissertation. University of Munich, Faculty of Social Sciences.

Fraser, Nancy. 1989. *Unruly Practices: Power, Discourse and Gender in Contemporary Social Theory.* Minneapolis: University of Minnesota Press.

1995. "What's Critical about Critical Theory," pp. 21–55 in Johanna Meehan (ed), *Feminists Read Habermas.* New York and London: Routledge.

1997a. "Rethinking the Public Sphere: A Contribution to the Critique of Actually Existing Democracy," pp. 69–98 in *Justice Interruptus.* New York: Routledge.

1997b. *Justice Interruptus.* New York: Routledge.

Freeman, Jo. 1975. *The Politics of Woman's Liberation: A Case Study of an Emerging Social Movement and Its Relation to the Policy Process.* New York: Longman.

Friedan, Betty. 1976. *It Changed My Life: Writings on the Women's Movement.* New York: Random House.

Friedrichsen, Gisela. 1991. *Abtreibung. Der Kreuzzug von Memmingen.* Frankfurt/M.: Fischer.

Fuchs, Dieter. 1991. "Zum Wandel politischer Konfliktlinien: Ideologische Gruppierungen und Wahlverhalten," pp. 69–88 in Werner Süß (ed), *Die Bundesrepublik in den achtziger Jahren.* Opladen: Leske und Budrich.

2000. "Die demokratische Gemeinschaft in den USA und in Deutschland," pp. 33–72 in Jürgen Gerhards (ed), *Die Vermessung kultureller Unterschiede. USA und Deutschland im Vergleich.* Opladen: Westdeutscher Verlag.

Fuchs, Dieter and Hans-Dieter Klingemann. 1989. "The Left-Right Schema," pp. 203–234 in Kent M. Jennings, Jan W. van Deth, et al. (eds), *Continuities in Political Action: A Longitudinal Study of Political Orientations in Three Western Democracies.* Berlin und New York: de Gruyter.

Gal, Susan 1994. "Gender in the Post-Socialist Transition: The Abortion Debate in Hungary." *East European Politics and Societies* 8(2): 256–287.

Gamson, William A. 1990. *The Strategy of Social Protest,* second edition. Belmont, CA: Wadsworth Press.

1992. *Talking Politics.* New York: Cambridge University Press.

1999. "Policy Discourse and the Language of the Life-World," pp. 127–144 in Jürgen Gerhards and Ronald Hitzler (eds), *Eigenwilligkeit und Rationalität sozialer Prozesse (Festschrift in Honor of Friedhelm Neidhardt).* Opladen, Wiesbaden: Westdeutscher Verlag.

2001. "How Story Telling Can Be Empowering," in Karen A. Cerulo (ed), *Culture in Mind: Toward a Sociology of Culture and Cognition.* New York: Routledge.

Gamson, William A. and David Meyer. 1996. "Framing Political Opportunity," pp. 275–290 in Doug McAdam, John D. McCarthy, and Mayer N. Zald (eds), *Opportunities, Mobilizing Structures, and Framing: Comparative Applications of Contemporary Movement Theory.* New York: Cambridge University Press.

and André Modigliani. 1989. "Media Discourse and Public Opinion on Nuclear Power: A Constructionist Approach." *American Journal of Sociology* 95: 1–37.

Gans, Herbert J. 1980. *Deciding What's News. A Study of CBS Evening News, NBC Nightly News, Newsweek, and Time.* New York: Vintage Books.

Gans, Olivia. 1989. "The cultural experience of abortion in America." *Life Cycle* 9 (N/112): 10.

Gante, Michael. 1991. *$218 in der Diskussion. Meinungs- und Willensbildung 1945–1976.* Düsseldorf: Droste.

Garrett, Geoffrey. 1997. *Partisan Politics in the Global Economy.* Cambridge: Cambridge University Press.

Gaventa, John. 1980. *Power and Powerlessness: Quiescence and Rebellion in an Appalacian Valley.* Urbana: University of Illinois Press.

Gerhards, Jürgen. 1995. "Framing Dimensions and Framing Strategies: Contrasting Ideal- and Real-Type Frames." *Social Science Information* 34(2): 225–248.

  1996. "Soziale Positionierung und politische Kommunikation am Beispiel der öffentlichen Debatte über Abtreibung," pp. 83–102 in Wolfgang van den Daele and Friedhelm Neidhardt (eds), *Kommunikation und Entscheidung. Jahrbuch des WZB 1996.* Berlin: Sigma-Verlag.

  1997. "Diskursive versus liberale Öffentlichkeit: Eine empirische Auseinandersetzung mit Jürgen Habermas." *Kölner Zeitschrift für Soziologie und Sozialpsychologie* 49: 1–39.

  1999. "Wie responsiv sind die Massenmedien? Theoretische Überlegungen und empirische Ergebnisse zum Verhältnis von Medien und Politik," pp. 145–173 in Jürgen Gerhards and Ronald Hitzler (eds), *Eigenwilligkeit und Rationalität sozialer Prozesse (Festschrift in Honor of Friedhelm Neidhardt).* Opladen: Westdeutscher Verlag.

Gerhards, Jürgen, Friedhelm Neidhardt, and Dieter Rucht. 1998. *Zwischen Diskurs und Palaver: Strukturen öffentliche Meinungsbildung am Beispiel des Abtreibungsdiskurses in der Bundesrepublik.* Opladen: Westdeutscher Verlag.

Gerhards, Jürgen and Dieter Rucht. 1992. "Mesomobilization, Organizing and Framing in Two Protest Campaigns in West Germany." *American Journal of Sociology* 98: 555–595.

  2000. "Öffentlichkeit, Akteure und Deutungsmuster: Die Debatte über Abtreibungen in Deutschland und den USA," pp. 165–187 in Jürgen Gerhards (ed), *Die Vermessung kultureller Unterschiede. USA und Deutschland im Vergleich.* Opladen: Westdeutscher Verlag.

Ginsberg, Faye. 1989. *Contested Lives: The Abortion Debate in an American Community.* Berkeley: University of California Press.

Githens, Marianne and Dorothy McBride Stetson (eds). 1996. *Abortion Politics: Public Policy in a Cross-Cultural Perspective.* New York: Routledge.

Gitlin, Todd. 1980. *The Whole World Is Watching.* Berkeley: University of California Press.

Glendon, Mary Ann. 1989. *Abortion and Divorce in Western Law.* Cambridge, MA: Harvard University Press.

Goggin, Malcom (ed). 1993. *Understanding the New Politics of Abortion.* Newbury Park, CA: Sage.

Goffman, Erving. 1974. *Frame Analysis.* Philadelphia: University of Pennsylvania Press.

Gordon, Linda. 1976. *Women's Body, Women's Right: A Social History of Birth Control in America.* New York: Penguin.

1982. "Why 19ᵗʰ Century Feminists Did Not Support 'Birth Control' and 20ᵗʰ Century Feminists Do: Feminism, Reproduction and the Family," pp. 40–53 in Barrie Thorne and Marilyn Yalom (eds), *Rethinking the Family.* New York: Longman.

Gould, Carol C. 1996. "Diversity and Democracy: Representing Differences," pp. 171–186 in Seyla Benhabib (ed), *Democracy and Difference.* Princeton, NJ: Princeton University Press.

Granberg, Donald. 1981. "The Abortion Activists." *Family Planning Perspectives* 13: 158–161.

Green, John C., James L. Guth, Corwin E. Smidt, and Lyman A. Kellstedt. 1996. *Religion and the Culture Wars.* New York: Rowan & Littlefield.

Grossman, Atina. 1995. *Reforming Sex: The German Movement for Birth Control and Abortion Reform, 1920–1950.* New York: Oxford University Press.

Gutmann, Amy and Dennis Thompson. 1996. *Democracy and Disagreement.* Cambridge, MA: Harvard University Press.

Haas, Tanni. 1999. "What's Public about Public Journalism?" *Communication Theory* 9: 346–364.

Habermas, Jürgen. 1984. *The Theory of Communicative Action.* Thomas McCarthy, trans. Boston: Beacon Press.

1996. *Between Facts and Norms.* William Rehg, trans. Cambridge, MA: MIT Press. (Originally 1992. *Faktizität und Geltung: Beiträge zur Diskurstheorie des Rechts und des demokratischen Rechtsstaats.* Frankfurt/M: Suhrkamp.)

1962. *Strukturwandel der Öffentlichkeit. Untersuchungen zu einer Kategorie der bürgerlichen Gesellschaft.* Neuwied: Luchterhand.

1989. "Volkssouveränität als Verfahren: Ein normativer Begriff von Öffentlichkeit." *Merkur* 43: 465–477.

1992a. "Drei normative Modelle der Demokratie: Zum Begriff deliberativer Politik," pp. 11–24 in Herfried Münkler (ed), *Die Chancen der Freiheit. Grundprobleme der Demokratie.* München und Zürich: Piper.

1992b. "Concluding Remarks," pp. 462–479 in Craig Calhoun (ed), *Habermas and the Public Sphere.* Cambridge, MA and London: The MIT Press.

Hallin, Daniel and Paolo Mancini. 1984. "Speaking of the President: Political Structure and Representional Form in U.S. and Italian Television News." *Theory and Society* 13: 829–850.

Halva-Neubauer, Glen. 1993. "The States after Roe: No 'Paper Tigers'," pp. 167–189 in Malcolm Goggin (ed), *Understanding the New Politics of Abortion.* Newbury Park, CA: Sage.

Hampele-Ulrich, Anne. 2000. *Der unabhängige Frauenverband. Ein frauenpolitisches Experiment im deutschen Vereinigungsprozeß.* Berlin: Berliner Debatte Wissenschaftsverlag.

Harrington, Mona. 1999. *Care and Equality: Inventing a New Family Politics.* New York: Knopf.

Harsch, Donna. 1997. "Society, the State and Abortion in East Germany, 1950–1972." *American Historical Review* 102(1): 53–85.

Heinz, Donald. 1983. "The Struggle to Define America," pp. 133–148 in Robert C. Liebman and Robert Wuthnow (eds), *The New Christian Right.* New York: Aldine.

Held, David, Anthony McGrew, David Goldblatt, and Jonathan Perration. 1999. *Global Transformations. Politics, Economics and Culture.* Stanford: Stanford University Press.

Hertel, B.R. and M.C. Russell. 1999. "Examining the Absence of a Gender Effect on Abortion Attitudes: Is There Really No Difference?" *Sociological Inquiry* 69: 364–381.

Hilgartner, Stephen and Charles L. Bosk. 1988. "The Rise and Fall of Social Problems: A Public Arenas Model." *American Journal of Sociology* 94(1): 53–78.

Hirst, Paul. 1994. *Associative Democracy: New Forms of Economic and Social Government.* Cambridge, MA: MIT Press.

Holland-Cunz, Barbara. 1994. "Öffentlichkeit und Intimität – demokratie-theoretische Überlegungen," pp. 227–246 in Elke Biester, Barbara Holland-Cunz, and Birgit Sauer (eds), *Demokratie oder Andokratie? Theorie und Praxis demokratischer Herrschaft in der feminististischen Diskussion.* Frankfurt a/M: Campus.

Hunter, James D. and Carl Bowman. 1994. "The Anatomy of Ambivalence: What Americans Really Believe about Abortion," pp. 85–121 in James D. Hunter (ed), *Before the Shooting Begins.* New York: The Free Press.

Hunter, James Davison. 1994. *Before the Shooting Begins.* New York: The Free Press.

Inglehart, Ronald. 1983. "Traditionelle politische Trennungslinien und die Entwicklung der neuen Politik in westlichen Gesellschaften." *Politische Vierteljahresschrift* 24: 139–165.

Jochimsen, Luc. 1971. "§218 (1871–1971) – Hundert Jahre Elend," pp. 14–36 in Luc Jochimsen (ed), *§218. Dokumentation eines 100jährigen Elends.* Hamburg: Konkret.

Joffe, Carol. 1995. *Doctors of Conscience: The Struggle to Provide Abortion Before and After Roe v. Wade.* Boston: Beacon.

Joppke, Christian. 1993. *Mobilizing Against Nuclear Energy: A Comparison of Germany and the United States.* Berkeley: University of California Press.

Kalberg, Stephen. 1987a. "West German and American Interaction Forms: One Level of Structured Misunderstanding." *Theory, Culture and Society* 4(4): 603–618.

1987b. "The Origin and Expansion of *Kulturpessimismus*: The Relationship Between Public and Private Spheres in Early Twentieth Century Germany." *Sociological Theory* 5(2): 150–164.

Kaplan, Gisela. 1992. *Western European Feminism.* New York: New York University Press.

Kaplan, Laura. 1995. *The Story of Jane: The Legendary Feminist Underground Abortion Service.* New York: Pantheon.

Kelly, James R. 1992. "Learning and Teaching Consistency: Catholics and the Right to Life Movement," pp. 152–168 in Timothy Byrnes and Mary Segers (eds), *The Catholic Church and the Politics of Abortion: A View from the States.* Boulder, CO: Westview.

Kennedy, Randall. 1998. "The Case Against 'Civility.'" *American Prospect* 41 (Nov–Dec): 84–90.

Köcher, Renate. 1986. Spürhund und Missionar. Eine vergleichende Untersuchung über Berufsethik und Aufgabenverständis britischer und deutscher Jouralisten. Universität München: Dissertation.

Koonz, Claudia. 1986. *Mothers in the Fatherland: Women, the Family and Nazi Politics.* New York: St Martin's Press.

Koopmans, Ruud and Hanspeter Kriesi. 1997. Citizenship, National Identity and the Mobilization of the Extreme Right. A Comparison of France, Germany, the Netherlands and Switzerland. WZB – Paper FS III 97–101.

Koopmans, Ruud and Paul Statham. 2000. "Migration and Ethnic Relations as a Field of Political Contention: An Opportunity Structure Approach," pp. 13–56 in Ruud Koopmans and Paul Statham (eds), *Challenging Immigration and Ethnic Relations Politics: Comparative European Perspectives*. Oxford: Oxford University Press.

Kornhauser, William. 1960. *The Politics of Mass Society*. New York: The Free Press.

Kraiker, Gerhard. 1983. *Paragraph 218. Zwei Schritte vorwärts, einen Schritt zurück*. Frankfurt/M.: Fischer.

Kuklinski, James H., Ellen Riggle, and Victor Ottati. 1991. "The Cognitive and Affective Bases of Political Tolerance Judgments." *American Journal of Political Science* 35: 1–27.

Lambeth, E., P. Meyer, and E. Thornson (eds). 1998. *Assessing Public Journalism*. Columbia: University of Missouri Press.

Landfried, Christine. 1988. "Introduction," pp. 7–20 in Christine Landfried (ed), *Constitutional Review and Legislation: An International Comparison*. Baden-Baden: Nomos.

Leibholz, Gerhard. 1967. *Strukturprobleme der modernen Demokratie*, 3rd enlarged edition. Karlsruhe: C.F. Müller.

Leidner, Robin. 1993. "Constituency, Accountability, and Deliberation: Reshaping Democracy in the National Women's Studies Association." *NWSA Journal* 5(1): 4–27.

Lepsius, M. Rainer. 1989. "Das Erbe des Nationalsozialismus und die politische Kultur der Nachfolgestaaten des 'Großdeutschen Reiches'," pp. 247–264 in Max Haller, Hans-Joachim Hoffmann-Nowotny, and Wolfgang Zapf (eds), *Kultur und Gesellschaft. Verhandlungen des 24. Deutschen Soziologentags, des 11. Österreichischen Soziologentags und des 8. Kongresses der Schweizerischen Gesellschaft für Soziologie in Zürich 1988*. Frankfurt/M.: Campus.

Lieberson, Stanley. 1969. "Measuring Population Diversity." *American Sociological Review* 34: 850–862.

Liebman, Robert C. 1983. "The Making of the New Christian Right," pp. 227–238 in Robert C. Liebman and Robert Wuthnow (eds), *The New Christian Right*. New York: Aldine.

Lichterman, Paul. 1996. *The Search for Political Community: American Activists Reinventing Commitment*. New York: Cambridge University Press.

Lovenduski, Joni and Pippa Norris. 1993. *Gender and Party Politics*. Thousand Oaks, CA: Sage.

Lovenduski, Joni and Joyce Outshoorn (eds). 1986. *The New Politics of Abortion*. Thousand Oaks, CA: Sage.

Luker, Kristin. 1984. *Abortion and the Politics of Motherhood*. Berkeley: University of California Press.

Maleck-Lewy, Eva and Myra Marx Ferree. 2000. "Talking about Women and Wombs: Discourse about Abortion and Reproductive Rights in the GDR during and after the 'Wende'," pp. 92–117 in Susan Gal and Gail Kligman (eds), *Reproducing Gender: Politics, Publics and Everyday Life after Socialism*. Princeton, NJ: Princeton University Press.

Maleck-Lewy, 1994. *Und wenn ich schwanger bin? Frauen zwischen Selbstbestimmung und Bevormundung*. Berlin: Aufbau Taschenbuch Verlag.

Manin, Bernhard. 1987. "On Legitimacy and Political Deliberation." *Political Theory* 15: 338–368.

Mansbridge, Jane. 1980. *Beyond Adversary Democracy*. New York: Basic Books.

1986. *Why We Lost the ERA*. Chicago: University of Chicago Press.

Mansbridge, Jane J. 1996. "Using Power/Fighting Power," pp. 46–66 in Seyla Benhabib (ed), *Democracy and Difference*. Princeton, NJ: Princeton University Press.

McCarthy, John. 1987. "Pro-Life and Pro-Choice Mobilization. Infrastructure Deficits and New Technologies," pp. 49–66 in Mayer N. Zald and John D. McCarthy (eds), *Social Movements in an Organizational Society*. New Brunswick, NJ: Transaction.

McDonagh, Eileen L. 1996. *Breaking the Abortion Deadlock*. New York: Oxford University Press.

Meehan, Johanna (ed). 1995. *Feminists Read Habermas*. New York and London: Routledge.

Mezey, Susan Gluck. 1992. *In Pursuit of Equality: Women, Public Policy and the Federal Courts*. New York: St. Martin's Press.

Michels, Robert. 1998 (originally 1911). *Political Parties*. Notes by Seymour M. Lipset. Piscataway, NJ: Transaction Publishers.

Mill, John Stuart. 1991 (1861). *Considerations on Representative Government*. Amherst, MA: Prometheus Books.

Miller, David. 1992. "Deliberative Democracy and Social Choice." *Political Studies XL* Special Issue: 54–67.

Mills, C. Wright. 1956. *The Power Elite*. New York: Oxford University Press.

Moeller, Robert. 1993. *Protecting Motherhood: Women and the Family in the Politics of Postwar West Germany*. Berkeley: University of California Press.

Mohr, James C. 1978. *Abortion in America*. New York: Oxford University Press.

Monangle, Katie 1995. "How We got Here." *Ms.*, May–June: 57–58.

Mouffe, Chantal. 1996. "Democracy, Power, and the 'Political'," pp. 245–256 in Seyla Benhabib (ed), *Democracy and Difference*. Princeton, NJ: Princeton University Press.

Mushaben, Joyce. 1993. "Concession or Compromise: The Politics of Abortion in United Germany." Paper presented at the Annual Meeting of the American Political Science Association, Washington, DC.

Mushaben, Joyce, Sara Lennox, and Geoffrey Giles, 1997. "Women, Men and Unification: Gender Politics and the Abortion Struggle Since 1989," pp. 137–172 in Konrad Jarausch (ed), *After Unity*. Providence, RI: Berghahn.

National Abortion Federation (NAF). 1993. *Incidents of Violence and Disruption Against Abortion Providers*. Washington, DC: NAF.

Negt, Oskar and Alexander Kluge. 1972. *Öffentlichkeit und Erfahrung. Zur Organisationsanalyse von bürgerlicher und proletarischer Öffentlichkeit*. Frankfurt/M.: Suhrkamp.

Neidhardt, Friedhelm. 1996. "Öffentliche Diskussion und politische Entscheidung. Der deutsche Abtreibungskonflikt 1970–1994," pp. 53–82 in Wolfgang van den Daele and Friedhelm Neidhardt (eds), *Kommunikation und Entscheidung. Jahrbuch des WZB 1996*. Berlin: Sigma.

O'Connor, Karen. 1996. *No Neutral Ground? Abortion Politics in an Age of Absolutes*. Boulder, CO: Westview.

Olasky, Marvin N. 1988. *The Press and Abortion, 1838–1988*. Hillsdale, NJ: Lawrence Erlbaum.

Oldfield, Duane M. 1996. *The Right and the Righteous: The Christian Right Confronts the Republican Party*. Lanham, MD: Rowman & Littlefield.

Oliver, Pamela E. and Hank Johnston. 2000. "What a Good Idea! Ideologies and Frames in Social Movement Research." *Mobilization* 5(1): 37–54.

Oliver, Pamela E. and Gregory M. Maney. 2000. "Political Processes and Local Newspaper Coverage of Protest Events: From Selection Bias to Triadic Interactions." *American Journal of Sociology* 106(2): 463–505.

Orloff, Ann Shola. 1993. "Gender and the Social Rights of Citizenship: The Comparative Analysis of Gender Relations and Welfare States." *American Sociological Review* 58(3): 303–328.

Pacensky, Susanne and Renate von Sadrozinsky. 1988: *§218 – zu Lasten der Frauen. Neue Auskünfte zu einem alten Kampf*. Reinbek: Rowohlt.

Pateman, Carol. 1988. *The Sexual Contract*. Stanford, CA: Stanford University Press.

——— 1992. "Equality, Difference, Subordination: The Politics of Motherhood and Women's Citizenship," pp. 17–31 in Gisela Bock and Susan James (eds), *Beyond Equality and Difference: Citizenship, Feminist Politics, Female Subjectivity*. New York: Routledge.

Peattie, Lisa Redfield and Martin Rein. 1983. *Women's Claims: A Study in Political Economy*. New York: Oxford University Press.

Penrose, Virgina, 1990. "Vierzig Jahre SED-Politik: Ziele, Strategie, Ergebnisse." *IFG: Frauenforschung* 8(4): 60–77.

Petchesky, Rosalind Pollack. 1984. *Abortion and Woman's Choice: The State, Sexuality and Reproductive Freedom*. New York: Longman.

Peters, Bernhard. 1994. "Der Sinn von Öffentlichkeit," pp. 42–76 in Friedhelm Neidhardt (ed), *Öffentlichkeit, öffentliche Meinung und soziale Bewegungen*. Opladen: Westdeutscher Verlag.

Pfetsch, Barbara. 1998. "Government News Management," pp. 70–93 in Doris Graber, Denis McQuail, and Pippa Norris (eds), *The Politics of News. The News of Politics*. Washington, DC: Congressional Quarterly Press.

——— 2000. "Journalistische Professionalität versus persönliches Vertrauen: Normen der Interaktion in der politischen Kommunikation in den USA und Deutschland," pp. 141–163 in Jürgen Gerhards (ed), *Die Vermessung kultureller Unterschiede. USA und Deutschland im Vergleich*. Opladen: Westdeutscher Verlag.

Piven, Frances Fox and Richard Cloward. 1971. *Regulating the Poor*. New York: Random House.

Pole, J. R. 1978. *The Pursuit of Equality in American History*. Berkeley: University of California Press.

Rattinger, Hans. 1994. "Attitudes Toward Abortion Law in Germany 1990–1992: Determinants and Implications," *German Politics* 3(2): 249–264.

Riemer, Jeremiah. 1993. "Reproduction and Reunification: The Politics of Abortion in United Germany," pp. 167–187 in Michael Huelshoff, Andrei Markovits, and Simon Reich (eds), *From Bundesrepublik to Deutschland*. Ann Arbor: University of Michigan Press.

Robinson, William I. 1998. "Beyond Nation-State Paradigms: Globalization, Sociology, and the Challenge of Transnational Studies." *Sociological Forum* 13: 561–594.

Roller, Edeltraud. 2000. "Marktwirtschaftliche und wohlfahrtsstaatliche Gerechtigkeits-prinzipien in Deutschland und den USA," pp. 89–110 in Jürgen Gerhards (ed), *Die Vermessung kultureller Unterschiede. USA und Deutschland im Vergleich.* Opladen: Westdeutscher Verlag.

Rosen, Jay. 1994. "Making Things More Public: On the Responsibility of the Media Intellectual." *Critical Studies in Mass Communication* 11: 363–388.

Rousseau, Jean-Jacques. 1998 (originally 1762). *The Social Contract.* Maurice Cranston, transl. New York: Viking Penguin.

Rucht, Dieter. 1994. *Modernisierung und neue soziale Bewegungen. Deutschland, Frankreich und USA im Vergleich.* Frankfurt/M.: Campus.

   1995. "Parties, Associations, and Movements as Systems of Political Interest Media-tion," pp. 103–125 in J. Thesing and W. Hofmeister (eds), *Political Parties in Democracy.* Sankt Augustin: Konrad-Adenauer-Stiftung.

   1999. "Linking Organization and Mobilization: Michels's Iron Law of Oligarchy Reconsidered." *Mobilization* 4: 151–169.

   2000. *Jugendkulturen, Politik und Protest (Youth Cultures, Politics and Protest).* Opladen: Leske & Budrich.

Ruzek, Cheryl. 1978. *The Women's Health Movement: Feminist Alternatives to Doctors' Control.* New York: Praeger.

Ryan, Charlotte. 1991. *Prime Time Activism.* Boston: South End Press.

Ryan, Mary P. 1992. "Gender and Public Access: Women's Politics in Nineteenth Century America," pp. 259–288 in Craig Calhoun (ed), *Habermas and the Public Sphere.* Cambridge, MA: MIT Press.

Sainsbury, Diane. 1994. *Gendering Welfare States.* Thousand Oaks, CA: Sage.

Sanders, Lynn. 1992. "Against Deliberation." Paper presented at annual meeting of the American Political Science Association.

Sauer, Birgit. 1995. "'Doing Gender': Das Parlament als Ort der Geschlechter-konstruktion," pp. 172–199 in Andreas Dörner and Ludgera Vogt (eds), *Sprache des Parlaments und Semiotik der Demokratie.* Berlin: Walter deGruyter.

Schenk, Christina. 1994. "Feministische Politik im Bundestag – Erfahrungen und Per-spektiven." pp. 35–71 in Elke Biester et al. (eds), *Demokratie oder Androkratie. Theorie und Praxis demokratischer Herrschaft in der feministischen Diskussion.* Frankfurt am Main: Campus.

Schreiber, Robert, Marianne Grunwald, and Carol Hagemann-White. 1994. *Frauenver-bände und Frauenvereinigungen in der Bundesrepublik Deutschland.* Schriftenreihe des BMFJ Band 16. Stuttgart: Kohlhammer.

Schudson, Michael. 1998. *The Good Citizen.* Cambridge, MA: Harvard University Press.

Schulz, Bud and Ruth Schultz. 1989. *It Did Happen Here: Recollections of Political Repres-sion in America.* Berkeley: University of California Press.

Schumpeter, Joseph A. 1942. *Capitalism, Socialism, and Democracy.* New York: Harper.

Scott, Joan. 1986 "Gender: A Useful Category for Historical Analysis." *American Historical Review.* 91: 1053–1175.

Scott, Jacqueline and Howard Schumann. 1988. "Attitude Strength and Social Action in the Abortion Dispute." *American Sociological Review* 53: 785–793.

Segers, Mary C. 1992. "The Loyal Opposition: Catholics for a Free Choice," pp. 169–184 in Timothy A. Byrnes and Mary C. Segers (eds), *The Catholic Church and the Politics of Abortion.* Boulder, CO: Westview.

Sichterman, Barbara. 1986. "Der Feminismus der CDU," pp. 133–148 in Helmut Dubiel (ed), *Populismus und Aufklärung*. Frankfurt: Suhrkamp.

Simonds, Wendy. 1996. *Abortion At Work: Ideology and Practice in a Feminist Clinic*. New Brunswick, NJ: Rutgers University Press.

Skocpol, Theda. 1997. "The Tocqueville Problem." *Social Science History* 21(4): 455–479.

Smith, Dorothy E. 1987. *The Everyday World as Problematic: A Sociology of Everyday Life*. Boston: Northeastern University Press.

1990. *The Conceptual Practices of Power: A Feminist Sociology of Knowledge*. Boston: Northeastern University Press.

1999. *Writing the Social: Critique, Theory and Investigations*. Toronto: University of Toronto Press.

Snow, David and Robert D. Benford. 1988. "Ideology, Frame Resonance, and Participant Mobilization," pp. 197–217 in Bert Klandermans, Hanspeter Kriesi, and Sidney Tarrow (eds), *From Structure to Action: Comparing Social Movement Research across Cultures*. Greenwich, CT: JAI Press.

1992. "Master Frames and Cycles of Protest," pp. 133–155 in Aldon Morris and Carol Mueller (eds), *Frontiers in Social Movement Theory*. New Haven, CT: Yale University Press.

Solinger, Rickie (ed). 1998. *Abortion Wars: A Half Century of Struggle, 1950–2000*. Berkeley: University of California Press.

Soskice, David. 1999. "Globalisierung und institutionelle Divergenz: Die USA und Deutschland im Vergleich." *Geschichte und Gesellschaft* 25: 201–225.

Spalter-Roth, Roberta and Ronnie Schreiber. 1995. "Outsider Issues and Insider Tactics: Strategic Tensions in the Women's Policy Network During the 1980s," pp. 105–127 in Myra Marx Ferree and Patricia Yancey Martin (eds), *Feminist Organizations*. Philadelphia: Temple University Press.

Staggenborg, Suzanne. 1991. *The Pro-Choice Movement. Organization and Activism in the Abortion Conflict*. New York: Oxford University Press.

Taagepera, Rein and James Lee Ray. 1977. "A Generalized Index of Concentration." *Sociological Methods and Research* 5: 367–384.

Terkel, Susan Neiburg. 1988. *Abortion: Facing the Issues*. New York: Franklin Watts.

Terry, Randall. 1988. *Operation Rescue*. Springdale, PA: Whitaker House.

Thietz, Kirstin (ed). 1992. *Ende der Selbstverständlichkeit? Die Abschaffung des §218 in der DDR*. Berlin: Basis Druck.

Tribe, Lawrence H. 1990. *Abortion: The Clash of Absolutes*. New York: W. W. Norton.

Tuchman, Gaye. 1978. *Making News*. New York: The Free Press.

Ulrich, Kerstin. 1998. Soziale Bewegung und kollektive Identität. Der Diskurs über Abtreibung und Reproduktionstechnologien als Beispiel feministischer Identitätskonstruktion. Unpublished PhD dissertation, European University Institute. Department of Political and Social Sciences.

von Beyme, Klaus. 1991. *Das politische System der Bundesrepublik Deutschland nach der Vereinigung*. Munich: Piper.

Vultejus, Ulrich. 1990. "Das Urteil vom Memmingen," pp. 9–34 in Ulrich Vultejus (ed), *Das Urteil von Memmingen. Vom Elend der Indikation*. Köln: Volksblatt Verlag.

Walker, Nancy J. 1988. "What We Know About Women Voters in Britain, France, and W. Germany." *Public Opinion* 55(May/June): 49–52.

Warren, Mark. 1992. "Democratic Theory and Self Transformation." *American Political Science Review* 86: 8–23.

Williams, Patricia. 1988. "On Being the Object of Property." *Signs* 14(1): 5–24.

Williams, Rhys H. and Jeffrey Blackburn. 1996. "Many Are Called but Few Obey: Ideological Commitment and Activism in Operation Rescue," pp. 167–185 in Christian Smith (ed), *Disruptive Religion.* New York: Routledge.

Wobbe, Theresa. 1989. *Gleichheit und Differenz. Politische Strategien der Frauenrechtlerinnen um die Jahrhundertwende.* Frankfurt/M.: Campus.

Worgitsky, Charlotte. 1992. "Meine ungeborenen Kinder: Entstehungs- und Wirkungsgeschichte," pp. 127–143 in Jeanette Clausen and Sara Friedrichsmeyer (eds), *Women in German Yearbook* 9. Lanham, MD: University Press of America.

World Values Survey, 1981–1984 and 1990–1993. [machine-readable data file]/World Values Study Group]. Ann Arbor, MI: Inter-University Consortium for Political and Social Research.

Wuerth, Andrea. 1999. "National Politics/Local Identities: Abortion Rights Activism in Post-Wall Berlin." *Feminist Studies* 25(3): 601–631.

Yishai, Yael. 1992. "Public Ideas and Public Policy: Abortion Politics in Four Democracies." *Comparative Politics* 25(2): 207–228.

Young, Brigitte. 1996. "The German State and Feminist Politics: A Double Gender Marginalization." *Social Politics* 3(2/3): 159–184.

   1999. *Triumph of the Fatherland: German Unification and the Marginalization of Women.* Ann Arbor: University of Michigan Press.

Young, Iris Marion. 1996. "Communication and the Other: Beyond Deliberative Democracy," pp. 120–135 in Seyla Benhabib (ed), *Democracy and Difference.* Princeton, NJ: Princeton University Press.

Zippel, Kathrina. 2000. Policies against Sexual Harassment: Gender Equality Policy in Germany, the European Union and the United States in Comparative Perspective. Unpublished Ph.D. Dissertation. UW – Madison.

Zirakzadeh, C. Ernesto. 2000 "Framing and alternative theories of social movements in politics" Unpublished manuscript, Department of Political Science, University of Connecticut.

Zwerenz, Ingrid (ed). 1988. *Frauen. Die Geschichte des §218.* Frankfurt/M.: Fischer.

Index